Curried Cultures

CALIFORNIA STUDIES IN FOOD AND CULTURE

Darra Goldstein, Editor

Curried Cultures

GLOBALIZATION, FOOD, AND SOUTH ASIA

EDITED BY

Krishnendu Ray and Tulasi Srinivas

UNIVERSITY OF CALIFORNIA PRESS

BERKELEY LOS ANGELES LONDON

Elizabeth Buettner's "'Going for an Indian': South Asian Restaurants and the Limits of Multiculturalism in Britain" was first printed in slightly different form in *The Journal of Modern History, 80*(4), 865–901. It is reprinted here with permission. Jayanta Sengupta's "Nation on a Platter: The Culture and Politics of Food and Cuisine in Colonial Bengal" was first printed in slightly different form in *Modern Asian Studies, 44*(1), 81–98. It is reprinted here with permission. Krishnendu Ray's "Global Flows, Local Bodies: Dreams of Pakistani Grill in Manhattan" was printed in different form (and under a different title) in *Food, Culture & Society, 14*(2) 243–273.

University of California Press, one of the most distinguished university presses in the United States, enriches lives around the world by advancing scholarship in the humanities, social sciences, and natural sciences. Its activities are supported by the UC Press Foundation and by philanthropic contributions from individuals and institutions. For more information, visit www.ucpress.edu.

University of California Press
Berkeley and Los Angeles, California

University of California Press, Ltd.
London, England

Library of Congress Cataloging-in-Publication Data

Curried cultures : globalization, food, and South Asia / edited by Krishnendu Ray and Tulasi Srinivas.
    p.   cm.
Includes bibliographical references and index.
ISBN 978–0-520–27011–4 (cloth : alk. paper)
ISBN 978–0-520–27012–1 (pbk. : alk. paper)
    1. Food—Social aspects—South Asia.   2. Food habits—South Asia.
3. Cosmopolitanism—South Asia.   4. Nationalism—South Asia.
5. Globalization—Social aspects.   I. Ray, Krishnendu.   II. Srinivas, Tulasi.
    GT2853.S64C87   2012
    394.1'20954—dc23

                                                    2011029711

11   20   19   18   17   16   15   14   13   12
10   9   8   7   6   5   4   3   2   1

*To my mother Rukka Srinivas for stirring in me a fascination
for all things gastronomic.
To Rudra and Babul for keeping me sane.
To Sierra Burnett Clark and Jackie Rohel for all the
unacknowledged work.*

CONTENTS

PART ONE

Opening the Issues

PART ONE

Opening the Issues

ONE

Introduction

Krishnendu Ray and Tulasi Srinivas

SOUTH ASIA IS A NEW HUB of intersecting global networks nourished by proliferating material and symbolic transactions propelling bodies, things, and conceptions across national boundaries. In this book, traversing national boundaries is the contingent operational definition of globalization. That implies at least two things: globalization becomes more visible after national boundaries crystallize; and we witness a new kind of self-consciousness about the connections between various locales and between the local and the supralocal in this phase of globalization. Furthermore, the affiliation of food to the body makes comestibles intensely local, in spite of their long history of distant circulation. Thus food is a particularly productive site to interrogate a new iteration of something old, because it links not only the global to the local, but the mind to the body and beyond. By weaving densely local stories, this book draws attention to processes of globalization as they play out at particular places and on specific peoples' conceptions of themselves and their world.

In the last quarter of the twentieth century, new nodes in the global traffic in capital and culture joined previous flows of the capitalist world-economy from the edges of the Mediterranean and the Atlantic. Works such as *The Globalization of Chinese Food* (Wu & Cheung 2004), *Asian Food: The Global and the Local* (Cwiertka & Walraven 2001), *The Globalization of Food* (Inglis & Gimlin 2009) and *Globalization, Food and Social Identities in the Asia Pacific Region* (Farrer 2010) bear witness to those transformations. Until now there has been no comparable work centering on the South Asian wellspring of unconventional flows of bodies, edible commodities, and cultural conceptions. Although South Asian cookery is transforming the everyday world of urbanites everywhere, there has been little attention given to this process.

Curried Cultures closes that gap in our knowledge about South Asia, its connections to the larger world, and to the cultural environment that urban middle classes almost everywhere face with increasing potency. It draws attention to timeless processes of creolization and conservation, flow and counter-flow, and transvaluation of the old and production of the new in the food cultures of globalizing middle classes. The title, *Curried Cultures,* is ironic, self-consciously playing on a stereotype, and earnest enough to appropriate the curry as a sign for the people it talks about. These are people who are born of the transaction between India and elsewhere, no different from the genealogies of Chicken Tikka Masala or Curry Raisu, not wholly belonging to the subcontinent and yet oddly defined by it.

Partly what is new about the current conjuncture that is marked by the term *globalization* is that numerous spatially distributed urban middle classes have been dramatically pulled into transnational transactions in taste, and they have left a legible imprint of their experience, often in multilingual mediums. Paying attention to this practical-linguistic ecumene is important here so as to redress excessive attention to nation, religion, and commodity in the literatures on the global-cultural link. In addition, numerous chapters in this volume are written by scholars who are themselves of the middle class and who often write about people who belong to that class to whom English is available, at least as one in a bilingual or multilingual world. The anglophone middle class comes with a location in a social hierarchy with a shared feeling of middleness, either precariously or assuredly so. Some of the brash assertion of middleness of this class is a product of the novelty of their location in an emerging economic and cultural powerhouse such as India (Dickey 2010, 2000; Fernandes 2006; Deshpande 2003; Fernandes & Heller 2006; Dwyer 2000; Derné 2008; Harriss 2006; and Fuller & Narasimhan 2007).

This book is neither about globalization from above, nor is it about globalization from below. Instead it is mostly about globalization from the middle, with its derivative and deviant relationship to neoliberal globalization (that Bhabha characterizes as "performative, deformative" translation—1994: 241), and the imaginative reconstitution of the global elsewhere. This book is about that middle class precisely because it is a class that has emerged as a major player in the conceptualization of globalization and counterpositions to globalization. Much has been written about globalization from above, but very little from elsewhere. A subaltern history of globalization that Akhil Gupta challenges us to conceive in the next chapter is yet to be born. We see the field of cultural globalization as constituted both by questions of the perimeter, marked by the nation-state, and of hierarchy, in terms of class and profession.

Curried Cultures joins an array of work that interrogates culinary cultures (separate from agricultural food production)[1] to address issues of globalization, nation-making, nation-breaking, and beyond. In particular, we develop what is suggested in Warren Belasco and Philip Scranton's *Food Nations* (2002) and James L. Watson and Melissa L. Caldwell's *The Cultural Politics of Food and Eating* (2005) about the relationship between place, power, and comestibles. These issues have been developed further in studies such as Jeffrey Pilcher's *Que vivan los tamales!* (1998) on Mexico and Richard Wilk's *Home Cooking in the Global Village* (2006b) about Belize. We draw on their work to argue that in some ways globalization makes national boundaries porous as people, goods, and signs move from one part of the world to another with greater velocity and ubiquity. New links are forged between the social structure and commodities, between global markets and local governments, and between diverse peoples and conceptions. In the process, categories of the local and the global, which previously appeared to be distinct, now become increasingly interwoven and reproduce each other.

In other ways, globalization solidifies boundaries of the world and the mind, often by naming, codifying, and standardizing everyday practices that middle-class men in previous epochs rarely paid attention to. We explore these changing ratios of legibility of everyday practices by interrogating culinary cultures in South Asia and by South Asians elsewhere. In the process, we examine dynamic formulations of identity and its maintenance in various uprooted "worlds"—a world of people who feel the pull of other worlds in the double oralities of taste and talk.

To elaborate a little further on the theme of the local and the global reproducing each other, we find that the jostling of class, profession, and nation within the interstate system and the global cultural ecumene, produces a variety of localisms and cosmopolitanisms. In Equatorial Guinea, for instance, "the national elite are assembling the favourite foods of different ethnic groups and repackaging them as part of the Equatoguinean national cuisine" (Cusack 2000: 218). In this case the national impetus seems to come as much from the old metropolitan center, Spain, as from local elites. Specific bureaucracies, such as the Spanish "Aid Agency and the Ministry of Health and Consumer Affairs, and Spanish religious orders" are "implicated in the building of a national cuisine" (2000: 219).

In the Belizean story, local and authentic foodways, which emerge from current conditions of globalization, are crafted for tourists looking for diversity and difference (Wilk 2006b). This manufacturing of locality *is* the global phenomenon, argues Wilk, sometimes done in a densely lived, unselfconscious way and sometimes done as pure Disneyfied performance. "It took more *globalization* to bring local food out of the kitchen" and assert its presence in the public domain of Belizean national identity (Wilk 2006b: 166). We do not get "'Belizean cuisine' until migrants who had lived for years in the USA began to return home in the 1980s," demanding authenticity and backing it up with capital (Wilk 2006b: 172–173). The first "Belizean restaurant" in Belize City was opened by an expatriate family from Los Angeles in 1989.

What unites the Equatoguinean and Belizean experience, and is rarely commented on, is that these tenuous national cuisines are sometimes a product of the interstate system with its own hierarchy of values espoused by development bureaucrats and tourism bureaus. Meaning, Belize and Equatorial Guinea are said to have a cuisine because it is now expected that nations have cuisines, as much as flags, anthems, and airlines. Or in Sidney Mintz's words, "is having a cuisine important—is it because other people have one?" (2002: 24).

Longer networks, faster flows, and intensifying relationships between here and there, both real and imagined, demand reformulations of locality, identity, and notions of the self. The provisioning, preparation, and consumption of food among South Asian middle classes affects various aspects of identity such as ethnic affiliation, linguistic facility, gender constructs, notions of hierarchy, national identity, and so on. Food can be used variously as a signifier of cosmopolitanism, localism, traditionalism, or nationalism, in implicit or explicit negotiations with global hierarchies of value (Herzfeld 2004). What happens to these constructs of identity when they are subject to both the collapsing and expanding patterns of recent global flows? That is the larger question that this book seeks to examine. More specifically, some of the allied questions that emerge are: How are classifications of the self and the other impacted for those drawn into the vortex of the translocal? What notions of historicity, locality, or authenticity rest in food in a world of expanding ambit and frequency of transactions between distant places? How do places such as homes, restaurants, and cafés—places designed to contain bodies in specifically demarcated activities, such as eating and sleeping—relate to and how are they imagined to relate to other places? How are bodies and places made and remade to fit each other in authorized and unauthorized activities? What kinds of relationships ensue from the real and imagined places and peoples?

Current understandings of cultural globalization and transnationalism often rely upon a particular kind of spatial understanding, where the world is divided into nation states and culture is linked to territory. Even the amorphous notion of civilization in Samuel Huntington's famous essay (then book) (1993, 1996) falls within bounded regions, which are more or less closed. Goods and ideologies move across this space aided by hastening technologies of transportation and communication. But compared to commodities and conceptions, peoples' mobility across national boundaries is much more frictional. When people do move, globalization leads to a paradoxically persistent questioning of identity among migrants and natives alike. Thus, migrating food practices bridge and buffet bodily conceptions of the self and the other, insinuating themselves into conceptions of home and abroad, this place and that other one, private and public.

Identity is no longer "taken for granted" (Berger 1997), especially for urban middle classes drawn into the vortex of recent global flows; rather, it becomes an all-absorbing project that is often enacted through consumption. In Arjun Appadurai's cogent conception: "As group pasts become increasingly parts of museums, exhibits, and collections, both in national and transnational spectacles, culture becomes less what Pierre Bourdieu would have called a habitus (a tacit realm of reproducible practices and dispositions) and more an arena for conscious choice, justification, and representation, the latter often to multiple and spatially dislocated audiences" (1996, 44). Recent ethnographic work that describes cultural consumption among the Indian middle classes (Osella & Osella 2000; Fernandes 2006; Varma 1998) links it repeatedly to the shaping of a nation, imagined or otherwise. But how this consumption, especially of comestibles, actually plays out in the everyday lives of South Asians in their quotidian particularity, whether among the urban Indian middle classes or among their diasporic compatriots, and what it means to them and to others, is rarely explored. We hope to fill that lacuna.

Furthermore, globalization has been seen by many theorists as the dominance of the culture of Euro-America (Barber 1996; Berger 1997; Friedman 2000, 2005). That is a plausible claim about a number of subjects discussed in this book, such as the idea of a restaurant and the related standard of judgment through the frame of professional French haute cuisine. Furthermore, elite restaurants in Indian cities (see chapter 7) or the traffic in chefs between princely states (see chapter 3) can be treated as derivative forms of a metropolitan standard. Yet we think such instances could be more productively engaged with as vernacular forms of modernity, derived at some point and in many of its elements from the Euro-American West, but exceeding it, much like Anglophone Indian literature today. In other words, the superimposed cultural-linguistic matrix can be understood as the "cosmopolitan vernacular" (Pollock 2006) that implies certain affiliations and summons membership of certain locals in translocal networks. That, of course, keeps the possibility open that the cosmopolitan vernacular may be challenged by more regional idioms with a far more proximate lexical radius. That is a potentially interesting scenario, which nevertheless is not our story here. Instead, how some South Asians today practice being cosmopolitan in the realm of foodways, and how others challenge such scripts are some of the issues we are after.

We argue that food—the provisioning, preparation, presentation and consumption of it—can help us to unearth subtle changes in the social and cultural worlds that connect the local to the global: remind us of older and perhaps more robust networks of globalization (chapter 2 in this volume); suggest movement along the spokes of a wheel radiating outwards from a metropolitan center (chapter 7); as backwash along these lines of conveyance (chapters 8, 9, 10); or as rhizomic patterns (chapters 5 and 11). Of course, it is also true that globalization in the late twentieth and early twenty-first centuries may at times be an appropriate synonym for Americanization. Yet, we find that patterns of dispersal and connection are plentiful, especially among transmigrating middle classes. *Curried Cultures* argues that another place, another's food, is not merely the "global's presumptive victim, its cultural nemesis, or its coerced subordinate," but an increasingly assertive player in transactions of taste (Kraidy & Murphy 2008: 339). We will show how in the pages below.

"Curried" cultures also allows us to distinguish this work as culinary, hence closer to everyday sensory experience than "food" or "nutrient" would have allowed us. That indicates a certain practical proximity to dishes and diets that is often missing in discussions where food is only considered a lens to investigate other things. Of course, we do look at food to comment on other matters, but the practice of cooking matters to us because we consider it an important way of knowing the world and acting on it. We do not think it necessary to narrow our sensory horizons to sharpen our intellectual vision, contrary to what dominant Western epistemologies have assumed since the eighteenth century. To us, first principles are no more important than mouth-watering aromas and we want to convey some of that sensory exuberance even within the confines of visual marks on paper. Food is not only a lens, but something we pay particular attention to—its material and symbolic constitution. In that, we have learned from Francesca Bray's complaint that materialists have shown little interest in the material (1997: 39).

Food allows us theoretical possibilities more fecund than almost any other material object precisely because of its ability to be at one moment inside and at another outside the body, to be a-routine-and-a-ritual, and for its ubiquity-and-specialty (Bennett 2010). Food, when aligned with body and place, allow us to imagine both rootedness and routes of dispersal. This is a feature that R. S. Khare and M. S. A. Rao drew attention to long ago, when they stated that food "mediates body and mind, work and thought, and individual person and society" (1986: 6).

Another's food is sometimes the most accessible product of a cultural complex; sometimes too easily digested without acknowledging the others' presence (Hooks 1992; Heldke 2003; Nandy 2003b). We wrestle with both those aspects of access and taken-for-grantedness, and in the process we try to delineate the possibilities of a migrant, minoritarian, food-related cosmopolitanism, while acknowledging its possible conflation with a neoliberal commodification of everything, including food culture. Several scholars have argued for a new cosmopolitan theory of globalization that accounts for difference (Hannerz 1996; Harvey 2001; Breckenridge, Pollock, Bhabha, & Chakrabarty 2002). Martha Nussbaum has argued effectively for a cosmopolitan morality in which we need to know the culture of the other to create a truly plural social environment (1996; cf. Calhoun 2007). In the anguished wake of the ethnic bloodbath that accompanied the collapse of Yugoslavia and subsequent instances of virulent terrorism and predatory modes of counter-terrorism, Carole Breckenridge, Sheldon Pollock, Homi Bhabha, and Dipesh Chakrabarty (2002), working with South Asian material, have sought a minoritarian cosmopolitanism of refugees, migrants, and exiles, as a critique of nationally constituted nativist modern spaces. We provide flesh and bones to those unspecified aspirations. Yet we are attuned to Craig Calhoun's retort that "nationalism is not a moral mistake," in spite of recognizing that it is unequivocally implicated in numerous atrocities and banal injustices of the twentieth century. It is, nevertheless, "also a form of social solidarity and one of the background conditions on which modern democracy has been based" (2007: 1). We are amenable to a cosmopolitan ethic and aesthetic precisely because we are people who have come from elsewhere, another nation. It is for us, then, a very pragmatic case of actually existing cosmopolitanism that accounts for multiple national loyalties and attachments both close by and at a distance. We find Robbins's contention incontrovertible that "If people can get as emotional as [Benedict] Anderson says they do about relations with fellow nationals they never see face-to-face, then now that print-capitalism has become electronic- and digital-capitalism, and now that this system is so clearly transnational, it would be strange if people did *not* get emotional in much the same way, if not necessarily to the same degree, about others who are *not* fellow nationals, people bound to them by some transnational sort of fellowship" (Robbins 1998: 7). Furthermore, cosmopolitanism is no more an apology for capitalism than nationalism was when it was the dominant mode of middle-class identification (Robbins 1998: 8). Of course, there is nothing naturally virtuous about transnationality, although it is worth making the case against the "thousand gross and subtle ways in which we are told every day that people outside our borders are too distant to matter" (Robbins 1998: 12). We do not find such distant people too remote for our moral compass. Yet we are acutely aware that such a posture is unavailable to many. To those for whom it is accessible, we think cosmopolitanism is a more productive attitude than nativism and we will show how in the following pages. Nevertheless, globalization establishes relations of power, including practices by which we appropriate that power for ourselves. "Globalization is ours because it is in the dimension of globalization that we fashion our ethics and bodies, that we imagine the way we conduct our lives, that we suffer and desire, that we submit others to ourselves and are made subordinate to them" (Bayart 2007: xi). We are subjected by globalizing processes, and yet we are tasting, thinking, dreaming, acting, and living subjects, who use, shape, and resist globalization's flows. We couldn't agree more with Bayart's sober judgment that globalization "will probably transform us, but it will not damn us any more than it will redeem us" (2007: 8). Yet it remains a challenge to be global without being imperial.

Food studies, because of its genealogy in European scripts, has been too focused on Western national food cultures. Sometimes, as a retort to globalization, food studies can also be seduced by a purifying provincialism, often visible in nationalized and racialized readings of the local that is territorialized as terroir (see, for instance, the discussions surrounding the sale of kebabs and curry in Lucca, Italy).[2] In contrast, Sheldon Pollock shows in *The Language of the Gods in the World of Men* (2006) that certain South Asian versions of the relationship between the local and the supra-local, sedimented in long-circulating elite networks of Sanskritic aesthetic cosmopolitanism, permitted vernacular appropriations, such as Balinese Hinduism and Sinic Buddhism, allowing options beyond a bland homogenizing culture or a closed ethnolocalism. Such choices may also be possible again in contemporary patterns of circulation of peoples, commodities, and conceptions.[3] The discussion of culture and place as it pertains to South Asian cities and South Asians abroad can teach us alternative forms of cosmopolitanism that neither universalize a metropolitan culture, nor posit a nativistic relationship between terrain, tongue, and taste. We elaborate on those possibilities in the following pages, while acknowledging that cosmopolitanism as a form of identification is not readily available to everyone, and that cosmopolitanism does not escape the hierarchical structures of globalization (or can be allowed to be comfortable in its own universal strictures). Yet like feminist and antiracist cosmopolitanism that preceded it, we seek to understand solidarities along with situatedness while reaching across barriers of nation and tribe. *Curried Cultures* takes the problem of building translocal models of globalization seriously by fully engaging in meaningful and critical dialogue that not only spans our gustatory differences, but makes inhabitance in a distant locale viable, while illuminating the poetics and politics of place-making through diet and desire. The middle classes play a particularly important role in those transactions in transnational taste-making in the current instance precisely because they are not bereft of the basic material and symbolic resources necessary to play that game.

SCHOLARSHIP ON INDIAN FOOD CULTURE

When India emerged from under colonialism in 1947 with the recent memory of the Bengal Famine seared into middle-class consciousness it was not surprising that hunger dominated public discussion on Indian food. Michael Worboys (1988) and David Arnold (1994) have provided us with famine's prehistory in British imperial concerns about diet and malnutrition and its relationship to colonial science from the 1860s to the interwar years. The nationalist response to this colonial "reconnaissance and categorization of India" (Arnold 1994: 4) developed hesitatingly and did not acquire full force until the third decade of the twentieth century. "By the late 1930s what had once clearly been a branch of colonial science *about* Indians, and an aspect of the colonial 'discovery' of India and its resources, was becoming part of an Indian scientific research agenda *for* Indians" (Arnold 1994: 26). A robust thread of that discussion continues in Amartya Sen's Nobel Prize–winning work in the political-economy of hunger, which came out of those discourses and was developed within modern Western epistemologies (see Drèze, Sen, & Hussain 1995).[4] More recently in the United States, Mike Davis's *Late Victorian Holocausts* (2001) is an inspired example of where such research can lead—as a critique of market-state relations within the frame of political-ecology. In some ways Davis pursues the argument of the first generation of Indian nationalist economists such as Dadabhai Naoroji in *Poverty and Un-British Rule in India* (1901).[5]

The torch for the technological response to hunger, by way of the Green Revolution, has been carried famously by plant geneticists Norman Borlaug and M. S. Swaminathan of the Indian Agricultural Research Institute in New Delhi. Swaminathan eventually came to occupy the chair of the U.N. World Food Congress in Rome in 1984.[6] That technological optimism and policy intervention has not gone unanswered. Vandana Shiva has emerged as the most vociferous critic of the ecological and social consequences of the Green Revolution in India (1993, 2005). These directions of research remain robust within the conceptual and disciplinary frame of political-economy and political-ecology. *Curried Cultures* engages with what comes after that and takes us in a different direction, towards the culture of consumption (and reproduction), a sphere that Mary Douglas and Baron Isherwood contended "is the very arena in which culture is fought over and licked into shape" (1996: 57).

The two ends of this incongruent polarity, colonial famine and post-colonial gastronomy, are surprisingly tied together by a remarkable book, *Alimentary Tracts* (2010), by Parama Roy. Heavily theorized and deeply entangled in the thicket of literary criticism, it is chronologically selective, hopping, skipping, and jumping from the 1857 Indian Mutiny (against East India Company rule), to Gandhi's austere vegetarianism and spectacular fasting, through hungers of the low-caste poor in Mahasweta Devi's fictions, to the gastronomic reclamation of curry powder by Madhur Jaffrey. In doing so Roy walks the fertile borderlands of the ethical and the aesthetic consequences of eating the other—animal and human. In allowing the other to enter one's body without the desperate need of purgation, she expertly inverts the critique of Hooks (1992), Heldke (2003) and Nandy (2003b). She does that by drawing on Jacques Derrida's (1991) suggestion of anthropophagy, not as an abomination but as a "parabolic instantiation of unexpected somatic and ethical engagement with the other" where the "refusal to partake of the other is an important breakdown in or rejection of ethical reciprocity with the other" (P. Roy 2010: 14). Yet this attempt to yoke the political-economic to symbolic-aesthetic analysis remains an exception. The field of engagement with Indian food is polarized into a number of foci: one pole coalescing around crop science; another around development economics; one around culture; still another around nutrition and public health; and another around food science.

The cultural dimension acquired a new kind of visibility by the 1980s and created new tributaries of discussion that eventually severed its connection to the more traditional scope of crop science, political-economy, and anthropology's durable concern with caste and commensality. It is the cultural dimension that will be the focus here, because those concerns have come to define food studies. For scholars working in the realm of interpretive cultural analysis, R. S. Khare's *The Hindu Hearth and Home* (1976b) and Arjun Appadurai's "How to Make a National Cuisine: Cookbooks in Contemporary India" (1988) became important new touchstones. Unsurprisingly, both came out of anthropology, which has a century-long tradition of taking the aesthetics of food seriously. Khare's work was produced within the frame of symbolic anthropology and was based on dense ethnographic description. On the other hand, drawing on ethnography but eventually transcending its confines, Appadurai's reconceptualization of the Indian (and subsequently the global) social landscape allowed scholars to escape the burdens of the long-festering discussion on caste and commensality that had dominated Indian sociology at least since Louis Dumont's *Homo Hierarchicus* (1970; also see Marriott 1990). That escape may have been too fully and easily executed[7] and the byproduct of such a turn was to divert the attention of emerging scholars (outside of anthropology) from the work of the researcher who has done the most sustained work on Indian food (Khare 1976a, 1976b, 1992, 1994, 2006). The postscript of this volume draws attention to what might be gained by returning to the classics.

Curiously, a similar fate has befallen the equally original work of Francis Zimmermann (*The Jungle and the Aroma of Meats* 1987), which is increasingly confined to an audience of anthropologists working on ethno-medicine. Keeping Zimmermann's work in view could afford us the opportunity to develop a theory of taste and knowledge that is tethered to location, in his case the Doab between the Indus and the Ganges, prefiguring a theory of terroir, yet a very Indic one that could enrich the European conception. Zimmerman suggests that a different body and body of imagination may be at work here, reminding us again that all classifications are local. In the process he tries to retrace the system of classification of the natural world that was superseded by the colonial episteme. This is promising, notwithstanding two shortcomings of his method. The first is Zimmerman's overenthusiasm for structuralism's binary oppositions, in this case, the opposition between *anupa* (wetlands) and *jangala* (drylands), and its relationship to disease classification and therapeutics in ancient Ayurvedic texts. That opposition ignores the centrality of the in-between positions of *sadharana* and *sama* (average or everyday), which are central to clinical practice. Zimmerman's second shortcoming is an excessively easy move from the classical texts and their spiritual geography to modern empirical ecology and epidemiology. This ends up caging the totality of Indic tradition within what is seen as scholastic and ideological, against the putative scientific empiricism of the West (Obeyesekere 1991). This is a posture, it appears, that is quite popular in the French mode of Indology, in this case perhaps borrowed from his teacher Louis Dumont.

Charles Malamoud's sharp textual analysis in *Cooking the World: Ritual and Thought in Ancient India* (1996) is similar to Zimmerman's method. Malamoud picks the Sanskrit phrase *lokapakti* in the Satapatha Brahmana, translating it as "cooking the world." At the heart of every Brahmanic rite, Malamoud asserts, is cooking the world. Every sacrificial operation employs a derivative of one of the roots signifying cook, "PAC or SRA (or one of their partial synonyms, such as US, GHR, TAP, or DAH)" (1996: 36–37). This is a powerful, almost magical claim that declares an unwillingness to place everything under the aegis of Western logic, intelligibility, and translatability. It clarifies much about both the ancient Vedic tradition and its contemporary Indic appropriation. Nevertheless, Malamoud's litany of rites is not exhaustive, because it excludes the ultimate offering of the uncooked soma that the Vedas go on about. Yet, in the case of the soma, too, it is food and food for thought. So, it is not always cooking exactly, but at all times it is the offering of food that ties the world together across ritual cleavages. Zimmerman's and Malamoud's texts promise rich conceptual possibilities for contemporary analysts. Yet eventually both authors give in to speculation that ranges too widely from text to practice and between the past and the present. To move from classical text to current practice one could do no better than Paul Toomey's *Food from the Mouth of Krishna* (1994) that zeros in on Govardhan as an exemplary Vaishnava pilgrimage place in northern India, at the intersection of folk and sectarian traditions, focusing on the "kinds of food events observed at temple and feasts; food classification systems and coded sequences followed by ritual specialists in cooking, offering, and distributing food; and finally, meanings conveyed by menu changes and changes in quantities of food offerings in different groups" (Toomey 1994: 4). Toomey successfully ties together ritual and everyday practice that has a tendency to fray in academic anthropological Indology.

Recently, anthropology, of which the just-mentioned texts are some of the thickest instantiations, and its more proximate subcontinental cousin, sociology, have ceded ground to expatriate South Asian scholars working outside those academic traditions—perhaps partaking of a form of émigré nostalgia—in the fields of history, cultural studies, and postcolonial studies (P. Roy 2010; Mannur 2010). In contrast, the definitive, two-volume, *Oxford India Companion to Sociology and Social Anthropology* (2003), edited by Veena Das, has almost nothing pertaining to food consumption (actually less than half a page in a 1,600-page collection). Those attuned to the Indian intellectual space have not yet considered public edibility to be a domain worthy of theoretical attention (beyond that is the traditional anthropological concerns of caste and commensality). Perhaps theoretical attention to culinary matters comes with affluence and at the end of public spectacles of hunger.

Outside of anthropology, K. T. Achaya's encyclopedic *Indian Food: A Historical Companion* (1998b) remains the standard text to develop an overview. Within the field of history a new generation of scholars is producing highly theorized texts on the relationship between discourse, diet, and domesticities that moves past Achaya's endless (although rich) empiricism (Arnold 1994; Chaudhuri & Strobel 1992; Zlotnick 1996; Harrison 1999; E. M. Collingham 2001; S. Prasad 2005, 2006). Conceptually, Bernard Cohn's attention to the materiality of clothes, the body, and forms of knowledge since the mid-1950s, and his productive harnessing of methodologies in anthropology and history provided the opening to reconsider diet, disease, and the body (see Cohn 1996). Nupur Chaudhuri's "Shawls, Jewelry, Curry and Rice in Victorian Britain" (1992) and Susan Zlotnick's "Domesticating Imperialism" (1996) provided a template of this direction of inquiry leading into food. A rich seam of research on domesticity and intimacy has subsequently been uncovered, using new sources such as domestic manuals in vernaculars (especially in Bengali) and by revisiting old manuscripts in Persian and English (Walsh 2004; Banerjee 2004; Lal 2005; Sengupta 2010).

Chapter 4 in this volume—"Nation on a Platter"—provides a substantial historiographical analysis of these developments.

New kinds of work have proliferated in at least two other directions. On one hand, edibles in semi-public spaces, such as restaurants and hotels in cities around the globe, have been made legible (Conlon 1995; U. Narayan 1997; T. Srinivas 2007; Buettner 2008). A number of chapters in part 3 provide recent examples of this direction of research. They draw on the analysis of popular urban culture, restaurants, and status, which in some ways returns us to the much older discussion of commensality and hierarchy, but this time focused on the city and commerce, rather than the village and the community (B. [Bhaskar] Mukhopadhyay 2004; T. Srinivas 2007). Both iterations of these themes—old concerns about caste and commensality, and the new issues of city and consumption—have recently figured in special food issues of the journals *South Asia Research* (2004), *China Report* (2007, about the Chinese of Kolkata), and *South Asia* (2008).[8] *Curried Cultures* brings together these recent developments in three separate chapters on Indian restaurant food, making amends for the remarkably long silence on public edibility in South Asia.

On the other hand, work has flourished on diets and diasporic domesticities drawing on the study of immigrant households, ethnic sensibilities, and questions of postcolonial identities (U. Narayan 1997; Ganguly 2001; K. Ray 2004; T. Srinivas 2006; Mannur 2010; P. Roy 2010). Each one of these works, along with the final substantively empirical chapter by Srinivas (chapter 11), is an exploration of the unsettled boundaries between private and public, home and away, which are often assumed to be clearly demarcated. They deal with shifting concepts of the domestic and of the public in urban foodscapes. They explore conceptions of ethnicity, caste, and identity for diasporic Indian communities, while simultaneously looking at narratives of health and fitness that such communities contend with and incorporate into their foodscapes.

Common use of terms such as foodscapes, flows, and transnationalism shows our immense debt to Arjun Appadurai's imaginative formulations, which frame almost any current discussion of globalization, modernity, and food. The challenge is to say something more than what is already intimated in "Playing with Modernity" (1995) and *Modernity at Large* (1996). We see our task as retaining the startling illumination of his suggestions in those works by paying attention to movement, by way of various scapes, and yet doing so without sacrificing attention to the density of bodies, things in close proximity, and to communities that are still bounded in other ways. Food studies can draw attention precisely to the weight of localized bodies caught in globalized motion. On the other hand, Appadurai makes a number of exemplary points about migrants and media reconstituting our worlds, which must be made to bear on food studies' tendency to territorialize taste and naturalize locality. For instance, he insists that ethnographers must find ways to represent the links between imagination and social life. If traditional anthropology's historical role was to fill the "savage slot in an internal Western dialogue about utopia," he proposes, then a "recuperated anthropology must recognize that the genie is now out of the bottle and that speculations about utopia are everyone's prerogative" (1996, 65). A number of chapters in this book, especially on restaurants, develop that theme, while others argue against it, even while taking his recommendations seriously. Appadurai also forces us to rethink the relationship between diasporic publics and the private sphere of migrants.[9]

In "Public, Popular, and Other Cultures," Christopher Pinney (2001: 1–34) points to the vivid materiality of popular visual culture in South Asia, decisively drawing it into the realm of academic analysis. Such a move is possible precisely because of popular culture's frisson of marginality, which makes it desirable for an academic fabrication of a countercultural posture. This is in part why films, television serials, and rickshaw- and calendar-art have been studied, yet the academic middle classes' own exemplary sites of everyday publicness, such as restaurants and coffee houses, are rarely investigated. Another reason for ignoring eateries may be that the audiences they produce are smaller and more fragmented than those of a film or a television show, and thus less amenable to distant modes of representation and argumentation. However, restaurants, located as they are in the space between the public and the domestic, provide a view from the middle of those two un-bridged categories. For this reason alone, analytical investigation of restaurants would be instructive to the nature and means of transactions in literal tastes and how they shape aesthetic taste. Furthermore, urban eateries are worth paying attention to because unlike cinema, television, cricket, and film music, restaurants might heighten the divergent trajectories of class-based spaces. That is to say, elite restaurants might re-cleave Indian public culture similar to Peter Burke's reading of early modern European culture as divided between two unbridgeable domains of elites and masses, replicated in nineteenth-century Calcutta studied by Sumanta Banerjee (1998), which would qualify, if not nullify Ulf Hannerz's claim that postcolonial popular culture emerged as a "field of activity more or less uniting elites and masses in shared pastimes and pleasures" (Hannerz 1992: 240–241). Yet, it is also true that, much like cinema, street foods—*chaats, samosas, bhelpuri, vada, pakora,* and kebab—are equally popular among elites, middle classes, and the poor. They are often consumed in shared spaces (produced by street vendors) in ways that elide and obscure such divisions, borrowing from high and low cultural universes at the same time and combining them in unexpected ways. Which way South Asian public culture is headed is a question worth posing through the medium of commodified cuisines. A notable exception to the paucity of attention to public eateries is Frank Conlon's "Dining Out in Bombay," in the pages of Breckenridge's *Consuming Modernity* (1995), where the incongruity of the public and popular is developed with great felicity and empirical richness. It is instructive that Conlon's work finds room within Appadurai and Breckenridge's capacious composition of "public culture" as the "space between domestic life and the projects of the nation state—where different social groups . . . constitute their identities by their experience of mass-mediated forms in relation to the practices of everyday life" (1995: 4–5). Conlon's work prefigures almost any work on modern Indian restaurants, hence it is not at all surprising that a number of chapters here draw on it to illuminate their work or argue with it. Two instances of the fecundity of "Dining Out in Bombay" have to suffice for our argument here. The first is his glancing but prophetic attention to the intricate logistics of the lunch delivery system—the *dabbawallas* (lunch-box-carriers) of Bombay—that preceded its entrée into business school curricula as an example of bottom-up, capillary networks of remarkable efficiency and robustness. Second, he warns us not to ignore recent developments in Bombay's elite restaurants, not be blinded by the temptation to view them "merely as interesting, possibly amusing, manifestations of the cultural consumption on the periphery of a Euro-centered world capitalist system. Such a reaction should be resisted insofar as it slips too easily into a comfortable assumption that Indian public culture is merely a derivative, if colorful, form of global modernity" (1995: 115).

Lastly, two important caveats about what this book does not do. *Curried Cultures* does not address the concerns of the more than twenty percent of the Indian population that the United Nations estimates is faced with acute hunger.[10] In the early sections of this chapter we have pointed to work that addresses those concerns, and note here that it is outside the scope of this work. Nor does this project address the concerns of subalterns about whom

Gayatri Chakravorty Spivak has written as those "who have stayed in place for thirty thousand years" (Spivak 1999: 402). *Curried Cultures* is about those who have been drawn fully into the vortex of globalization in its current form, which in our estimation is mostly the South Asian middle and upper classes.[11] What Frank Conlon wrote at the early stages of the discussion on public dining cultures in a South Asian world continues to carry weight: "If India's cosmopolitan public culture is to be the object of scholarly analysis, its essentially elite qualities must be acknowledged" (1995: 108). While acknowledging those limits, we think it is important not to draw excessively rigid boundaries between the categories of middle-class and mass consumption, or luxury and more mundane goods, precisely because of the hegemonic reach of such middle-class, middle-brow things, which are its exact analytic potentialities. It is truer now than when Conlon was writing almost two decades ago that most of India's "population has existed between the extremes of great wealth and abject poverty and that at many intermediate levels people have experienced a growth of purchasing power ... [enabling] an ever widening popular participation in the phenomenon of restaurant dining" (1995: 116). Such analysis can, for instance, teach us ways of reimagining and interrogating this strange but naturalized institution we have come to call a *restaurant* after eighteenth-century Parisian taste-makers. We are reminded most clearly of those potentialities in the chapters by Madsen and Gardella (chapter 5) and Shaffer (chapter 6). Furthermore, *Curried Cultures* is mostly about Indians in India and abroad without sustained attention to other South Asians. Here we touch the surface of an urbanized, multi-lingual middle class, and although we are aware that is not the whole story, it will have to suffice for now. We will dig deeper into provincial towns and vernaculars of public eating in future work. We just do not know enough about the protagonists in such towns yet. We are currently developing research in those directions in a project we are calling "Cities without Restaurants: Cookshops and the Provincial Middle Classes in a Small Indian Town." But that has to await its time. The study of restaurants in India is worth pursuing in some detail not only because they are ubiquitous, but also because it will afford us theoretical insights that will complicate our ideas about cuisine, culture, and cities, which at present are mostly derived from Euro-American spaces. Hopefully, in the process we will also learn about what lies below the bourgeois restaurant, such as tea stalls, *dhabas* (roadside eateries), boiled-egg stands, paan and cigarette shops, and food vendors, which have not yet been the focus of academic analysis.

The first part of this book wrestles down the concept of globalization as something old (movement of people, things, and ideas across national boundaries) and yet as something new (density of transportation networks, communications flows, circulation of signs) by way of this introduction and the next chapter, by Akhil Gupta. Gupta wonders why questions of globalization in popular and scholarly discussions in the West have for the most part retained a temporally shallow frame. He argues that food and foodstuffs have played a critical, and underappreciated, role in the long history of globalization. While much has been made about the impact of the global circulation of news, films, music, and fashions, not enough attention has been paid to how identities have been shaped by the movement of cuisines and foods. A deeper history of globalization as seen through crops and cuisines takes us past several moments of theoretical consolidation of the culture of consumption, hurtling us from this overelaborated neoliberal moment, backwards through Fordism, the mid-Victorian Glass Palace, past Wedgewood's china, to early modern Europe and the imperial expanse of a world of exotic goods and consumption (Slater 1997; Schivelbusch 1992; Freedman 2008).

The second part highlights the history of South Asian food within the circuits of exchange in colonial times and the nationalist reaction to it. These chapters trace the development of the culture and aesthetics of what comes to be called Indian food through an analysis of historical documents. While some attention is paid to the British importation of flavors and cooking methods from India, most of it explores the changing face of Indian food in India. In chapter 3 Angma Jhala examines the material culture and aesthetics of the *zenana,* including the history of courtly cuisine in colonial princely households. In particular, she explores how imperial cultural norms, such as cooking styles; ideas of taste; and ingredients introduced from Europe, the Americas, and the Middle East, influenced the politics of food in ceremonial and political functions (*durbars,* viceregal visits to princely states, state marriages) in the public theater of the Raj. Attention is paid to the role of gender in the preparation of dishes and menus for state functions, such as marriages, celebrations for the birth of children (especially the male heir), pregnancies, and other auspicious events (*pujas* and festivals, for instance) that are of particular relevance to the female members of the courtly household. This chapter argues that the history of cuisine (and cooking) in the zenana reflects the changing hybrid nature of colonial rule in India, whereby recipes incorporated both precolonial, indigenous culinary traditions as well as European ingredients and food preparation systems to merge in a dynamic, transnational, cosmopolitan style of courtly cuisine. Indeed, the "indigenous" itself would have been cosmopolitan in nature, reflecting the vast differences in local courtly households (for there were nearly six hundred princely states before Independence in 1947) based on region, religion, and ethnicity.

Chapter 4 examines the relationship between dietary practice and health in late nineteenth-century and early twentieth-century Bengal, where Jayanta Sengupta argues that food and cuisine represented a vibrant site on which a complex rhetorical struggle between colonialism and nationalism was played out. Insofar as they carried symbolic meanings and "civilizational attributes," cooking and eating transcended their functionality and became cultural practices, with a strong ideological-pedagogical content. The Bengali/Indian kitchen, so strongly reviled in European colonialist discourses as a veritable purgatory, became a critically important symbolic space in the emerging ideology of domesticity in the colonial period. The gastronomic excesses of gluttonous British officials—crucial in asserting the physical superiority of a "masculine" Raj—became an object of ridicule in Bengali culinary texts, signifying the grossness of a materialistic Occident. The cooking and eating of food thus became deeply implicated in the cultural politics of *bhadralok* nationalism.

Between Independence (1947) and Liberalization (1991), with the expanding size of the middle class, rising incomes, and transvaluation of modes of public edibility, cultures of consumption have proliferated. In recent years, we have witnessed a robust restaurant culture in major Indian cities, although little has been written about them outside the realm of the restaurant review and the gastronomic essay (see N. S. Roy 2004). Cities large and small have begun to brim with *Barista* and *Coffee Day*. Yet, not everything is discontinuous. Modern Indian eateries also draw on older patterns of urbanization and circulation of classes through urban spaces such as Brahmin Udupi hotels that remarkably combined the purported fixity of caste with the fluidity of commerce and commensality.

Chapter 5 examines the evolution of traditional Brahmanical food practices by narrating the story of Udupi restaurants (known as "Udupi hotels") from the early twentieth century, when entrepreneurs from the Udupi area on the Kanara Coast made their first moves outwards, until today, when the culinary power of Udupi hotels has reached as far as the Silicon Valley in California. Stig Toft Madsen and Geoffrey Gardella argue that Udupi hotels have contributed to the processes of secularization and modernization by exposing traditional dietary practices associated with temple and village rituals to the combined forces of the market, state law, and politics. Thereby, Udupi catering and hoteliering have been instrumental in the transformation of commensal orthodoxies lying at the very root of Hindu religious identity and Brahmanical tradition, thus enlarging the public space for civic intercourse. However, Udupi entrepreneurs have also contributed to a religious revival. Part of the profits entrepreneurs have earned in urban centers have been used to renovate old temples and to sponsor rituals. The end result of the increased ritual activity is the creation of a highly charged religious landscape awash with revitalized *devtas,* reempowered *bhutas,* and sanskritized temples—courtesy the migrants. The chapter ends on the note that "a Great Tradition that modernizes, globalizes, and secularizes is also likely to Brahmanize and revitalize."

Is the Udupi-style restaurant a modern westernized thing or a traditional Indian one? Such questions and others in the following chapters on restaurants and chaat cafés in Mumbai, London, New York, and Berkeley draw interesting comparative insights about gastronomic discourse, urban spaces, hierarchy of global cities, and immigrant bodies and imaginations. The discussions in these empirically rich chapters attend to a long-festering but muted—muted about the food and the space—commentary on publics, publicity, and popularity, as produced in European coffeehouses in the work of Jürgen Habermas (1991), Wolfgang Schivelbusch (1992) and Benedict Anderson (1983); a space that presumably produced the bourgeois national publics via proximate conversation and distant newspapers. Subsequent critiques of the singularity and masculinity of such publics by Nancy Fraser (1992) and their provincialism by Dipesh Chakrabarty (2007) incite our attention to such spaces again. How is the process of transplanting such Euro-American institutions happening in India and among Indians in the West, and what does that do spatially, imaginatively, and gustatorily to peoples' imagined, real, and sensorially experienced worlds? Further research will have to go beyond such spaces and focus on different kinds of eateries and the potential of gatherings around tea stalls in Queens, New York, paan shops in Toronto, and pubs in Southhall, London, which constitute different kinds of publics (still curiously amassed around edibles) with varied intentionalities and reach in terms of publicity and modalities of being public and private.

Here we stick to the restaurant to provide a more detailed look than usually accorded such places.

In chapter 6, Holly Shaffer interrogates the invention of a "historical" cuisine. She traces the method of cooking—*dum pukht*—from the 1970s, back into its Persian, Mughal, Nawabi, and British histories, and forward into its contemporary history in Lucknow. The goal is to take one dish (or method) and use it, through oral histories, interviews, and ethnography, as a material trace to uncover contemporary questions of culinary authenticity, nostalgia for "lost" Muslim culture, and historical cuisine as a commodity, while also reaching into the past that the contemporary seeks to hold.

Susan Dewey, in chapter 7, shows that food consumption is a powerful means by which individuals demonstrate their membership in a privileged group. As global commodities continue to penetrate post-Liberalization Mumbai, they offer fantasies of happiness through the phantasmagoria of consumer capitalism—fully but critically engaging with Appadurai's world of lives and dreams. Although the idea of the "international Indian" is inextricably tied to European and North American notions of taste and discernment, membership in this subculture, with its associated privileged forms of knowledge, offers a powerful tool with which to establish authority and social status that are beneficial in other spheres of professional and personal life. It examines the construction of such consumption practices using research in two Mumbai-based sites: India's nascent wine industry and the rapid expansion of three themed restaurants, all of which have sought to "teach modern India how to eat." In examining how "international Indians" and others they interact with make sense of these sites as relatively new cultural phenomena, it comes closest to affirming Ulf Hannerz's other important contention that postcolonial popular culture "appears to be above all a manifestation of metropolis-oriented sophistication and modernity" (1992: 240; also see Dwyer & Pinney 2001: 11).

In chapter 8 Elizabeth Buettner argues that in Great Britain, a nation where the consumption of "foreign" food has grown exponentially since the 1950s, South Asian cuisine occupies a unique place. In the postcolonial era, preexisting public conceptions evolved in tandem with mass immigration from the subcontinent. Other favored foreign cuisines, particularly Italian and Chinese, that took root in British diets and dining-out habits were not widely associated with immigration to any comparable extent. West Indians were the only minority group to compete with South Asians in terms of numbers and the level of public attention and anxiety they attracted. But

Afro-Caribbean cuisine (as distinct from Caribbean-produced commodities such as sugar) never featured significantly in white British diets, nor did Caribbean restaurants become popular destinations for other ethnic groups. Whereas music has been the cultural form postwar Britons most commonly associate with the Afro-Caribbean community, South Asian food and peoples typically merged in white understandings—a distinction aptly summarized in critiques of the tokenistic multiculturalism long taught in British schools as revolving around stereotypes of "saris, samosas, and steel bands." The history of South Asian food's rise in popularity reveals an uneasy coexistence between ongoing racism and exclusion on one hand, and the gradual and conditional development of enthusiastic appreciation of "celebratory multiculturalism," on the other hand.

In chapter 9, Krishnendu Ray argues that in the sociology of food we have learned a lot about what customers seek and get in eating ethnic food, which nevertheless summarily dismisses any volition or aspiration on the part of the immigrant producer of food, outside of economic necessity. Even when born of necessity, there is more to the story of immigrant restaurants than distinction, domination, and deployment of cultural capital by its white anglophone customers. By inserting the habits, memories, work, and dreams of immigrant entrepreneurs into the discussion of taste, this chapter contributes to a fuller understanding of global flows and modes of localization—bodies are always somewhere and they are often trying to make room for themselves in that place, by drawing on their own resources and the work and imagination of others.

In chapter 10, Arijit Sen examines an Indian fast food restaurant concept that has become popular in the United States. Called "chaat cafés," these restaurants produce everyday Indian street food for urban cosmopolitan customers in America. According to Sharon Zukin (1995) restaurants such as these exemplify a symbolic economy of globalization. The fronts of these restaurants are fashionable meeting places for cosmopolitan "foodies," while also drawing on immigrant customers. The backroom food preparation areas are populated by low-paid immigrant workers of all ethnicities. Although chaat—a form of piquant street food—may be served in Indian restaurants across the world, the American chaat café is unique in its layout, location, menu, and behavior. Unlike traditional Indian "curry-restaurants," chaat cafés sport self-serve delis and informal decor. The author argues that chaat cafés aren't isolated ethnic enterprises catering to an immigrant niche market, but rather new public spaces emerging out of demographic, economic, and political restructuring and urban revitalization in major American cities. Based on spatial analysis, urban investigation, participant observations, interviews, and an analysis of urban development plans of the city of Berkeley, this chapter argues that this café is located at the intersection of multiple public realms.

Chapter 11 deals with shifting norms of food provisioning in both the city of Bangalore in South India and the city of Boston in the United States. It argues that women are primarily involved in food provisioning in Indian households in both cities. Through interviews and other ethnographic tools, Tulasi Srinivas looks at the changing nature of the Indian foodscape and its implications for Indian women. As more prepared food and packaged food enters the Indian marketplace and more women are absorbed into the global economy, the notions of food provisioning undergo a serious shift. A new moral narrative accompanies these shifts in everyday behavior that privilege global capitalist ways of being. In Bangalore the author finds that the moral narrative of food shifts from local understandings of health and home grown and cooked food where purity is important, to one of time and speed where access to luxury food and quick foods become key. Furthermore, purity concerns are often replaced with concerns over hygiene and modern notions of health. In Boston, on the other hand, the narrative often encompasses fears of loss of ethnicity and of identity, and concerns over a return to a "purer," simpler life. Both concerns are linked to authenticity in process and in aesthetics, and in both locations are often interwoven with secrecy as to ingredients, process, and availability. The moral positioning of food becomes a revealing narrative of the hazards that these women feel they face in providing for their families.

Finally, in the postscript, R. S. Khare returns us fully to anthropology's long engagement with foodways, precisely where the modern quest began to figure out the relationship between locals, their foods, and their place-making and time-marking practices. It is fitting that Khare, a pioneer in studying food in the South Asian context, guides us through the arc of his research. He interrogates what has stayed the same in food research, what has changed, with what kinds of problems and potential. Within that over-arching frame he discusses some distinct conceptual issues, collaborative efforts, and new research directions (especially anthropological) in Indian investigations. This is where we take the measure of giants in the field such as Louis Dumont, McKim Marriott, Mary Douglas, and Sidney Mintz. In the process he draws attention to the sensually rich but undertheorized moments of the great-anthropologist-in-the-world. By doing so he disturbs our expectation of an ethnographic text that excises the kind of material that leads Clifford Geertz, in *The Interpretation of Culture,* to characterize *Tristes Tropiques* by Claude Levi-Strauss as not "a great anthropology book, or even an especially good one," but "surely one of the finest books ever written by an anthropologist" (1973: 347). Precisely because it includes the kind of sensory material full of feeling and action that the anthropologist Paul Stoller sees as otherwise relegated to informal settings, because the genre rules of a consecrated ethnography disallow such sensory detours (1990). In this chapter we find Khare feeling his way towards the new materialism of food and bodies that succeeds the old ideal-material divide that valorized symbol over practice, and signification over sign (see Lock & Farquhar 2007). It is a new materialism that pays attention to bodies and minds, and to built environments and urban geographies that distinguishes this collection.

Much of what we call globalization today is not new and that is evident only if we dig a little deeper into the lineages of our foods and anthropological research on it. Yet what we suggest with the phrase globalization here is that things are quite different today from what preceded it. We use the term to draw attention to transnational flows and to denote a sense, or a structure of feeling, at least among urban dwellers, and especially among the middle classes, that people from all over the world have been pulled together in sharper and more proximate juxtaposition to each other. In that sense, cultural globalization is new. It is a new thing in urban middle-class conceptions of self and the other, and food plays a central role in that imaginary.

NOTES

1. Agro-industrial food production is in itself a rich and substantial field, which can only be illustrated with a few references here (McMichael 1994; Bonanno, Busch, Friedland, Gouveia, & Mingione 1994; Barndt 1999; Johnston, Gismondi, & Goodman 2006; Gupta in this volume).

2. The municipal council of Lucca (a town in Tuscany, Italy) ruled on January 26, 2009, that "with a view to safeguarding culinary traditions and the authenticity of structure, architecture, culture and history, establishments whose activities can be tracked to different ethnicities won't be allowed to operate." See the Bloomberg article: http://www.bloomberg.com/apps/news?pid=20601092&sid=aSqbıksisZaI &refer;.

3. Pollock confines that possibility to the past instances of translocalism and not the current one.

4. We are here confining ourselves in two directions: first, to the discussion of food in the modern social sciences and humanities, thereby excluding the conversation on food in the century-old disciplines of nutrition and food science (for recent instances, see Islam & Sarkar 2010; Ratnawali 2010); and second, we are also unable to comment on the extensive discussion of food, taste, and health as developed within local Indian systems of medicine and good living such as in Ayurveda (see Zimmermann 1987; Wujastyk &Meulenbeld 2001; Wujastyk 2003; Smith & Wujastyk 2008). We do not have adequate competence in either of those fields to comment on their development. For a recent work that bridges the historiography of indigenous and Western medicine, see Digby, Ernst, & Muhkarji 2010.

5. Much of the current work on hunger is undertaken by institutions such as the Food and Agriculture Organization (FAO) of the United Nations and numerous non-governmental organizations. For the Food and Agriculture Organization, see http://www.fao.org/docrep/011/i0291e/i0291e00.htm; for the International Food Policy Research Institute (IFPRI), see http://www.ifpri.org/sites/default/files/publications/2020anhconfpaper01.pdf. IFPRI is one of fifteen centers supported by the Consultative Group on International Agricultural Research (CGIAR), an alliance of sixty-four governments, private foundations, and international and regional organizations.

6. Borlaug was accorded the second-highest civilian recognition—the Padma Vibhushan—by the government of India in 2006.

7. See the postscript of this volume and the special food issues of journals such as *South Asia,* April 2008, and *South Asia Research,* May 2004.

8. In February 2009 the School of Oriental and African Studies (SOAS) hosted a conference on food and immigration and a collection of papers from that meeting was published in June 2011 as a special issue of the American journal *Food, Culture & Society*. Outside the academy a robust new direction has developed in popular food writing, mostly in the genre of travel writing and memoir. Combining the two superbly, Chitrita Banerji has produced a long line of work (1997, 2006, 2007, 2008). Two less poetic but much more comprehensive popular studies of Indian food are by Colleen Taylor Sen (2004, 2009).

9. See Fraser (1992) for public and Dwyer and Pinney (2001) for popular as a specifically South Asian inflection of the "public." Furthermore, public-ness cannot be exhausted by face-to-face meeting, but could also be mediated from a distance by print and electronic media (Taylor 2004). Aiwha Ong (1999) theorizes the formation of ethnicized transnational publics that are neither dependent on critical rational face-to-face dialogue nor on consumption, but on the proliferation of information technology.

10. According to the *Times of India* (February 27, 2009): "India is failing its rural poor with 230 million people being undernourished—the highest for any country in the world. Malnutrition accounts for nearly 50% of child deaths in India

as every third adult (aged 15–49 years) is reported to be thin (BMI less than 18.5). According to the latest report on the state of food insecurity in rural India, more than 1.5 million children are at risk of becoming malnourished because of rising global food prices."

11. We just do not know enough about the other worlds yet, even if we keep in mind Appadurai's contention that the most localized of Indian worlds have become "inflected—even afflicted—by cosmopolitan scripts that drive the politics of families, the frustrations of laborers, the dreams of local headmen" (1996, 63).

TWO

A Different History of the Present

THE MOVEMENT OF CROPS, CUISINES, AND GLOBALIZATION

Akhil Gupta

INTRODUCTION

GLOBALIZATION AS A PHENOMENON has captured the popular and scholarly imagination in the First World in the last two decades. Much of this discussion of globalization has turned on trade and economic issues, and on the very visible worldwide diffusion of media and popular culture. Thanks to a series of highly visible protests against the World Trade Organization, the International Monetary Fund, and the World Bank, first in Seattle, and then successively in Prague, Washington DC, Genoa, and New York, globalization has become a contested term in popular discourse. Nowhere is this more evident than in recent controversies about the safety, reliability, and sustainability of food. Issues of food safety hit the headlines because of the export of contaminated milk from China, but have also been raised with regard to the long-term health effects of genetically modified foods. Concern about the reliability of food supplies was underscored by global food shortages that resulted in food riots in many countries for the first time in living memory. Droughts in food-exporting countries such as Australia, which may be caused by global warming; long and complex commodity chains, especially when they involve the processing and transportation of fresh meat, fruits, and vegetables; and the use of commodities such as corn for fuel and animal feed have all been identified as causes of global food shortages. Finally, a growing interest in sustainability, alongside concerns about safety and reliability, have prompted a movement to consume food that is grown locally. Known by several names—locavores, slow food—this movement emphasizes buying food directly from the farmer, thereby reducing the commodity chain to its minimum, and eating food that is grown sustainably (itself measured by land conservation, the carbon footprint of the commodity, or the measure of virtual water that it contains).[1]

I will use the movement of crops, changing culinary practices, and shifting habits of food consumption to argue that food and foodstuffs have played a critical, and perhaps under-appreciated, role in the long history of globalization. In the contemporary moment, much has been made about the impact of the global circulation of news, films, music, and fashions. However, not enough attention has been paid to how cultures, histories, and identities have been shaped by the movement of cuisines and foods. What does a deeper history of globalization as seen through crops, cuisines, and consumption tell us about the historical shaping of identities?

FOOD AND GLOBALIZATION

I will begin by offering some theoretical reflections on the location of food in the broader debate about "globalization." One can identify at least two broad positions on the phenomenon of globalization, which have to be understood sequentially. In response to the paeans to globalization that accompanied the neoliberal expansion of capitalism in the last quarter of the twentieth century, came the response that there was nothing new about globalization. Although the energy of the first position came largely from the business world (Friedman 2000, 2005), it found strong support in a kind of multi-culturalist discourse that was unaware of its own imperial centrality, and it also received encouragement from commercial cultural production in spheres like film, television, and music. In academic fields, it produced broadly convergent positions between disciplines that normally are on opposite sides, like economics and literary and cultural studies. The opposition to this view also sometimes came from the same disciplines, but mainly from historians (Hopkins 2002; F. Cooper 2001).

In food studies, these two trends coexisted, but while the globalization of food has attracted a great deal of attention in the last decade, it has not led to the dichotomies and polemics that characterize the literature on globalization more broadly. Why is that the case? I suggest that here we need to pay attention to the relative autonomy of intellectual fields. The rise of "fusion" food, exotic ingredients, and the relentless and never-ending search for the "new," fueled by an enormous rise in popularity of food shows on television, food films, travel shows that were mostly about food, do draw upon some of the same energies of capitalist consumerism that have informed the celebratory wing of globalization in other domains. However, these trends have been accompanied by the enormous popularity of books on the history of food. The question of the origins of foods, and the circulation of foodstuffs from their places of origin to their place of consumption, has become of abiding interest to "foodies" as well as to scholars.[2] The result is that, at least in the West, an awareness of the history of the origins of food and its global circulation has developed alongside the trend toward consuming the global.

This fact has significant implications for how globalization is understood. The knowledge of globalization that has been propagated in popular culture and scholarly circles through food has largely avoided the dualisms and polemics that often seem to have settled onto the general literature on globalization. This difference in understanding between food studies and other fields leads to a question about what is lost analytically when we talk of globalization in the singular. Is globalization one phenomenon, or many different ones that have converged to create the illusion of unitariness? Alternatively, are these different phenomena simply confused with one another?[3] Food studies helps push the position that we need to think of globalizations as discrepant and diverse rather than singular and unified.

Globalization is not a unique "thing" that can be charted in a unitary and definitive fashion for at least three reasons. First, the meaning of globalization diverges according to the phenomenon or sector being analyzed: thus an understanding of globalization derived from an examination of global financial flows differs substantially from another that looks at the exchange of biogenetic materials. Secondly, globalization appears very different in distinct geographical and spatial settings. Finally, globalization means very different things to diversely situated groups of people. Food studies help us make the argument that we need to move beyond the sweeping character of some of the pronouncements about globalization in the contemporary world by attending to the situational and conjunctural nature of "the global." Even as we engage from our various subject positions the ethico-political imperative to name, define, and debate "the global," we should be keenly aware of the futility of the task. An acknowledgment of the impossibility of mapping globalization in the face of the necessity of doing so makes it possible to more clearly engage the politics of what Tsing has called "the culture and politics of scale making" (2000: 330).[4]

Despite the pronouncements of some economists and politicians, the contemporary form of globalization does not represent the inevitable march of history.[5] Many aspects of life in the twentieth century appear to have reversed earlier processes of globalization. One such process involved the movement of food through the *people* who transported foods and foodways from one location to another.[6] If one looks at the mobility of populations, the absolute numbers of people who moved from one state boundary to another in the nineteenth century may very well have been comparable to immigration in the world today. Despite the fact that we like to think that the population movements in the world today are historically unprecedented, the *proportion* of the population that migrated in the nineteenth century certainly exceeded anything in the present. Just think of the millions of people who migrated from Europe to the far corners of the world: the Americas especially, but also South Africa, Australia and New Zealand, and different colonial areas in Africa and Asia, and in addition there were those who traveled, temporarily or permanently, from one nation-state in Europe to another. As many as one hundred million people are estimated to have moved in the nineteenth century, half of whom were European (Held, McGew, Goldblatt, and Perraton 1999: 311–314; Mintz 1985: 71). They took with them their own food cultures and knowledges, and this has profoundly altered the character of "national" cuisines (Möhring 2008). The construction of a "national" cuisine often rests on the "forgetting" or suppression of the foreignness of its foods and foodways, which are, not surprisingly, associated with immigrant food and immigrant peoples.[7] However, there are important exceptions to such a statement. For example, the "national" cuisine in the United States is seen as a result of the various cuisines of dominant European immigrant groups.

This brings me to my second point, which has to do with the unevenness and contradictoriness of globalization. Globalization is best seen not as a set of flows, but pathways for transactions or exchanges that depend on the reconfiguration of existing structural and social conditions (Held et. al. 1999: 1–28; Tsing 2000: 460). These pathways ensure that flows are highly unequal and asymmetrical. In its late-twentieth-century form, globalization in fact has sharply differentiated the ease, speed, and direction in which different things have flowed. On one end are finances, images, and communications, which now move around the globe at dizzying speeds; on the other end are flows of people and biogenetic resources, which move much more haltingly and unidirectionally. Somewhere in the middle are flows of goods, technologies, and ideas. From immigration laws to regimes of intellectual property rights, multiple barriers to mobility exist; these are stratified by geopolitical location, class, gender, and race. The acceleration of financial transactions is often commented on as a distinctive feature of globalization, but the increasing barriers being placed on the movement of immigrants should also be seen as part of the same phenomenon.

It is interesting that many of the contemporary movements and protests against globalization have targeted fast-food companies. For example, French farmers led by José Bové protesting global trade agreements chose to attack a McDonald's restaurant in 1999. The asymmetry of global "flows" is clearly seen in the fact that corporations based in the West have been able to expand rapidly in the rest of the world, particularly catering to a fast-growing middle class in countries like India, whereas farmers from the Third World who wish to sell primary goods in First World markets have a much harder time negotiating the regulatory apparatus, and often have to face protective tariffs, in places such as Europe.

The third point that I have to make about globalization is that globalization is the name for a process that is observed from somewhere, by someone.[8] The breathless excitement with which globalization has been greeted by some may be intimately related to the anxiety that it has provoked in others in that both sets of people seem to be operating with a common narrative about the nation-state. To caricature this narrative, it goes something like this: for the first three quarters of the twentieth century, economic and social life was carried out within a framework in which the territorial state was paramount, and where nationalism provided the ideology of community, which allowed for a regime of regulation characterized by a tripartite relation between capital, labor, and the state apparatus. This is the Fordist compact, which was realized perhaps most fully in social democratic regimes or welfare states. (Harvey 1992). However, in the last twenty-five years, the territorial pact between capital and labor has been broken, so that a gap has opened up between the territorially expansive reorganization of capital on a global scale and the nationally limited character of state regulation and of labor organizing. "The economic" and "the social," which used to map onto the same territory, are now separated; and this separation has given rise to a crisis of representation and meaning on one side (which I think is expressed in the contentious character of nationalism today, ever more strident and xenophobic) and a crisis of regulation on the other, as the regulatory mechanisms that were founded on territorial nation-states and the international system of states find themselves out of sync with dominant economic institutions.

Notice the kind of story that is being caricatured here: first there was the sovereign, territorial nation-state, and then there was globalization, with its attendant gains and painful effects. This raises an important question: Can a different history of the present be narrated? It becomes clear that such a narrative of globalization makes little sense if one sees it from the perspective of a poor person in Bangladesh, Trinidad, or Lesotho. Only in a few nation-states in the First and Second Worlds was the sovereign, territorial state and the provisioning of social welfare a convincing fiction to the majority of their populations. For most other parts of the world, and particularly for subaltern peoples, the twentieth century has not been so much an interruption, as a continuation, of processes of globalization that date at least to the age of European exploration, and in the case of most of Asia, to a much earlier period. A global history of globalization would account not only for non-Western genealogies (Hopkins 2002: 2) but also for subaltern histories. The production, distribution, and consumption of food provides us with excellent material to pursue such a history.

If one looks at the Indian Ocean, for example, in an area that includes coastal East Africa, the Red Sea, the Persian Gulf, the Indian subcontinent, and what is now Southeast Asia (and beyond the Indian Ocean region, coastal China and Japan), one finds a long history of connection. These connections probably reached their zenith from the twelfth century onwards, and especially during the century between the latter half of the thirteenth century and first half of the fourteenth (i.e., from 1250–1350). During this time, long-distance trade over land, but especially over sea, had resulted in a truly spectacular set of economic relations and cultural encounters. Economies around the world connected by these routes boomed, as did new forms of cultural expression (Abu-Lughod 1989).

If one wished to explain the nature of politics, societies, and cultures in these places, one needed to look not just at a culture area or empire, not at their encounters with peoples over the next hill, but around the Indian Ocean. For example, goods such as silks and porcelain flowed out of China and rapidly affected tastes around the Indian Ocean (hence we talk even now of dining on "fine China"); Arabian horses were exported to India and changed transportation and military strategy in the subcontinent (Chaudhuri 1985: 108); coffee went from the Yemeni port of Mocha via Egypt to Amsterdam and London in the late seventeenth century, and then was grown in Java to meet European demand, becoming a part of their and our lives to such an extent that many people would be unable to function without it (Hattox 1985: 23; Wickizer 1951: 66–67; Chaudhuri 1985: 31); and incense from the Middle East became central to the ritual life of South Asia and China (Chaudhuri 1985: 18).[9] The point I wish to make here is that premodern globalization, much of which took place before the fifteenth century, was not a "shallow" phenomenon. It did not merely influence the lives of those who lived in coastal areas, along the great ocean trade routes, and those who lived on the vast, intercontinental land routes like the Silk Route, but affected the intimate lives of people far from these places. Religion and ritual, typically regarded as intimate and community centered, were profoundly shaped by these global movements, as were ideas and images, and material artifacts in which people dressed and ate; in short, if one thinks of the extensiveness, reach, and sociological importance of these earlier moments of globalization, they may have been even more far-reaching than anything we might observe today.

Such a claim, of course, immediately raises important question of metrics and methods: how is one to measure the "degree" of globalization? Nowhere is this question more problematic than in the realm of ideas and everyday practices. Held, McGew, Goldblatt, and Perraton argue that if one weighs the extensiveness, intensity, velocity, and impact of global interconnections, then the period before European empires was characterized by *thin globalization* (1999: 21–27). From the perspective of a devout Indonesian Muslim, Held, McGew, Goldblatt, and Perraton's assertion that the "impact" of global flows before European empires was "low" might appear rather puzzling, if not blatantly Eurocentric.[10] It might be helpful to remember that the great diffusion of world religions took place well before the period of European empires, that is, in the era that Held, McGew, Goldblatt, and Perraton term as a period of "thin globalization." Hopkins proposes a different historical genealogy of globalization, dividing it into four phases: archaic, proto-, modern, and post-colonial (2002: 3). While this has the virtue of decentring the West, and positioning contemporary globalization in a long arc, the categories, by being defined in relation to the modern phase of globalization, unwittingly restore the rise of the West as their central narrative.

The efflorescence of historical studies of food in the last two decades strenuously reject a version of history that privileges the last quarter of the twentieth century as a watershed in the grand narrative of globalization. In fact, if anything, such writing for the most part tends to reinforce a version of history that stresses the continuous flow of foods and foodways over time. Food preparation and consumption, as the most intimate, everyday, household activity, is a wonderful metric for the "depth" of globalization, and there is perhaps no better topic that is better explored in this regard than the global flow of spices.

MONOPOLY AND THE MAKING OF A DISTINCTIVE "EUROPEAN" CULINARY CULTURE

We are accustomed not to thinking of sugar as spice, but, rather, to thinking of 'sugar and spice.'

SIDNEY MINTZ, *SWEETNESS AND POWER*

In their study of cooking techniques in southern Europe in the fourteenth and fifteenth centuries, Redon, Sabban, and Serventi conclude that "the main difference between a medieval master cook and a modern-day chef lay in the wealth of spices in his cupboard" (1998: 19). Lest there be any misunderstanding, they are not making this comparison in favor of the modern chef! Spices played an important role in medieval culinary arts, particularly as practiced among aristocratic and urban households, and were by no means limited to the elite; and spice merchants played a prominent role in the social order. (Why are spices so important to medieval Europe? Freedman's *Out of the East* proposes some answers.)

What were the commonly used spices and why were they so routinely found in the kitchens of the wealthy in medieval Europe? Pepper was by far the most important, both in terms of quantities imported, and in its everyday utility (Pearson 1996a: xx), reaching humbler tables and more rural surroundings than its "finer" counterparts (Redon, Sabban, & Serventi 1998: 8). Cloves, nutmeg, cinnamon, and mace were the other important spices, with the first two considered the most precious (Freedman 2008: 108). In addition to these, there were long pepper, ginger, grains of paradise, and cumin; and saffron too played an important role as a flavoring and coloring agent.[11] The extent to which spices were employed can be gauged from the fact that a random sample of twenty-six dishes chosen from *The Medieval Kitchen* yielded eighteen that used at least one spice from Asia, of which eleven employed black pepper.[12]

The surprising popularity of spices, particularly pepper, in the diet of medieval Europe has often been attributed to a simple reason. Most cattle and other major livestock were slaughtered in the late autumn, as it was not possible to feed the animals through the long winter. The meat then had to be preserved by smoking or salting for consumption in the next few months. It has been argued by some that pepper and other spices were used to disguise the semi-putrid smell of the rotting meat, especially as meat consumption increased in a prospering Europe (Pearson 1996a: xvi; Mintz 1985: 81).[13] However, others dispute such functional explanations, since they cannot account either for the subtlety and precision with which spices were often used, or for the fact that fewer spices came to be used before improvements in the methods of preservation; and it certainly does not account for why a smaller quantity of spices were not used when meat and fish was fresh (Dalby 2000: 156; Mennell 1985: 53; Redon, Sabban, and Serventi 1998: 29).[14] Whatever the merits of this argument, one thing is clear: spices served a large range of functions in the medieval European kitchen, and were used in a wide range of foods such as meat, fish, jam, soups, and drinks (Pearson 1996a: xvi).

What no one disputes is that the appetite for spices increased voraciously as Europe moved into its Age of Discovery. Cooking was only one of the many uses to which spices were put; they were important for their medicinal properties, as preservatives, and as an addition to wine (Mintz 1985: 78).[15] Since most wine was drunk within a year, and techniques for preserving it were not yet well developed, spices made the coarse wines of the poor palatable and the mulled wines served on noble tables tastier (Pearson 1996a: xvii). A sweet, spiced red wine called *hypocras* was often served as the last course of a meal, along with cheese, candied fruits, and light cakes (Henisch 1976: 105; Redon, Sabban, & Serventi 1998: 15). "Spices for the chamber" such as candied coriander and ginger, were also served after dinner, often in a private room to select guests, to aid in digestion and to sweeten the breath (Henisch 1976: 105; Redon et al. 1998: 11).[16] Such a use no doubt followed from a belief in the medical efficacy of spices. The medicinal use of spices was well established in South Asia and the Islamic world, and it slowly entered European medical practice through Arab pharmacology (Mintz 1985: 80; Pearson 1996a: xv). In fact, some of the earliest Portuguese sources on Indian spices were written by healers and pharmacologists (of whom Garcia da Orta and Tomé Pires are the best known).[17]

An important place among the spices was held by sugar. This is difficult to understand for the modern observer, as sugar's role has been drastically redefined over the last few centuries. In the Europe of the fourteenth and fifteenth century, sugar was as precious and difficult to obtain as other spices, and was used in much the same manner. Mintz makes this clear: "When it was first introduced into Europe around 1100 C.E., sugar was grouped with spices pepper, nutmeg, mace, ginger, cardamom, coriander, galingale ... saffron, and the like. Most of these were rare and expensive tropical (and exotic) imports, used sparingly by those who could afford them at all" (1985: 79–80). Unlike other spices, sugar gradually "changed from being a specialized medicinal, condimental, ritual, or display commodity into an ever more common food" (Mintz 1985: 37–38). Redon, Sabban, and Serventi comment that what "is most surprising to us about medieval cooking is its lack of interest in distinguishing sweet dishes from salty. . . . Sweet and salty were simply not culinary categories" (1998: 27–28). Sugar was commonly added to dishes that contained other spices, dishes whose dominant flavor was not sweet. Like other spices, sugar played an important medicinal role. In fact, we have no reason to distinguish sugar from other spices (sugar and spice) but rather to think of sugar as one spice among others.[18]

All of these spices came to Europe through a flourishing trade that tied Southeast Asia and South Asia to the Red Sea and the Arabian Gulf, from where they were transported overland to the southern Mediterranean, eventually finding their way into Europe, mainly through Venetian merchants (although Genoa was also an important center). Sugar cane cultivation came to Andalusia and Sicily with the Arabs, but sugar was also imported from North Africa; once again, Venice was the center for the European redistribution of sugar (Mintz 1985: 24). All spices, including sugar, thus shared some common characteristics.

Spices, and the spice trade, were to shape profoundly the nature of European "exploration" in the "Age of Discovery."[19] As is well known, in this story of trade, monopoly, and colonization, the Portuguese were to play a pivotal role.[20] Without understanding the conflicts over spices (including sugar), one cannot understand global geopolitics in this age. Nor can one appreciate the rich history of global connections before the rise of sovereign states. Perhaps yet to be told is a detailed history of the role of colonization in the story of the rise of sovereign nation-states in Europe, which we know occurs much the same time as the Age of Discovery, and which could not have been unaffected by the resources and rivalries unleashed by the effort to monopolize the spice trade. This might, after Edward Said and postcolonial theory, appear to risk stating the obvious, yet such a project remains, so to speak, largely unexplored. What makes such Eurocentrism even more surprising was that this was a time, after all, when Europe was clearly not in the center, but on the margins of a world system centered around Asia and the Middle East. The Peace Treaties of Westphalia in 1648, taken to inaugurate the model of the sovereign nation-state in Europe, occurred in the middle of what Boxer has called "The First World War." This was the fight between the Portuguese and the Dutch for control of the former's colonial possessions, a struggle that "was waged in four continents and on seven seas" (Boxer 1969: 106) and that unfolded for a large part of the seventeenth century (1600–63).[21] The principle of sovereignty—"the entitlement to rule over a bounded territory" (Held et al. 1999: 37)—was formulated in an historical context in which rule over colonial territories and the division of such lands was already a subject of some concern to European states. Tilly notes that "the construction of external empires provided some of the means and some of the impetus for the fashioning of relatively powerful, centralized, and homogenized national states within the continent [of Europe]" (1990: 167).[22] But even on those occasions when there is an acknowledgment of the imbrication of colonialism in the rise of sovereign states in Europe, it rarely forms an integral part of the analysis (Tilly 1990; Houbert 1998).[23]

The growth of European involvement in the spice trade no doubt altered ecologies, production systems, and economies in the spice-growing areas as well, but little is known on that score. Were there changes in the methods and areas devoted to the cultivation of spices? Of course, we do see the dramatic example of the use of slaves and indentured labor in the production of sugar cane, but that coincided with sugar's transformation from a spice to an everyday commodity.

I do not intend to add to the rich primary literature that explores the Portuguese role in the spice trade in Asia (see especially Subrahmanyam 1993). What I wish to do is to draw certain links between processes of globalization whose affinities are often overlooked because of the scholarly divide between different bodies of water. On the one hand is an Atlantic Ocean–based scholarship that focuses largely on Spanish and Portuguese (and later English and French) connections with the New World and the west coast of Africa; on the other hand is a Pacific Ocean–based (really Indian Ocean–based) scholarship that focuses on Portuguese and Dutch (and later English and French) connections with South Asia, Southeast Asia, the east coast of Africa, and the Middle East.

In the Atlantic circuit, sugar emerges as a key product; in the Pacific circuit, black pepper is central, although other spices are important as well.[24] These two circuits were linked through the consumption of beverages such as tea and coffee, which married a product from one circuit (tea from China, later India; coffee from Arabia, later Java) with a product from the other circuit (sugar from the New World).[25] But they were linked as well in the role played by the Portuguese in attempting to corner the European market for spices. Once sugar is incorporated into the story of spices, one begins to see a thread between Portuguese colonization in the New World and Portuguese actions in Asia. (It then makes it possible for me to link Brazil and India in the same story about globalization in the Age of Discovery).

It was not long after Vasco da Gama first reached Calicut in 1498 that the Portuguese managed to occupy the center of the European spice trade. Lisbon displaced Venice as the port that landed the largest volume of spices. These spices were then distributed to the rest of the continent through Antwerp, which became an important center of financing and redistribution. Lisbon and Antwerp bypassed Alexandria and Venice just seven years after Vasco da Gama's maiden voyage (Chaudhuri 1985: 69). In fact, between 1505 and 1515, four times more spices entered Lisbon than Venice (Pearson 1996a: xxvi–xxvii). When he heard about the return cargoes of Portuguese ships in 1501, a contemporary in Venice glumly remarked: "to-day, with this new voyage by the King of Portugal, all the spices which came by way of Cairo will be controlled in Portugal, because of the caravels which will go to India, to Calicut, and other places.... And truly the Venetian merchants are in a bad way, believing that the voyages should make them very poor" (quoted in Chaudhuri 1985: 64–65). Such an observation turned out to be on the mark: by 1515, Venice was humiliated into buying spices in Lisbon (Pearson 1996a: xxvii).

The rapidity with which the center of the European spice trade shifted to Lisbon had its parallels in that Atlantic spice, sugar. Portugal and Spain encouraged a new industry in sugar cane in their islands in the Atlantic, first in Madeira and Sao Tome after 1450, and later in the Canary Islands (Mintz 1985: 29–32). From the Spanish Canary Islands, Columbus took sugar cane with him to the New World in his second voyage in 1493. In the New World, sugar cane was first grown in Santo Domingo, and was being shipped back to Europe as early as 1516. And in the wake of sugar cane came slavery: "Santo Domingo's pristine sugar industry was worked by enslaved Africans, the first slaves having been imported there soon after the sugar cane" (Mintz 1985: 32). The Portuguese took cane with them to Brazil, which took over as the leading supplier of sugar to Europe in the sixteenth century. In the century leading up to 1625, Portugal was supplying nearly all of Europe with sugar from Brazil (Mintz 1985: 38). Once again, Lisbon depended on Antwerp for processing and distribution. Between the thirteenth and mid-sixteenth centuries, Antwerp was the center for refining sugar in Europe and its subsequent sale (Mintz 1985: 45).

There were other connections between the Atlantic and the Pacific circuits of European colonization during the Age of Discovery. Although I have so far emphasized what the Europeans took from Asia, the crops that they took to Asia from the New World were to have enormous consequences for agricultural patterns and eating habits.[26] For example, the diet of the poor in South Asia is composed heavily of chilies and potatoes (and in some parts of the subcontinent, tapioca), all crops that were first introduced to India from the New World. Much of what passes for Indian food today in restaurants from Delhi to Birmingham to Rio is composed of foods native to the New World: chilies, potatoes, tomatoes, maize, groundnuts, and cashews. Fruits such as pineapple, papaya, cheeku, guava, avocado, and passion fruit have also found their way into the culinary cultures and eating habits of South Asians, who regard most of these products as a part of their inherited traditions.[27] The extent to which New World crops have found their way into "Indian" food is revealed by a random sample of fifty recipes from a contemporary Konkani cookbook, the *Rasachandrika*. The sample demonstrates that 74% of the recipes included at least one crop from the New World, and that 66% included red or green chilies.[28]

Similarly, pasta and red sauce might be associated with the great traditions of Italian cooking, yet Europeans first encountered the tomato only after Columbus. Although it is taken as a truism in the literature in economics that the hardest thing to change are people's preferences for the kinds of foods they like to eat (and hence that demand for certain types of food is relatively inelastic), the historical evidence demonstrates a truly remarkable plasticity in tastes and consumption patterns. Perhaps no other arena of social life demonstrates the hybridity of cultural encounters as thoroughly as the preparation, display, and consumption of food.[29]

These new foods changed not only eating habits but also affected cropping patterns, land and water use, and forest cover as well. This is an area about which we know very little: What were the agricultural and ecological implications of this shift to New World crops? We know something about how the growing demand for spices altered the rhythms and patterns of pepper production as well as of other spices. Even at the height of European demand for spices, however, the major share of spice production was being shipped not to Europe, but to China and India, with their enormous domestic markets and flourishing economies. But this story of the impact of New World crops and of changes in spice production is not very well researched compared to the major plantation crops, such as sugar, tea, coffee, and palm oil.

Even less explored is the link between agricultural shifts and the construction of people's ethnic and religious identities. In Goa, for example, there is a highly elaborated distinction between "Christian cooking" and "Hindu cooking" that relies on the selective use of ingredients, preparation techniques, and patterns of consumption. During the infamous Inquisition, which began in Goa in 1540 and lasted for about 200 years, one of the ways in which the Portuguese authorities discovered whether someone had genuinely converted or was merely pretending to have done so was by checking if they still followed the Hindu custom of cooking rice without salt.

CONCLUSION

I began this chapter with the observation that the last quarter of the twentieth century, rather than heralding a new age of globalization, might better be understood as a particular crisis of "high sovereignty" for the nation-state form in the First World. Viewed from what became the peripheral areas of a world system centered in northern Europe (this includes India as well as Portugal), what changed since 1250 was not the fact of globalization, but the forms that it took. From a system of open trading across land and sea that connected Southern Europe, North Africa, the Middle East, South Asia, Southeast Asia, and East Asia, we moved to a situation characterized by monopolistic practices, mass deportation of slaves, and enforced subjugation of peoples through colonialism. This too was a form of globalization, albeit an unhappy form for the hitherto flourishing civilizations around the Indian Ocean and in the New World.

This chapter demonstrates that by focusing on crops and cuisines, one can uncover some of the dynamics of the colonial phase of globalization. It is clear that colonization followed the spice trade, both in the East Indies and in the West Indies. A form of sovereignty emerged in which "mother countries" claimed different territories for themselves, and divided the globe amongst them. The Portuguese were soon displaced of their monopoly of the spice trade by the more efficient Dutch, who in turn were successfully challenged by the British.[30] After a few years in which they wrested control over the spice trade from Venice, the Portuguese had in any case lost the initiative because of the revival of the spice trade through the Red Sea.[31] On the sugar front, too, after the middle of the seventeenth century, the British started producing sugar in their own colonies. Processes of displacement and internecine struggle among colonizing powers became the hallmarks of this phase of globalization. But globalization in the colonial phase went along with the consolidation of a model of Westphalian sovereignty for the European colonizers. This was a model of sovereignty more than a practice because its ideological form eventually became dominant with the end of official colonialism, but its practice was never more than a fiction for the majority of dependent and peripheral nation-states. We have yet to come to terms with the various ways that colonialism and imperial expansion have shaped the formation of nation-states in Europe during the Age of Discovery and in the North more generally in subsequent eras.

A history of globalization that does not take the ideology of sovereign nation-states as its basic premise, or the self-understanding of Western industrial nation-states as its starting point, might better help us interpret the present. Hopkins, for example, has stressed that it is important "to prevent the history of globalization from becoming simply the story of the rise of the West—and the fall of the rest—under another name" (2002: 2). Few questions are as fraught today as that of identity. The paramountcy of national identity, never secure in most Third World nation-states, is being challenged as well in the dominant nation-states of the West. The problem of how to inculcate a national identity among people who shared nothing but a border had preoccupied modernization theorists in the aftermath of decolonization. Now, the need to create a national identity has been replaced by the fear that "ethnic" or "fundamentalist" identities are a problem for dominant states in the West.

Why is the question of identity rarely posed in terms of cuisine and crops in the scholarly literature while so much of the popular celebration of multiculturalism is in terms of a cosmopolitan consumerism? Is it because we scholars fear taking on a topic that is "shallow," or can too easily be co-opted into a new round of capitalist gluttony? Crops and cuisine offer us an intimate window into how people construct class hierarchies, ethnic identities, gender differences, religious borders, and distinctions between the sacred and profane.[32] When it is clear that such distinctions are not created out of eternal, stable substances and practices, but rapidly incorporate new commodities and relations, such as New World crops in Asian cuisines, the connection between globalization and identity becomes especially interesting. Crops, cuisines, and consumption offer us a uniquely informative and important thread in the understanding of the history of globalization.

NOTES

I wish to thank Manishita Dass, Lalaie Ameeriar, Nejat Dinc, and Bhavna Mukundan for research assistance.

1. Virtual water is a measure of the water footprint of a commodity. In the case of a crop, it includes all the water that goes into its production and distribution, including the water needed for the machinery or the other commodities that go into its production.

2. Many of these books are histories of particular commodities: Coe & Coe (1996) on chocolate; L. Collingham (2006) on curry; Corn (1998), Dalby (2000), Milton (1999), and J. Turner (2005) on spices; Dharker (2005) on salt; Fischer & Benson (2006) on broccoli; Fussell (2004) on corn; Freidberg (2004) on French beans; Jenkins (2000) on bananas; Weaver (2000) on vegetables; Zuckerman (1998) on potatoes; and Willard (2001) on saffron. There are numerous ambitious or encyclopedic histories of food. Some examples include Toussaint-Samat (1998); Flandrin and Montanari (1999); Tannahill (1995).

3. Other sources that I have found useful in thinking about globalization include Appadurai (1996); Beynon & Dunkerley (2000); Held, McGrew, Goldblatt, & Perraton (1999); Inda & Rosaldo (2002); McMichael (2000); Sassen (1996); and Tsing (2000).

4. This point emerged in an engagement with a paper presented by R. Radhakrishnan.

5. For example, Hopkins writes, "Today, as in the past, globalization remains an incomplete process: it promotes fragmentation as well as uniformity; it may recede as well as advance; its geographical scope may exhibit a strong regional bias; its future direction and speed cannot be predicted with confidence—and certainly not by presuming that it has an 'inner logic' of its own" (2002: 3).

6. See especially the account of the knowledge that African slaves brought to the cultivation of rice in the southern United States (Carney 2001).

7. On the construction of a national cuisine, see Möhring (2008) and Appadurai (1988). In this article, Appadurai does not focus on the role of immigration.

8. Tsing (2000: 344) writes, "This task requires that we study folk understandings of the global, and the practices with which they are intertwined, rather than representing globalization as a transcultural historical process." The point that Tsing is making here is that *any* attempt to represent globalization is someone's folk understanding of "the global," and that it is important for us to relate all theories of globalization to the sociological location from which that particular construction has arisen. Most discussions of globalization do not acknowledge that their own

maps are not "views from nowhere" but arise from particular structural and cultural locations.

9. The origins of coffee are often traced to Ethiopia (Hattox 1985: 13). However, Yemen was the major supplier of coffee to the Middle East and Europe until the early eighteenth century.

10. One could similarly argue that the diffusion of major "world" religions, technologies, and ideas (Buddhism, Hinduism, Islam, Christianity, and Judaism; processes of making paper, silk, and gunpowder; knowledge of medicine, astronomy, and agriculture) before Europe's "Age of Discovery" has had a more profound impact on human civilizations than anything that came after. My point is not to make the case for one side versus another, but to caution that there is no one scale by which "impacts" can be measured.

11. Saffron and rose water had clearly been introduced to European palates by the Arabs, who were also the chief intermediaries in the spice trade.

12. The recipes reviewed were for split pea or dried fava bean soup, chickpea soup, lasagne, white ravioli, extemporaneous soup, white poree, white porrata, green poree, watercress poree, black poree, asparagus with saffron, sauteed mushrooms, Le Menagier's civet of hare, sweet and sour cive of venison, chicken with fennel, chicken with lemon, brouet of capon, roast kid with sauce of gold, stuffed suckling pig, bourbelier of wild boar, chicken with orange sauce, sweet and sour fish, roast shad, grilled fish, dover sole with bitter orange juice, and cuttlefish in black sauce.

13. This may be the origin of such recipes as "pepper steak" or beef tongue or roast studded with cloves.

14. Mennell (1985: 53–54) seeks to explain why fewer spices came to be used in medieval recipes by pointing out that using a smaller number and quantity of spices may have been one way in which finer cooks distinguished their art from inferior ones. But there is no reason why this effort at distinction should have necessarily led towards fewer spices, rather than their more precise combinations or more selective use, as in Thai or Indian cuisines.

15. Mintz mentions the five principal uses or "functions" of sucrose: as medicine, spice-condiment, decorative material, sweetener, and preservative.

16. This was not the only occasion at which spices were consumed. A historian writing of the eating habits of the rich has this to say, "Even when they are not at table they made free use of spiced comfits, partly for the sake of aiding digestion and partly to gratify the appetite" (Mead, quoted in Mintz 1985: 81).

17. See da Orta (1996) and Pires (1944).

18. "This usage of sugar as spice may have reached some sort of peak in the sixteenth century. Soon thereafter, prices, supplies, and customary uses began changing rapidly and radically" (Mintz 1985: 86).

19. I will use quotes for these terms for the first time only as it is not possible to use them without irony.

20. The story of the Portuguese empire is most famously told in Boxer (1969). See Pearson (1987) for a more detailed account of the Indian part of this story.

21. The fight between the Dutch and the Portuguese (Spain and Portugal were under a common crown from 1580 to 1640) began with an attack by Dutch warships on Príncipe and São Tomé in 1598–99 and ended with the capture of Portuguese settlements in Malabar in 1663 (Boxer 1969: 109).

22. Tilly does not follow through the implications of this statement for his own study of the European state system. Furthermore, as Radhika Mongia (2007) has pointed out, it is misleading to trace the rise of nation-states in Europe to such an early period; in fact, European nation-states can only be said to exist after the end of colonialism. Before that, European states were empire-states, since the colonies were an integral part of the state but not of the nation.

23. I have not dealt with the more difficult question of the role of colonialism in the ideology of the sovereign state.

24. The story of sugar has been brilliantly narrated by Mintz (1985).

25. On tea, see Forrest (1973); Pettigrew (2001); Scott (1964); and Ukers (1936).

26. A wonderful example of New World crops transplanted to the Indian subcontinent for colonial purposes is provided by *cinchona,* the antimalarial drug found in "tonic" water (Desmond 1992: 220–230).

27. The definitive guide to the origins of Indian food is two volumes by Achaya (1998a, 1998b).

28. The Konkan is a narrow strip on the west coast of India that was perhaps most profoundly altered by the ocean trade. The sample of recipes surveyed includes such staples as *sukke, talasani, ghashhi,* and *ambat.* I am grateful to Lalaie Ameeriar for sifting through this data.

29. Writing about the period 1600–1800, Hopkins (2002: 5) says, "Sugar, tobacco, tea, coffee, and opium entered circuits of exchange that created a complex pattern of multilateral trade across the world and encouraged a degree of convergence among consumers who otherwise inhabited different cultural spheres."

30. See chapter 5 of Boxer's *The Portuguese Seaborne Empire 1415–1825,* which focuses on the global struggle between the Portuguese and the Dutch.

31. For details and controversies about the nature of the spice trade, see Steensgaard (1996) and Wake (1996).

32. For instance, the literature on ethnic identity rarely mentions the role of cuisine in the construction of ethnicity. Clothing is sometimes analyzed in these terms (especially in Orientalist analyses of Otherness through practices such as veiling). The role of cuisine in national identity has been analyzed to some extent.

PART TWO

The Princely-Colonial Encounter and the Nationalist Response

THREE

Cosmopolitan Kitchens

COOKING FOR PRINCELY ZENANAS
IN LATE COLONIAL INDIA

Angma D. Jhala

A STATE BANQUET AT THE PALACE of an Indian prince during the late nineteenth or early twentieth century would have presented a "hybrid mélange of Hindu, Mughal and English court customs" (Dwivedi 1999: 28). Highly spiced and scented Mughal delicacies, perfected at the kitchens in Awadh, would be presented alongside Anglo-Indian staples such as Mulligatawny soup or Christmas pudding. Just like dress or religion, food had become a signifier of cultural accommodation as well as divergence. While an aesthetic pleasure, it was also innately connected with the larger political and economic climate of the era. In this manner, local, regional, or national (culinary) histories became inherently interwoven with global narratives of sociopolitical change long before the current temporal frame for globalization (Bayly 2004; also see chapter 2 in this volume). In this chapter, I will argue that the courtly women of princely India were particularly important players in the transmission and cultivation of different culinary styles and food appreciation in colonial India.

Royal and aristocratic Indian women resided in the *zenana*, which literally means the "women's quarters" of the palace or home in Persian, and many practiced the traditions of *pardah* (literally, "veil" or "seclusion"), whether they were from Muslim, Hindu, Sikh, or Buddhist ruling dynasties. The zenana refers not only to a separate, gendered architectural space, but also to a separate sociopolitical entity, controlled and inhabited by women, distinct from a male arena of power within the ruler's court.[1] Zenana women were invariably the producers, patrons, or transmitters of food in the royal household, and through the act of dynastic marriage they further spread different cuisines and recipes across the diverse regions of the subcontinent. They were also crucial in creating new ideas of fusion cooking during the colonial period, both in hybridizing the exchange between European and Indian traditions of cooking as well as through the merging of different regional culinary systems across India, which had more limited interaction before Pax Britannica. I suggest that this cultural cross-pollination makes the late nineteenth- and early twentieth-century zenana uniquely cosmopolitan (see Appiah 2006; Breckenridge 2002; Dharwadker 2000; Cheah and Robbins 1998). Mongrel and hybrid institutions, these female courts adopted aspects from different Indic practices across religious, class, regional, and culinary lines, as well as from European, American, and other non-Indian cultural points of reference (see Rushdie 1991; Bhabha 1994).

Historically, royal Indian kitchens were connected to a vibrant system of global trade, which saw the introduction of foreign ingredients, cooking techniques, and recipes. From 100 B.C.E. to the fifteenth century C.E., the Silk Road linked China to the Mediterranean via India and Persia, leading to a continuous movement of foodstuffs alongside the flow of religious movements and pilgrims (such as Hinduism, Buddhism, Christianity, Zoroastrianism, Judaism and Islam) (Findley & Rothney 1998). A lively maritime trade economy from the fifth century C.E. further facilitated the transport of spices, rice, sugar cane, oranges, lemons, limes, bananas, and melons, among other ingredients, across the known world (Cohn 1996; Gupta [chapter 2] in this volume). With the ascent of the Mughal Empire in sixteenth-century India, Turkic, Persian, and Afghan traditions of dress, architecture, and cuisine were adopted by non-Muslim indigenous elites in South Asia (Lal 2005; L. Collingham 2006). In this manner, Central Asian cooking merged with older traditions within the subcontinent to create such signature dishes as *biriyani* (a fusion of the Persian *pulao* and the spice-laden dishes of Hindustan), and the Kashmiri meat stew of Rogan Josh (L. Collingham 2006). It not only generated new dishes and entire cuisines, but also fostered novel modes of eating. Such newer trends included the consumption of Persian condiments, which relied heavily on almonds, pastries, and quince jams, alongside Indian *achars* made from sweet limes, green vegetables, and curds as side relishes during Mughlai meals (L. Collingham 2006: 30).

Much of this culinary innovation occurred through social interactions between different ruling elites, often fostered through political marriage and the transmission of women between dynastic families. Non-Muslim rulers, such as the Hindu Rajputs of western India, married their daughters to Mughal emperors, and they in turn influenced the development of Mughlai cooking (Lal 2005: 167–175). These women brought their own cultural practices—religious worship, vernacular language, regional dress, and forms of toilette—to the imperial court. Food ranked high among these cultural products. Filmmaker Ashutosh Gowariker, in his 2008 historical biopic of Mughal emperor Akbar (1542–1605) and his Rajput bride, Princess Jodhaa of Amber (an earlier name for the kingdom of Jaipur), devotes an entire scene to the young bride's entrance into and eventual colonization of, after a period of initial resistance, the royal kitchen. Jodhaa eventually convinces the imperial cooks to allow her to prepare Rajasthani cuisine. While Gowariker's suggestion that the Rajput princess introduces vegetarian cooking to the Mughal court is highly suspect, as Rajputs have historically been meat-eaters, this scene is useful in showcasing the role of women as cultural ambassadors, particularly in creating new definitions of desired food and methods of food presentation and preparation. Gowariker emphasizes this aspect of Jodhaa's influence in the Mughal harem alongside her observance of religious devotion (*bhakti* Hinduism), traditional dress (Rajasthani *gagra* and *oodhani*) and language (Hindi, in contrast to Akbar's Urdu) (Gowariker 2008). Akbar's court thus reflected a "controlled diversity of styles," where the practices of different regional communities were displayed and supported (Bayly 1986: 300).

In this manner, food was deeply entwined with the larger political environment, as regional kingdoms navigated their relationships of fealty to the imperial power: Mughal or later British. The royal court, whether it was established at the Mughal seat or the capitals of smaller regional kingdoms, recognized that food was a central element in political theatre. The connoisseurship of food reflected a host of sensibilities: cultural sophistication, hospitality to foreign guests (wanted or unwanted), and proximity to the conquering entity. The paraphernalia of eating—adoption of certain cuisines or dishes to supplement preexisting culinary traditions, the style of table manners observed, the presentation of a menu, the use of chefs, and the importation of foreign ingredients and cooking utensils—all became reflective of who, and what, was in power. It highlighted the ascendency or descent of particular regimes, empires, or subcultures. Thus, from the late fifteenth to the eighteenth centuries, both Muslim and non-Muslim states emulated Ottoman, Mughal, or regional Muslim forms of cooking, table etiquette, and modes of sitting during meals.

While this precolonial period saw the growth of a vibrant Indo-Islamic culture, the arrival of European imperialism allowed for an even greater exchange between different subregions of the subcontinent, which may have had little contact previously, as well as the cross-pollination of European and Indic ideas of food enjoyment (L. Collingham 2006). After 1780 there was a wholesale westernization of courtly tradition, particularly within the regional successor states, or what were later termed the "princely states" under British paramountcy (Bayly 1986: 306). Following the failed Mutiny of 1857, at which time Indian native rulers both fought for and against the British East India Company, many indigenous princes adopted Western cultural practices. With the end of warfare, they exchanged the lance and spear for the tennis racket and the cricket bat. Indian rulers embraced Western architecture for their palaces; the use of the train (and, later, the automobile and the airplane); and an admiration for European jewelry, dress, cuisine, recreation, and entertainment (Dwivedi 1999: 31). They acquired European-styled education through a British tutor or governess, and the auspices of an English public school and university, or its Indian equivalent. They began wearing suits, going dancing, eating Western food, and hiring Western cooks (Allen and Dwivedi 1984: 87). They employed Europeans, as well as Indians from outside the boundaries of their traditional states, in areas of government and household management. Europeans worked as architects, engineers, chefs, heads of the mint, teachers, couturiers, jewelers, doctors, and lady companions, among a host of other professions, in the princely states. Some princes even married Europeans or Europeanized Indian wives (L. Collingham 2006: 170–172). New forms of architecture, furniture, interior design, and the practice (or not) of *pardah* changed the patterns of eating for many of these Western-educated Indian elites.

Thus from the late eighteenth through mid-twentieth centuries, Indian elites introduced Euro-American styles of food, the written menu, eating at table with knife and fork, and dining on European plate into their feasting rituals (Kapurthala 1954: 28; Jaffer 2007: 142–143). In particular, colonialism fostered new trends of fusion cooking and the juxtaposition of different cuisines side by side. It was an uneasy intermingling of precolonial and colonial gastronomic and dining trends.

Courtly and royal women, in particular, played an important part in the making of this culinary cosmopolitanism. They influenced this dynamic exchange within and between royal kitchens. As several princely families practiced polygamy and married for political motivations of alliance making, their zenanas invariably housed women who came from "outside," who brought their own culinary practices from their father's state (and often their mother's and paternal grandmother's as well). Thus it was through women that various regional practices from different kingdoms or subregions found themselves absorbed within the same royal court.

Since it was the women who came from elsewhere, traversing geographical, cultural, and psychological spaces in the act of dynastic marriage, it was they who invariably introduced external influences. Thus the zenana of the king, or those of his nobles, often housed women with different religious, caste, regional, linguistic, aesthetic, and clan affiliations, thereby creating a heterogeneous world within the already cosmopolitan universe of the princely state. A Hindu Rajput zenana, for example, might have included Kshatriya, Brahmin, Sudra, and Vaisya women as well as Muslims, Jains, and Christians.

There are many examples of such heterogeneous zenanas. For instance, during the nineteen teens and twenties, Begum Sultan Jahan, the then Muslim regnant queen of Bhopal, employed a Muslim ayah, a German Jewish nanny (whom she protected during the Second World War) and a Christian Irish governess, for the instruction of her young granddaughter, the heir apparent, Abida Sultan (Sultaan 2004: 13–15). She also arranged her youngest son's marriage to the great-granddaughter of the king of Afghanistan, in part to hybridize the Bhopal zenana by bringing in foreign women (Sultaan 2004: 7; S. M. Khan 2000: 169). In 1941, the Nepalese Rana aristocrat, Vijaya Raje, married the Maratha ruler of Gwalior. Rana-Maratha marriages were still something of a novelty, as were Sikh-Hindu unions at the time. She would promote lifelong connections between the mountain kingdom and the Gwalior court after her marriage, as well as bring various Nepalese family members, retainers, and cooks with her to Gwalior. Through her and later her Nepalese daughter-in-law, the Gwalior kitchens became particularly well known for their preparation of Nepali delicacies (Holkar & Holkar 1975: 169). The third wife of Maharaja Sawai Mansingh II of Jaipur, Maharani Gayatri Devi, was born into the Brahmo family of the Cooch Behar royals in eastern Bengal in 1919. While the Cooch Behars were nominally Hindus, their reformist version of Hinduism deemphasized ritual and highlighted Theism, in contrast to the Hindu Rajput practices of her husband's home. She would bring Bengali styles of cooking to Jaipur as well as her maternal grandmother's Marathi cuisine from the Gujarati kingdom of Baroda. In the Buddhist kingdom of the Chakma Raj in the Chittagong Hill Tracts of East Bengal, Raja Nalinaksha Roy had an arranged marriage to the cousin of Gayatri Devi, the Hindu, Brahmo granddaughter of Keshub Chandra Sen from Calcutta

(R. T. Roy 2003: 64). After her marriage in 1926, Benita Sen introduced both Bengali and Anglo-Indian food to the Chakma Rajbari kitchens.

There were also numerous examples of Western women who married into princely Indian families. In the Sikh state of Kapurthala, Maharaja Jagatjit Singh married Spanish and Czech women in 1908 and 1942 respectively, in addition to his previous Hindu Rajput wives, who brought their own attitudes toward food to the court. The Maharajas of the Hindu Maratha state of Indore wed American brides for three successive generations, from the 1920s to the 1990s, who introduced American cultural trends to Indore (Younger 2003; Jhala 2008). The last American daughter-in-law, Sally "Shalini" Holkar, wrote a cookbook on the cuisine of princely India in the 1970s entitled *Cooking of the Maharajas,* just as the princes were losing their Privy Purse under Prime Minister Indira Gandhi.

This cultural mixing during the colonial period markedly influenced modes of eating and forms of cuisine in the princely households. Gayatri Devi's mother, the princess Indira Devi of Baroda, had three cooks in her private kitchen when she became Maharani of Cooch Behar: one for Bengali cuisine, native to Cooch Behar; one for Marathi dishes (which she had grown up with in Baroda); and one for European food (Devi 1995: 47). British Empire staples such as the Christmas pudding became popular in princely kitchens, as they involved bringing ingredients from across the empire. In this way, British culinary products became emblematic of "family, nation and empire, accommodating tradition while adapting to change," even as local modes of cuisine were radically shaped by European and colonial influences (O'Connor 2009: 13).

This is an underexplored topic and there has been no previous study of the cuisine of the princely zenanas. While there is a growing literature on South Asian food history, very few have delved specifically into the culinary traditions of the princely states (see L. Collingham 2006; introduction to this book). Much of the writing on royal food and cooking has found itself in the pages of popular cookbooks, often composed by women who were married, born, or grew up in zenana contexts. These books often have little discussion of the origins or historical trends in relationship to specific dishes (Devi 1969; Holkar & Holkar 1975; Singh 2002). In the wider context of South Asian history, the princely states, and the women of the zenana, have often been marginalized by the dominant discourses of colonial or national-ist historiographies. For this reason, this chapter hopes to throw some light on a largely uninvestigated topic. It utilizes a wide range of source material, including biographies, autobiographies, interviews, oral histories, cookbooks, menus, letters, and private unpublished papers.

In addition, investigating the kitchens of the zenana is significant to a broader understanding of imperial history, as it complicates the narrative of the colonial encounter and breaks down rigid cultural, racial, national, religious, and class boundaries. Building upon the work of David Cannadine, William Dalrymple, Durba Ghosh, and Maya Jasanoff, I argue that there was a cross-cultural exchange between imperial actors and colonized subjects in India.[2] As Cannadine has argued in relationship to class, Ghosh and Dalrymple in terms of domesticity and family, and Jasanoff in regards to imperial collecting, the colonial encounter was often a conversation of reciprocal rapport, exchange, and influence based on the diversity of particular life histories, which cannot be neatly encapsulated into monolithic paradigms (Cannadine 2001; D. Ghosh 2006; Dalrymple 2003; Jasanoff 2005). These findings critique the earlier Orientalist thesis introduced by Edward Said of a binary relationship, where a hegemonic Europe re-created a distinct and inferior East in its own words and image (Said 2001). Indeed, as this chapter will reveal, the food patterns of the princely states were influenced by a multivalent definition of modernity and identity, which had locus points both in native practices and colonial influences.

This chapter is divided into three parts. It will begin by giving an overview of the history of the princely states and their relationship to British paramountcy. The second part will examine the role of zenana women in creating hybrid, pan-regional cuisines within royal kitchens during the colonial period. It will then address the introduction of European cuisine into princely kitchens during the nineteenth and twentieth centuries.

THE PRINCELY STATES AND BRITISH COLONIAL RULE

Princely India, and the zenana kitchens within it, was historically a heterogeneous entity, which encompassed some five to six hundred semiautonomous kingdoms that existed alongside British India until 1947. These "native" or "princely" states, as they were termed, formed a diverse and powerful polity. Indian kingship itself was not static or homogenous, and each princely state had its own history, culture, religion, language, and kinship groupings, which differentiated it from other "little kingdoms," as did the zenanas within them. They ranged from the Hindu Rajput and Maratha states of western India; the Sikh kingdoms of the Punjab in the north; the Muslim states of Bhopal and Hyderabad, which had Mughal, Persian, and Afghan antecedents; the Buddhist tribal kingdoms of eastern Bengal, such as the Chakma Raj, which had ties with Burma; and the powerful southern states of Travancore and Mysore. As an entity, princely India was by no means a homogenous whole. Some states were as large as European countries and as wealthy, such as Kashmir and Hyderabad (Copland 1997). Some upheld male primogeniture; others were matrilineal in succession, such as the South Indian kingdoms of Travancore and Cochin (Ramusack 2004: 34).

The conquest of Bengal in the mid-eighteenth century by the British East India Company augured the subsequent spread of British imperial power within the subcontinent. By the time of the treaties of 1818 and the defeat of the Marathas and the Pindaris during the decline of the Mughal Empire, the East India Company had emerged as the single paramount power on the Indian subcontinent. The aim of British paramountcy, however, was not to directly rule the whole of India, but rather only those areas that were financially profitable and politically expedient, such as Bengal and the presidencies of Bombay and Madras. For the remaining "terra incognita," the British implemented a policy of "indirect rule," which provided "a cheap means of pacifying and subordinating regions not under their own direct control" by forming subsidiary alliances and treaties with the native rulers (Ashton 1982: 7).

Under the umbrella of the Pax Britannica, the princes held full authority in internal matters of state governance such as taxation, state revenue collection, criminal and judicial law, and the development of educational and cultural institutions (Ramusack 2004: 2). However, they could not conduct foreign policy and were obliged to maintain a body of Company troops, which would be stationed in their kingdoms under the control of a British political officer (Ashton 1982: 7).

In the mid-nineteenth century, the crisis of the 1857 Mutiny, which threatened to topple British colonial rule in the subcontinent, highlighted the vital role of the Indian princes in Britain's policy of "indirect rule" (Ramusack 2004: 87). During the revolt, certain princes in the native states, such as Gwalior, Hyderabad, Patiala, Rampur, and Rewa, proved to be "breakwaters in the storm," which would have otherwise "swept away" the British, in the words of the first viceroy, Lord Canning (GOI 1860). Thereafter, the princes were "accorded a permanent position as part of the British Empire" (Ashton

1982: 17). The Queen's 1858 Proclamation, which was announced shortly after the events of the Mutiny, sought to "'respect the rights, dignity and honour of native princes as our own,' because they were the quintessential 'natural leaders' of South Asian society" (Cannadine 2001: 44). In shifting from Company to Crown rule, the Proclamation aimed to establish a new social order with the British monarchy as the focus of sovereignty, capable of structuring into a single hierarchy all its subjects, Indian and British (Cohn 1987: 648). It encouraged and embellished a "language of feudal loyalty" among the Indian princes (Bayly 1988: 197).

In 1876, Prime Minister Benjamin Disraeli proclaimed Queen Victoria Empress of India during the opening of Parliament. In his speech, Disraeli emphasized the heterogeneity of the princes in regards to race, religion, and legal tradition, and eulogized their rare histories as "highly gifted and civilized." He claimed that the luster of these royal lineages rivaled the antiquity of the English monarchy itself. The princes, he intoned, "occupy Thrones which were filled by their ancestors when England was a Roman Province" (Hansard's 1876: 409). Disraeli suggested that these kingdoms represented India's extraordinary diverse heritage, which could have no "coherent community" unless it was incorporated into the "integrating systems" of the Empire (Cohn 1987: 653).

The Delhi Imperial Assemblage held one year later, in 1877, to officially crown Victoria Empress of India served even further to associate the empress's authority and that of the British with India's "traditional" rulers (Rai 2004: 89). Lord Lytton, the newly appointed viceroy and governor-general, orchestrated the highly ornate ceremony. His hope was that the public pageantry would establish the queen's authority by placing her rightfully "upon the ancient throne of the Moguls" (Lytton 1876, April 21). Lytton believed that the strong support of the Indian princely order was crucial to the interests of the Crown. The "sympathy and cordial allegiance" of the "native aristocracy of the country," he wrote to Queen Victoria, "is no inconsiderable guarantee for the stability . . . of the Indian Empire" (Lytton 1876, May 4). Those who attended, some three hundred princes, were seen as the "flower of the Indian nobility," were thanked for their participation in the suppression of the Mutiny and were awarded new honors for meritorious service in a similar tradition of *nazar,* or fealty, as that which was performed earlier at Mughal *durbars* (Cohn 1987: 660). The ceremony combined both Anglo-Norman and Mughal conceptions of royalty and visual display, which would be mirrored in the ateliers of the princely courts (Bayly 1988: 197).

In the subsequent period, a system of "personal" relationships between the Indian rulers and their British sovereigns, as romantically portrayed in the literature of the late nineteenth and early twentieth century, began to emerge. The British realized that they had to woo their princely allies if they wished to protect and strengthen this symbiotic relationship. In return for services rendered during the Mutiny, and with the hope for continued future partnership, the Crown devised a system of gifting honors to Indian dignitaries, such as gun salutes, knighthoods, and titles, in a similar manner to that with which it favored its own aristocracy and gentry in England. Royal Indian women, such as wives and other female relatives of Indian rulers, were included in this process of "ornamentation" and were awarded the Order of the Crown of India for meritorious acts of service, as Sunity Devi proudly displayed in her 1902 portrait (Cannadine 2001: 90). With an image of the queen in its centerpiece, the necklace interspersed Tudor roses with the Indian symbol of lotuses (Ramusack 2004: 92).

The ceremonial of the durbar, where members of the British administration officially met native princes, was perhaps the most telling public display of the Raj's incorporation of the symbols of indigenous leadership. Such grand occasions reflected the theatricality of imperial power and the relationship between the Crown and its subsidiary allies, which was an emulation of the pageantry of both Mughal and European royalty. In such settings, appropriate etiquette and deportment were essential elements of political dialogue and exchange. Seating placements, ceremonial dress, and stylized modes of speech between Indian royals and British proconsuls were all of great importance (Ramusack 2004: 90). The 1877 Delhi Durbar, where Viceroy Lytton officially declared Queen Victoria Kaiser-I-Hind, or Empress of India, was expressive of this trend of visual ornamentation, replete with both Anglo-Saxon and Indic symbols of kingship (Cohn 1987: 656–661).

The viceroy, as a Crown representative, transplanted the majesty of the queen or king-emperor to India and effectively symbolized the British monarch's suzerainty over India's own "native" leaders. Curzon, who served as viceroy from 1899 to 1905, took Lytton's concept of pageantry to a more ornate level. He was a man who thrived on spectacle and was captivated by the aristocracies of the East (Cannadine 1994: 78–79). While on tour in Asia, he wrote detailed descriptions of royal palaces and royal etiquette. In his opinion, India's grandeur lay in its princes and titled wealth, which made England, in comparison, appear "dingy and unimaginative" (Cannadine 1994: 79). Curzon particularly appreciated pomp in the display of the Raj, which he believed would preserve India's princes from the diluting influence of the West.

In 1903, he personally orchestrated the imperial durbar at Delhi to announce the coronation of Edward VII. He wrote to a friend that it would be the "biggest show that India will ever have had" (Cannadine 1994: 83). He believed it would bring together people from all over the subcontinent and radiate the glory of the empire outwards through the unity of India. The symbolism of kingship was forefront in his pageantry and he wanted the princes to be "prominent actors in the ceremony," not "mere spectators at it" (Cannadine 1994: 85). He invited twice as many princes as had arrived for Lytton's 1877 assemblage, and his festivities lasted two weeks, with around 150,000 people gathered (Cannadine 1994: 85). The Duchess of Marlborough, who was present, described the occasion as something out of the *Tales of the Arabian Nights* (Cannadine 1994: 88). These were markers of a clear link between the traditions of monarchy and the power of empire: "the relationships between the aristocracies of the metropolis, and the aristocracies of the periphery ... [are] integral to our understanding of any patrician order and any imperial system" (Cannadine 1994: 110). In such a manner, the Raj manufactured a hierarchy along British lines and transported it to India, while simultaneously incorporating local elements. Princes mingled easily with members of the Raj bureaucracy, as social equals through the honours system, which tied them with the British (Cannadine 2001: 89). Several of the ornaments designed by zenana ateliers, such as costumes, jewelry, and footwear, would have been fashioned for such ceremonial occasions and reflected these political relationships of shared power and mutual ornamentation.

Acquiring the support of India's traditional leadership helped to legitimate Britain's paramountcy in South Asia. As Michael Fisher observes, "by ensuring the loyalty of India's 'princes' and the continuity of its traditional institutions—primarily through the careful guidance of the Resident—the British Empire was intended to be eternal" (Fisher 1991: 32). In her famous proclamation, Queen Victoria emphasized her hopes for indirect rule by underlining the Crown's tolerance towards the religious traditions and customs of the princes.

> We hereby announce to the native Princes of India that all treaties and engagements made with them by or under the authority of the Honourable East India Company are by us accepted, and will be scrupulously maintained, and we look for the like observance on their part. We desire no extension of our present territorial possessions.... We shall respect the rights, dignity

and honour of native Princes as our own; and we desire that they, as well as our own subjects, should enjoy that prosperity and that social advancement which can only be secured by internal peace and good government. (Harlow & Carter 1987: 210)

Queen Victoria herself, it was claimed, was fond of her Indian subjects. Indeed, it has been argued that she was more "passionate" about India than any earlier British monarch. In particular, the queen was enamored by the princes, whom she regularly invited to Windsor and Sandringham, and incorporated them into her larger kinship networks, in several cases acting as godmother to the children of rulers and their wives.[3]

The princes were accepted as integral elements into this larger project of paramountcy for several reasons. Indigenous leadership was an inexpensive method for the British to patrol and administrate large areas of land that were often inaccessible: an essential element of indirect rule. The princes were also important contributors to the British imperial military by financing campaigns and providing recruits, not only for battles on Indian soil, but also overseas. They symbolized the grandeur of the empire and the eloquence of ancient monarchies, when played out in the setting of "public consumption" such as durbars, viceregal visits and tours by the English royal family when visiting the crown colony (Ramusack 2004: 130–131; Copland 1997: 33).

To European observers, their martial prowess, at "once fierce and out-landish," added to their glamour as rulers (Copland 1997: 24). The customs of the native courts appeared to the "untutored gaze of English romantics, immensely old," leading Disraeli to admiringly reflect that their dynastic lineages were far older than that of the English monarchy itself (Copland 1997: 22). The lifestyle of pageantry appealed to certain European travelers as well. During Lord Irwin's 1929 viceregal visit to the kingdom of Kolhapur, a *Times* correspondent described the zenana ladies as adorned in gorgeous saris, peering through "nebulous curtains" and the courtiers as dressed in "vivid sashes and pagris and jeweled swords"(Copland 1997: 24; *The Times of India* 1929, 19 November).

Outside the perimeters of their kingdoms, native princes could not hold diplomatic ties with other states or countries (Mathur & Sukhwal 1991: 28). While they could maintain standing armies, they could not exceed a predetermined number, nor employ Europeans, Americans, or members of other Asiatic countries in their ranks (Mathur & Sukhwal 1991: 31). They were also barred access to foreign capitalists. Rulers themselves could not leave their kingdoms without first informing their Residents and Political Officers of their travel itineraries (Vyas 1991: xii). Paramountcy effectively stripped the princes of external influence outside their kingdoms, and they were dependent upon the Crown in matters relating to foreign policy and defense of their states.

At the same time, many of the princely states were internally autonomous, and the presence of the paramount power was rarely felt within their borders. As William Lee-Warner noted: "In a Native State, large or small, the Queen's writ does not run; that is the main point: it is foreign territory in the midst of the Queen's dominions" (Lee-Warner 1899: 271). The nineteenth-century treaties allowed the princes to maintain a fair degree of autonomy within their principalities, and by the early twentieth century they pushed for greater visibility in all-India affairs. As Vijaya Raje Scindia, Rajmata (Dowager Queen) of Gwalior suggested, it was in this period that in many ways "the princes had become real kings" (Scindia 1987: 144).

However, divided by divergent loyalties on the lines of religion, language, ethnicity, and culture, the princes were unable to maintain a unified front once the lineaments of a modern nationalist India became visible (Copland 1997: 10). The princes were the losers in the battle for power between the British Empire and Indian nationalists with Independence and Partition in 1947 (Ramusack 1978: xv). At the end of World War I, the princely states were still relatively secure, having been active in providing war aid, particularly in the form of troops. Indian rulers were often admired by their subjects and even by nationalists. In the 1920s, Mahatma Gandhi, whose father and grandfather had served as chief ministers under Indian princes, was himself "positive" toward the states, which were close to his ideals of Ram Rajya, the "acme of swaraj" (Rudolph & Rudolph 1984, 18). Yet, a few years later they were virtually extinct and nonexistent players in the construction of the Indian republic (Copland 1997: 2).

As the nation won independence from foreign rule, the princely rulers were stripped of their executive rights, and their territories were merged with the new democratic republic. In 1971, under Prime Minister Indira Gandhi, the erstwhile princes lost their last major entitlement, their constitutionally granted incomes, the "Privy Purse," which was based on an annual percentage of the revenue from their former kingdoms. With the absorption of the princely states, their systems of administration and land tenure were gradually abolished. Nonetheless, many of these erstwhile sovereigns remained active in the public life of the nation and continued to engage in politics and influence the aesthetics, fashion, and arts of Indian popular culture.

THE MAKING OF NEW HYBRID CUISINES: PRINCELY WOMEN AS GASTRONOMIC ENTREPRENEURS IN COLONIAL INDIA

The shifting political landscape of late nineteenth- and early twentieth-century India allowed for the creation of new marital and political alliances between families, regions, and religions, and thus created new pathways for food transmission. Under the larger umbrella of paramountcy, the British implemented a railway system across India, built modern megalopolises where regional princes met for imperial durbars, such as Calcutta and Delhi, and engineered steamship travel to Europe, where Indian princes engaged in the wider world of European travel and international cosmopolitanism (Jaffer 2007: 19–22). Through these innovations, Indian rulers from different caste, clan, religious and religion boundaries met and entertained ideas of political (or love) marriage.

Often the journey between the marital and natal home itself would entail the experience of new foods, and modes of eating. Train travel was first conceived by Lord Dalhousie in 1843 and finally implemented in 1853 with the first railway journey from Bombay to Thana (Kanwar 2006: 25). By the twentieth century, travel by train was de rigueur for many princely households, several of whom had their own private cars called "saloons." For courtly women who often had to traverse far distances, they would often travel by train from their father's to their husband's homes. During the 1930s, Gayatri Devi, then a princess of Cooch Behar, would often journey with her siblings between her father's state in Bengal to her mother's natal home, Baroda, in Gujarat. Her mother, who was the only daughter of Maharaja Sayajirao and Maharani Chimnabai II of Baroda, would annually make the trip across the breadth of India to visit her parents, like many royal brides.[4] In the process, her children would be introduced to a new pan-Indian cuisine, what Gayatri Devi describes as "railway curry" in her memoirs. This curry was devised to offend no particular tastes or religious persuasions, Hindu or Muslim, as it was devoid of beef or pork, consisting mainly of lamb or chicken and vegetables (Devi 1995: 3). In addition, the mode of eating reflected a new gastronomic sensibility with the development of railway travel in British India. As she writes:

> The cooks prepared "tiffin-carriers," a number of pans, each holding different curries, rice, lentils, curds, and sweets. The pans fitted into each other, and a metal brace held them all together so that you could carry in one hand a metal tower filled with food. . . . You could give your order to the railway man at one station and know that the instructions would be wired ahead to the next station and that your meal would be served, on the thick railway crockery, as soon as the train pulled into the next one. Another waiter would be ready to pick up empty containers, glasses, cutlery and plates at any further stop that the train made. (Devi 1995: 2)

Not only did the travel between different locus points through marriage foster novel food experiences as it did for Gayatri Devi, but transregional marriage also led zenana kitchens to become more heterogeneous in nature, as brides brought foreign culinary traditions with them, many even arriving with cooks and preparers of food from their natal homes (Allen & Dwivedi 1984: 272). The eating of dishes and ingredients native to childhood became one way these women retained a identity distinct from that of their new in-laws, palace staff, and the larger *praja* (people) of their married homes. It was also one way to distinguish themselves from fellow co-wives and thus advance their own positions within a large, hierarchical, joint family. With the birth of their own royal offspring, food became an even greater indicator of cultural difference within the zenana, as children often ate from their own biological or adopted mother's kitchen. In those households where there was amicable exchange between co-wives in one or multiple generations, royal children often ate at several zenana kitchens, imbibing numerous regional cuisines. Female children would take this pluralistic culinary knowledge with them in turn as brides to their married homes.

After the young Hindu Rajput princess of Kashipur, Sita Devi, married into the Sikh kingdom of Kapurthala in the Punjab, she brought her Nepalese cooks with her. Sita Devi, who was a devout Hindu noblewoman, married into the progressive Sikh royal family in 1928. Her father-in-law, Maharaja Jagatjit Singh, had taken such a fancy to the French way of life that he constructed his palace in the style of Versailles, banned the practice of *pardah* for the palace ladies, demanded that his court speak French as well as the requisite English, and employed French cooks trained at the Cordon Bleu as well as chefs from Lahore for Indian cuisine. In many ways, his appreciation for all things French bespoke an underlying anti-British attitude, developed as a young boy in response to the attitudes of his English tutors (Rajkumar Martand Singh, personal interview, June 10, 2009). In contrast, Sita Devi's cooks would have been familiar with the cuisine of her childhood as well as the food requisite for Hindu religious rites, such as *vratas*. These different food practices would have given her a sense of identity distinct from the larger Sikh, and Francophile, universe of Kapurthala.

On the opposite end of India, the daughter of a powerful and cultured Hindu Kshatriya Calcutta family was married to the young ruler of the Buddhist state of the Chakma Raj. Benita Sen was the granddaughter of the famed Hindu reformer, Keshub Chandra Sen, and was intimately connected with the literati circles thriving in turn-of-the-century Calcutta. Her mother's family was one of noted lawyers, her grandfather serving as the Advocate General of Burma, and her uncle as a judge of the Calcutta High Court. Benita grew up an intimate of the Tagore family, and the Nobel laureate poet, Rabindranath, would coin the name for her eldest daughter. She was a gifted student and was loath to give up her studies when her parents arranged her politically advantageous marriage to a Raja (R. T. Roy 2003: 84). The Sen family was keenly active in marrying their daughters to eastern royal families. Benita's elder sister was married into the Kapurthala royal family, and her two aunts had respectively married the Maharajas of Cooch Behar and Mayurbhanj.

In joining the Chakma royal family, Benita Sen, like Sita Devi, entered a completely foreign environment. She was from a Kstatriya family and had grown up practicing Brahmo traditions in a larger, if reformist, Hindu context. Her family was part of the legal and intellectual elite of British India and saw themselves as culturally and ethnically Bengali. In contrast, the Chakmas practiced Buddhism, tracing their origins to the Shakya Buddhists; spoke a Tibeto-Burmese language that had no written script (unlike the Sanskrit-derived Bengali); lived in rural mountainous and riverine environments rather than an urbane colonial cityscape; and physically appeared East Asian, having historically had ties with the Arakon region of Burma. As a new bride, Benita Sen felt her married home to be completely alien on the basis of religion, language, ethnicity, dress, and social etiquette.

Over the years she would revolutionize her husband's home and court. She introduced Bengali plays and literature, sent her children to British boarding schools in Darjeeling, and radically changed prevailing attitudes relating to accepted gender roles, rarely differentiating between her sons and her daughters in regards to education (R. T. Roy 2003: 86). She also influenced the nature of food, bringing both her Bengali heritage as well as her British-Indian tastes from urbane Calcutta to the table of the Chakma Rajbari.

Through her influence, at least three different types of cuisine were served in the Raj kitchens. The first was traditional Chakma or "hill" food, often served in large amounts to visiting guests and relatives on specific holidays—such as the Chakma Buddhist New Year, Bizu. This cuisine relied heavily on freshwater fish curries and such delicacies as fermented yogurt cooled and settled into bamboo shoots. Into this environment, Benita Sen introduced Bengali cuisine, which she had cooked for everyday meals and birthdays. These Bengali staples included *dal, lucchis,* and *baigan baji.* In addition, she would serve European food for state functions and particular meals of the day. Like many princely households across India, breakfast had become an English meal. The family would have eggs of some kind (scrambled, poached, fried, boiled, or in omelets), toast and tea. In particular, they would eat Western food for Christmas and New Year's, which would further hybridize the eating patterns of the Chakma royal family (Rajkumari Rajasree Roy, personal interview, May 30, 2009).

In addition to the influence some women had within their household, certain royal or aristocratic women became widely known as gourmands. In Baroda, the wife of the progressive Sayajirao Gaekwad was famously meticulous in the preparation of menus, Indian or European. She was particularly conscious of the training required for her cooks. She sent them to France to learn French cuisine, and to Awadh for Mughlai cooking (Allen & Dwivedi 1984: 274). In Baroda, Indian food was served on *thalis* (trays) with matching silver bowls of pulao; meat, fish, and vegetable curry; lentils; pickles; chutneys; and sweets. Planning menus was an art form, on which she lavished much time, molding it around the tastes of each of her guests. Her kitchen was particularly famous for pickles and cooked prawns taken from the estuary (Devi 1995: 8–9).

In 1941, the Nepalese Rana aristocrat, Vijaya Raje, married the Maratha Scindia ruler of Gwalior. As Maharani of Gwalior, she had twelve head cooks; each of whom played their own "game of one-upmanship," trying to prepare local delicacies with the greatest skill. As in many of the princely states, *shikar* food was often prepared in Gwalior during the shooting season. The family would be presented with wild duck, partridge, green-pigeon, quail, or deer. When there were no European guests or officials to entertain, they practiced Indian styles of dining in their Indian dining room, which involved squatting down on individual silver boards with silver *thalis* (trays) and gold matching *katoris* (bowls) (Scindia 1987: 137). As she recalled: "we sat on silver boards, with our legs folded under us in a standard yoga position, and before each of us was a low silver table. On this table was kept one large plate surrounded by as many bowls as there were dishes to eat. My husband and I ate and drank from gold plates, bowls and glasses; the others, not in our row, from silver" (Scindia 1987: 146). With the demands of so many cooks and rival culinary groups, the Maharani would be forced to sample each dish, even if she preferred one over the other (Scindia 1987: 147).

In particular, Vijaya Raje was instrumental in introducing Nepali cuisine into the Maratha kitchens of Gwalior. By the mid-1970s, the Gwalior kitchens would become as well known for Nepali delicacies as Marathi ones, such as Allu ka Acchar and Nepali Muttar. As Shivaji Rao Holkar and Shalini Devi Holkar suggest in *Cooking of the Maharajas,* the Nepalese brides of the Maharajas of Gwalior brought "along with their dowries, their jewels, and their maids, . . . excellent cooks. Now the kitchens of the palace are fragrant with spices unique to the food of Nepal" (Holkar & Holkar 1975: 169).

Similarly, after Gayatri Devi's marriage in 1940 to the Maharaja of Jaipur, Jaipuri cuisine reflected the culinary heterogeneity she brought as a new bride, as well as the North Indian Rajput principality's historic connections with the Mughal imperial center. At the Jaipur court, Afghan, Mughal, Bengali, Bombay, Parsi, and Gujarati dishes were served (Singh 2002).

In this manner, courtly Indian women served as gastronomic innovators and entrepreneurs, bringing new cuisines with them in marriage as well as creating fusion-cooking patterns in their married homes. They facilitated the development of varied and textured systems of eating and food enjoyment in princely India. As many had strong connections and proudly identified with their natal homes, they were constant links between the semi-autonomous princely state and the outer world. In particular, as the next section will discuss, they were instrumental in encouraging and facilitating the introduction of Western cuisine in the princely kitchens.

COSMOPOLITAN CREATIONS: EUROPEAN CUISINE
IN PRINCELY KITCHENS

While the British Raj altered the geography of princely India, allowing for intermarriage between families that ordinarily did not, as well as for the transmission of peoples, ideas, and practices across the subcontinent in an unprecedented manner, it also introduced European culinary traditions, ingredients, and recipes, creating new modes of cooking as well as fusion dishes. In addition to facilitating the transmission of different regional cuisines across the subcontinent through dynastic marriage, the colonial period also witnessed the introduction of European styles and attitudes regarding food. Dressing for dinner, sitting at the table, and observing a certain sequence of courses through the formal menu became essential ingredients for appropriate social intercourse. Dinners for foreign dignitaries, from the local British Resident to the English royal family on tour in India, acquired elaborate political and theatrical functions, where all the splendor of the Raj was on full display. Indian princes and their wives, when out of *pardah,* were meant to represent all that was best of Indian leadership—native chivalry as well as English gentlemanliness in a larger creed of "enlightened" imperialism. No colonial education for the Indian princes was complete without a debriefing on table manners, drawing-room etiquette and an appreciation for European food and liquor.

By the late nineteenth and early twentieth century, many princely kitchens, both those in the zenana and mardana (masculine domain), were serving European cuisine. In some royal households, Indian food was rare. In the Rajput states of Jamnagar and Chota Udaipur, located in Gujarat, the young princesses ate a completely European meal—a five-course French-styled menu—during the 1930s and 1940s. In Jamnagar, Mahendra Kunverba recalls that the European food was prepared by a French chef. Dinner began with soup accompanied with breadsticks, then fish, either in white sauce or fried, followed by meat (often meat cutlets) accompanied with vegetables such as potatoes. Afterwards, Indian food would be served on a *thali,* including a pulao, rotla, mutton, dal, and vegetables. As they had been instructed by their governess, an Englishwoman by the name of Mrs. Birch, the children all ate with fork and knife, and never with their fingers. Lastly, they would be served dessert, often of stewed apples, caramel custard, or fruit salad and never any Indian specialties for the end of meals, such as *paan* (Mahendra Kunverba, personal interview, June 6, 2009). In Chota Udaipur, her sister-in-law, Jairaj Kunverba had a similar-styled meal. She only sat on European-styled chairs at the table and was served on silver *thalis.* Meals comprised several courses, beginning with soup, followed by fish, then a chicken or meat dish, a European dessert, and finally imported chocolate. The men might additionally eat cheese and cream cracker biscuits, and finally have brandy and cigars to finish off the dinner. Both Rajkumari Mahendra of Jamnagar, whose uncle was the famed cricketer Ranjitsinh, and Jairaj Kunverba of Chota Udaipur did not encounter an Indian-style menu until after their marriages in the 1950s, when they entered the princely home of Dhrangadhra.

Other households observed both European and Indian cuisine for different meals during the day. In the Muslim state of Rampur, Princess Mehrunissa recalled that breakfast in the palace zenana was solely on European lines. She and her siblings ate a typical English breakfast with porridge, orange juice, fruit, eggs, and toast (M. Khan 2006: 16). At the same time, her father, Nawab Hamid Ali Khan, was renowned across India for the preparation of fine Indian food. He had ninety to one hundred cooks, and each cook mastered a particular dish. His meals were described as having at least thirty types of chicken, twenty-five of meat, forty *shikar* (game food), fifty types of dals, and ten kinds of pulao. According to some reports, it took nearly two and a half hours to complete a meal at his table (Allen & Dwivedi 1984: 275).

Royal women themselves cultivated and patronized European chefs or introduced European cooking in their households. In Baroda, Maharani Chimnabai II had her chefs sent to France to learn French cooking (Allen & Dwivedi 1984: 274). In Cooch Behar, her daughter Maharani Indira Devi brought her Indian cook to Rome, where he apprenticed at the restaurant Alfredo's to master the art of lasagna for her own kitchens (Devi 1995: 57). She also employed a Russian chef who prepared French food in the Cooch Behar's Calcutta home, Woodlands (Devi 1995: 97). In Jaipur, during the 1940s, both European and Indian cooks served the royal household. Indira Devi's daughter, Maharani Gayatri Devi was instrumental in overseeing the daily menu, as were many royal women. In one instance of wartime rationing, she personally cut down the expenditure for crème brûlée (Devi 1995: 206).

Many royal households, such as in Indore, employed Portuguese chefs from Goa for their European cooking (Holkar & Holkar 1975, 183). In the Chakma Raj in eastern Bengal, Maharani Benita Sen introduced Portuguese cooks from Burma who were skilled European pastry chefs to make confections (Rajkumari Rajasree Roy, personal interview, May 30, 2009). When the Spanish dancing girl Anita del Gado arrived in India as the Maharani of Kapurthala, she would eat French food and drink Evian water on her rail journey in the Kapurthala royal carriage from Bombay to her husband's royal seat in the Punjab (Moro 2006: 63).

There were also various restaurants and food establishments in British India that were particularly favored by royal patrons. Firpo's, an established

Italian restaurant in Calcutta and very much part of the city's social scene, would fete many a princely gathering. A typical meal would include soup, roast chicken or meat, dinner rolls, fish, lemon custard, lemon or chocolate soufflé, and fruit salad, eaten to the sounds of Big Band music. In 1922, when Begum Sultan Jahan of Bhopal hosted the Prince of Wales during a royal visit to India, she had Western food and drinks catered from Firpo's Bombay outfit (Sultaan 2004: 29). Firpo's would also serve as an institution where prospective royal spouses could meet, accompanied by appropriate chaperones. When Gayatri Devi was a teenage Cooch Behar princess courted by her future husband Maharaja Mansingh II of Jaipur, she met him at the Calcutta location of Firpo's for an informal dinner (Devi 1995: 102). It was at this same restaurant that Vijaya Raje Scindia, then an unmarried Rana noblewoman, met Maharajkumar Durjay Kishor Dev, a junior prince of Tripura, also for the purpose of marriage talks (which ultimately did not result in a union). Firpo's, as Vijaya Raje wrote, was a place where "men, Indian and English, in well-cut business suits and accompanied by women in flowered dresses or saris, sipped tea and nibbled at [its] famous cakes; [while] others ordered their ritual sundowners" (Scindia 1987: 54).

The Willingdon Club in Bombay was another such location in British India that attracted princely patronage. As Gayatri Devi noted:

> The Willingdon held a rather special place in Bombay life. It was the first really elegant club that was open to both Indians and English, and where the elite of both societies mingled on equal terms. It had excellent facilities for all manner of sports and glorious grounds and lawns edged with the blazing colors of tropical flowers, floodlit in the evenings. In the daytime people met in the fashionable Harbour Bar in the Taj Mahal Hotel for drinks before lunch, but in the evenings all of Bombay's smart society went to have drinks at the Willingdon, sitting in wicker chairs out on the lawns, knowing they would meet all their friends there and that tables would be shifted and enlarged as parties merged or new guests arrived. The waiters in their long white tunics with green cummerbunds and turbans flitted between the tables serving drinks and delicious hot, spicy hors d'oeuvres. (Devi 1995: 135)

Perhaps nowhere was food as important in princely households than in the hosting of British dignitaries or their fellow princes. The art of the banquet was itself a highly nuanced political skill. Invariably, meals to celebrate a British honored guest were of a European bent and carefully orchestrated. In Hyderabad, banquets included the serving of cocktails or tomato juice while the state band played selections from "The Gondoliers" or "The Arcadians."

"The Roast Beef of Olde England" would be performed later as a "harbinger of the muttons and curries to follow" (Armstead 1987: 136). European dishes would be accompanied with a sorbet and Russian cigarettes to relieve the palate, as well as punch a la romaine and Evian water. For a dinner celebrating the visit of Viceroy Wavell, the meal involved a watery soup, boiled mutton and sweets from Madras wrapped in paper.

But it was the celebration of Christmas, both for formal state dinners as well as private observance, in princely households that witnessed the full adoption of colonial cuisine. Most princely households observed a host of religious holidays and their associated feasts. Hindu states invariably observed feasting for the major holidays of their Muslim, Parsi, or Jain subjects, as did Muslim royal courts for their non-Muslim subjects. Therefore, it was not surprising that Indian princes added Christmas as part of their religious and social calendar after the arrival of the British. Several states also had Britons and other Europeans living within them, whether they were representatives of the Crown Raj or state employees. Appropriately feting Christmas was an important part of public political consumption during this time. In 1943, the Rajput Maharaja Umaid Singh gave a lavish Christmas dinner for his European guests, which is representative of the kind of menus prepared by the palace's Western cooks.

For a supper, the starters included fish mayonnaise with lobster patties, chicken and ham mousse in aspic, boar's head, game pie, and pork as well as salads. This was followed by a variety of sweets, including trifle, fruit jelly, mince pies, meringues, éclairs, pastries, and ice cream. The whole menu was finished off with coffee. At departure (presumably the following day), the guests were served the Anglo-Indian staple Mulligatawny soup, sausages and mashed potatoes, eggs and bacon (Nath, Holmes & Holmes 2008: 122). Similarly, in the kitchen of the Chakma Raj, Maharani Benita Roy observed Christmas as a state and private festival. Christmas and the Western New Year on January 1st, as well as dinner parties for British dignitaries such as the local district commissioner, would have English-styled menus, with the eating of Christmas pudding and crystallized sugar pastry baskets on the twenty-fifth of December. Maharani Benita would also order Christmas stockings from Calcutta full of candies and toys for her children every year, which would be put up on Christmas Eve (R. T. Roy 2003: 84).

By the time of Independence in 1947, the observances of such European holidays had become an ordinary event in the homes of elite westernized Indians. In the years since, many princely kitchens, whether those that serve palace hotels or private residences, continue to prepare similar menus. As Manju Shivraj Singh, an aristocratic woman from a Jaipur *thikana,* writes in 2002: "But still there are prestigious tea parties on the lawns of the [Jaipur] City Palace where guests are served wafer-thin cucumber sandwiches" on Lalique silverware (Singh 2002: 13). The culinary legacy of the Raj still lives on in postcolonial India and is often mimicked by subordinate classes.

CONCLUSIONS

In this chapter, I have argued that understanding the colonial history of food in the zenana sheds light on a world that straddles various cultural and political identities, which break neat binary paradigms. This culinary mélange demonstrates the cosmopolitanism of Indian courtly kitchens during the height of Empire and provides a richer portrait of domestic life in colonial India as well as female homosocial spaces generally. These dishes were the products of women, who crossed the boundaries of India and Britain, province and princely domain, Europe and Asia, and the old and the modern. Cooking in the zenana kitchens highlights a relationship between various colonial actors: chefs from Britain and the Continent, princely Indian men and women from various different religious, ethnic, and regional backgrounds, and local Indian cooks, who served these indigenous courts. These dishes and the women for whom they were made complicate the transnational character of imperial historiography, South Asian history, and colonial ideas of food and taste.

Furthermore, the food history of the royal zenanas is not only something of the past but also lives in the present. Several former palaces and princely estates, particularly in Rajasthan, have been turned into hotels, which cater to an international, as well as domestic, clientele. The Maharaja of Jaipur was the first to convert his palaces into hotels during the 1960s, and subsequently the rulers of Jodhpur and Udaipur, as well as number of smaller former princely states, have made their homes into hotels. These palace resorts market the grandeur of royal India and are equipped with luxury spas, equestrian holidays, British colonial–styled safaris, local dance and musical entertainments, and (invariably) meals or social functions with the royal families who own these properties. They present dishes that are unique to those regions and royal households, whether Mughal-styled cuisine at *mehfils* or *shikar* food in game reserves. Where once princely kitchens prepared banquets for viceregal parties or the British royal family in a diplomatic game of gastronomic power-sharing, now it is global multinationals, Russian plutocrats, and Hong Kong billionaires, as well as ordinary middle-class tourists, who are the tasters and patrons of palace cuisine—contemporary inheritors of "railway curries." The innovations of colonial zenana kitchens continue, albeit in a modified manner, to influence ideas of regional upper-class cooking in India today with the development of heritage tourism.

NOTES

1. Originally a Persian concept, which entered India with Muslim invasions in the thirteenth century, the zenana altered local customs as Hindu dynasties emulated the mannerisms of the Muslim court. Although the concept of gender-segregated living spaces was ancient to India, finding reference in the Sanskrit epics and the *Kamasutra* as well as classical Hindu architecture, such as the Rajput fort of Chittor in Rajasthan, it was not rigidly enforced until the arrival of Islam. During Mughal emperor Akbar's reign in the latter half of the sixteenth century, there was a marked move towards the confinement of women and the creation of a harem structure.

2. While I do not wish to undermine the atrocities related to empire, I do want to suggest that relationships between indigenous and colonial peoples was more complex than a simplistic story of unilateral domination.

3. For example, Queen Victoria served as godmother to the son of Maharaja Nripendra of Cooch Behar in 1888, being a close friend of his wife, Maharani Sunity Devi. Their son, Victor, was named in honor of the empress (Moore 2005: 106–7).

4. These trips, however, would be observed only after the first few years of her marriage, which was a scandalous one and in many ways a product of imperialism. Indira Devi met her future husband during the Delhi Durbar of 1911, when his sister, a classmate of hers at the prestigious British boarding school Eastbourne, introduced them. She subsequently broke her engagement to the Maratha ruler of Gwalior and eloped with the junior prince of Cooch Behar, who later became the Maharaja. To marry for love was a largely unheard-of act in princely India at the time, and for several years her parents did not acknowledge the union.

FOUR

Nation on a Platter

THE CULTURE AND POLITICS OF FOOD AND CUISINE
IN COLONIAL BENGAL

Jayanta Sengupta

RECENT CRITICAL WORK on nationalism has tended to shift the emphasis from long, drawn-out anticolonial political struggles for emancipation from political subordination to the more complex and nuanced struggles or contestations over cultural or intellectual domains or sites. It has been argued that the political movement of nationalism often derives new strength from, or is supplemented by, antihegemonic or contestatory exercises in cultural forms like writing about and remembering historical events, literature, performing arts, or philosophical and scientific deliberations.[1] This chapter seeks to establish the cuisine and culinary art of a nation as one more site in which the hegemonic aspects of colonial culture may be adapted, emulated, subverted, or resisted. For colonial India, such a study of cuisine holds out immense promise because of the infinitely rich and complex heritage of India's "traditional" cuisine, the variegated nature of the non-Indian influences to which the latter was subjected, and the many ways in which the cooking and eating of food came to be implicated in histories of intimacy and in the cultural politics of the body. Bengal makes an appropriate case study because of its early exposure to colonial rule, because of the vibrancy of nationalist thought in Bengal, and because of the availability of a substantial vernacular-language literature on subjects related to cooking, food and nutrition, and the relationship between dietary practice and health.

The three sections in this chapter deal with three different discourses on food and cuisine in colonial Bengal. The first one examines British perceptions of "ideal" food habits in tropical Bengal, and how these perceptions were linked—through a gendered politics of the body—to specific ideologies of the Raj. The second examines late-nineteenth-century Indian nationalist constructions of an ideal and healthy diet, and the ways in which these constructions were related to notions of masculinity and effeminacy. The third and final one examines the space that was given to cooking in the new ideologies of domesticity at the end of the nineteenth century, and to the growing debate on vegetarianism and nonvegetarianism, which became a surrogate commentary on the contrasting natures of Western and Eastern cultures.

A CAUTIONARY TALE: FOOD IN THE TROPICS

European attitudes towards India and its inhabitants were varied and often ambivalent, yet there was one basic assumption underlying all colonial medical texts from 1770 until at least 1858. That is a belief in the uniqueness of the Indian environment and its maladies, and the need for a fundamental reappraisal of European medical knowledge in the light of these new circumstances. Belief in the distinctiveness of the tropical disease environment raised the fundamental question of whether or not it was possible for Europeans to acclimatize their bodies to their new surroundings. Most medical men believed that there was nothing inevitable about sickness in the tropics and that much could be done to prevent it. In this context, attention was frequently drawn to the inappropriate diet of Europeans. Charles Curtis, a surgeon attached to the naval hospital at Madras in the 1780s, believed that overconsumption of meat was the root of many of their ills. "They cannot too soon . . . accustom themselves to what are called the native dishes," he maintained, "which consist for the most part of boiled rice, and fruits, highly seasoned with hot aromatics, along with meat items and sauces, but with a small proportion of animal matter." He regretted that the majority of Europeans injured themselves "from a kind of false bravado, and the exhibition of a generous contempt for what they reckon the luxurious and effeminate practices of the country" (Curtis 1807: 280–281; Harrison 1994: 40–41). Curtis's sentiments were echoed by the Calcutta surgeon Adam Burt, who warned that "the too liberal use of wine combines with the climate to render Europeans ill-qualified for digesting the great quantity of animal food which most of them continue to devour as freely as before they left their native country." Although he did not think it advisable to emulate Indian dietaries in every respect, they seemed to suggest "very useful hints" for survival in hot climates (Burt 1785: 9–10, 14; Harrison 1994). Other contemporaries— like the naval surgeon James Johnson—however, unambiguously prescribed "the slender and unirritating food of the Hindoo," especially for those whose daily routine did not include strenuous activities like travel (Johnson 1837: 11; Harrison 1999: 82).[2]

By and large, such medical exhortations were lost on the British in Calcutta, who ate huge amounts of every sort of meat, including pork and beef, both roast and curried. "We were very frequently told in England, you know, that the heat in Bengal destroyed the appetite," wrote Eliza Fay in 1780.

> I must own that I never saw any proof of that: on the contrary, I cannot help thinking that I never saw an equal quantity of victuals consumed. We dine too at two o'clock in the very heat of the day.... I will give you our bill of fare.... A soup, a roast fowl, curry and rice, a mutton pie, a fore-quarter of lamb, a rice pudding, tarts, very good cheese, fresh churned butter, fine bread, excellent Madeira (that is expensive but eatables are very cheap). (Fay 1908: 140)

Stomach disorders, inevitably, were common, but everyone blamed the climate rather than the unsuitability of their diet. The governor, Philip Francis, wrote in 1775: "I am tormented with the bile and obliged to live on mutton chop and water. The Devil is in the climate I think" (D. Burton 1993: 7).

During the early decades of Company rule in India—as Elizabeth Collingham's work has shown—such ostentatious and unhealthy dining habits "served well to underline the status of the Company grandee in India." However, with the increasing racialization of the Raj after 1857, the body of the British official in India became an even more powerful signifier of "Britishness," and diet and dress became, accordingly, cultural sites on which a sense of bodily difference between the British and their Indian subjects was maintained (E. M. Collingham 2001). Though this entailed a refinement of the eating etiquette compared to the meat-eating excesses of the earlier period, elaborate meals continued to be the norm, as indicated by the Bengal civil servant John Beames's account of the average Anglo-Indian official's fare in the late nineteenth and early twentieth centuries:

> Our *chota haziri,* or little breakfast, was at five-thirty to six, and consisted of tea, eggs boiled or poached, toast and fruit.... Breakfast at eleven consisted of fried or broiled fish, a dish or two of meat—generally fowl cutlets, hashes and stews, or cold meat and salad followed by curry and rice and dessert. We drank either bottled beer—the universal Bass—or claret.... Between four and five there was tea and cakes.... Dinner at half past seven or eight

consisted of soup, and entrée, roast fowls or ducks, occasionally mutton, and in cold weather once or twice beef, an entremet of game or a savoury, and sweets. (Beames 1961: 197; E. M. Collingham 2001: 156)

Similarly, Dipesh Chakrabarty's work on the culture of managerial power in Bengal's jute mills around the end of the nineteenth century shows that the lifestyle—and especially the food habits—of the British jute mill managers contained an element of spectacle as an important aspect of their physical superiority vis-à-vis the millhands. In such circumstances, as Chakrabarty suggests, "eating was a ritualised expression of a colonial ruling-class culture ... signifying ... excess and plenitude." Thus an early-morning *chota haziri* of a handful of toasts, a few eggs, and a large pot of tea was duly followed by a regular breakfast consisting of "fish, stewed steak and onions, eggs, curried fowl and rice, with the usual addenda of tea or coffee, with bread, butter and jam." Some went further and gleefully downed a few pegs of whiskey and soda before going back to work (Chakrabarty 1989: 167).

Just as these ostentatious eating habits were deployed as the cultural markers of a masculine, physically superior British Raj, the native kitchen or cookhouse was very bleakly portrayed as symbolic of all that was filthy, dirty, and uncouth about Oriental cultures. The author of a cookbook described a typical kitchen in an Anglo-Indian compound as "a wretchedly mean, carelessly constructed, godown [outbuilding] ... inconveniently far from the house, and consequently open to every passer-by" (Wyvern 1885/2007: 499). Further, because of inadequate equipment, the cook had to use "his cloth for a sieve, and his fingers for a spoon or fork" (Wyvern 1885/2007: 499). Given this description, it is perhaps not surprising that yet another cookbook cautioned: "The native ways are not our ways and the less you see of them over their cooking operations the more appetite you will have for the food set before you" (*An Anglo-Indian* 1882: 68).

To cut a long story short, the gastronomic habits of the British in Bengal—including conspicuous consumption bordering on gluttony in the early days of Company rule, and more refined but elaborate meals in the second half of the nineteenth century—served as a metaphor for the racial/physical superiority of the Raj. Although such dietary habits were firmly castigated from the scientific viewpoint—most frequently by climatologists and medical men—the table manners of the Raj obviously valued symbolism more than science. The Indian kitchen as an object of revulsion was the other part of the same worldview. The dark mysteries of the Orient manifested themselves within the cookhouse in many ways—through the heat, smoke, and filth, as well as through the cunning of foxy cooks, or *bawarchis,* who pinched provisions, padded their accounts, and—worst of all—used their curry powder to enliven what a 1906 cookbook described as "superannuated fish or meat" (Shalot 1906: 89).[3]

The majority of medical men, however, sought to emphasize cultural, as opposed to physiological, differences between whites and nonwhites. The prevailing ethos of the 1830s is best demonstrated in the work of James Ranald Martin, presidency surgeon of Bengal and later president of the East India Company's medical board, who held climatological factors responsible for the "degenerate" culture of the Bengalis. "When we reflect on the habits and customs of the natives," he wrote, "their long misgovernment, their religion and morals, their diet, clothing, etc., and above all their *climate* we can be at no loss to perceive why they should be what they are" (J. R. Martin 1837: 43, 45, 52, emphasis in original).

MASCULINITY, EFFETENESS, AND DIET

The growth of the idea of Indian "effeminacy," as Thomas R. Metcalf has contended, can be traced to eighteenth-century theories of climatic determinism, in which "heat and humidity were seen as conspiring to subvert manliness, resolve and courage" (Metcalf 1994: 105). According to the eighteenth-century historian Robert Orme, the diet of the "people of Indostan" exacerbated these shortcomings, dependent as it was on rice, an "easily digestible" food, obtained with little labor, and thus "the only proper one for such an effeminate race" (Orme 1971: 42–45; Metcalf 1994). Even among such "generally lethargic" people, Bengalis were especially known for their feeble, "effeminate" ways, and for their slothful habits. Herbert Risley, the amateur British ethnologist and physical anthropologist, observed that Bengali effeminacy had much to do with the "relaxing climate," the "enfeebling diet," and the premature maternity of women (Risley 1908: 57; Sinha 1995: 20–21). The self-perception of effeminacy, as John Rosselli has pointed out, was recognized by Bengali intellectuals and political leaders to be a peculiarly middle-class phenomenon. They offered various explanations for this effeminacy—the decline of native physical pursuits under the material security provided by British rule, the Bengali diet of rice, and the hot and enervating climate among them (Rosselli 1980).

The relationship between *bahubal* (physical prowess) and civilization came to be debated in the 1870s in the meetings of the Hindu Mela, a social and cultural association in nineteenth-century Calcutta. Dietary practices became one of the keywords of this debate. As early as 1866, the Brahmo reformist intellectual Rajnarayan Basu's influential pamphlet *Prospectus of a Society for the promotion of national feeling among the educated natives of Bengal* submitted an alternative to Western modernity by proposing a return to indigenous custom and etiquette after cleansing them of "native" superstitions (R. Basu 1866, cited in Ghatak 1991: 35). Based on the cultivation of physical culture, appropriate dress, and "proper" dietary practices, this programmatic agenda was quickly adopted by the Hindu Mela, whose sessions reverberated with emotional exhortations on the colonial comparison between a martial race and a nonmartial one. Manmohan Basu's keynote address at the second Hindu Mela, in 1868, stated that by introducing physical education within the country, the organizers of the Mela would successfully rid the Bengali of the humiliating reputation he had amongst the British and other Indian communities of being "fainthearted" and "rice-eating" (S. S. Mukhopadhyay 1960: 141; Chowdhury 1998: 23).[4] The principal crop of Bengal and an integral part of Bengali identity, rice—with its supposedly enervating attributes—thus cast a gloomy shadow over the Hindu Mela's anxiety-ridden project of overcoming the allegations of effeteness through the cultivation of an active physical culture.[5] Such anxieties were unmistakably present in Rajnarayan Basu's comparative evaluation of old and present times, *Se kal ar e kal*, published in 1873. Comparing "those days" with "these days," he spoke of health as one of the several key areas of Bengali life where lack of nutritious food, consumption of adulterated and harmful food, and excessive drinking had conspired to engender a decline. "We have seen and heard in our childhood," he lamented, "of numerous examples of how much people could eat in those days. They cannot do so now" (R. Basu 1873: 28–40, cited in Chatterjee 1998: 196–197). Basu thus set the tone for an increasingly vocal strand of *bhadralok* (gentleman) thought on physical debility and "proper" dietary practices that examined these themes from both a medical and a cultural point of view in the last quarter of the nineteenth century and the initial decades of the twentieth.[6]

By the early decades of the twentieth century, the late-nineteenth-century ruminations on the debilitating effects of the Bengali diet had given way to "scientific" explanations. By this time the medical colleges were well-established institutions, and for many chemists, attention had come to focus on the science of health, hygiene, and nutrition. Interestingly, however, even such "scientific" explorations into the chemical ingredients of the average Bengali daily fare—and their character-molding properties—were imbricated with the cultural politics of self-conscious attempts to historicize the gastronomic trajectory of the nation. Consider, for example, the following passage from a treatise on food written by Chunilal Bose, a chemistry professor at the Calcutta Medical College and one-time Chemical Examiner to the Government of Bengal:

> The health and physique of the Bengalis were not so poor a few generations ago. *Time was when the people of this province were not unaccustomed to military life and service,* for they formed regiments which successfully fought against the disciplined army of the Mughal Emperors of Delhi. In the latter half of the 18th century . . . *they showed their prowess, courage, endurance and the other manly qualities of a soldier* in successfully counteracting the military operations of the French in the struggle for supremacy in South India. There was then plenty of nourishing food (such as milk and fish) available in the land, and people could afford to take them in the right quantity. It is the dearth of these two staple articles of food in Bengal at the present moment that has made the diet of the generality of the people so poor in its nutritive value and has contributed to the deterioration of the health and the lowering of the resisting power against the onslaught of diseases. It is the duty of every true son of Bengal to devise means and adopt measures for the increased supply of milk and fish throughout the province. This will improve the diet of the people and make the country smile once again in health and prosperity. (C. Bose 1930: 93–94, emphasis added)

In Bose's view the Bengali diet was far too rich in carbohydrates but markedly deficient in protein, the "muscle-forming element." Such a "one-sided" diet, according to Bose, led to retardation in one's growth and development, disinclination for physical exercise and any kind of active work, weakening of the powers of endurance, lowering of vitality, loss of the natural powers of resistance against infectious disease, and premature old age as well as mortality. In order to make up for the deficiency in protein, he prescribed "*a more liberal allowance of protein-foods of animal origin* [e.g., milk, fish, meat, and eggs] *in the present-day diet of the people*" (109, emphasis in original).

In short, by the turn of the century the scientific quest for a suitable diet had become inextricably linked with the cultural politics of bhadralok identity. So much so, in fact, that the scientific explanation was often offered as *a posteriori* justification of a project that was already under way in political terms. The bhadralok needed to beef themselves up in order to lay a better claim to a historically unsustainable "martial tradition." What was a better way of doing this than imitating the flesh-eating ways of the West? But, as we will see in the next and final section, the culinary nationalism of the bhadralok shied away from mere emulation and came to focus on what it perceived as the distinctive identity of Bengali cuisine.

A RECIPE FOR MODERNITY: THE ART
OF FINE CUISINE

That leads us to an exploration of the new importance accorded to food and cuisine by bhadralok publicists in Bengal in the late nineteenth and early twentieth centuries. This was, of course, part of a larger discourse of new domesticity that was emerging not only in Bengal, but also in other parts of India in the period in question, and occupied a key space in the nationalist politics of gender.[7] In its turn, this new ideology of domesticity was embedded in the vernacular print culture that mushroomed in different parts of India in the late nineteenth century and opened up a broad discussion on issues related to family, household, and kin relationships to newly literate audiences, including middle-class women. Compared to the middle decades of the century, the much wider circulation of these vernacular texts represented a shift of literary culture and spawned a public sphere in whose discussions women came increasingly to participate—initially as consumers, but subsequently also as authors, of ideas on education, family life, and social etiquette.[8]

This period witnessed the emergence of a new cultural artifact—cookbooks—that were used to advise a newly wed woman in the culinary arts and to reassure the young wife that skills in the kitchen would ensure a happy married life. It is obvious that these cookbooks were part of a larger discourse that sought to limit women's roles to those of wife, mother, and homemaker. But, interestingly, they did more than that. Quite often they defined Bengali/Indian cuisine in contradistinction to European cuisine, and, in doing so, took positions on the distinction of Western and Eastern cultures as a whole.

Cooking was a skill in which the capacities of the "modern" woman came under attack from the 1870s onwards. It was said that the "New Woman" (*nabina*) was no longer able to cook and relied on the skills of professional cooks to perform a function traditionally handled by the women of the household. One can cite numerous instances from didactic manuals on normative ideals of domesticity and femininity, and from contemporary periodicals like *Bamabodhini Patrika, Antahpur,* and *Sadharani.*[9] These were accompanied by occasional exhortations to include cooking in the school curriculum for girls, thus institutionalizing the transmission of a traditional domestic ability (*Somprakash* 1887).

What made these lessons necessary was as much a change in taste and food habits as a perceived loss of competence. As the bhadralok fanned out to different parts of India and came into contact with non-Bengalis and Europeans, greater experimentation in cuisine became the rule. The ideal modern *grihini* (housewife) was one who was skilled in the new ways of cooking as well as the old. Girish Chunder Ghose noted of Bengali women in 1868 that they no longer collected fame by cooking "a simple soup or a dish of porridge," but "must master the mysteries of pillaos and know exactly the true colour of a kebab in order to pass for learned in the art." "Some even aspire," he continued, "to the glory of preparing fowl curry and cutlets in exact imitation of the Great Eastern Hotel" (Ghose 1972: 58–59). A writer in the *Bamabodhini Patrika* in 1874 similarly enumerated the types of cooking a *bhadramahila* (lady) should learn:

> Native Brahmin dishes of rice and curry; meat in the Moghul style; sweet-meats made from *chhana,* coconut, semolina, lentils, pumpkin, and thickened milk; western-style pickles and jams, cakes, biscuits, puddings, and bread; and Indian *roti, luchi,* and *puri.* (Garhasthya darpan 1874: 130; Grihasthalir katha [n.d.]: 5–6; both cited in B. Ray 2002)

It needs to be noted, firstly, that though such skills were integral to the emergence of an essentially Hindu nationalist ideology of domesticity, the range of dishes included in the bhadramahila's expected culinary repertoire displayed an eclectic, cross-communal mix, granting Islam its rightful place on the bhadralok's table. Secondly, exhortations against employing the professional cook were hardly motivated by considerations of mere economization. On the other hand, in the didactic manuals on the norms of femininity, cooking by the *grihini* was given an inalienable affective dimension. It was repeatedly asserted that the real zing in a recipe came from the love and nurturing care of the *grihini,* which professional cooks were unable to provide (Banerjee 2004). In other words, while revulsion against the professional cook distanced Anglo-Indian women from the kitchen even further, the same sentiment had precisely the opposite kind of effect on the Bengali bhadramahila at the end of the nineteenth century.

It was in this context that the first cookbooks began to appear in Bengal. The very first Bengali cookbook, *Pakrajeswar*, was published as early as 1831, and a second edition came out, with financial assistance from the Raja of Burdwan, in 1854. Full of esoteric recipes collected from royal households in Mughal India, the book was hardly suitable for use in ordinary bhadralok homes (Sripantha 2004). The gap was filled in 1883 with the publication of *Pak-Pranali*, a monthly magazine devoted entirely to cooking and edited by Bipradas Mukhopadhyay, a well-known author of instructional manuals on different aspects of family life. The magazine aimed to teach "modern" women the culinary skills allegedly lost through education and refinement, as well as to help them keep up with changing tastes in food and save money by preparing food at home themselves. Women's journals soon followed suit. *Bamabodhini Patrika* had an occasional recipe column from 1884, and *Mahila* had one from 1895. *Punya*, which was not specifically for women, carried recipes by the editor, Prajnasundari Debi, from its inception in 1897. *Antahpur* also had a regular cookery column from 1900, written by women contributors. From around this time, books on general household topics, too, started routinely to include recipes for both ordinary household cooking and for festive dishes.[10]

But, insofar as the bhadramahila's perceptions were concerned, was cooking an art or a science—to be approached with the same meticulous, systematic orderliness that had made the European scientific/material civilization such a powerful entity? The publisher of Prajnasundari Debi's *Amish o Niramish Ahar* had no doubt at all that the turn-of-the-century culinary opus represented an ideal mix of "the poetic imagination and the scientific spirit." The "scientific bit" lay in the precise directions and exact measurements[11] that accompanied each recipe in the book. In the foreword, the author herself presented a very strong case for the necessity of preparing an orderly inventory of Bengal's eating habits and culinary practices:

> In our Bengal, some aspects [of life] are characterized by a lack of orderliness *(bidhibaddha bhav)*. In this country, there is no discipline *(srinkhala)* and finesse *(paripatya)* in any matter. This [distinctively] Bengali trait is especially noticeable in the way we eat. Fish and cream *(kshir)* freely go together to make an abra-ca-dabra of our diet; such a diet is as much detrimental to health as it is against the scriptures *(shastra)*. One of my principal objectives is to rescue the Bengali cuisine from this chaos, and to give it a disciplined character. Unless this is done, Bengali cuisine will never develop a backbone. It is not of much use to collect a few recipes and publish them in a book. Just as a

disciplined regiment of even a few soldiers is of much greater use in war than the mobilization of millions of troops, so is discipline a crucially important matter in the writing of cookbooks. This discipline is not evident in the few books on food that have been written in Bengal. It is for this reason that I have started with the staple vegetarian food of rice, and [then] systematically moved on to other categories. (Debi 1900/1995: 13–14)

The publisher's preface set great store by vegetarian food, taking this as a mark of distinction between Oriental and Western foods. Because of the cold climate of their habitat, the "Western Aryans" of necessity had to develop meat-eating habits. But the gathering of animal flesh entailed relatively greater hardship, and so cut down on the time available for leisure and, thereby, for "progress." This led to the attainment of a comparative superiority on the part of the Oriental civilizations. This historical debilitation had even a contemporary touch, as the publisher concluded: "Till this day the Europeans have not learnt the magnificent art of combining a variety of vegetables [in a dish]" (Debi 1900/1995: 17).

In the late-nineteenth- and early-twentieth-century discourse on food, the issue of vegetarianism versus nonvegetarianism became a cultural question, with much significance for nationalist thought. Whether one ate animal flesh or not became a marker of civilizational characteristics or distinctions. The material/spiritual dichotomy—a rhetorical creation of nationalist thought, in which the difference between Western and Indian civilizations was reflected—was used freely in the comparative discussion of food as well. The flesh-eating habits of the West were argued to have contributed to what was considered to be a grossly materialistic civilization, thriving on crude physicality/coarse vulgarity. Conversely, the refinement and spiritual superiority of Indian civilization was reflected in the immense variety of its vegetarian cuisine.

A compelling force in favor of vegetarianism in India is the ethical one against the consumption of food that necessitates the taking of life. Such perceptions have a long history in the country, and thus being a vegetarian occasions little surprise here. And even as long ago as 1000 B.C.E., so extensive was the range of cereals, pulses, oilseeds, vegetables, fruit, milk, condiments, spices, and sweetening agents available, that vegetarian meals of high nutritional quality, and with gustatory and aesthetic appeal, could be fashioned. As K. T. Achaya suggests, "perhaps nowhere else in the world except in India would it have been possible 3000 years ago to be a strict vegetarian" (Achaya 1998a: 263).

The advanced creativity of Indian cuisine was argued to blossom in its vegetarian cuisine. In the foreword of one of the most popular, modern cookbooks of the turn of the century, the publisher proclaimed that the vegetarian diet was "discovered" by the early Aryans living in the west of the Urals. He argued that meat-eating, as a habit, was more difficult and time-consuming and, therefore cut down on leisure time. Since leisure was essential to the "progress" of any civilization, this meant that at the height of the Aryan civilization of the East, the West lagged far behind in civilizational refinement. "To this date, the Europeans have not mastered the exquisite art of combining different vegetables [into a marvelous dish].... Many a century will pass before the Western race will manage to learn these mysteries of vegetarian cooking" (Raychaudhuri 1995: 17).

The *dharmic* argument against flesh-eating was also frequently used to mark out the Hindu diet as a spiritually superior one. Bipradas Mukhopadhyay, the author of the first truly popular Bengali cookbook, *Pak-Pranali,* made no bones about the claim that "when human society arrives at the crest [*uchcha sikhare*] of *dharma,* the urge to fill one's stomach by the killing of animals declines." He then went on to quote "an Englishman" who supposedly compared the dining table of the English to "a great cremation ground" (B. [Bipradas] Mukhopadhyay 1987, 29).

Prajnasundari Debi herself traced the divine origin of vegetarian food and related the origin of flesh-eating to the dietary practices of *asuras* (demons). But she also ascribed the primacy of vegetarianism in India to the hot, tropical climate, and to the privileging of nonviolence in the Hindu and Buddhist religions. The sages of ancient India, she contends, did not refrain from eating nonvegetarian food. In fact, she argues that even the varieties of nonvegetarian cuisine were picked up by the Islamic Orient (Arabia, Persia, etc.) and Europe from the Indian dietary practices (Debi 1900/1995: 52–51).

But the person who brought the vegetarianism versus nonvegetarianism issue directly within the orbit of contemporary nationalist concerns about masculinity and physical culture was Swami Vivekananda. To him, nonvegetarianism —especially meat-eating—was a compulsion imposed by the material/practical realities of modern life. He even went to the extent of saying that it was meat-eating that created the difference between the power to rule others and the abject surrender to physically more robust peoples:

As long as men have to practise *rajas,* as required by the modern age, there is no other alternative than meat-eating. It is true that king Asoka saved the lives of a couple of millions of animals by his sword, but is not a thousand years' slavery even more terrible than this? Which is a greater sin—to kill a few goats, or to fail to protect the honour of my wife and daughter, and to fail to prevent others from plundering the food meant for my children? Let those who belong to the elite, and do not have to win their bread by physical labour, shun meat. But as for those who have to provide for their subsistence by means of continuous physical toil, forcing them to be vegetarians is one of the reasons for the eclipse of our national independence. Japan is an illustration of what good, nutritious food can achieve. (Vivekananda 1897/1987: 537)

In other words, Vivekananda cared little for vegetarianism as a possible cultural/nationalist marker of Indian cuisine. For him, meat-eating provided the only way to a robust health, which was indispensable for a host of things—like a community's "honour," labor's productivity, and nation's "progress." Vegetarianism, on the other hand, was an emasculating habit that put insurmountable obstacles on the path of nation-making. Subsequently, the debate continued well into the twentieth century without being completely resolved, despite the participation of prominent bhadralok nationalist publicists like Prafulla Chandra Ray, Ramendrasundar Trivedi, and Rajsekhar Basu, among others.

CONCLUSION: NATION ON A PLATTER

To conclude, by the end of the nineteenth century, food and cuisine represented a vibrant site on which a complex rhetorical struggle between colonialism and nationalism was being played out. It can be argued that for the Bengali bhadralok, food became a politically charged tool of contestation, from both a gastronomic and a culinary viewpoint, that is, relating to the ways in which the bhadralok ate their food, as well as to the ways in which the bhadramahila cooked dainty dishes. Insofar as they were shot through with symbolic meanings and "civilisational attributes," cooking and eating transcended their functionality and became cultural practices, with a strong ideological-pedagogical content that continued to inhabit the discursive space of nationalist thought through the late colonial period. The Bengali/Indian kitchen, so strongly reviled in European colonialist discourses as a veritable purgatory, became a critically important symbolic space in the emerging ideology of domesticity in the late nineteenth century. The gastronomic excesses of gluttonous British officials—so crucial in asserting the physical superiority of a masculine Raj—became an object of ridicule in bhadralok culinary texts, signifying the grossness of a materialistic Occident. And yet, serving the "nation" on a platter did not involve, for the Hindu bhadralok, a simplistic drawing of exclusivist communal boundaries in matters of food. As evident from the repertoire of dishes expected of an ideal *grihini,* food belonging to other religious and cultural traditions found its way to the bhadralok's table, and Bengal's manifold local traditions were freely drawn upon in an effort to delineate a regional palate. And, for all of the contestatory character of this cultural politics of food, the perceived discipline and orderliness of the Western kitchen were considered things worthy of emulation. It was through this curious interplay of emulation, adaptation, contestation, and resistance that some of the least noticed but nevertheless most important cultural practices of bhadralok nationalism unfolded in the Bengali kitchen. And if this kitchen appeared to be mysterious in a negative sense in the colonizer's gaze, we do need to think through these mysteries in a much more nuanced manner in order to unravel some of the less explored intricacies of nationalism.

NOTES

1. The literature on the role of these forms and practices in shaping the cultural politics of nationalism is substantial and expanding. For just a few selected examples, see Chatterjee (1993) for history writing; Guha-Thakurta (1992) for the visual arts; Bakhle (2005) for music.

2. For another in-depth examination of late-eighteenth- and early-nineteenth-century British medical ideas on the ideal diet for a tropical environment, see Arnold (1993), especially pp. 36–43.

3. For a study of the deep-seated Anglo-Indian misgivings about the native "bazaar" and the Indian cook, see Procida (2003: 123–149).

4. For an examination of colonial thinking on the role of diet in producing physical strength, martial valor, and such other "manly virtues" among particular Indian communities—and the "debilitating" effect of a rice-based diet on Bengalis in this respect—see Arnold (1994).

5. Both rice and physical exercise were major topics in contemporary Bengali texts on healthcare. See, for instance, Jadunath Mukhopadhyay (1868); Radhika Prasanna Mukhopadhyay (1868); and Bandyopadhyay (1872). Interestingly, in the early twentieth century, as the Bengali bhadralok became increasingly concerned with the dwindling opportunities of an urban colonial-commercial economy and the rising influence of non-Bengali business communities, the earlier anxieties about

the "enfeebling" characteristic of rice were reconstituted in late-colonial bhadralok discourses on food into a defiant cultural stance about the "desirability" of rice in comparison to the North Indian staple of wheat, which became a synecdoche for a number of non-Bengali communities. For an interesting discussion of this discursive transformation, see S. Prasad (2006: 78–81).

6. The increasing importance of this theme is attested to by the space that diet and nutrition regularly commanded in medical journals like *Chikitsa Sammilani, Bhishak Darpan,* and *Swasthya*. Between 1885 and 1935, more than six hundred Bengali-language books, pamphlets, and periodicals dealt with issues related to health and hygiene (see S. Prasad 2005: 6). For representative late-nineteenth-century samples of the treatment of diet in such periodicals, see P. K. Bose (2006: 120–133).

7. For an account of this, see T. Sarkar (2001); Chatterjee (1989); Chakrabarty (1994); Walsh (2004).

8. The role of vernacular print culture in the creation of such public spheres in colonial India is particularly well documented. For five representative examples, see Naregal (2001) for Bombay; Orsini (2002) for northern India; C. Gupta (2002) for the United Provinces; A. Ghosh (2006) for Bengal; and Mitchell (2009) for Madras. For additional accounts of how these vernacular literatures treated the theme of domesticity and women's relationship with it, see Hancock (2001); M. E. Hancock (1999); Joshi (2005); Sreenivas (2008); and Donner (2008).

9. See, for instance, the articles contained in the anthology of women's writings from *Bamabodhini Patrika* (B. Ray 2002).

10. For a discussion of the increasing importance that food and cooking commanded in Bengali vernacular publications in the last quarter of the nineteenth century, see Borthwick (1984).

11. The original editions of the book replaced "spoonfuls" with *tolas* (approximately 11.66 grams) and *chhataks* (approximately 58 grams) as units of measurement. Metric measurements, however, were only used as late as in the 1995 reprint, and at the behest of the editor, Prajnasundari's granddaughter.

PART THREE

Cities, Middle Classes, and Public Cultures of Eating

FIVE

Udupi Hotels

ENTREPRENEURSHIP, REFORM, AND REVIVAL

Stig Toft Madsen and Geoffrey Gardella

And then in Madras it was different. The restaurants and hotels that were vegetarian were clean (though the popular non-vegetarian or "military" places, as they were quaintly called, were as bad as anything in the North). The cleanliness and the vegetarianism were connected; they were both contained in the southern idea of brahminism. At the Woodlands Hotel I stayed in a clean room in an annexe, and ate off banana leaves (for the sake of purity, and the link with old ways) on marble tables in the air-conditioned dining-room. There were gardens and an open-air theatre or stage in the hotel grounds.

V. S. NAIPAUL, *INDIA: A MILLION MUTINIES NOW*

THIS CHAPTER EXAMINES the evolution of a traditional Brahmanical food practice in the modern world. Traveling in southern India, as Naipaul did, one sooner or later encounters Udupi restaurants and hotels, such as the Madras Woodlands.[1] We will pursue the historical and geographical origins and the economic developments of some of these hotels and restaurants, and tell the story of the circular movement that transforms Brahmanical orthopraxy into a wider force for secularism that, in turn, revives religious beliefs and practices. We will narrate the story of Udupi restaurants (confusingly - known as "Udupi hotels" in India) from the 1920s, when entrepreneurs from the Udupi area on the Kanara Coast made their first moves outwards, till today, when the culinary power of Udupi hotels has reached as far as the Silicon Valley in California. We will argue that Udupi hotels have contributed to the processes of secularization and modernization by exposing traditional dietary practices associated with temple and village rituals to the combined forces of the market, state law, and politics. Thereby, Udupi hoteliering and catering have been instrumental in the transformation of commensal orthodoxies lying at the very root of Hindu religious identity and Brahmanical tradition.

In her book *The Consuming Body,* Pasi Falk observes that, "the rituals involving not only eating (meal) but also other activities concerning food function as the integrative mechanism of society. The primitive society is in a fundamental sense an 'eating-community'" (Falk 1994: 20). This is true of Hindu communities too. As noted by Appadurai, "food is a central trope in classical and contemporary Hindu thought, one around which a very large number of basic moral axioms are constructed and a very large part of social life revolves" (Appadurai 1988: 10). Thus, Hindu dietary custom prescribes rules that dictate who cooks and who serves, who may have commensal relations with whom, and the purity or vulnerability of the food or drink consumed (Weber 1958: 43). Among these, commensality, or "interdining," has been held by Conlon (1979: 157) to lie at "the root of all caste distinction." Commensal apartheid has existed at least since the time of the *Manusmriti* (generally dated between 200 B.C.E. and 200 C.E.), as commensal rows or "feeding lines" consisting of people of the same caste or subcaste have repeatedly defined or objectified group identity (Derrett 1968: 176).

As commensality has been a principal structuring mechanism in Hindu caste society, both in its civilizational centers and in the agrarian hinterlands, reform of the social and religious matrix of Hindu civilization is integrally tied to changes in dietary practices. In modern times, civic organizations, such as caste associations, and the state have endeavored to eliminate dietary discrimination between various castes, especially those against the untouchable castes. While these attempts at social and legal reform have been important, we find that commensal reform in the public sphere has, to a considerable extent, ensued by the operation of market forces unleashed by entrepreneurs. It is not that the Udupi Brahmins and other entrepreneurs saw themselves as reformers promoting new norms of "compulsory table community," to use Weber's terminology (Weber 1958: 24). They may rather have been the unconscious accomplices of history, but by earning a living, in contravention of the norm that food is for giving and not for selling, they have taught South Indians to eat old and new types of food in a commercial, and yet culturally acceptable, setting.[2] They have also created a model that could be emulated by other castes, thereby setting in motion a process of "ethnic succession" in a key sector of the modern economy.[3]

In North India, courtly Muslim etiquettes and traditions created a public sphere. In South India, however, civic space and public facilities were few and far between until Indians were attracted to new and secularized forms of cultural hybridity under the Indo-British empire (Frykenberg 1982). Thus, Udupi restaurants and hotels enlarged public space in a part of India that had hitherto sealed off civic intercourse. However, as we shall argue in the end of the chapter, Udupi entrepreneurs have eventually contributed to a religious revival.

THE UDUPI WAY OF EATING OUT

As Naipaul experienced, Udupi restaurants serve wholesome, cheap, clean, and ritually pure South Indian food, mostly vegetarian. The general atmosphere is one of fast ordering, fast service, fast eating, fast clearing, fast billing, and fast exit. There is neither a Western idea of slow, polite, and hushed service, nor a North Indian concept of elevating the customer to the level of *nawab*.

Food is divided into meals and tiffin, corresponding to the heavy and light refreshments served in temples. Typically, Udupi restaurants have a set menu of only one type of meal. This means that everybody eats the same thing at almost the same time, as is also the case in religious rituals. The art of the cook consists in reproducing the same taste again and again. The introduction of various types of rice meals (Madras *thali*, Bombay *thali*, etc.) modified this conservative ideal. The major innovation, however, was the introduction of North Indian, Chinese, and Continental dishes in the 1970s, and North Indian *tandoori* items in the 1980s. In Bombay, the menu often contains nonvegetarian dishes, which are not part of Brahmanical tradition.

Food and beverages are served at tables by suppliers in more or less complete uniforms and assisted by water boys. The suppliers walk quickly, ladling out the food from big containers—the rice from veritable buckets—like suppliers do in mass feedings in temple rituals and at other religious occasions. However, the restaurant suppliers do not have to bend down to the ground, and they do not work in pairs, servicing two feeding lines at a time, as is done in a religious context.

The supplier occupies the central role in restaurants, a role that is defined less in terms of caste purity than the role of the cook, but which, nevertheless, establishes a dividing line between the pure and the impure. This is achieved through a rather strict division of labor between the suppliers who handle cooked food, such as rice, which is specially vulnerable to ritual pollution, and the cleaners. The cleaners clear the tables of all utensils and drop the utensils into a bucket or a container on a pushcart. They also mop the table. This relatively polluting work is typically done by non-Harijan boys, Bunts, Naiks, Gaudas, or even Brahmin hotel boys *(hotel mani),* or alternatively by permanently employed older men in half-pant uniforms. The cleaners are clearly deemed capable of doing their ritually impure work properly and are given the tools to do so. In North India, by contrast, the more polluting jobs are generally performed by workers from the lowest castes, who are typically denied the implements that would enable them to work efficiently.

Behind the scenes, in the kitchen, cooks are traditionally Brahmin, many of whom have gained their experience cooking for large groups at temples. The cooks work in groups with assistant cooks, *idli* grinders, and vegetable cutters, among others. Often there is a main kitchen where meals are cooked, and a snack kitchen where coffee and tiffin are prepared. The kitchen workers are the only staff members who have maintained a distinctly traditional look, even when those workers are not Brahmin. Dressed, most often, in ritually pure dress of loincloth and shawl, they resemble temple priests.

The kitchen is located at the back of the restaurant. As in a temple or a house, it is not open to outsiders. The food is not advertised by being put on view, but by a conspicuous signboard on the pavement announcing "meals ready." Only pollution-resistant items, such as sweets, are displayed. In contrast, the small restaurants in North India *(dhabas)* are open at the front portion, where the food is cooked. Despite the ritual significance of the cooks in Udupi restaurants, their role is less central than that of the cook in religious mass cooking. While maintaining the idea of purity, the restaurants shift the stress from the kitchen to the dining hall.

The flow of customers is regulated by utilizing some sections of the restaurant and closing off others by small wooden "no service" signs. The dining halls are well-lit rooms furnished with rows of wooden or marble-topped tables and wooden chairs or benches. The sparseness of the furnishings often leads to Udupi restaurants being quite noisy: the walls and floors are generally bare, the ceiling fans screech, the customers chat freely, and music may be playing. The staff, apart from the cleaners, openly communicates orders and messages.

Although food was traditionally served on banana leaves, as Naipaul described, Western utensils have become more commonplace. The traditional banana leaves have given way to stainless steel *thalis* and crockery. Stainless steel was introduced for tiffin and only used later for meals. When served light refreshment, a customer is liberally provided with cutlery. Indeed, at times, a customer is provided with a veritable profusion of spoons.[4] Meals, however, are usually eaten with the right hand, perhaps with the help of a single small spoon for the curd. The light refreshments, being more resistant to impurity, are more adaptable for modernization than rice meals.

The supplier presents the customers with the bill, which is prepared by a bill clerk, who also communicates orders to the kitchen. The customers pay at the exit to the cashier—perhaps the owner himself—strategically positioned near the exit with a desk in front of him and with photos of the founder and lithographs of selected gods and goddesses decorating the wall behind him. This hardly leaves any possibility of tipping. The bill is surrendered to the cashier and spiked: it is meant for the internal accounts of the hotel. As the customer carries no proof of payment with him or her, the owner of the hotel may destroy as many bills as he likes at the end of the day in order to doctor the accounts. On the other hand, the bills are so small that the bill clerk often does not itemize the order, which makes it more difficult to match consumption with the releases from the store. Altogether the billing system is fairly straightforward and utilitarian, presuming an ability to write among the suppliers.

BRAHMINS AND COOKING

To understand the origins of these restaurants and the traditions that lie behind them, let us first turn to the men who pioneered them: Udupi Brahmin cooks-turned-entrepreneurs.[5] This had to do, in no small part, with the role Brahmins played in South Indian cooking. Being the priestly caste, their sacerdotal duties have traditionally included "procuring sacrifice, study of *veda,* alms-giving, conducting sacrifice, teaching *veda,* accepting donations" (Conlon 1977: 225). Though these priestly roles may not have predetermined Brahmins to become software engineers (Nanda 2009: 155; Madsen 2009: 92–93), they have helped contemporary Brahmins to enter fields such as science, education, and administration, where they have been able to redeploy their traditional skills. They have been less prominent in trade (Sheth 1974: 165), but, surprisingly, Brahmins have been in the forefront of modern industrial development in the southern and western parts of India.

Apart from the sacerdotal duties, Brahmins have pursued another specialization not included in Conlon's *shatkarma* list: cooking and serving food. As Brahmins rank highest in the *varna* status hierarchy, they are the only ones who can cook for any caste. Brahmin male cooks have therefore traditionally prepared food for Brahmins as well as for some other twice-born Hindus on ritual occasions. Other castes have acted as cooks for castes that Brahmins have been unwilling to serve. Some dominant castes ranking below the Brahmins refuse to cook for any caste but themselves (Barnett 1973: 184). Thus, Brahmin cooks have worked in a ritually restricted, but not entirely closed, occupation.

There are numerous different regional traditions of cooking and mass feeding that could have acted as a model for commercial restaurants. In the east, the Jagannath temple cult in Puri provided the theoretical underpinnings for a huge walk-in restaurant: there the devotees of different castes received cooked divine meals, or *mahaprasad,* in return for the uncooked food offered to the priestly establishment (Rösel 1983). The mass commensality in Puri, however, did not occur elsewhere in Orissa, and the sacred complex in Puri has not provided a model for secular catering. In Mathura and elsewhere in northern India, Vaishnavaite sects have championed mass feeding. The Vallabhites, in particular, "attach great importance to food offerings, and their sophisticated cuisine makes them the undisputed gourmets of Krishnaism" (Toomey 1986: 64). It seems possible that this tradition has contributed to the development of restaurants in the north. In the south, the Tirupati hill-temple has played an important part in the rise of mass commensality. Noting the connections between feeding the gods and goddesses, feeding the pilgrims, and the role of food redistribution in the political economy of Tamil Nadu, Breckenridge points out that its temple kitchens specialized in dry *prasadam* items, which were portable, and measurable, and could be preserved (Breckenridge 1986: 32).

Arguably, the most direct and commercially successful redeployment of traditional priestly cooking skills to the modern world has come from the Brahmins from Udupi in the South Kanara district of Karnataka. This area has a strong tradition of religious mass feeding and pilgrim management. The Udupi Brahmins successfully adapted this *model of* Brahmanical hospitality to a *model for* secular catering and hoteliering.

Udupi is a city with a population of around 120,000 on India's west coast, in the state of Karnataka. The Udupi district and the South Kanara (or Dakshin Kannada) district, which formed one district until 1997, combine forested hills with an open green landscape. The Hindus on the Kanara coast had been Shaivaites for centuries until the teachings of Madhvacharya (c. 1238 to c.1317) strengthened Vaishnavism. Madhvacharya was a Brahmin and his followers are almost exclusively Brahmins, known alternatively as Madhva Brahmins, Shivalli Brahmins, Tulu Brahmins or Udupi Brahmins. After the death of Madhvacharya, a Krishna temple was established in Udupi. The temple is situated close to seven other temples, the heads of which take turns as the head of the Krishna temple. The head pontiff, *paryaya swamier,* holds this position for two years before relinquishing it (Mutt 1989: 66).

The Krishna temple has three kitchens. The *paryaya swamier*'s own kitchen (the *chawki*); the *mristanna* for invited guests such as Brahmins, scholars, and donors; and a third kitchen in an building known as the *bhojanashala,* which caters to the pilgrims irrespective of caste. The *bhojanashala* was inaugurated in 1989. Three to four thousand people, including school and college students living in the various monastic establishments attached to temples, or *mutts,* eat there daily. When a new *paryaya swamier* is installed, between ten and thirty thousand people are fed a meal that all the *mutts* cooperate in preparing. The firewood needed for cooking this meal is stacked in a huge mound the shape and size of a temple car. Pilgrims rest houses, *choultries,* are now attached to the *mutts,* but about sixty years ago individual Brahmin families also housed pilgrims.

Not only the city of Udupi, but the South Kanara district as a whole has a vibrant temple culture. Its 687 villages have total of 2173 *muzrai* (religious and charitable) institutions registered under the Madras Hindu Religious and Charitable Endowments Act (1951). Of these, 353 are major institutions assessed by the government. Udupi subdistrict had the largest number of *muzrai* institutions in the district (*Karnataka State Gazetteer,* South Kanara District 1973, 6: 670–673). Many of the temples have cooking facilities. The food is generally cooked on a wood fire in huge brass vessels, but in the 1960s some temples introduced steam boilers heated by wood to reduce the temperature in the kitchen and avoid soot. Utensils are often borrowed or rented from other temples. While some cooks are permanently employed by one temple, others are hired on a temporary basis to do *roz kelsa,* "cooking jobs" (Murthy 1989: 131).

Attending a mass feeding event at a temple in this region, one recognizes the similarities to the Udupi restaurants. Vegetarian food dishes, such as *sambar, rasam, payasam,* and rice are prepared in huge pots the size of bath tubs by teams of Brahmin cooks working long hours. Feeding takes place in a quick and efficient manner. A large covered area is prepared into which devotees are brought in waves and seated in rows. Each receives a banana leaf, and then suppliers come by in rapid succession. The meal only takes about twenty minutes before the now-sated crowd is ushered out. A crew of cleaners sweeps through, clearing banana leaves and cleaning the ground. Quickly the next group is brought in, and the process starts over. Both in method of preparation and serving style, these mass feeding events are echoed by Udupi restaurants.

Mass feeding also takes place in connection with *nagamandalas* and *bhutakolas. Nagamandalas* are rituals of snake or cobra propitiation around an intricate geometrical design drawn on the ground. *Bhutakola* is worship of potentially malevolent spirits who appear in the form of possessed religious specialists. The rituals are typically organized by a family for the welfare of themselves and their village (Carrin & Tambs-Lyche 2003; Upadhyaya & Upadhyaya 1984; see also Karanth 1975).

THE MOVE OUT

The South Kanara region has long produced a surplus of rice (Conlon 1977: 24, 42), but land was scarce. The numerous Bunts and the Jain landlords controlled most of it, while the Shivalli Brahmins, centered on an old village called Shivalli close to Udupi, remained a small and relatively insignificant caste without a tradition of migration or trade to secure a homeward flow of remittances. As South Kanara was located at the western extreme of the Madras Presidency, its inhabitants, even those residing in Mangalore, stood little chance of competing with the Tamil "Revenue Brahmins" who held a near-monopoly on government positions in the Presidency as a whole (Seal 1968: 112). Locally, Konkani-speaking Gauda Saraswat Brahmins, Christians, and others were able to secure most government jobs (Conlon 1977: 54–61). Hence, service, however humble, did not pull the local Shivalli Brahmins out of their traditional occupations. When poverty "flushed them out," as noted scholar and litterateur K. S. Haridasa Bhat expressed it, they had to depend on their main cultural capital, that is, "pleasing the mass by feeding rice" (*anna santarpana* or *samaradhana*). The flexibility and management skills built up around the many small and big shrines and temples in Udupi constituted their comparative advantage when they started moving out of their district in the beginning of the twentieth century.

THE FIRST UDUPI RESTAURANTS

K. Krishna Rao became the first major South Kanara hotel owner. He was born in 1898 in the village Kadandale in the south-central part of the district. His father was a small landholder, priest, and ayurvedic practitioner. He received little formal education, and was "practically illiterate—his parents took him out of school for he was required to help with family chores" (Krishnan 1983: 9). His work in food service began when an uncle managed to get Krishna Rao a job in the Puthige *mutt* in Udupi. Later he worked in another *mutt* as an attendant of the *swamier* and in a small nearby restaurant. In Madras he worked first as a domestic servant, then ran off to join Sharada Vilas Brahmins Hotel in George Town as a kitchen boy. In 1925 his employer offered Krishna Rao one of his restaurants for Rs. 700, to be paid in monthly installments.[6] In just three years, he had gone from cleaning the kitchen to owning his own restaurant. He quickly made his new business into a success. In 1926–27 Krishna Rao moved out of George Town and opened two restaurants on Mount Road—an area considered "the land of the Sahibs." There was not "a single, decent vegetarian restaurant" in this centrally located area until Krishna Rao opened Udupi Sri Krishna Vilas and Udupi Hotel (Krishnan 1983: 34).

In 1939 Rao opened the present Old Woodlands. In 1952, after the economic boom associated with the war, he opened the New Woodlands further south on Cathedral Road in the Mylapore locality, inhabited chiefly by Tamil Brahmins. Subsequently he started a drive-in restaurant and expanded his operations to such cities as Bangalore, Coimbatore, Salem, Ahmedabad, New Delhi, and Bombay, as well as London, New York, and Singapore. K. Krishna Rao died in 1990. Several of his restaurants and hotels are now owned and managed by his sons by his two marriages. When alive, Krishna

Rao often "advised, lessoned and blessed" his cashiers, receptionists, and suppliers when *they* started on their own, and who at times borrowed the name "Woodlands."

The second prominent chain of Udupi hotels is the Dasaprakash group. The group was founded by K. Seetharama Rao, who was born in 1899 in the village Kuthethoor. In contrast to Krishna Rao, Seetharama Rao had an education, but gave up a low-grade salaried position in Mangalore to join his brothers' tiffin business in Mysore in 1921. Whereas K. Krishna Rao expanded into the world of the sahibs along a metropolitan axis, the Dasaprakash group expanded along the colonial axis of leisure from Madras to Mysore and the hill station Ooty. In recent years, Dasaprakash has opened several new restaurants in California (*History and Origin of Dasaprakash* 2009).

The Dasaprakash Hotel in Madras, inaugurated in 1954, is a kind of earthly home for the gods, with Krishnas and Radhas placed in halls, on staircases, and in porticos. The hotel has a regular *pooja* room and an attached wedding hall, *kalyan mantapam*. The *swamiers* from Udupi have paid "voluntary visits" to the hotel. Though the idea was to transform the hotel into a sacred and auspicious space, the hotel also hosted functions unrelated to Hinduism.

From early on, Bangalore provided an alternative migratory destination. While the southern and central portions of the old South Kanara district are the provenance of most of the migrants to Madras, Kota Brahmins from Kundapur in the northern part of the district went to Bangalore. As their mother tongue is Kannada, migration to Bangalore did not isolate them linguistically to the extent that migration isolated Tulu-speaking Udupi Brahmins in Madras. Udupi Sri Krishna Bhavan and the Jnanardhana Hotel in Bangalore were founded in the early 1920s by a Kota Brahmin who came via Shimoga. Mavalli Tiffin Rooms, or MTR, was started in 1924 by two Kota Brahmin brothers who earlier worked as cooks.[7] Until the 1950s these two families were the main Udupi establishments catering to purist Brahmins and also arranging "palace parties" for the Mysore raja.[8]

The careers of Krishna Rao and Seetharama Rao were typical in many ways of the entrepreneurs of the *Gründerzeit* (Hanák 1982) in the 1920s to 1940s. Such pioneers often left their families—if they had any—behind in the district. Some studied on the side to join the salaried class. In Bombay, philanthropic hotel owners encouraged their workers to join Kannada Night Schools (Iversen & Ghorpade 2010). Other workers tried to utilize their place of employment to "come up" in the business. The pattern established by Krishna Rao of acquiring restaurants and hotels on lease or in partnership, later to become the sole owner, is typical of the South Kanara entrepreneurs. The founders generally did not diversify into other lines of business, and their sons generally took over as a group or individually. These joint families often shared a feeling that "manpower is limited," which meant that no son can be spared for other business ventures. Further, Brahmin hotel owners often marry among themselves. For example, the daughter of Seetharama Rao was married to a son of Krishna Rao, creating bonds of affinity between the two main Udupi hoteliers.

SECLUSION AND SEGREGATION

The Udupi and Kota Brahmins carried with them discriminatory traditions from the South Kanara region. One such feature was caste segregation. In temple rituals, Brahmins have often been served separately with food made in a separate kitchen. The tradition of separate kitchens has not been transferred to the Udupi restaurants, but many Udupi hotels originally had dining areas exclusively for Brahmins. Some of these facilities have been simple small rooms with low wooden chairs. Major Udupi restaurants and hotels, including Udupi Sri Krishna Vilas and the New Woodlands Hotel, maintained separate dining sections for Brahmins till the late 1960s. Udupi Sri Krishna Vilas also had a separate section for Muslims (Krishnan 1983: 37). Other restaurants went so far as to bar Muslims until 1947 (Iversen & Raghavendra 2006: 22). A gross form of discrimination, common to religious and commercial settings, has been the exclusion of Dalits. Many restaurants, including Udupi restaurants, have denied Dalits admittance, or demanded that they eat outside from special utensils to be cleaned or disposed of by themselves. Restaurants agreeing to admit Dalits did so at the risk of boycott.

According to Galanter, access to hotels and restaurants has been a central political issue since 1923 when "the Bombay Legislative Council resolved that Untouchables be allowed to use all public watering places, wells, schools, dispensaries, etc." (Galanter 1972: 237). Thirty years later, cases of discrimination relating to the use of shops, restaurants, hotels, and places of public entertainment constituted the majority of cases registered under the anti-disabilities legislation (Galanter 1972: 264, table 10.2). In the 1950s and 1960s Madras courts were more active than courts elsewhere pursuing cases of discrimination, but nowhere did the move to abolish untouchability lead to massive litigation (Galanter 1972: 273).

In Madras, activists staged repeated demonstrations against the extension of orthodoxy into restaurants. The Dravidian leader Ramaswami Naicker personally painted over the word *Brahmin* on a restaurant signboard (Naipaul 1990: 254).[9] In 1938, he incited anti-Hindi riots during which crowds attacked "coffee stalls run by Brahmans" (Irschick 1986: 222). Again, in 1957, a campaign was launched to "erase the word Brahmin from hotel name-boards . . . since such display is irrelevant in a secular state" (Rudolph & Rudolph 1967: 417). Slowly, commensal seclusion and the practice of untouchability have been eroded by commercialization, political activism, and legal reform. The establishments run by Udupi Brahmins played an important part in the expansion of civic space by exposing caste-centered traditions of ritual purity to the forces of change. As a result, seclusion and segregation are now much less frequent.

The broadening of the customer base is paralleled by the changing demographics of the workers. According to a survey by Iversen and Raghavendra (2006), in one small village restaurant, the kitchen staff is still Brahmin, though even here tiffin and coffee preparation is done by non-Brahmins. As one moves to larger towns and cities, most cooks are not Brahmins, but from castes such as Bunt and Billava. Iversen and Raghavendra attribute this change to the expansion of the menu to cover North Indian and Chinese food, which are not part of the traditional repertoire of the South Indian Brahmin cooks. This has opened the door for other cooks. Moreover, fewer Brahmins are choosing to enter the cooking trade, encouraging owners to become flexible in their hiring. In both cases, it is market forces that have prompted the change. Exposing traditional commensal apartheid to capitalism has led to inclusivist secularization, but as Iversen and Raghavendra's title, "What the Signboard Hides" indicates, change may hide behind an unchanging facade.

ETHNIC SUCCESSION IN BOMBAY:
BRAHMIN, BUNT, AND BILLAVA

Udupi restaurants also reached Bombay, the commercial capital of India. Here South Kanara entrepreneurs replaced each other in the business, those of lower castes replacing those of higher. Udupi Brahmins and

Konkani-speaking Gauda Saraswat Brahmins were the pioneers. Later the nonvegetarian Bunts—many of whom had been employed by Brahmins—established their own restaurants. More recently, the Billavas or Poojarys, a backward caste of toddy tappers, have entered the business after having worked in Bunt-owned hotels and restaurants. The success of one group has had a demonstrative effect on others, but none of these groups has affected a complete ethnic closure. The success of "Udupi Hotels" has led entrepreneurs from outside South Kanara to open businesses under that name.

The early restaurants in Bombay were referred to as Madrasi Hotels or Madrasi Brahmin Hotels, indicating that they served vegetarian food. Bombay, however, became the site for nonvegetarian restaurants. The Second World War favored Udupi restaurants, which knew the art of stretching watery *rasam* and feeding twenty-five people from a single chicken. In 1948 prohibition was enforced. This allowed Bunts, often in collaboration with Goan women, to prosper from illicit liquor and gambling. The profits were used to buy up Parsi and Muslim Irani restaurants in the 1950s and 1960s (A. S. Bhatt, personal communication). In the last thirty years, old Udupi joints started to expand with air-conditioned bars and restaurants serving exclusively Chinese and North Indian nonvegetarian dishes. Pizzas, hamburgers, and Chinese snacks were added and *idli* started to be marketed as "steam idli" (it has always been steamed) to highlight that it is a healthy dish. Rich youngsters, housewives, and working women were the new target groups (Shetty 1991).[10]

The most prominent Udupi chain in Bombay is the Kamath group, which was started in 1954 by Venkateshwar Kamath, a Gauda Saraswat Brahmin from North Kanara. The vegetarian Kamath restaurants have spread all over South India, particularly at nodal traffic points. They have also reached Atlanta and Tokyo (Irani 1991). Unlike the founders of Woodlands and Dasaprakash, Venkateshwar Kamath helped entrepreneurs of various castes to set up Kamath restaurants by financing them. Moreover, he created a recognizable style that recurs in all Kamath restaurants. The Kamath restaurants represent a more efficient and more contemporary attitude to managing a chain, whereas Woodlands and Dasaprakash represent a nineteenth-century style of capitalism, which established the Udupi brand with a modicum of standardization.

The secularization of the restaurants in Bombay and elsewhere can be seen in the layout of restaurants. As the cashiers often sit in the non air-conditioned part of the restaurant to save on the electricity bill, this section contains the images of gods and goddesses. This means that the dimly lit nonvegetarian air-conditioned section is often devoid of religious imagery. As regards the lodges, Udupi residential hotels do not place a Gideon Bible or a copy of the Bhagavad Gita in a drawer for the private contemplation of the boarder, as five-star hotels often do. Thus, the most expensive and prestigious facilities in a hotel, the nonvegetarian air-conditioned restaurant and the rooms, are also the most secular, while the purest space, the vegetarian restaurant, emerges as the cheapest.

A GREAT TRADITION GLOBALIZES

As mentioned, Udupi restaurants have spread beyond the borders of India. There are now several kosher Udupi restaurants in the New York City area. In California's Silicon Valley, restaurants expanded in the wake of South Indian information technology workers settling in the valley. The area is home to both a Dasaprakash restaurant and a chain called Udupi Palace. As with restaurants in India, the demands of the market have forced the owners of these restaurants to be flexible in their interpretation of doxa. Because it is difficult to obtain visas for cooks, the kitchen staff has become diverse and there are almost no Brahmins (A. N. Narayanswami, personal communication). The role-differentiation between cook and supplier is also sometimes obliterated (Rune-Christoffer Dragsdahl, personal communication).

Apart from the restaurants, other products with roots in Udupi have also been subject to globalization. Decades ago the Mavalli Tiffin Rooms expanded into the prepared foods market offering ready-to-eat meals, snacks, and spice mixes. Such prepared products now provide both Indians staying on in India and migrants with culturally appropriate food. Tulasi Srinivas goes so far as to say about Indian immigrants to the United States that "the MTR packaged food promotes secrecy and subterfuge among certain women whereby a facade of authenticity and traditional eating is maintained when in fact multiculturalism and cosmopolitanism have changed both eating and cooking habits" (T. Srinivas 2006: 208). The facade of traditionalism masks a hybrid reality both in the private house and the corporate world—in 2007 the Norwegian group Orkla bought MTR Foods for Rs. 450 crore (*Times of India* 2007).

Thus far this chapter has detailed how skills of cooking and playing host have been used as a model for a capitalist business allowing Udupi and Kota Brahmin and their ethnic successors to effect a transition from ritualist purity to capitalist entrepreneurship. We have attempted to show how Udupi hotels and restaurants have been significant catalysts in transforming a religious tradition in a direction consistent with the overall Indian policy of social reform. The Udupi hotels have given South Indians, who have had less contact with courtly forms of commensality, the possibility of eating and staying outside the home and the temple. To some extent, this was a marriage of convenience, as these Brahmin entrepreneurs had few other avenues for advancement other than their traditional role as cooks. This contingency notwithstanding, the way they redeployed their skills has proved sustainable both in India and abroad. This is no mean feat. Karl Marx famously argued that the expansion of the railway network in India would "dissolve the hereditary divisions of labour, upon which rest the Indian castes" by forcing Indians of all castes to rub shoulders (Marx 1853). Certainly, the commodified commensality brought about by the Udupi hotels has also had an effect in this direction. Marx stressed technological change. In contrast, this chapter has tried to grasp, equally and mutually, the inner design of a traditional society and the modern world with its changing consumption patterns.

There is a certain irony in the transformation of a sacred space into a secular space for what Appadurai (1988: 9) calls "the exploration of the culinary Other." Tulasi Srinivas points out that "as globalization erodes the traditional notions of hierarchy, breaking down caste barriers through commensality and marriage, the anxiety over identity becomes rooted in the symbolic value of consumption. The retrieving of the self through the eating of the cuisine of one's caste, ethnic group, region, and locale, becomes a precious experience" (T. Srinivas 2006: 209). Therefore, Udupi hotels are simultaneously the sites where caste barriers are broken and where what she terms "gastro-nostalgia" is provided. This combination of change and nostalgia is exemplified by the customers of the Udupi Sri Krishna Bhavan described by Iversen and Raghavendra. While this restaurant did not admit Muslims before 1947, Muslims now account for a quarter of the customer base. At the same time, "old customers repeatedly tell [the owner] how much they appreciate that the taste of the food has changed so little over the years" (Iversen & Raghavendra 2006: 22).

The story does not end there, for there is a pinch of *hing* (asafoetida) left to be added. This leads us, in a circular pattern, to where it started, namely to the rituals and temples of South Kanara. Successful entrepreneurs maintained familial and economic ties to the region of their birth. Part of the profits they had generated in urban centers was used to renovate old temples, thereby increasing the prestige of the donors in their home region. K. Krishna Rao of the Woodlands, for example, spent Rs. 10 lakhs renovating the temple in his native village (Bannanjee G. Acharya, personal communication). That set a standard that encouraged migrants to plow enough money back into the hinterland to effect a religious revival. In the estimation of some informants, hoteliers (including caterers) have contributed about ninety percent of the funds that have been used to renovate the temples and shrines in the district (Bannanjee G. Acharya, personal communication). Perhaps some 400 to 500 temples in the district have been renovated to varying degrees. As already mentioned, the number of major assessable temples in the old district of South Kanara exceeds 300. An average outlay of just Rs. 2 lakhs per temple would mean a hotelier contribution of about Rs. 7 crores for 400 temples. Hoteliers also contribute to the daily worship, for example, by dedicating funds held in fixed deposits for various *pujas* (rituals of worship). A very large portion of the daily worship in the Krishna Temple in Udupi is financed in this way (N. A. Madhyastha, personal communication). In addition, hoteliers also contribute to *nagamandalas* and *bhutakolas*. The hoteliers do donate to secular activities, such as educational and social institutions, but they do so more sparingly. Most of the donations for the schools come from local people. "The new uneducated rich give to God because God and not education helped them," an experienced educator remarked during fieldwork in 1991.

While entrepreneurs of different castes may not develop antagonistic relations in the metropolitan cities, their sponsorship of religion may sharpen conflicts back home. Donors and temple boards may disagree about the best ways to utilize funds. Bunts and Brahmins often seem to clash over temple management. As Brahmins are generally priests while Bunts are often temple trustees, this type of conflict repeats itself. The end result of the increased ritual activity is the creation of a highly charged religious landscape awash with revitalized *devtas* (divinities), reempowered *bhutas* (spirits), and sanskritized temples—courtesy of the migrants.

The spiritual elite of Udupi town partakes of this Hindu revivalism, which has become politically potent in many parts of India since the 1990s. In 1991, Bharatiya Janata Party (BJP) leader L. K. Advani started his national election campaign with a short visit to Udupi hosted in the temple area. Vasudeva Rao notes about the Madhva sect in Udupi that most of the members of the sect are either active or passive supporters of the BJP and the Vishwa Hindu Parishad (VHP). The senior Pejavara matha swamiji belongs to the Dharma Sansad of the VHP. As Nandy points out, the Dharma Sanad "is a synod of saints and seers of all faiths prevalent in Hindu society" (Nandy et al. 1995: 91). Gifts create problems; the economy of affection has its discontents. Gifts made by men to thank the gods and spirits for their good fortune provoke visions of ancient and future glory, which in turn link up with religious and political revivalism more broadly.

It is not difficult to see the parallels to the manner in which the flow of migrants' "gratitude money" from the West has played an important role in the religious violence sponsored by Islamic, Sikh, and Hindu organizations in recent years.[11] It is more difficult, perhaps, to see any parallel to the manner in which temple restoration has taken place historically, but it can be argued that Richard Davis's enchanting stories in *The Lives of Indian Images* provide the background against which to judge recent revivalism. Stretching his contention, it can be argued that everywhere the construction of a mosque or a temple or a church outside an area of immediate political control can be read as an act of symbolic conquest, and everywhere the reconstruction of a mosque or a temple or a church on home ground can be read as an act of resistance or self-assertion (Davis 1997: 194 et passim).

As regards South Kanara, religious riots broke out several places in the coastal belt in late 1998 and early 1999, leaving several people dead and causing substantial material damage. According to Muzaffar Asoodi, the riots were caused by economic competition between caste groups and by religious revivalism among both Hindus and Muslims (Assadi 1999: 13). Subsequently, Karnataka became the first southern state to have a BJP government. In 2008–9, the liberal city of Mangalore experienced a Hindu form of "Talibanization" as gangs of young men tried to rein in young pub-going women (People's Union for Civil Liberties 2009).

Thus, South Kanara has proved not to be immune to religious riots despite its tradition of civility, its impressive record in commerce and education, and its orderly ethnic succession. It would be nice if a densely structured local religious society would render itself immune to the virus of communalism as critical traditionalists are wont to imagine. However, the chicken has found a way to come home to roost even here in the best of all possible Hindu worlds (Madsen 2005). This circular movement between modernization and religious revival is likely to continue, as the government of Karnataka has called on Indians abroad to support temple renovation at home (*Times of India* 2008).

Max Weber was disinclined to believe that capitalism would have any future in India. Indians, he argued, would be incapable of running modern industries in an efficient and nonpredatory manner on account of the Hindu "law of rituals." When Milton Singer studied Madras entrepreneurs, he realized that Weber was wrong. According to Singer, modernization among these entrepreneurs was helped along by a series of adaptive strategies. These strategies enabled industrial leaders to thrive in the modern world without unbearable mental strains resulting from a failure to conform to inherited notions of purity. To account for the coexistence of Hinduism and capitalism, Singer developed the notion of "compartmentalization." The industrialists in Madras, he argued, did not experience a clash between their identity as Hindus or Brahmins and their identity as industrialists because these two roles were compartmentalized or separated into different life-worlds (Singer 1972: 320–25). In 2000, when John Harriss restudied some of the same entrepreneurial families that Singer had interviewed, he found the notion of compartmentalization misleading (Harriss 2003). Instead, Harriss observed a similar interpenetration between capitalism, Hinduism, and Hindutva politics that we have drawn attention to, namely, politicized Hindu capitalism without compartmentalization. Thus, a Great Tradition that modernizes, globalizes, and secularizes is also likely to Brahmanize and revitalize as it stands forth.[12]

NOTES

This chapter originates in discussions between Sujatha M., K. Ramachandra Rao, and Kate and Stig Toft Madsen around November 1988. The Danish Research Council for the Humanities enabled Rao and Stig Toft Madsen to do fieldwork in Karnataka and Tamil Nadu from March to June 1991. In 2009 Geoffrey Gardella, in consultation with A. N. Narayanswami, brought their knowledge from India and California to bear on the project. For details see Madsen (1992).

    1. A description of Udupi Hotels is found in *Karnataka State Gazetteer, South Kanara District* (1973: 362–363). For literary works see Ramdas (1976) and Laxman

(1988). For a portrait of K. Krishna Rao, the founder of Woodlands, see Krishnan (1983), an extract of which may be consulted in Muthiah (1989).

2. "A modern restaurant represents a total refutation of the entire orthodox culinary and jati commensal rules that the tradition inculcates at the level of the domestic hearth," wrote Khare (1976b: 246).

3. On ethnic succession, see Light (1981: 65) on the smooth uncontested occupation of jobs left vacant by upwardly mobile ethnic groups, and K. Ray (2006) on American restaurants.

4. See Dubois (1906: 184) for the abhorrence in which Brahmins held metal plates, forks, and spoons in the early nineteenth century.

5. Although there are examples of women entrepreneurs opening eating establishments, the vast majority of Udupi restaurant owners, including the successful ones, are men.

6. It has been and still is possible to rent fully furnished small restaurants on a short-term or even daily basis. By renting progressively bigger places, a person may eventually become the owner of a restaurant.

7. Nair (2005: 64) dates the first vegetarian hotels in Bangalore to the aftermath of the plague around 1898, when many Brahmins sent their wives out of the city and thereby opened a niche for restaurants.

8. Practically all the waiters in MTR have been from South Kanara and the cooks have been Brahmins. Perhaps, this rootedness explains why the MTR has felt free to dispense with many of the standard rules for the division of labor, cultivating, instead, a certain bohemian style.

9. Many Udupi hotels used the word *Brahmin* in their name to indicate ownership and that the cooks were Brahmin. The term *Udupi* itself became a marker of purity.

10. The Bombay tiffin-trolley system distributing lunches to working males presumes that wives or other female relatives cook the meal. This system only partly competed with the Udupi restaurants and canteens, which deliberately targeted bachelors. For more on the tiffin-trolleys in Mumbai, see Nilesh (2008).

11. The role of diasporic remittances in Hindu revivalism may be gauged from Sabrang (2002).

12. Warren Hastings, it will be remembered, "stood forth" as the *diwan* (high government official) and de facto ruler of Bengal in 1772, putting an end to the subterfuge under which the East India Company had hitherto operated.

SIX

Dum Pukht

A PSEUDO-HISTORICAL CUISINE

Holly Shaffer

ISHTIYAQUE, AMIN, AND I drive in a green car, snaking through the old city of Lucknow. Darkness is punctured by the purple shades of fluorescent light reflected off whitewashed walls. We are debriefing, while peering through the windows, searching for the tell-tale sign of open-air cooking: flame close to the ground. We have just completed an unsatisfying yet rather expensive meal at the Taj Hotel's five-star Oudhiana, a grey, alcoved space with oriental touches like arches, patterned fabrics, and a hookah, that exults in Lucknow's historical, now mythical, cuisine. Our main interest is in *dum pukht*—the sealed pot cooking technique that renders meat tender, and rice divinely moist yet dry, fragrant yet pungent.

"Now, what did you think of the rice," Ishtiyaque asks, which is an entirely unfair question. Not only is he the chef of multiple restaurants in multiple cities, including Chote Nawab in Lucknow, a restaurant that specializes in "authentic Lakhnavi cuisine," where I have been learning his techniques; but he is also the eldest son of Imtiaz Qureshi, perhaps still the most famous chef in India even after thirty years. Imtiaz's, and therefore Ishtiyaque's, story is as follows: in the 1970s, the chairman of the Indian Tobacco Company (ITC), Ian Aksar, decided to enter the high-end hotel business. One of his tactics, considering he was a gourmand and competing with the lure of luxury historic buildings like the Taj and modern buildings like the Oberoi, was to specialize, even brand, luxury restaurants offering "traditional" Indian cuisine. At this time, restaurants in five-star hotels mainly offered European or Chinese food, with a small static menu of Indian. Major S. S. Habib Rehman, the former business manager of the ITC, and a key player in its promotion of Indian cuisine, recalls:

When I entered the hotel business, the five star hotels were dominated by Western influence. Our cuisine, kitchens and service were focused around this palate, and the Indian kitchen used to occupy a corner space with the menu prospect quite small. It quite honestly offended our sensibilities for two reasons. What was offered in no way represented the accomplishments and diversity of Indian cuisine, and secondly, I discovered or rediscovered that I myself had a good background in Indian cuisine by virtue of my environment and upbringing [in an upper-class family in Hyderabad, like Lucknow a former Mughal capital]. This made me resolute to change the equation and I was quite determined to resurface Indian cuisine to its rightful place. It happened that I had joined a company, ITC, which in a sense, was also inclined to discover, Indian-ness and Indian roots in its ventures and initiatives. That created a good blend to propel my own desire to rediscover or bring forward the magic, width and depth of Indian cuisine. It is that desire or search that led us to the establishment of a broad classification of cuisine in our restaurants: *Bukhara/Peshawri* which brought tandoor food; *Dum Pukht* which brought traditional breads, curries, kebabs, rice and *Dakshin* which put together regional cuisine of peninsular India (Tamil Nadu, Kerala, Andhra . . .). Happily for us Indians also were woken up to such a wide range of Indian cuisine.[1]

A key part of this plan was obviously the chef. The man they were searching for, someone grounded in tradition yet able to innovate for an international and national audience and a linen-clothed table, china, and silverware context with a bill at the end, turned out to be Imtiaz Qureshi. They found him in Lucknow, where he was working for a hotel, the new patronage with the loss of the nobility's wealth, but with a proper chef's lineage to the Nawabs, or former Mughal rulers. For his trade test, Imtiaz prepared foods from the northwestern frontier (a.k.a. Pakistan and Afghanistan): succulent kebabs tingling in spice and limbs of goat or lamb tenderized and roasted. This is the menu now served at Bukhara, his first restaurant (1977), still consistently rated one of the best in India, as well as in the world.

After two years working at the ITC, he traveled to America and England to see what the situation of Indian food was abroad. He found that "Mughlai" food was all that was represented, but that it depressingly consisted of butter chicken, chicken tikka, and naan. So he started thinking about this, that the original food was not locatable in any authentic form. He began to research the food of Lucknow, his home. Imtiaz is, in ways, the origin of the movement towards "historical" cuisine and the concept of "preservation." He practiced for five years in banquet halls, and tested his menu in another

ITC restaurant, Mayur. In 1989 he opened Dum Pukht, also to international fame, which specialized in Lucknow's aristocratic decadent cuisine, particularly meats, such as leg of lamb, or *raan,* slow cooked in richly spiced and thickened sauces fluttered in gold, and aromatic layered rice and meat dishes, *pulao.*

Lucknow's cuisine is inherited from the Mughal court (itself a mix of the Turkish/Central Asian/Persian/North Indo-Pakistan); the declining Safavid Court in Iran, where the first Nawab, Sadat Khan, emigrated from; the European (French, English, Portuguese); and the Awadhi regional influences, but refining itself further on its own demands. In a comparison to Mughlai food, its greatest influence, Lakhnavi food has less spice (due to the Persian influence); smoother textures (supposedly Nawab Asaf ud Daula had lost his teeth—but there was an equal attitude that considered chewing boorish); multiple strainings (from the French); attention paid to aromas and colors (such as keora and rose water; or feeding animals on specific diets, like saffron pills to infuse their flesh); a theory of spices that included arrangements with the Hakim and ground spices for taste and whole ones, wrapped up in an easily removed bouquet so as not to offend the palate, for aroma; and a predilection towards richness: the generous use of ghee, cream, and nuts (besides dish after dish of meat). Lucknow's cuisine is also known for its theatricality, such as "riddle" dishes where one food seemed or tasted like another, or spectacle like an opium-dozed monkey hiding within a puffed fried bread, or *puri* (see Sharar 2005: 155–70; Bhatnagar & Saxena 1997; True 2004; and Shaffer 2007).

So this is not an easy question, the offhand: what did I think of the rice? We are talking of centuries of refinement, first in the aristocratic court culture of eighteenth- and nineteenth-century Lucknow, subsequently recalibrated through the apprentice system that Imtiaz, on to Ishtiyaque, was trained under; and second in the forty-odd years of hotel cooking—the two methods sometimes conflicting. I recall my advisor, R. K. Saxena, Principal of the Institute of Hotel Management in Mumbai, formerly of Lucknow, telling me the one question he would have for Imtiaz: "It is not about complicated dishes. Garlic *kheer* [a smooth rice pudding] not tasting of garlic, bones of fish melting into flesh—no, no, it is about rice. How does Imtiaz manage to maintain each grain separate, aromatized, plump, and infused, yet dry. Each one singular, yet within them all?"[2]

Rice is clearly metaphysical. I do not take that route. "The texture of the rice was sticky. . . ." I begin entirely without elegance.—"Yes, yes, and . . ."—"The scent was gone; they used false coloring."—"Aha," Ishtiyaque beams. He is thirty with a pony-tail, hip yet quite serious: "Did you notice, they brought the pulao without a lid—what is *dum* cooking without unsealing the dough, the opening, and that first intake of breath?"

The Taj's restaurant, Oudhiana, never had a chance. We were competitors after all: Ishtiyaque, the chef; Amin, the manager; and me, their humble acolyte. "You've had pulao at the restaurant right?" Ishtiyaque asks me, probing, "We let you open the lid," he stresses, but then pauses, "but even the restaurant isn't quite the real dum pukht. . . ." Which is what we are after now. It is why we are driving slowly through the streets of the old city at 11 at night searching for flame against the inky blackness.

Ishtiyaque and I have the same story in our head. It is guiding us towards the pulao or biriyani[3] made outside, by the dum pukht method: in a cauldron, or *degh,* sealed with dough, with fire beneath and coals on top, slow baking. It is the story written on the menu at his father's restaurant, Dum Pukht:

> History remembers the Nawabs [Mughal governors turned rulers] of Awadh for their love of music and dance, of epicurean delights and grand gestures.
>
> When famine ravaged the state, Nawab Asaf-ud-Daulah decreed the neverending construction of a giant edifice, the Bara Imambara [a Shia building housing objects related to the mourning period of Muharram and a gathering place during that time], creating unceasing employment. By royal decree, too, arrangements were made to provide food. Enormous containers were filled with rice, meat, vegetables, spices and sealed. Hot charcoal was placed on top and fires lit underneath while slow cooking ensured that food was available day and night.
>
> The result was extraordinary, for when the vessels were unsealed, the splendid aromas attracted royal attention. "Dum" means to breathe in and "Pukht" means to cook. By order of the Nawab the "dummed" cuisine was now perfected for the royal table. Exotic dishes were evolved, in which, flavours and fragrances intermingled with exquisite results. Before long, the new cuisine was fashionable at many other royal courts. . . .[4]

It is a story repeated in the media regarding the restaurant, the technique, and frequently the cuisine of Lucknow as a whole.[5] It is a story still current on the streets of Lucknow, repeated many times (to me) when I asked about dum pukht cuisine. It is a story I was seduced by—it is why I came to India.

What a fabulous concatenation of factors: street food and courtly food, gift-giving and reciprocation, Muharram—the Shia commemoration of the martyrdom at Karbala in C.E. 680 [6] and its relationship to Lucknow's population and architecture, and might I repeat—food. This is a gorgeous food story, with much potential in the gustatory imagination. Yet, as the facts revealed themselves, I realized that the story is not entirely true, yet neither is it entirely false.

There was a famine and the Imambara was built, though they were not necessarily related.[7] However, the story was in place by the time Abdul Halim Sharar was writing in the 1880s, though not without its own coloring of the facts. In his book *Lucknow: The Last Phase of an Oriental Culture,* he writes:[8]

> In 1784 there was a famine in Avadh and even the well-to-do of the town were starving. At that difficult time, the work of building the Imam Bara was started in order to alleviate the suffering of the population. As the better class people considered it beneath their dignity to work as labourers, the construction was carried on by night, as well as by day, and the impoverished and starving gentry of the town came in the darkness of the night to join with the labourers and work with the aid of torches. The Nawab had entered upon the construction of the building from sincere religious motives and, in the same way, the people threw themselves into the work with immense energy and feeling. (Sharar 2005: 47)

He does not mention food in relation to this story, which he does explicate in detail in his book, itself a compilation of articles for the Urdu newspaper he edited, *Dil Gudaaz.*

However, the plausibility of food gifted out at such a religious occasion is entirely accurate. Part of the tradition of Muharram, as well as of many other ceremonies for Muslims and Hindus alike across India, is the gifting of food during ceremony. For instance, on the twelfth day of Rabi'ul, the anniversary of the Prophet Muhammad, the nobleman "Raushan-ud Daula observed it on a grand scale . . . every day sent abundant supplies of various preparations such as pulao and sheer birunj (milk dressed with rice) during the entire period of the festivities." Itmad-ud Daula Qamauddin Khan also "distributed daily from his kitchen, among the poor and the indigent" (Umar 1998: 413) food in large quantities. Hafiz Rahmat Khan gave thousands cooked food and water daily during Muharram (Umar 1998: 406); and Nawab Asaf ud Daula, the ruler of Lucknow, daily (not just during festivals) distributed food (Umar 1998: 418).

It is rather the particular cobbling of the facts generated in the 1980s by Qureshi and Rehman that reveals the fabrication. This became explicit in two interviews that bookended my time in India. The first was during my third week, with Imtiaz, who is now nearing eighty, with a white handlebar mustache and belly belying his craft. We sat in the marble, porticoed lobby of the Andheri branch of the ITC hotel in Mumbai. I asked him the meaning or origin of the phrase *dum pukht*.

"The word *pukht*," he explained to me, "means a sacred thing, a temple, a mosque or a 'kitchen.' It is meant to be very hygienic and of high standards. So there is *dum,* which is a method of cooking . . . with fire from both sides [of the sealed vessel] so the food gets cooked in its own moisture . . . and *pukht,* which is cooking food in a hygienic condition." He paused, "So I put the two words together and opened a restaurant, which became very famous."

Even this is not entirely true (what is truth, after all), *dum pukht* simply as a phrase has a documented history, which I will explore below, but it is how Imtiaz expressed it, and utilized the phrase *dum pukht* that seems to have altered its definition as a specific technique or a particular dish to become a "catch-word," as Saxena defined it, if not elided with the differentiated cuisine of Lucknow.

The second interview was my next to last day in India with Rehman. We were in his lovely home, talking for long enough that I was invited to stay for a dinner party he was hosting. Among many dishes, one stood out: a delicate rich nuanced *salan,* or thin sauce, fire-speckled with delicate spice and small round balls, or *kofta,* some of vegetables, some of meat, disguised so you couldn't tell the differce until you bit. This was one of the *pehle,* or riddle dishes, akin to the famous *shub degh,* from Kashmir, yet popularized in Lucknow. It is a dish slow cooked overnight (*shub* means night) in the dum pukht method. It consists of roundels of ground meat and roundels of ground turnip—the two indistinguishable by sight.

About an hour into our discussion, to my question of the origin of dum pukht he explained, "I am also a student of history, there is a reference to a Nawab in a book, but a reference to many of those fellows. So someone gave blankets and labors and citizenry, so in that we came up with the story. I don't know whether it is true or not but *we took advantage of this romance* to bring the food to well off compatriots" [my italics].

I giggled. I couldn't help it—well, it was a romance—a delightful one in fact, and at that point I was no longer disgruntled that this distinct weaving was an invention of the 1980s. The story, in a way, did indeed speak to that time. It was far enough away for the newly wealthy, in an independent capitalist India, to feel nostalgic for an aristocratic past, and even some of its values, including a moral economy of gift giving—specifically the relation-ship between the people, their ruler, and religion that perhaps was not as extant, or at the very least, diluted.

But I had initially been dismayed—I felt lied to—as if some moral bound-ary had been crossed. Could it be, that word I so despised, *authenticity?* But I knew that stories were not authentic, or their very authenticity depended on their ability to change. That is what stories do. They zoom about shifting according to their teller, much like recipes and dishes of food do by their maker. A dish cannot stay the same by the virtue of the changing nature of products, seasons, locality, the very water used; and that does not even enter into the character of a cook's hand or taste. So what was it? Was it the actual fixedness of the story, and its repetition, that was so bothersome? Was it that it seemed to leave something out, something not only essential to dum pukht, but to the culinary culture of Lucknow as a whole?

Yet Ishtiyaque and I believe in this story, the menu one, when we pull up expectant to the Bara Imambara, which, when it was built in the late eighteenth century, "contained the largest vaulted hall in the world" and still today is overwhelming in its immensity. (Chelkowski 2006: 107) It is also Muharram now, and the Shia part of the city has shifted into mourning the martyrdom at Karbala. Muharram is in part commemorated through proces-sions of *taziyeh,* portable shrines or mausoleums for the martyrs, through the streets. We have just missed the end of a procession; men barefoot, wear-ing mourning black, still walk about. Remnants of paper, sparkles, from the *taziyeh,* have settled on the ground. It seems as if the two times merge—the seventh century and now—that the loss is a current through the present,[9] just as now merges again with the eighteenth century as if we might find Nawab Asaf ud Daula descending from his elephant to breathe in the gorgeous hearty scent from one of the hundreds of potentially steadily simmering pots.

We continue on through the looming, scalloped gate; go right, left, right, right, until another smaller gate angles out between shops. To the left a crowd stands in front of a stage hung with light bulbs—small stitched leaf bowls are being passed out hand over hand. I look left, and see three great iron cauldrons defining themselves against the darkness.

Ishtiyaque propels himself out of the car, motioning me to stay, then to come—"I've never seen this, but I thought maybe. . . ." And he goes up to the man, holding up three fingers. I remember that Ishtiyaque grew up in Delhi and Bombay, not Lucknow, that he is once-removed. "Eat with your fingers," Ishtiyaque says, handing me a leaf bowl, then taking a bite for himself, "it tastes different, it is a different experience." Each grain is coated with reddened oil, and the bright orange of false saffron colorant, but here it doesn't matter. The spice is quiet but present, the broth of the meat hot and healing on the throat. We stand and eat.

The comparison is too sharp to the Oudhiana with its linen draped table, stuffed chairs, and silver cutlery to be entirely meaningful. We have placed ourselves in the same position as the nineteenth-century painting[10] of Ghazi ud din Haidar, one of the last of the Nawabs of Awadh, pressed uncomfortably close to a table overladen with delicacies. His British designed crown is too tight, his surrounding entourage, including Lord and Lady Moira, pressed too close. This king is no longer a Mughal, portrayed in regal profile on the crisp white cloth, or *dastarkhan,* spread on the ground, yet nor is he British. We also are neither the aristocracy nor the poor, the British or the Indian, the then or the now; we are not Shia Muslims. And yet the taste holds, or something holds. Is it just romanticism that this food, this dum pukht, tastes somehow more *real* than the restaurant; that at least one of its meanings, beyond just food, has come through? Or is it just that we've inhabited a story that feels right, if only for a moment.

· · ·

Dum pukht, as a culinary technique with recipes, has a documented history. First and foremost it is labeled as one of the ten types of meat cookery in the Mughal courts according to the *Ain-i Akbari* (1590), or History of Akbar. The author, Abu'l Fazl, gives a recipe (Abu'l Fazl 1994: 61–4): "10 sers meat; 2 sers ghi; 1 ser onions; 11 misqals fresh ginger; 10 misqals pepper; 2 dams cardamoms." Here the dish seems to be only of slow cooked and spiced meat, but a couple of centuries later, Francis Joseph Steingass, as the erudite Robert Skelton informed me, "in his Persian-English dictionary (1892: 535) has *dum pukht* as 'a kind of pilaw,' or meat and rice dish. He defines *dam* as breath, air, life, scent, smell, fume, breath of an oven, the mouth of a stove or a hot bath; bellows; the stewing over a slow fire plus many other meanings including time, season, hour, moment—of which the last is so commonly used, as in the Urdu phrase ek-dam- 'one moment.' *Pukhtan,* is of course the verb to boil, cook, etc. from which we get the past particle pukhta: cooked."[11]

Dum pukht is both a method of cooking and specific recipes, like a pulao or meat dish. K. T. Achaya defines "dumpukht, dumpoke" in his *Historical Dictionary of Indian Food* (1998a: 62): "These terms refer to the baking of meat in a seal of dough. The Persian word dumpukht literally means air-cooked (i.e. baked). . . ." He further states that "the word was anglicized to dumpoke in colonial India, and frequently denoted a boneless stuffed duck cooked in a seal of dough."

Thus dum pukht, as European travelers witnessed it, was a slow-baked dish of meat, which the Hobson Jobson dictionary of Anglo-Indian terms compiled in the late nineteenth century corroborates. John Fryer writes (1698: 93): "These eat highly of all Flesh Dumpoked, which is baked with spice in Butter." He also writes (1698: 404) of "baked meat they call Dumpoke which is dressed with sweet Herbs and Butter, with whose Gravy they swallow with Rice dry boiled." This is likely close to the contemporary dish, *Murgh Musullum,* a whole chicken dressed with spices and ghee baked in a low sealed vessel or *lagan,* with coals beneath and on top, sealed with a rope of dough.

I made this with Sangeeta Bhatnagar, who co-authored *Dastarkhwan-e-Awadh* (1997) with Saxena, on the roof of her house in Lucknow. It took at least three hours, not including the overnight marination, and the staged additions of fragrance: rose, keora, the delicate interplay of ground and whole spices. She motioned me close near the end, when she was about to lift the lid: "This is it," she said, "the reason for *dum* cooking: now when I tell you, breathe in deep." And I did.

Reverand Ovington writes (Ovington & Rawlinson 1689/1929: 397): "a dumpoked Fowl, that is boil'd with Butter in any small Vessel, and stuft with Raisins and Almonds in another (Dish)." Begum Nur Bano of Rampur related a story about a dish like this to me on the telephone while I was on the train on my way, her voice bumping along the tracks: "The chicken had to be of a certain age, two to three years and the meat had to be tender. There was a lot of pure ghee, with raisins, almonds, pistachios, and rice. The rice, and chicken stuffed with the dry fruit were cooked separately—he would also mix sugar and salt, sprinkle it over the chicken; that taste was so different to any other taste. I've eaten dum pukht all over. It's a name now . . . lost is that taste, you see, it's a different dish." Maybe not so curiously, the travelers of the seventeenth century experienced a similar dish to the one in the *Ain-i Akbari* of about a hundred years earlier. Perhaps by the late nineteenth century, when Steingass's dictionary was published, the method was also applied to the meat and rice dish, pulao.[12]

Achaya writes further (1998a: 62) that dum pukht, as a "style of cooking was not confined to the north. Even in 1068 C.E., the Kannada writer

Shantinatha in his Sukumaracharite refers to slow cooking under a seal of wheat dough used to hold down the lid, as *kanika*." Dum pukht as a technique was used elsewhere, frequently under different names, which is not too surprising given its basic simplicity. There are many stories of a simpler form of dum pukht where the earth is indeed the seal. The Nawab of Kakori, a hamlet famous for their melt-in-the-mouth kebabs so tender that it is an art simply to form them on the *seekh*, or long metal skewer, explained to me:

> Before dum there was a food called *gil-i hikmutt*. There are no records, only one recipe I know about. They would take a whole fish and clean it from inside and outside, take out the fins and wash it properly, then pure oil was put all over and in between the *masalas* and it was filled with dried fruit. The fish was stitched from the stomach, was dipped in *ghee* and covered with *mulmul*, which is muslin. The mouth was opened and then they put clay all over the fish. They made a hole in the ground, leaving about 4" diameter and put the fish with its mouth sticking out. They made an outer circle, where they put the fire. When there was a heat on the fish, the ghee would come out, meaning the fish would open its mouth by force of the heat. This ghee with saffron was given to the honored guest. When the temperature would rise from the steam inside, the fish would again open his mouth and the Nawab would take out another spoonful and give to a guest, and so on. When the fish was done it was taken out of the cloth, and no clay remained, but the fish was tenderly cooked. This ghee given to a guest is the greatest of compliments.

I heard a similar story in Faizabad, when I dined with the lawyer V. K. Singh's family. I commented to his daughter-in law that all of the women in the family seemed to be wearing shades of green—and that it was beautiful. She must have been reminded of the jungle because she nodded and told me joyfully of her hometown Rae Bareli, surrounded by forests. Her husband joined her and commented: "We would go hunting, then dig a pit, start a slow fire, bury the prey (frequently wild boar), and cover the pit with sweet-smelling grasses and let it cook for hours. The taste is like nothing else."

Raja Sulaiman Khan of Mahmudabad confirmed this notion one day while I sat in his spare study with walls of books. We had been discussing Muharram, both regarding dum pukht cooking, which is used during this period—in part because the technique is easy to adapt to mass feeding, but also regarding the gifting of food, called *tabarukh*. Certain foods, including but not confined to dum pukht cuisine, were associated with certain days in the mourning period and certain people. But we shift from this to the discussion of the origins of dum pukht. "Dum pukht probably has its origin in hunting food. There is a strong tradition of hunting, especially across

North India. It is probably Hindu; they often cooked in the jungle. One of the ways of cooking was to dig a hole in the ground, to bury the pot, seal the pot and let it cook while they went off to do something else. There is a similar dish from an area religiously connected to this part, but has a terrain very different: Arabia. There it is called *mandi.* So dum pukht is a sophisticated version of something very basic. In dum pukht you do not grind the masalas; whatever you put in, you put in unground. Don't put many spices. Black pepper, red chilies, onions, and garlic, rose water, and ghee, no water. Rose water is considered to be a tenderizer. And rose petals."

Rose petals and water are also a medicine, the domain of *hakims,* the doctors of Yunani (Greek medicine adapted into the Arabic-speaking world through Avicenna), whom Sulaiman sends me to. Sulaiman's hakims, Khawwar and Akbar Nawab, who are also Ishtiyaque's, live near the Odeon cinema in a large brick house adjacent to the street. Up the steps, if the gate is open, the pharmacy to the right is stacked with bottles in varying hues, and the waiting room to the left full of ailing people. I pass right through to the courtyard, which is turning blue in the twilight, to ask on scents. "Perfumes here have a medicinal value," Khawwar Nawab says, "the smell of perfume, especially in sweets, dilates the heart so the blood passes easily." I then ask on *dum.* "I have thought about this," he says. "In preparation. There is one technique called *gil-i hikmat* [which is the same as the Nawab of Kakori described], *gil* being the Persian word for mud, for medicines of animal origin. For example, you remove the intestines of a crab and place in an earthen pot. Cover with an earthen plate and seal with special mud—put this in fire and roast for 3–4 hours until it becomes almost powder, an ash. Similarly while cooking food we close the opening with flour. This was started by hakims to treat the rice. When rice is prepared in this way it is easily digested by the body." An elderly Ayurvedic doctor in Varanasi also told me of this method, but with pearls, instead of crab intestines.

By now we seem far away from dum pukht's supposed origin in Iran. A twentieth-century thread indicates the Persian connection, again with Robert Skelton's generous help. In Dr. Muhammad Mu'in's *Farhang-i Farsi* (1963, 2: 1104), a twentieth-century dictionary, *dam pukht* is defined and equated with *dampoxt-ak* as a food resembling pulao, where rice is cooked, but without water (this is likely the steaming/baking method) and with lentils or peas.[13] *Dampoxt-ak,* which is a lentil and rice dish, is also in the contemporary Persian cookbook *New Food of Life* by Najmieh Batmanglij (1992).

But all of these sources, which attest to dum pukht being a technique, existing in multiple periods in multiple forms, leave out an emotional undercurrent to my interviews: slight annoyance, if not simple boredom. "Dum pukht!" people would say, surprised, when I asked. Well, they would proceed, like Zahoor Rizvi, of the spiced and perfumed tobacco company, closed now for ten years, did: it is "not actually the name of some food, dum pukht is a way of cooking." Then after talking for three minutes about dum pukht, they would move on to other, far more colorful aspects of the cuisine of Lucknow. These latter halves of the conversation lasted hours. Eventually, Kanwar Ratanjit Singh of Kapurthala, fondly called Reggie, told me plainly, a day into cooking such delicate and exquisite foods in his house in Shimla, a mountain town quite far from Lucknow: "Dum pukht is a catch phrase, it is a term popularized, but the technique is the basis, the essential method in Awadhi cuisine. . . . If you cook a dish and then take it off the fire to just sit, breathing in its own aromas for twenty minutes, or half an hour, the taste is completely altered. This takes time and patience, not many places do this, definitely not in restaurants. . . ." Farid Faridi went one step further boldly claiming one evening in Lucknow that "there is no such thing as Awadhi cuisine" at all. "It's a myth, an invention."

· · ·

"Dum pukht," Sulaiman told me, "is an Awadh stroke, but it is actually a Mughal dish." And before that a Persian one, and before that. . . . He continued, "the dishes are names, so anyone can do things, can invent tradition, we are in flux all the time, we have to recognize, although attempts can be made to preserve skills, tastes, recipes, we have to recognize that the time has passed. It will never be the same, it cannot be the same, that context. I believe there is a context."

What happens when historical food loses its context? Such as when it moves into a hotel restaurant? That cobbled story of dum pukht, written on the menu, taps into the context of Lucknow's food, though not always explicitly (such as with the Shia backstory, the essential aspect of Muharram)—but is that enough? Or should it even be a question? Imtiaz revitalized a slowly dying cuisine. He translated that food for a new audience—he *allowed for the story to continue.* But now it is a different story. How does this aspect, of a story that by necessity must adapt, link into the concept of the preservation of historical cuisine, which is somehow built into that very model "authentic"?

A name, a technique, even a recipe does not imply that the product is the same because of *context*. Do we care about context?

"I am trying with my family to preserve," Reggie Singh of Kapurthala, explains to me in his Tudor manor house, the former summer home of one of the British viceroys to India, in the foothills of the Himalayas. "But there are dishes that I know the names of, but I have no idea how to make them— *anar pulao* (pomegranate), *angoor pulao* (grape), *moti pulao* where the meat is formed into pearls. I've tried it but never gotten it right."

This is reminiscent of the list in Abdul Halim Sharar (2005: 158), which, even by that time in the late nineteenth century, had also become only names: "There are seven well-known kinds of pulaus in Lucknow. I can remember the names of only *gulzar,* the garden, *nur,* the light, *koku,* the cuckoo, *moti,* the pearl and *chambeli,* jasmine; but in fact scores of different pulaus are served." There is no reference to what these dishes are, how they tasted, what they looked like.

Reggie continues, "Also you don't know if the pomegranate is actually pomegranate or simply what looks like it. Like one chef was able to put × kilogram of sugar into one grain of rice—he had his own technique no one knows what it was. The pomegranate and grape pulaos, I had a school friend who was the son of a small Nawab, they lost everything—he described these dishes to me."[14]

"Tomorrow" he tells me, "I will make with you two of Wajid Ali Shah's pulaos, a mango and an orange. My great-grandfather was good friends with Wajid Ali Shah, we had many lands in Lucknow, this was how Awadhi cuisine entered our cuisine (though much of it stems from the Mughals). . . . Yet you do not have the authentic," he tells me, "because no one remembers the authentic, and those that claim authenticity are not providing it. Most of those chefs died, the rest is approximation."

However, he is doing a pretty good job. Or maybe he is just an excellent cook; the mango pulao, traced with raw mango syrup and strips blending elegantly into the perfectly tender perfumed rice, was divine. Did it make it more divine when I thought about Wajid Ali Shah also dining on such a dish? Yes, it did. Did it help that I knew there had been a quest to get here, sleuthing by Reggie, and even by me? Yes. Things taste better when you think you have found a story.

"I am searching for pulao recipes," Reggie muses. "It is both preservation and personal enjoyment—the only way to keep this art form alive is to practice it. It is a living form, a recipe is a guideline, it helps to form the shape of the dish, but anyone that cooks has his own taste, his own hand, but the recipe gives some form—that is why I am writing things down, and maybe people started that a bit ago, but it was not the tradition, to write."

. . .

I suddenly wonder if I am the one that wants to fix dum pukht in place—to give it a definition, a clear track, a story—to find some impossible truth. The change, the shift, the very movement is intrinsic—what *was* never works for what *is*. "Historical cuisine" works against its own interests. Did the branding of dum pukht stop the movement by proliferating this one story about Lucknow's cuisine? Or did it in fact spur on research particularly by those who weren't satisfied with that particular fixing? The fluidity of the story, and of the recipe allows for it to continue. I return to where I started, with Imtiaz, in those first few weeks. "There is no secret recipe," he says, "No ingredient is hidden, what is hidden is the heart and the hand. In fact, there is no written recipe. I have learned from my teacher, I have passed on to my students, and it will go on. My student, as I did, has used his brain, he has modified and changed. . . ."

NOTES

1. All interviews in this chapter were conducted by the author in 2006 while on a Fulbright Research Fellowship and Dartmouth Reynolds Grant; this endnote will stand as citation for them. The concept of creating a national yet regionalized cuisine is, though propelled by big business, reminiscent of the Central Cottage Industries Emporium (1948) and the All India Handloom and Handicraft Board (1952), which under a nationalist, economic, and preservationist rubric promoted artisans to continue or rediscover regional crafts and designs for a national consumer base; both are rooted in Gandhi's *swadeshi* movement. See: "The Handicraft Movement" in Dhamija 2007: 66–98. The discourse on regional restaurants but for a cosmopolitan audience also fits into the discourse of cookbooks (see Appadurai 1988).

2. The answer Imtiaz Qureshi gave to this question on rice was understandably vague, and has to do with the age of the rice. "If the rice is new it generally gets to stick together. I wash the rice three or four times, so all of the surface dirt drains off, and generally I do not soak it for too long. Normal rice you soak for an hour if not old or new. Then I drain the rice, after washing properly, and apply a little oil to the rice, a little lime juice and salt. The rice gets clean, takes the scent of lime, and it also doesn't stick together. This is not the case with new rice [it will stick], if the rice is too old it gets spoiled and smells."

3. There is debate about the difference between *biriyani* and *pulao,* and whether there is one at all (the opinion of Achaya 1998a: 29). From what I observed in Lucknow, and what is argued in Bhatnagar and Saxena (1997), technically in *pulao,* the rice and the meat are cooked separately and then layered before the final dum cooking, whereas in biriyani the soaked, but not par-boiled rice, is fried, and then cooked with the meat. Biriyani is also meant to have stronger spices, usually ground, as compared to whole (then removed). However, writing in the 1880s Sharar has a more subtle distinction: "In Delhi, the most popular food was biryani, but the taste in Lucknow was more for pulao. To the uninitiated palate both are much the same, but because of the amount of spices in biryani there is always a strong taste of curried rice, whereas pulao can be prepared with such care that this can never happen ... in the view of gourmets a biryani is a clumsy and ill-conceived meal in comparison with a really good pulao and for that reason the latter was more popular in Lucknow." (Sharar 2005: 157–158)

4. *Dum Pukht* menu, ITC Maurya Sheraton Hotel, Delhi, 2006.

5. See L. Collingham (2006: 96); Kalra & Das Gupta (1999: 57–58). This story is also in numerous articles, such as one by Sravanthi Challapalli called "Tasty bites and Titbits" in *The Hindu,* March 20, 2004; or a story called "Khana Khazana" in *Sunday Mid Day,* November 24, 2002. However, this story is repeated so frequently that it has become common knowledge.

6. As a description of Muharram, Peter Chelkowski writes: "In the year 61 of the Muslim calendar, a battle took place at Karbala, a barren desert in what is now Iraq. It was there that the rituals and myths surrounding Imam Husain originated. Husain—the champion of the Shia cause, the son of Ali and the grandson of the Prophet Muhammad—was on his way to join his fellow Shia partisans in the city of Kufa when he was ambushed in the desert. Along with his entire family, and (according to tradition) a group of seventy-two male followers, Husain was massacred by the numerically superior forces of the caliph Yazid, the leader of the Sunni Muslims. The battle took place on the day of Ashura, the tenth day of the month of Muharram. This tragedy has assumed immense historical, spiritual and cultural significance to the Shias, who view it as the greatest suffering and sacrifice in history. It has transcended time and space to acquire importance of cosmic magnitude" (Chelkowski 2006: 101).

7. See Keshani (2006: 219–250). He provides firm evidence that the Imambara complex was not built to relieve famine and was built later than most accounts describe, from 1786 to 1791.

8. By the time Abdul Halim Sharar was writing, in the 1880s, Lucknow's culture had already been in decline for years—particularly since the Uprising/Battle of Independence in 1857. The book is structured as a mixture of anecdotes, stories, and other types of facts—a written oral history.

9. I once asked my friend Maruqh Abdullah, daughter of Nawab Jafar Abdullah, during Shbein, the mourning period for the assassination of Ali during Ramzan, how do you mourn? She said "a family member dies and you mourn ferociously the first year, but then it lessens." She sat with a straight back, her long black braid

tucked out of sight, and her eyes purposeful. "Because of our love of God, with Ali, with Imam Husain, Hasan, every year we mourn, and every year we mourn ferociously; we mourn for them, for what they have done for us, more than we have ever mourned for the family, because it is God we are weeping for," Maruqh spoke in a careful staccato, trying to express to me, in a way that I might understand, "and it is also every year, each and every year, that we change our clothes, we come here, we chant the elegies, every year we are in mourning, it is this reason that it is so close to our breast." I also discussed this collapse in time with Sulaiman and Vijay Khan of Mahmudabad—that the loss of that time, during the Martyrdom at Karbala, runs like a current through the present, and are always in conversation.

10. *Ghazi-ud-din Haidar and Lord & Lady Moira at a banquet.* British Library Add. Or. 1815.

11. Robert Skelton, email communication, 2004. Steingass 1892, or see it online at http://dsal.uchicago.edu/dictionaries/steingass/.

12. The Persian meat and rice dish *pulao* is also know as *pilaf* in Turkish, and in most of India and the South and Southeast Asian world as *biriyani*.

13. Robert Skelton, email communication, 2004.

14. A similar series of stories involves the *moti,* or pearl pulao, and *moti kaliya,* when it is made in a sauce. Amir Naqi Khan of Mahmudabad described *moti kaliya* to me in complete darkness, since the electricity had gone out. He clearly loved to cook, and had experimented with this dish: "You take the goat's intestine, wash it and boil it, clean it completely, tie it on one end and on the other end put an egg's white in it, and when it is filled you put knots, tie the knots and again boil it. After it is boiled, you take out the 'pearls' and put them in the *salan* [thin gravy]." Sharar it seems made it with egg yolks along with numerous other things: *"Moti,* the pearl pulau," which "was made to look as if the rice contained shining pearls. The method of making these pearls was to take about two hundred grains in weight of silver foil and twenty grains of gold foil and beat them into the yolk of an egg; this mixture was then stuffed into the gullet of a chicken and tied around with fine thread. The chicken was heated slightly and the skin cut with a penknife. Well-formed, shining pearls appeared, which were cooked with the meat of the pulau." The *moti,* which refers to a nineteenth-century dish, could be working in multiple ways here. That dish could have passed undisturbed since the nineteenth century into the present family of Amir Naqi Khan, or been invented at some point in that period. Or, he might have read Sharar, been inspired and worked with his chef to prepare the dish. Amir Naqi Khan is referenced in True (2004: 66). True quotes Khan saying, "I wanted to try my hand also," then writes, "He [Khan] learned to make the pearl pulao, using egg whites for the pearls."

SEVEN

"Teaching Modern India How to Eat"

"AUTHENTIC" FOODWAYS AND REGIMES
OF EXCLUSION IN AFFLUENT MUMBAI

Susan Dewey

Today Americans especially seem to have a great desire to experience the "real" thing, an authentic taste, a different lifestyle. Anything fake is deplored, fake foods included.

MADHUR JAFFREY, *AN INVITATION TO INDIAN COOKING*

My main goal is to teach modern India how to eat, because that's something we as a country really don't know how to do just yet. So much of what we call "fusion cuisine" is really just confusion, so as a consequence of this I want to teach people how to explore their senses, to really understand that authentic cuisine is all about the subtleties of differences.

RAHUL, RESTAURATEUR

FRENCH PHILOSOPHER JACQUES DERRIDA contends that his law of genre embodies "order's principle: resemblance, analogy, identity and difference ... order of reasons, sense of sense" (1980: 81). Positing that genres' very existence engenders boundaries, limits and, by default, exclusion, Derrida draws our attention to the otherwise rather self-evident point that notions of authenticity rely directly upon their implied ability to distinguish what Rahul the restaurateur glosses above as "the subtleties of differences." Foodways constitute a powerful means by which individuals demonstrate their membership in privileged groups, one which anthropologist Sidney Mintz contends intimately links "novelty with knowingness, with sophistication; and certainly being open to new experience" (1996: 116). This process of establishing hierarchies of discernment has been elaborated and intensified in Mumbai, India's entertainment and economic center, following the advent of economic liberalization in 1991, with recent years often witnessing a two-hundred percent growth in restaurants (Dixit 2008: 6).

Indeed, the advent of post-Liberalization economic reform has created a highly visible urban subculture in which such discernment regarding foodways functions to distinguish an imagined community (B. Anderson 2006) characterizing itself through exclusive food and alcohol consumption practices. The key distinction in Mumbai between contemporary and historical forms of commensality lies in the powerful status presently accorded to particular types of cuisine and the manner in which it is obtained. Whereas even in ancient India, foodways "represented at once a medium of exchange and rank and a reflection of personal moral identity and . . . social relationship" (Conlon 1995: 92), the postcolonial period witnessed the emergence of new cultural traditions whereby "food [became] embedded in a different system of etiquette—that of the drawing room, the corporate gathering, the club event, and the restaurant" (Appadurai 1988: 8). These social changes reflect broader economic shifts, whereby the share of the hotel and restaurant industry to India's gross domestic product (GDP) has doubled from 8% in 1950–51 to 16% in 2003–04 (United Nations 2008: 2). India's GDP rose nearly 10% in 2007–08 during a wave of prosperity that allowed hundreds of American chain restaurants, among countless local counterparts, to become part of many urban consumers' daily lives (Prewitt 2008: 33).

A city of twelve million people and tens of thousands of eateries ranging from informal roadside affairs to extravagant restaurants in five-star hotels, Mumbai is a significant site for the analysis of foodways, because of its sheer power of place in South Asia. The anthropologist William Mazzarella, for example, notes that for many South Asians simply mentioning the city's name evokes "the transformative allure of modernity, both material (a new life in the city, the possibility of making a living, however precarious, on one's own terms) and the phantasmic (the spectacular imaginaries of Bollywood)" (2003: 179).

Indeed, Mumbai distinguishes itself relative to the rest of India through its possibilities for social mobility; its vibrant media industry; the number of women in the workforce; and the vast numbers of restaurants, nightclubs, and other sites for consumption-related entertainment. Combined with the relatively close living quarters that even wealthy families share with one another, restaurants and other consumption-related venues have increasingly become powerful symbols of membership in the minority community of individuals who have benefitted from India's expanded foreign investment and relaxed trade restrictions with the rest of the world. As one leading restaurateur noted, such eating establishments symbolize infinitely more than their cuisine: "In the Bombay [Mumbai] of my parents' generation, the routine used to be: go to work, then go home. Nowadays you finish work at seven, you go to Indigo [a lounge bar and restaurant] and have a drink, or you go to Olive [similar to Indigo] or something, even on a weekday. The average person in Bombay [Mumbai] goes out at least three or four nights a week now, it's not like that in the rest of India." The restaurateur's description of living in an India quite different from that of his parents' time distinguishes itself primarily through consumption and spending patterns, so that sociality outside the home is an increasingly important part of many young urban Indian lives. Historian Frank Conlon notes that "restaurants reflect, permit and promote the introduction of a wide variety of changes in modern Indian life, including modifications of urban budgets and work schedules, entry of women into the middle class workforce, new patterns of sociability and, perhaps, growth of new ways to enjoy wealth through conspicuous consumption" (1995: 91). Yet these changes are embedded in deeper South Asian norms and regulations regarding food consumption practices, which anthropologist Arjun Appadurai has referred to as "highly condensed social fact" (1981: 494). In his insightful analysis of the cultural meanings of food and its distribution in Tamil Brahmin households, Appadurai refers to these messages conveyed as a system of "gastro-politics" in which food announces social status far more powerfully than it nourishes.

Connections between food and power have extremely deep roots in Hindu South Asia, and prohibitions on the exchange of foods between individuals of different castes, genders and ethnicities are what Appadurai has elsewhere termed "carefully conducted exercise[s] in the reproduction of intimacy... [that are] never medically or morally neutral" (Appadurai 1988: 10). Although anthropologist R. S. Khare determined nearly three decades prior to Liberalization that food restrictions amongst communities such as Lucknowi Brahmins relaxed with each successive generation, taboos on food exchange and consumption are still alive and well in most of rural India (1976b). Anthropologists Susan Wadley (1980) and Sarah Lamb (2000) have both observed such proscriptions, with Wadley in particular noting the explicitly religious functions "of maintaining the proper balance of hot and cold in one's life and one's body" (1980: 33). In this highly charged gastronomic context, Rahul the restaurateur's notion of "teaching modern India how to eat" takes on a particularly profound moral weight.

Accordingly, this chapter discusses how the regimes of exclusion that have come to define post-Liberalization India manifest themselves in food consumption practices in affluent Mumbai. I explore how privileged consumers in the city use foodways to demonstrate social status amidst the rapidly expanding choices available to purchase touted "lifestyle" markers. The desire for so-called authenticity in food is not at all unique to a wealthy minority in Mumbai, as such discernment masks its deeper social function as an agent of class stratification throughout most of the world. Indeed, these regimes of exclusion rely upon such distinctions, which in turn demand intense cultivation of the senses. It is thus hardly surprising that one of the most profound post-1991 changes has been the construction of an enormous variety of spaces in which a well-chronicled group of media celebrities and businesspeople may engage in sensory experimentation. Examples of such venues range from staged grape harvests modeled on those of French villages to evenings of Moroccan belly dancing accompanied by Lebanese food on the terraces of five-star hotels.

It is important to note that this regime of exclusion exists in complete opposition to the post-Independence rhetoric of equality, which featured the elimination of poverty and social injustice as paramount in its social policies. Yet scholars of Indian popular culture consistently comment upon the extraordinary power fame commands in India (Dewey 2008; Dickey 2007; Dwyer 2000), noting that well-known individuals in a South Asian context can be seen as barometers of India's openness to "foreign" ideas (Inden 1999). Anthropologist Mark Liechty (2003) has similarly observed that Nepali middle-class consumers intrinsically link ways of being "modern" with purchasing power and imported commodities, thus highlighting the complex connections between class and South Asian ways of thinking about the world beyond its subcontinental borders.

It is little wonder that *The Times of India* section titled *The Bombay Times,* which includes *Page Three,* a feature chronicling high-profile social events attended by some of the city's wealthiest residents, often carries brief articles on where readers may obtain objects and experiences featured in its pictorials, ranging from Italian panini to Moroccan belly dance performances. As *The Bombay Times* editor Ayaz Memon explained to me, "the Bombay [Mumbai] jet set is not like the New York jet set, as there are only about a hundred people that you can keep talking about, whereas in New York it's nine hundred or one thousand." Although this difference in numbers is not as dramatic as Memon asserts, it is not coincidental that these *Page Three* depictions of the lives of designers, liquor barons, and media professionals are intimately tied to food consumption. In her humorous book about the subjects of *Page Three,* journalist Kanika Gahlaut divides those featured into a number of types: "the client hunter/visiting card dropper, the wine taster, the exhibitionist (Harvard-returned gay filmmaker), the cigar czar, . . . and the darling" (2001: 15). This eclectic blend of characters number about one hundred core members who appear on *Page Three* each morning in a variety of settings, usually in South Mumbai restaurants and nightclubs at parties sponsored by the purveyors of newly arrived sensory commodities from the United States and Europe, such as fragrances, alcohol, and beauty products.

All of these events feature the consumption of food and alcohol as prominent aspects of the entertainment, which in itself is planned to display the particular "identity" of the featured brand. For instance, a particular French perfume was launched at a fashion show featuring a line called "Vamp," with an announcer exhorting the audience, "welcome to the world of conspicuous consumption" as well-known Mumbai models appeared onstage in clothing that closely resembled lingerie. Uniformed waiters circulated throughout the crowd with chocolate *millefeuille* and glasses of French champagne, as the announcer made a great show of the fact that the French ambassador was present. This scene was a world away from the everyday realities of the vast majority of Mumbai's citizens, who travel on the city's notoriously overcrowded public transportation system, suffer from strikes, struggle to make ends meet in an increasingly unaffordable city, and, perhaps most notably, are part of the estimated 300 million consumers targeted by the vast majority of advertising campaigns featuring persistent themes of upward mobility.

Yet the connections between food consumption, the venues in which it takes place, and social class are familiar to any fan of Indian popular culture. A sample commercial for the insidiously ubiquitous skin-lightening cream Fair and Lovely opens with a shot of a weeping young woman riding the bus home to a suburban Mumbai apartment building from an unsuccessful job interview. Passing by the kitchen en route to her bedroom, she hears her mother refuse her father a second cup of coffee by reminding him about the need to economize in preparation for the young woman's wedding. Her tears continue to flow as she stares at her reflection in the mirror, despairing that she will never find a job and its associated economic independence. Yet after significantly lightening her skin with Fair and Lovely, she walks confidently into the lobby of a lavishly decorated hotel, where she is offered a job by the impressed interviewers. In the final scene, she sits with her parents at the hotel's restaurant, ordering a cup of coffee for her father.

This brief tale of upward mobility is problematic in its conflation of light skin and success, but nonetheless notable in its use of the restaurant as class signifier with its brightly lit interiors in sharp contrast with the dim space of the kitchen and bedroom of the family's cramped apartment. The sweating, exhausted, weeping young female of the first scene's bus ride features in direct opposition to the beautiful woman we later see striding toward her parents in air-conditioned comfort wearing a tailored pink business suit. Such stark visual differences underscore Mumbai's inescapable overpopulation and pollution as clearly as they illustrate how social class mitigates the degree to which individuals are able to insulate themselves from these environmental and sensory hardships.

In a city where over half of all residents live in informal housing settlements and six million people have no housing at all (D'Monte & Kakodkar 2002: 38), viewing crushing poverty is a daily part of life for everyone. There is no way to completely ignore the fact that, as Appadurai notes, the rich in urban Indian centers like Mumbai "seek to gate as much of their lives as possible, traveling from guarded homes to darkened cars to air-conditioned offices, moving always in an envelope of privilege through the heat of public poverty and the dust of dispossession" (2000: 39). One restaurateur I interviewed complained about the toll this reality took upon his clients' physical state, comparing Mumbai rather unfavorably with the less-populous cities of London and New York, where "businessmen walk, they get exercise. But here, public transportation and the roads are so degraded that you have to be driven everywhere, and so you constantly have to watch what you eat to stay in shape."

This sentiment echoes sociologists Harris and Lipman (1984: 418), who contend that social environments inscribe themselves on the landscape in situations of extremely inequitable wealth distribution. Such physical manifestations of social injustice have dramatically increased in the past decade, following economic liberalization, and are most evident in the demolition of Central Mumbai's mills, which formerly employed thousands of workers, to make room for shopping malls, restaurants, entertainment centers, and sleek apartment buildings advertised as built along the "international standards" used in the United States. Yet even those who benefit from such changes are not oblivious to the inequalities they perpetuate: driving past a newly cleared former mill site awaiting the construction of yet another nightclub-cum-restaurant one evening, the soon-to-be manager of the establishment commented to me, "that's our Bombay [Mumbai]. Take away the fucking bread of the people and put up a goddamned discotheque."

Scholars of Indian urban planning observe that India has "no great tradition of formally created secular public places" (Burte 1996: 46), which underscores how what goes on in the secular privacy of the aforementioned discotheque partly prompts and further reinforces its exclusivity. Urban planners describe their ideal ratio of open space to human inhabitants as four acres per one thousand people; while London has 4.84 acres per thousand inhabitants, Mumbai has 0.03 acres per thousand inhabitants (Radhan 1996: 56). Much of this tiny amount of space is in the form of "members only" spaces such as Priyadarshini Park, which charges an exorbitant thousand-rupee annual membership fee for use of its half-acre plot. This extreme class stratification combines with close living quarters in the regime of exclusion by necessitating a parallel space where sexualized behavior and romantic liaisons can only exist in the "private" realm of establishments featuring food and alcohol. The assistant manager of one of Mumbai's premier private restaurants and social clubs told me that discretion is one of the premier benefits of membership, noting: "Certainly, we have lovely food, but our main appeal is that if a guest does not want attention, we'll not even touch him. There are so many people, and I cannot name names, who come here for their own private reasons, not political or corporate, but for their own personal reasons. Things that cannot be done in society, in the public sphere, they come and do it here."

This "public sphere," then, exists in direct opposition to both the secluded physical space of the private restaurant and the relative moral and behavioral space that membership buys. Public space is rarely a forum for true (let alone equal) interaction between different class groups in Mumbai, and debates on the appropriate use of such areas are particularly contentious in reference to what is popularly termed "street food." Sociologist Arvind Rajagopal makes a powerful connection between urban Indian notions of modernity and "the education of the senses [that] occurs through the mass media and through localized struggles that disclose the particular historical changes being wrought" (2001: 93). Using the *pheriwala* (a mobile street vendor who often sells food) as a symbol of post-Liberalization modernity's contested nature, Rajagopal details state and private efforts to ban or restrict the activities of these mobile entrepreneurs on the unsubstantiated grounds that their practices are less hygienic than licensed restaurants. This is by no means limited to Indian popular discourse: a *New York Times* travel article on the wide variety of cuisine offered by both *pheriwala* and stationary salespeople praised an increasing number of licensed restaurants in Mumbai that offer varieties of snack foods usually only available from street vendors. The piece noted the dangers inherent in consuming "the wares from a street vendor who is casually mashing potatoes with his bare and grubby hands, as flies buzz happily around" (Rao 2009: 5).

This encroachment of the state and its regulatory bodies upon more areas of life is an inherent part of broader projects of discernment and exclusion among the powerful, and thus dramatically reveals their inherently classed nature. Such a focus on regulating the "disorder" of unlicensed food vendors underscores how neoliberalism's practice deliberately seeks to exclude the poor through its logic of classed discernment, with calls for order, hygiene, and other rather transparent masks worn under the guise of "international standards." Complaints about the persistence of *pheriwala* and other vendors in the South Mumbai neighborhoods that house both the vast majority of offices and the city's wealthiest residents creates an inherent conflict: office-goers require inexpensive midday meals, while wealthy residents wish to limit the amount of pedestrian traffic outside their homes.

Such a classed debate is by no means new; indeed, a persistent theme in Mumbai popular discourse is the difference between the city of Mumbai itself, which extends from the southernmost neighborhood of Colaba to the oceanfront curve of Worli, and the suburbs, which begin at Dadar and extend indefinitely northward. Most city residents characterize South Mumbai as rather wealthy and quite supercilious, whereas the suburbs are seen as a poorer, albeit more spacious and cleaner, imitation of their southern neighbor. South Mumbai's architecture, such as the Gateway of India and the famous Taj Mahal hotel, reflects its British heritage, which recalls historian Anthony King's (1990) observation that decolonized cities often retain their centers of power. Popular cultural accounts of these classed differences often use gustatory analogies, such as *The Times of India* column that jokingly claimed, "You know you're a South Bombayite (Mumbaikar) when the only thing you make for dinner is the time." Rather patronizingly citing the examples of parallel luxury eating establishments on opposite ends of the city, the column noted, "the north [the suburbs] hasn't always been original but it's been quick on the uptake. For every [South Mumbai] Indigo, there's an [suburban] Olive. For every [South Mumbai] Samovar, there's a [suburban] Prithvi Café" (Times of India 2002)

Yet efforts to remove *pheriwala* and other vendors confine themselves exclusively to South Mumbai streets, and often take on the rhetoric of cleansing: to "clean up" the streets, or to advocate for more "hygienic practices." Interestingly, this sort of language extends to the bodies of Mumbai's more privileged citizens as well, and is unmistakable in promotional literature and advertisements for a burgeoning number of gyms, spas, salons, and other establishments that promise to purify and refine the body. One such combined gym, spa, and restaurant, where I spent several months conducting research, had annual membership fees of just under $2,000; attracted clients who were featured regularly on *Page Three;* and would not look out of place in a large Western European or North American city. Its unique selling point was its oxygen bar and aromatherapy spa, which it claimed could rehabilitate damage done to the body in the outside world through pollution, lack of exercise, and overconsumption.

This regime of exclusion thus operates at a dual sensory level in which the privileged are urged to make use of gyms and spas to rid their bodies of contaminants introduced through rich food, pollution, and contact with public space, yet simultaneously encouraged to engage in new sensory experiences in class-specific arenas. "Because the good life is not so good for you," one spa's promotional literature read, "we offer a range of treatments and therapies to repair the damage caused by urban life." This rhetoric of balancing between two extremes is also evident in ways of thinking about ideal body types: the vast majority of men queried cited *mazdur* (manual laborers) as having the most attractive physiques because of their limited caloric intake and constant physical exertion, as opposed to specialized physical fitness knowledge. As one personal trainer put it, "the educated understand a perfect body, but the *mazdur* actually have the best bodies because they just work all day and don't get to eat all the rich, heavy kind of food we normally do." Thus, *mazdur* bodies happen as a consequence of deprivation, whereas those who are able to afford a personal trainer (as well as the sorts of foods and sedentary lifestyles that make his or her services necessary) are the product of sophisticated, privileged urban knowledge.

Many personal trainers unambiguously attribute the powerful social connection between various forms of food consumption and the *mazdur*-like svelte bodies desired by "the educated" to the introduction of international satellite networks to Indian television. One young woman I interviewed at a gym attributed these shifts to what she called "a whole new American way of life coming on TV" in the form of instructional fitness and cooking shows. She believed these combined with the newly deregulated economy to make people "more aware, eating new kinds of things and just wanting to look very, very good. When you look good, you smell good, you wear good clothes, then you get accepted into the best social circle." The use of the word *aware* to describe such changes in the way urban elites think about life is extremely common, prompting one gym proprietor to observe that these new developments reflected "an overall awareness . . . where you have to be that much more aware of your body, that much more attuned to the world around you." The sensory connections between being "aware," appearance, smell, and privileged experience with the world outside of India are an intrinsic aspect of the regime of exclusion in that those with the ability to discern (to be "aware") are not inconsequentially those with the greatest access to power.

This sensory manifestation of socioeconomic change may in fact be a worldwide phenomenon. For instance, anthropologist Judith Farquhar notes "the direct appeal to the senses" (2002: 290) made by changing norms regarding food, sexuality, and the body in postsocialist China. In India, the purveyors of these "correct" forms of awareness are notably often from outside India or have been educated in the United States, therefore constituting a "foreign authority" accorded an unusual amount of prestige regardless of the amount of fame they actually held in the country where they obtained their knowledge. In terms of the body, such authority holds a prominent position in gym and spa advertising: Reebok certification courses in aerobics conducted by trainers from South Africa and Australia, spa stylists trained at Vidal Sassoon in London, and highly publicized membership in international associations.

Despite their seeming ubiquity, there is no general agreement that being "aware" is the sole condition that guarantees immediate entry into certain realms that privilege sensory experience as an exclusionary measure. Anthropologist Sidney Mintz notes the existence of a double meaning for edible commodities that is particularly useful in understanding how regimes of exclusion operate through foodways in Mumbai, particularly in the context of the city's complex colonial history. Mintz observes that "outside meaning" refers to the structural position a particular thing holds for a culture, whereas "inside meaning" describes how individuals "impart significance to their own acts and the acts of those around them" (1996: 23). In his analysis of the ready adoption of sugar as a major caloric source by low-wage workers in newly industrialized Britain, Mintz describes how these dual meanings are in fact inseparable from one another: "At the level of daily life, the customary practices that working people developed in order to deal with the newly emerging industrial society in which they found themselves were answers, or "solutions" to conditions over which they had no real control. In these ways, *outside* and *inside* meanings are linked through the conditions created and presented to potential consumers by those who supply what is consumed" (1996: 31).

Lest we too quickly (and quite mistakenly) attribute total control to those who exercise the power to discern and exclude in Mumbai, it is important to examine the similarly nuanced forms of interlocking dual meaning taken by the condition of being "aware." Social theorist Ashis Nandy observes, "colonialism tried to supplant the Indian consciousness to erect an Indian self-image which, in its opposition to the West, would remain in essence a Western construction" (2007: 72). Yet this alone does not account for the relatively equal status of "knowing" and discernment accorded to Italian risotto Milanese (slow-cooked Arborio rice with saffron) and Thai khao soi (a dish composed of egg noodles, vegetables, and meat in spicy coconut sauce). Thai cuisine has enjoyed popularity amongst Mumbai residents, in particular those who are young, American-educated, and have partaken of the "backpacking" experience throughout Southeast Asia. One evening at Suzie Wong, which was then a new restaurant located on a houseboat moored in the Arabian Sea that served such fare, twenty-something South Mumbai residents were engaged in a lively discussion of their experiences in Thailand following their agreement that the food was authentic enough to have been made in Southeast Asia. A young woman spoke very emotionally about her difficulties with what she called the "poverty and desperation" she witnessed in northern Thailand. "We just can't understand how those people live," she noted as she sipped a cup of green tea, apparently oblivious to the fact that a great number of Mumbai residents live in similar conditions.

It could be argued that such statements are an inherent part of the regime of exclusion's sensory isolation from experiences deemed unpleasant or offensive in one's own immediate environment. Yet they are also a condition of postcolonial India, in which the sights and sounds of injustice are ubiquitous enough to be normalized and ignored. Yet how do risotto Milanese and khao soi attain equal status in the eyes of affluent Mumbai residents? The answer lies in a complex combination that Roy, in the context of the growth of regional Indian cuisine cookbooks in the United States, describes as a combination of the post-Independence "Nehruvian paradigm [with] the imperatives of a British and North American multiculturalism, the pluralist politics of which is heavily dependent ... on metaphors of culinary processing and prescription" (P. Roy 2002: 484). Most consumers of such cuisine in Mumbai have spent some time abroad (some even working in restaurants during college), but these individuals also grew up with a uniquely South Asian multiculturalism that raises questions about the meaning of authenticity in this context.

This is part of a broader phenomenon scholars have termed "auto-orientalism," a process anthropologist William Mazzarella, writing in the context in contemporary Mumbai, describes as a conscious, and sometimes ironic, phenomenon in which Indian-ness becomes a form of self-induced Othering. On the opening night of Suzie Wong, Sabina Singh, wife of the restaurateur who opened the venture, described how she arrived at the theme of "Chinese brothel" in designing its interior. Popularly known for her "Bollywood kitsch" line of ready-to-wear garments and accessories, including handbags made of see-through plastic trimmed in bright red with cardboard copies of 1970s Hindi film posters inside, Singh was quick to point out that her audience was limited to those who were aware of its irony. "It's funny for those who can see the joke, you know? Amitabh Bachchan in skin-tight white pants and roller skates, it's funny."

The popular chain restaurant Roti! has capitalized on this use of irony as well, billing itself as "a modern-day *dhaba*" in reference to the rustic roadside eating establishments frequented by long-distance truck drivers all over India. Roti! features enlarged, framed, professionally taken photographs of overturned trucks, a fairly common sight on Indian highways, and rope-covered walls in imitation of the décor of a real *dhaba*. The ironic force and popularity of Roti! however, stems from its location in Breach Candy, a neighborhood where real estate routinely sells for $500 a square foot.

To what can we attribute the popularity of these ironic statements, particularly in reference to the sensory pleasures of consumption? Anderson contends that "all communities larger than the primordial villages of face-to-face contact (and perhaps even these) are imagined. Communities are to be distinguished, not by their falsity/genuineness, but by the style in which they are imagined" (2006: 6). Certainly, the elaborate processes surrounding the regimes of exclusion that manifest themselves in food consumption in Mumbai could be characterized as such, but they also take concrete forms as well. For instance, Mumbai's most expensive combined gym-spa-café found itself on the outside of these regimes of exclusion when it attempted to establish a dual-membership arrangement with private social clubs and restaurants such as The Chambers, Bombay Gymkhana, and the Breach Candy Club, all of which have colonial origins and membership restricted to the hereditary Indian elite that emerged post-Independence. Management encouraged the dual-membership pitch to include a detailed discussion of the gym-spa-café's exclusivity, noting, "we don't take in anybody blind, we take only the quality young achiever professionals who are the leaders of business and films." There was a distinct sense of disdain toward this proposal on the part of the boards of the Bombay Gymkhana and the Breach Candy Club in particular, who felt that their members, despite the fact that such prospective entrants were also very wealthy, would not favorably regard the admission of individuals from the film industry. A manager of The Chambers explained his reason for declining rather politely, noting "our members are the crème-de-la-crème of Bombay [Mumbai], so when someone says, 'I am a member here,' generally you know the value of that person."

Indeed, the acceptance process for membership at The Chambers is comprised of an extremely selective two-month-long process that, as one member put it, "assesses your values, your status in the market." If a single member of The Chambers board of directors takes issue with the application, it is rejected. The Bombay Gymkhana has restricted its membership for the past decade to the heirs of current members, causing the chairperson of its board to note, "We can't have just anybody coming in here. This is not the fish market." Such regimes of exclusion are by no means unique to either India or the British colonial system. The Bombay Gymkhana was built in 1875 to provide a social space for British administrators to congregate, although even then, like many other clubs, membership was restricted to the administrative elite and was by no means open to any English national in India. Money is prohibited inside, with meals paid for through signatures, and an elaborate system of entry for visitors remains unchanged from colonial times. Although we hope not to conform to the school of thought historian Partha Chatterjee has criticized for allowing the relatively brief period of India's colonization by the British to "swamp" the history of India, it is important to acknowledge how contemporary Mumbai elites manipulate these complex webs of history and power to negotiate their own everyday lived experience.

Nonetheless, such imagined communities also take shape in what some might term neocolonial forms of sybaritic pleasure, particularly in the numerous launches and events designed to advertise newly available commodities. "A Walk in the Clouds," an invitation-only party sponsored by the champagne house Chateau Indage, is a prime example of this phenomenon.

Described by organizers as "a place where Indian culture and wine culture blend together, creating harmony between the two traditions in a festive atmosphere," the event celebrated the year's grape harvest and was attended by all of the individuals who guarantee an event *Page Three* coverage.

Chateau Indage spared no expense in the organization of this event, with experts from Burgundy, France, flown in for the occasion to advise participants and chefs, who created innovative fusion foods with a wine-based theme. Complete with fire-eaters, dance troupes, tattoo artists, magicians, palmists, and copious quantities of alcohol, the evening sought to mimic the harvest celebrations of Europe. Publicity literature for the event made no secret of its desire to introduce what it termed "wine culture" to Mumbai in a rather hedonistic setting:

> Experience the magic of traditional celebrations of the Old World vineyards of France, Italy and Spain, combined with the contemporary wine parties of the New World vineyards of Australia, Chile and South Africa—all right here in India. For the first time in India, sample the largest collection of fine international wines and champagnes with select world cuisine amongst the ambience of ancient Rome. The highlight of the Carnival is the traditional wine stomp, in which you can dance in a tub full of grapes to replicate the way village virgins in ancient France have traditionally welcomed the first harvest. (Chateau Indage 2003)

The evening closely corresponded to Ritzer's concept of the phantasmagoria, in which one is "immersed in a world filled with everything one could imagine . . . in a land of candy and all of it within reach" (2001: 21). As individuals in varying degrees of sobriety wandered around the displays of wine and wine-related products, commenting on their own experiences at vineyards in Europe (some more embellished than others), it became clear just how powerful alcohol had emerged as a fetish that announced social status. Baudrillard defines a fetish as "a functional simulacrum" in which "objects are not the locus of the satisfaction of needs, but of a symbolic labor, of a 'production'" (1998: 33). Like so many other consumption-related events that appear on the space of *Page Three,* "A Walk in the Clouds" was largely about being seen and the opportunity to evaluate oneself vis-à-vis others in a socially prestigious situation.

This process of social networking is masked in ways quite similar to the ways in which individuals explain the differences between bodies sculpted through "awareness" as opposed to physical labor. At a press conference held at the restaurant and lounge bar Indigo to mark the new availability of an imported scotch, spokespeople emphasized the authenticity of the brand employing connections between ethnicity, localized production, and knowledge. "If I want to eat South Indian food," the managing director explained, "I'll ask a South Indian friend. Same thing here—our finesse can be measured by the fact that ours is the most popular brand of Scotch among the people who know all about it, the Scots."

Observing that people should not only drink their scotch, but also "feel the Scotch way of life," the marketing director detailed the rugby and golf matches it sponsored in Mumbai and encouraged those present to attend. One might argue that such sponsorship and linkage to a lifestyle is made even more crucial for those who market imported alcohol, given that state and federal government taxes amount to 710% additions on an already high price. The marketing director explained consumers' choice to buy such a product, because "it's something absolutely unique, and by and large Indians like to drink in a social environment, to be seen."

Drawing on the power of "being seen," numerous objects and experiences have risen to ascendancy, as the example of the new popularity of wine illustrates. Ashok, a vintner in his early thirties, explained his decision to leave a lucrative career in the Silicon Valley in favor of returning to India and cultivating a vineyard on his family's ancestral land, several hours' drive from Mumbai. His story provides a fascinating example of how regimes of exclusion never exist independently of the broader imagined communities of which they envision themselves a part. Mumbai residents such as the vintner are painfully aware that the sort of "foreign authority" they bring with them from abroad counts for little outside of India. Over dinner one evening with Antoine, a French vintner on a visit to Mumbai to explore the growing wine industry, Ashok found himself rather humiliated when Antoine dismissively stated, "I know all the secrets of your sauvignon blanc." Nevertheless, Ashok issued a telling rebuttal, noting, "yes, but once you leave, in India these secrets will still be mine."

Antoine's disruption of Ashok's expertise narrative simply amplifies more subtle ways in which Mumbai residents find themselves playing by rules of discernment they did not set themselves; after all, "international standards" would not exist without the notion that these entail supremacy patterned on broader constructions of race. "In California I was making incredible amounts of money," Ashok explained in reference to his decision to return to India, "but I also got a very clear sense that I would always be just some brown guy. Here I have to deliberately choose to stay unmarried because

I know that I could never stay faithful with all of the opportunities that come along with my lifestyle, while we're in the midst of this so-called sexual revolution." Ashok's statement shines a particularly critical light on how the condition of postcoloniality both redefines and replicates the complex intermingling of race, sexuality, and consumption.

It is fitting, then, that a significant portion of Ashok's work involves educating consumers in order to sustain sales in ways that directly capitalize on the embedded histories that inform everyday life in the city. Ashok described the importance of what he termed "training sessions" both in Mumbai and, for more select groups, at the winery itself. "It's nothing that they've ever seen before" he explained, "and that experience really opens up the senses to much more than body and aroma, so that one can begin to actually understand the wine." Echoing restaurateur Rahul's notion of "teaching modern India how to eat" almost exactly, Ashok harnesses the realm of the sensual akin to that of "A Walk in the Clouds" in his description of the process of appreciating wine.

This regime of exclusion is obviously a major (and lucrative) point of reference for some Mumbai residents, and yet most are aware of the extremely unequal terms on which they participate. Interestingly, despite the heavily male associations that scotch and other hard liquors have, some newly arrived Western European brands make an effort to market their products to women in the form of cocktails. When I asked the merchandise manager for an imported brand of hard alcohol to characterize the lifestyle of the women to whom she markets cocktails, she responded by drawing explicit parallels between the lives of her peers and American television. "Our generation is different," she noted, "because we don't expect women to be locked up at night. You know 'Sex and the City'? My girlfriends are much more in tune with that lifestyle than all of this *saas-bahu* [relationship drama] crap that Indian TV keeps dishing up."

The merchandise manager thus envisions hers as a brand that is fetishized as foreign via the enormous amount of referencing that it employs in its marketing strategy. This is in many ways representative of the way in which individuals position themselves vis-à-vis the rest of the world, especially the United States and Europe, as people who are part of an international community who share in the same kinds of events and experiences. In his discussion of Benedict Anderson's *Imagined Communities,* Partha Chatterjee notes that "autonomous forms of imagination of the community" are overwhelmed by the history of the postcolonial state (1993: 11). As such, Chatterjee suggests that India has been placed in a category of "permanent Other." The regime of exclusion in which individuals act out fantasies such as "A Walk in the Clouds" is an intrinsic part of such an imagined community.

In this chapter, I have argued that regimes of exclusion are necessarily sensory in nature, and include the ability to insulate oneself from environmental disturbances and unpleasant smells, tastes, and sensations, but also from the very visible evidence of social injustice written into the social and physical landscape. Yet the neoliberal agenda that offers the seductive myth of fair reward (usually through consumption) for individual initiative is inseparable from the fact that it exacerbates socioeconomic inequalities wherever implemented. It must be noted as a cautionary measure, however, that such processes are not entirely new in character, given the way that Mintz credits the post–Industrial Revolution world system as having "distinguished itself by its success not only in producing the consumables, but also in specifying and defining the needs" (1996: 78). As such, it may be that the project of "teaching modern India how to eat" is in its essence little more than an elaborate set of justifications for why a small minority of individuals have the privilege of sensory indulgence while a significant number of Indians continue to experience hunger as a looming and ever-present threat.

EIGHT

"Going for an Indian"

SOUTH ASIAN RESTAURANTS AND THE LIMITS OF MULTICULTURALISM IN BRITAIN

Elizabeth Buettner

"GOING FOR AN INDIAN"—or "out for a curry"—has become an increasingly prominent aspect of British social, economic, and cultural life since the 1960s. In assessing the wide appeal of South Asian food and restaurants in April 2001, Britain's late Foreign Secretary Robin Cook proclaimed that "Chicken Tikka Massala"—one of the cuisine's mainstays among British diners—had become "a true British national dish, not only because it is the most popular, but because it is a perfect illustration of the way Britain absorbs and adapts external influences. Chicken Tikka is an Indian dish. The Massala sauce was added to satisfy the desire of British customers." Such cultural traffic did not threaten British national identity, Cook stressed; rather, it epitomized "multiculturalism as a positive force for our economy and society" (Robin Cook's Chicken Tikka Masala Speech, 2001).

Estimates reveal that Britain now has nearly 9,000 restaurants and takeaways run by South Asian immigrants and their descendants that employ more than 70,000 people and have an annual turnover exceeding £2 billion (S. Basu 2003: xi; Grove & Grove 2005: 208; Monroe 2005; L. Collingham 2006). The vast majority of their customers are white. Within the wider context of New Labour's proclamations valuing cultural and ethnic diversity after its electoral victory in 1997, Robin Cook was not alone in celebrating South Asian food, or culinary variety more generally, as a defining feature of Britishness in the early twenty-first century (Back, Keith, Khan, Shukra, and Solomos 2002). Recent scholarly work demonstrates food's central role in depictions of multicultural diversity in Britain as enjoyable and invigorating, but such assertions would have been inconceivable several decades ago (Cook, Crang & Thorpe 1999; A. K. Sen 2006). The cuisine's current cultural prominence within national identity follows a history that saw most

Britons either ignore or vigorously reject food understood as "Indian," just as many objected to the arrival and settlement of peoples from the subcontinent. While Indians were present in Britain before the end of empire, their numbers were small and their visibility and impact uneven when compared with their increase after India and Pakistan's independence in 1947 (Visram 2002; Fisher 2004; A. M. Burton 1998). Substantial immigration from former South Asian colonies, alongside that from the Caribbean and elsewhere, remade Britain in cultural and demographic terms after the Second World War, and the enthusiasm Robin Cook and others would later exhibit has repeatedly proved elusive or decidedly limited (Brown 2006; Brah 1996; Hiro 1993; Layton-Henry 1992). Multiculturalism has never indisputably been deemed "a positive force" for Britain—far more commonly, it has been imagined either as a problem or as a means of tackling a problem. Ethnic minorities and their cultural practices have long been, and to a considerable extent continue to be, widely met by racism, suspicion, and intolerance.

For many white Britons, food may well constitute what Uma Narayan and others have described as the nonthreatening, "acceptable face of multiculturalism." "While curry may have been incorporated . . . into British cuisine, 'the desire to assimilate and possess what is external to the self' did not extend to actual people of Indian origin, whose arrival in English society resulted in a national dyspepsia," she asserts (U. Narayan 1997: 184, 173; also see Hesse 2000; Heldke 2003; Kalra 2004). In a nation where the consumption of "foreign" food has grown exponentially since the 1950s, South Asian cuisine occupies a unique place (Warde 2000; Bell & Valentine 1997). Long considered the "Jewel in the Crown" of the British Empire, India was firmly ensconced in Britain's cultural consciousness by the late colonial period. In the postcolonial era, preexisting public conceptions evolved in tandem with mass immigration from the subcontinent. Other favored foreign cuisines, particularly Italian and Chinese, that took root in British diets and dining-out habits were not widely associated with immigration to any comparable extent, partly because Italian and Chinese communities were smaller and also deemed less culturally problematic in the postwar period (Roberts 2002; Parker 1995; Hardyment 1995; Colpi 1991). West Indians were the only minority group to compete with South Asians in terms of numbers and the level of public attention and anxiety they attracted. But Afro-Caribbean cuisine (as distinct from Caribbean-produced commodities such as sugar) never featured significantly in white British diets, nor did Caribbean restaurants become popular destinations for other ethnic groups (Cook & Harrison

2003). Whereas music has been the cultural form postwar Britons most commonly associate with the Afro-Caribbean community, South Asian food and peoples typically merged in white understandings—a distinction aptly summarized in critiques of the tokenistic multiculturalism long taught in British schools as revolving around stereotypes of "saris, samosas, and steel bands" (Gilroy 1987; Troyna & Williams 1986; Donald & Rattansi 1992; Between Two Cultures 1968).

The history of South Asian food's rise to popularity reveals an uneasy coexistence and tension between ongoing racism and exclusion and the gradual, and conditional, development of enthusiastic appreciation—what David Parker has termed "celebratory multiculturalism" (Parker 1995: 74). This particular framing illustrates the divergent, and changing, meanings of multiculturalism since it appeared on Britain's cultural and political horizon in the 1970s. While describing Britain as "multicultural" alludes to a demographic reality following immigration, "multiculturalism" refers to a succession of conscious efforts to make sense of, and manage, ethnically diverse communities at the local and national levels. The expectation that immigrants and their children would assimilate within British culture was replaced by a politics focused on integration starting in the mid-1960s. Signaling this shift in 1966, Home Secretary Roy Jenkins defined integration "not as a flattening process of uniformity, but cultural diversity, coupled with equality of opportunity in an atmosphere of mutual tolerance" (cited in Favell 1998: 104).

In the 1970s, "benevolent multiculturalism" as policy was most apparent within the British education system, where it was believed that racism could be combated by dispelling widespread white ignorance of ethnic minority cultures through sympathetic teaching (Troyna 1993). As a state response to discrimination—not just at school, but in the spheres of housing, employment, and social services—multiculturalism was, as Stephen May summarizes, "a well-meaning but ultimately vacuous approval of cultural difference" as opposed to an effective strategy to counter racism and inequality (2002: 129). Multiculturalism became subjected to vituperative critique by antiracists in the 1980s, who argued that teaching about other cultures and preaching tolerance failed to confront racial prejudice (Donald & Rattansi 1992). By the early 1990s, it had largely become a tarnished cliché and faded from the public policy agenda, yet enjoyed a new lease on life after New Labour came to power (Abbas 2005; Back et al. 2002). Throughout this period, however, and regardless of whether or not policymakers explicitly endorsed versions of multiculturalism, Britons of all ethnic backgrounds confronted the realities of living with diversity—an everyday multiculturalism involving differing degrees of social proximity and types of interaction (or lack thereof) with those seen as "other."

Yet how different was the multiculturalism displayed during the late 1990s and early 2000s from earlier manifestations that had been found wanting? Stanley Fish has called the "multiculturalism of ethnic restaurants, weekend festivals, and high profile flirtations with the other" "boutique multiculturalism," where there exists only a "superficial or cosmetic relationship to the objects of its affection"—a far cry from a full acceptance of either the cultures or the peoples in question (Fish 1997; Hall 2000). As this chapter will advance, multiculturalism as culinary celebration or as a white consumer practice constitutes only a limited form of tolerance; indeed, it can all too readily be seized upon as an easy substitute for a deeper accommodation of cultural and ethnic diversity in Britain. As will be argued below, multiculturalism in a broader, more encompassing sense proved extremely fragile in moments of crisis occurring not long after Robin Cook's speech extolling the virtues of chicken tikka masala.

South Asian restaurants and the cuisine they serve illuminate a persistent yet evolving dialectic between the rejection, and embrace, of the "other." At the same time, they call into question just what kind of "other"—or even *how* "other"—the cuisine is. Not only are restaurants in Britain labeled as "Indian" mainly run and staffed by Bangladeshis and Pakistanis, but their dishes normally differ markedly from what is consumed in the subcontinent and, for that matter, by most people of South Asian origin in Britain (Brown 2006: 145). Epitomizing a hybrid cuisine, it renders any distinctions drawn between "ethnic" and "British" food inadequate (Cook, Crang & Thorpe 2000: 113; James 1996). Calling chicken tikka masala "a true British national dish" raises the possibility that it has been, as Narayan phrases it, "assimilated" and "possessed" by a Britain in which national identity no longer hinges on what Paul Gilroy has termed "ethnic absolutism." Writing in the 1980s, Gilroy stressed how "the absolutist view of black and white cultures, as fixed, mutually impermeable expressions of racial and national identity" saw the distinction "race" and "nation" blur (Gilroy 1987: 45, 61). If "Indian" food now counts as "British," has a Britishness thus conceived replaced one that long revolved around whiteness with one that makes space for ethnic minority peoples and cultures? (see Parekh and the Runnymede Trust Commission on the Future of Multi-Ethnic Britain 2000). Alternatively, has Britishness become an identity which now validates and is predicated upon hybrid, syn-cretic cultural forms—and if so, in what ways? Or has the selective accom-modation of a "foreign" food left older notions of Britishness largely intact by "assimilating" and "possessing" it on British terms?

In the following pages I test these possibilities by charting these restau-rants' history since the late colonial era. The small handful existing before the end of Britain's Raj in India grew exponentially between the 1950s and the 1970s, when far larger numbers of Indians, Pakistanis, and (after 1971) Bangladeshis arrived to live and work in postcolonial Britain. As restaurants proliferated, their customer base changed, as did their social and cultural meanings. Although these establishments spread throughout Britain to be found even in small towns with few Asian residents aside from those involved in catering, they became particularly visible and numerous in cities with large Asian communities.[1] Starting in the late 1980s, ethnically diverse neighbor-hoods in London, Bradford, Birmingham, and elsewhere became self-styled "Curry Capitals" as "Going for an Indian" achieved the status of a national habit with locally specific contours.

Regardless of their expansion and popularity, Asian restaurants and their dishes always faced detractors, white and Asian alike. Positive and negative images of Britain's curry culture have remained in perpetual tension, reveal-ing much about the changing relationships between Asian and white Britons, the class connotations of producing and consuming this cuisine, and the diversity of Britain's Asian population. Asians working in catering often become sidelined as agents with their own agendas, as was the case when Robin Cook used the active voice when describing how Britain "absorbs and adapts external influences." Such phrasing that positions Asian producers largely as passive is clearly inadequate: the standardized forms that South Asian food and restaurants typically took by the 1980s illustrate strategic choices restaurateurs made to build a solid customer base among a white population that was initially skeptical, if not outright hostile.

South Asians in the restaurant sector have played a critical role in remak-ing Britishness, yet at the same time form a deeply riven rather than a uniform group. Between 85 and 90 percent of Britain's "Indian" restaurants and take-aways are owned and staffed by Bangladeshi Muslims (Gardner & Shukur 1994; Eade 1989; Choudhury & Sylheti Social History Group 1993; Evans 1973). Pakistani Muslims run most others, particularly in cities like Bradford and Birmingham, whose Asian communities predominantly originate from Punjab or from Mirpur District in Azad Kashmir (Ballard 1994; V. S. Khan

1977; Dahya 1974; Rex & Tomlinson 1979; Rex 1996). In light of the widespread paranoia about Islamic religious practices, politics, and culture in Britain since the late 1980s, it is surprising that this aspect of Britain's curry house culture has received so little scholarly attention. Despite these restaurants' popularity, Islamophobia markedly shapes responses to them—not only from white Britons but arguably even more visibly from other sectors of the South Asian diaspora. In recent years, new Asian entrepreneurs have led the chorus of critics who condemn standard curry-house fare for failing to be "authentic," or even "Indian." Through offering culinary alternatives, they challenge common British conceptualizations of an undifferentiated Asian population and culture and assert distinct national, regional, class, and religious backgrounds. With restaurants as their stage, South Asians perform their own acts of ethnic absolutism that work against reconfigurations of Britishness that include curry as much as they undercut notions of a monolithic diasporic culture. The fraught history of the status of South Asian food and peoples within British society, alongside the evolving struggles to delimit what culinary offerings might properly qualify as "Indian," illuminate some of the many forms a lack of consensus about multiculturalism can take.

FROM COLONIAL BEGINNINGS
TO POSTCOLONIAL DIFFUSION

Before British rule in the Indian subcontinent ended in 1947, Indian restaurants in the metropole were few and far between. Several came and went in the nineteenth century and others emerged in the early twentieth, largely in London. Most were run by and catered mainly for an Indian (and predominantly male) clientele who had come to Britain as lascars (seamen), students, or in a professional capacity. The majority were working-class establishments, particularly those providing for men from Sylhet (now part of Bangladesh) employed by merchant shipping companies who docked at British ports, most notably in London's East End (Fisher 1996; Adams 1987; Visram 2002; Choudhury et al. 1993, Choudhury 2002).[2] Of these early restaurants, the oldest that survives today is Veeraswamy's, off Regent Street. Dating from 1926, it was opened by a spice importer who became official caterer for the Indian Pavilion at the 1924 British Empire Exhibition held at Wembley outside London. Veeraswamy's served upper-middle-class and elite customers, including visiting Indian princes and other dignitaries as well as officer-class

Britons who had once lived in India (London News 1926; Veerasawmy [sic] 1953; Dining Out at Veeraswamy's 1982).

Like other early restaurants offering Indian-style dishes, Veeraswamy's was largely ignored by most Britons with the exception of repatriated ex-colonials.[3] Interwar accounts of its staff, clientele, and atmosphere suggest an establishment redolent of Raj culture. Turbaned Indian waiters provided service considered "an Oriental dream" amidst Indian carpets, chandeliers, punkahs (fans), and other decorative accoutrements intended to connote the luxurious "East." Diners who wanted to be treated like "sahibs" again by attentive "native" servants and cooks had come to the right place. Veeraswamy's allowed diners who had "been out East ... to eat again a real curry and remember the days when they were important functionaries on salary instead of 'retired' on pension," a 1928 restaurant guide noted (Smith 1928; Bon Viveur 1937). The Indian owner of another establishment recalled the 1930s as a time when former Indian Civil Servants enjoyed being addressed as "Sahib" when they called out, "Bearer! ... Bearer!" The waiters, not disinterestedly, reciprocated: "we wanted to have a little more tip, so why not?" (Qureshi in Adams 1987: 155).

Ex-colonials remained disproportionately numerous among white Britons patronizing Indian restaurants during the 1950s and extending into the 1960s. As the manager of London's Shafi put it in 1955, "the Indian Khichris, Curries, Bombay Duck and Chutneys and other delicacies have become a regular must" for Englishman who had lived in India (Where to Eat in London, 1955, 65). Some restaurants were described as serving food "in good Old Indian taste," a reference to British "Old India Hands" (Where to Eat in London 1955, 1960: 22). Another term former colonials used among themselves was "Koi Hais," which translated as "is anyone there?"—an expression used to summon Indian domestic servants. One "sahib" writing in *The Times* in 1964 referred to "Koi Hais" in London speaking Urdu at "our last refuge, the Indian restaurant" (The Sahib in a Graceful Thicket 1964).

British social sectors lacking personal ties to the Raj, meanwhile, showed little inclination to eat Indian cuisine (Postgate 1954, 1955). Although curry powder had been sold and added to a variety of English dishes during the nineteenth century, the wider market for establishments dedicated to serving Indian "curries" remained minute (Zlotnick 1996; L. Collingham 2006). Inasmuch as Britons contemplated them at all, Indian dishes usually carried resiliently negative connotations rooted in popular conceptions of colonial culture. In 1955 the British author of a series of Indian cookery books described the "impression, difficult to eradicate, that curry eating is bad for you; that it causes dyspepsia, makes you evil-tempered and tends to shorten your life"—an outlook perpetuated, he continued, "by writers who depict purple-faced, curry-eating colonels who retire to rural England and vent their spleen on the natives." Successive editions of his books that appeared in the late 1950s and early 1960s attempted to counter preconceptions of curry as an underhanded method of disguising spoiled food with pungent spices and the persistent idea "that Indian cooks are dirty and their dishes permeated by disease germs" (Day 1955: 8, 1964: 6).

In such understandings two stereotypes converged: that of the arrogant, privileged colonial, and that of unhygienic South Asian peoples and food (Buettner 2004). The latter perception derived from long-standing notions of the bodily dangers facing Europeans who resided in the "tropics," the digestive problems spicy food was thought to cause, and unclean "natives" who, nonetheless, might prove pleasurably servile and offer a visually appealing spectacle when dressed in "Oriental" fashion (E. M. Collingham 2001). In retrospect, returned colonizers and newly arrived (ex-)colonized subjects alike can be recognized as forming a vanguard of consumers and purveyors of South Asian cuisine in Britain. But at the time, both groups were widely imagined as marginal to metropolitan culture and tainted either through having led a decadent life in a harsh climate or because of racial difference.

Through the 1950s and into the 1960s most Britons continued to steer clear of South Asian food even when restaurants existed to offer opportunities for sampling unfamiliar dishes. Customers at establishments run by Asians were overwhelmingly Asian themselves, who grew far greater in number as immigration from the subcontinent increased in response to Britain's manpower needs at a time of economic expansion. Most restaurants in London and other cities with substantial numbers of Asian newcomers predominantly catered to transport and factory workers: in Birmingham, Pakistanis and Indians employed on busses or in manufacturing, and in Bradford those working in textile mills. Men who ran these casual, café-style establishments often had begun as factory workers before deciding to go into business for themselves by providing a service that fellow new arrivals in Britain wanted. Typically located near factories and mills relying on Asian labor, these eateries stayed open long hours to attract workers when the night shifts ended, providing inexpensive "home cooking," sociability, and a support network for Asians who worked and lived nearby (Their British Paradise Was Waiting 1965; Allen 1971).[4] Rarely, if ever, did an English customer cross the threshold

(Imran, Smith, & Hyslop 1994; Choudhury et al. 1993). For whites living in cities with high rates of immigration, Asian food was not what they consumed themselves; rather, it served as a key indicator of the newcomers' presence and cultural distinctiveness.

By the 1960s and 1970s, food acted as a common cultural barometer charting both the spread of South Asian settlement and white attitudes towards it. Indices of changing local demographics included sights—of "exotically" dressed people from the Indian subcontinent and Urdu or other Asian-language signs on shops (often selling Asian spices, vegetables, halal meat, or sweets)—and scents, as new cooking smells joined or replaced the old. A *Yorkshire Post* reporter said of Bradford in 1973,

> If the aroma of morning meals had wafted along the fringes of Oak Lane and other pavements in the area, the smell of fried bacon would have been overpowered by the scents of typical Punjabi day-starters such as chappatis and buffalo milk ghee and chilli-pepper omelettes.... Bradford is still a pork pie and black pudding town but two decades of largely Asian immigration have created a north of England curry capital covering several square miles. (Tyndale 1976)

While some wrote of these shifts in purely descriptive and even moderately appreciative terms, many more cited the smell of curry as a source of deep resentment. The view that Asians and their surroundings "stank of curry" abounded and became deployed by landlords to explain why they refused Asians as tenants (Housing Plight—All Combines to Create Ghettoes 1965; Landladies' Colour Bar on Students 1966; Aurora 1967). While West Indians' cooking smells were also criticized, the racist insults lobbed in their direction more commonly revolved around their supposed immorality (particularly if men sought sexual relationships with white women), loud music, and rowdy parties (Hill 1965: 77–78; Davison 1964: 23, 25; Buettner 2009). One Indian writer, Rashmi Desai, encapsulated white stereotypes of immigrants as "the West Indians are noisy and have all night parties ... [and] they do not conform to the sexual *mores* of the English, and hence cannot be trusted in a 'respectable' house or locality," whereas "Indians stink of curry" (1963: 20, 11). In this discourse of sensory assault on white Britons, West Indians were held responsible for that on the ears (as well as on the bodies of white women), whereas Indians and Pakistanis were the main culprits for that on the nose.[5]

White resentment of the smell of Asian food, and of Asians themselves, applied to public and private contacts alike. Desai described visiting a factory where "English workers had refused to work with the Indians and Pakistanis because they could not bear the smell of garlic." The managers' response was revealing: they "thought it better to isolate their existing Indo-Pakistani workers and stop recruiting more rather than tell them to stop eating garlic" (R. C. Desai 1963: 75). Confronting white workers' racism, which they may well have shared themselves, appears not to have been envisioned. Such attitudes, however, were more in evidence in discussions about Asians' presence in the neighborhood than in the workplace. Resentment of Asian encroachment on the community, penetrating into the private sphere as smells carried through doors, windows, and walls, proved much more vehement. One woman accounted for her desire to leave the Birmingham street where she had lived for more than thirty years by saying, "I want to get away from the Asians. . . . It's not the colour I'm against, far from it. I have an Asian couple living next door to me and they are the loveliest people you could meet. . . . [But] all the houses reek of cooking curry" (Lovely People but We Want to Get Away 1976). Some white residents of the Smethwick area of Birmingham considered cooking odors so offensive and detrimental to the neighborhood that they demanded rate reductions on their houses from the city council (Prem 1965). "White flight" from areas where immigrants had settled became a common response or aspiration.

Countless renditions of Asian immigrants' culinary culture dating from the 1950s to the 1970s and beyond dismissed it as little more than a social and economic problem. Disparaging references to the smell; repeated accusations of cruelty to animals through Muslims' ritual slaughter of halal meat; reports of Asians' alleged dietary deficiencies and the financial burden they thus placed on the National Health Service; complaints about the added costs of providing "curry on the rates" and halal food for Asians at schools, hospitals, and other public institutions—all recurred in local newspapers for decades (Clayton 1964; Danger of Too Much Chapatti 1972; Murphy 1987; Bell 1986). White British commentators widely considered the fact that "few change their dietary habits" as a primary example of how Asians "cling to their own culture" to their detriment (Clayton 1964). As one Birmingham writer complained in 1955, "their poor English, their liking for traditional foods and their loyalty to their own religions encourages them to stay in a tightly closed circle of their own races" (Little Harlems Must Go 1955). Gastronomic preferences, in short, ranked high in the panoply of reasons why Asians were criticized for failing to adapt to English culture in reports that reflected demands for immigrants to assimilate (and, later, to integrate) within British society.

Yet while negative assessments of Asian food persisted, more Britons gradually found the smell—and the taste—of curry enticing rather than repellent (Asians Have Made This Place Thrive 1976; Don't Turn Your Back on Us 1980). Signs of curry's popularity slowly became apparent by the later 1960s and 1970s, when some establishments that originally catered almost exclusively for Asians gradually witnessed a diversifying clientele (*British Eating Out* 1966).[6] Alongside Britons who had once lived in the subcontinent came others who were attracted by low prices, enjoyed the adventure of trying an "exotic" cuisine, or sought a spicy alternative to what they considered bland English fare. Young people featured prominently among Asian restaurants' newfound customer base. In an interview in 2005, Jim Taylor described his first visits to curry houses as a teenager in late 1960s Birmingham after an upbringing when meals at home consisted of "the normal stock 1950s, 1960s diet of lamb chops, boiled potatoes and peas, with a bit salt on if I was lucky." His father was "very anti-curry," he stressed; "my old man in the war used to have curry and it was basically, he reckoned, the chef's excuse to get dodgy meat cooked up and eaten by the troops" (Interview 2005, May 27).

Born in 1950, Taylor participated in a late 1960s youth culture engaged in a process of rejecting many established norms of his parents' Second World War generation. For this teenager living in a city that had attracted many Asians, opportunities to eat out informally with friends at their restaurants offered a means of shunning the plain-tasting "meat and two veg" meals favored by mainstream English society (Burnett 2004; D. Cooper 1967). "Like a lot of young people," he said, "you always want to try something that your parents won't give you, so I started to go out for curries." Moreover, "it was a bit of fun in that you'd try the hottest curry, even if it was so fiery it blew the roof of your mouth off.... You'd always try to have the hottest curry, you'd have a Madras, or a vindaloo, or a tindaloo."

The newly emergent social ritual Taylor described was an overwhelmingly young, male, and working- or lower-middle-class phenomenon. "Going for an Indian," he recounted, was "very much a boys' thing, a boys' night out" for the younger members of an increasingly affluent postwar society with money to spend on leisure and consumption.[7] Masculinity was displayed through competing with mates to choke down a vindaloo or "take the piss out of the waiter"—evidence that youth culture's "resistance through rituals" might well involve displays of racism, even when this took the arguably more benign form of reveling in unequal relations with staff in the course of consumption as opposed to more overtly aggressive forms of violence. "The waiters would all be dressed up in sort of white shirts and dickey bows, and be very servile sort of in nature," Taylor recalled, "and young people used to think, I suppose, they were a bit important, going to a place where the waiters were very servile." At the very least, other contemporary reports of young men's boisterous behavior at these restaurants suggest a lack of respect and courtesy for both the establishments and their staff. In 1968, *The Times* provided a glimpse of the casual and thoughtless conduct some diners clearly deemed acceptable in such surroundings, reporting that "Mr Dennis Scrivens, aged 22, swallowed a fork in an Indian restaurant in Wolverhampton ... while trying to balance it on the end of his nose" (Man Swallows a Restaurant Fork 1968).

The 1960s and 1970s thus marked a transitional phase in the evolution of Britain's curry house culture. While working-class, café-style restaurants continued to serve Asian customers, many establishments opened or adapted their offerings to attract a white clientele and spread from areas with large immigrant concentrations to become a nation-wide presence. The approximately 300 curry restaurants that existed in 1960 grew to 1,200 in 1970 and reached 3,000 by 1980 (Chapman 1991: 18). Young people remained a critical market and included not only wage earners but also students in search of affordable meals and foods that deviated from their parents' choices at home. Many of the first restaurants to cater to non-Asians opened near university campuses (Jamal 1996, Rafiq 1988). Groups of male customers predominated, but diners also included young couples or mixed parties. The 1980s witnessed the most dramatic increase in curry houses in Britain, which totaled 6,600 by the end of the decade (Chapman 1991: 18). Eating at curry houses had become a familiar social practice in much of Britain, generated an enthusiastic following among self-proclaimed "curry addicts," and acquired a range of cultural and social connotations that remain strongly in evidence even as they are challenged today.

With ever larger numbers of white Britons patronizing Asian-run restaurants, a new form of multicultural interaction had emerged: that of the freely chosen leisure activity. While encounters with Asians, the "smell of curry," and multiculturalism as official policy in mixed neighborhoods, at work, and at school had been—and often continued to be—widely resented and undertaken involuntarily, curry house cuisine gradually became accepted, appreciated, and ultimately celebrated. The growing popularity of "going for an Indian" and "white flight" from working-class neighborhoods with Asian communities occurred simultaneously. Multiculturalism as white consumption of "Indian" food produced to accommodate their tastes, enacted within the space of the restaurant, became distinct from the multiculturalism required by other everyday social interactions with Asians. As will be argued below, however, curry houses and their menus did not fully escape the contempt and racism that peoples of South Asian origin continued to experience in Britain. Rather, South Asian food and Britain's South Asian diaspora have remained closely intertwined in the white British imagination, even when the former was accepted and the latter rejected by, and as part of, British culture and society.

STANDARDIZING THE EXOTIC: REPRESENTING THE CURRY HOUSE'S PROLIFERATION

South Asian restaurants' ascent to popularity among white Britons marks but one manifestation of a modern transnational phenomenon occurring in Western Europe and North America. Following mass migrations to countries offering work opportunities, foodways altered among both immigrants and the host societies in which they settled (Diner 2001). Foreign foods associated with immigrant groups of low social status changed from being ignored, disdained, and widely deemed unpalatable to gain footholds within native food cultures. "Exotic" foods eaten only by immigrants (and, in the case of European nations with imperial histories, by colonizing and colonized populations who had resettled in the metropole) sometimes crossed over to become familiar and then eagerly consumed by wider society, often after an inexpensive restaurant introduction. Some dishes and cuisines failed to make the transition altogether, whereas others were modified to appeal to different palates. In the process, Italian, Chinese, and Mexican cuisine became Americanized; Italian food and Döner kebabs introduced by Turkish "guest workers" entered German diets; North African couscous became common in France; Indonesian and Chinese food gained acceptance in the Netherlands; and chicken tikka masala became British (Gabaccia 1998; Levenstein 1985; Roberts 2002; Çağlar 1995; Möhring 2008; van Otterloo 2002). Foods of foreign origin often led what Sylvia Ferrero, writing about Mexican offerings in Los Angeles, described as a "dual life": in this instance, "standardized food for Anglos, and specialties for Mexican-Americans and Mexicans" (Ferrero 2002: 216). On repeated occasions, the very standardization that proved decisive to a food's gaining wider acceptance beyond the migrant group was held against it by individuals who counted themselves better judges of quality and authenticity. Such was the case with South Asian restaurant fare in Britain.

In becoming ensconced within Britain's culinary landscape, curry houses took on an instantly recognizable stereotyped image. Founded in 1982, the Curry Club—an association of curry aficionados—testified to the wide following they had developed. Its quarterly magazine described what rapidly had become the characteristic cuisine, interior decoration, and staff appearance. Such restaurants offered dishes from the northern part of the subcontinent prepared cheaply by taking shortcuts and omitting ingredients, the result being "rather similar style curries, in rich spicy sauces which lacked the subtlety of the original recipes." New proprietors copied models that had proved successful for others, until,

> within a few years, every high street in the land had its identical restaurant.... They could have been cloned. No-one has counted how many Taj Mahals, Rajahs, Mumtaz's Stars of India, Curry Houses, Curry Gardens and ... Tandoori's exist in the U.K. The décor and the lighting are identical (red flock wallpaper, ornamental hardboard Indian arches, and red or orange lighting in Eastern lampshades.) The serving bowls, the candle lit warmers and, for all I know, the dinner jacketed waiters are all indistinguishable. But most fascinating of all is the menu. You are as certain to get the standard menu in the standard restaurant as you are to get a postage stamp from a post office whether you are in the coves of Cornwall or the Highlands of Scotland. (Indian Restaurant and Its Menu 1983: 12)

Significantly, this formula derived from owners' perception of its success with customers attracted by low prices, the overall curry house atmosphere, and the cuisine itself. Yet having become part of everyday life for many Britons, curry houses nonetheless were subjected to much ridicule and often to scathing criticism. Tawdry décor and poor quality, inauthentic food became the butt of jokes as seasoned customers poked fun at the "red flock wallpaper, the identical standard menu and the hot curries cooked in axle grease" (Restaurant Trade 1982: i). Restaurants and cafés geared towards a largely Asian clientele, meanwhile, received little attention during and after the 1980s. Public discussions revolved around those patronized mainly by whites, with most Asians becoming sidelined as consumers of a cuisine that was purportedly "theirs," however inauthentic such food was accused of being.

Denunciations came not only from white customers but from selected Asian commentators as well—in short, from a range of self-proclaimed experts who claimed to know better. An early critic was the Indian actress Madhur Jaffrey who, by the mid-1970s, was well on her way towards becoming the most recognizable media figure promoting Indian cooking through her cookery books and subsequent television shows broadcast in the 1980s. Jaffrey's *An Invitation to Indian Cooking* first appeared in Britain in 1976, and—not disinterestedly in light of her own recent reinvention as a key culinary spokesperson—recommended learning to prepare Indian dishes at home on the basis of restaurants' shortcomings. Dismissing the vast majority as "second-class establishments that had managed to underplay their own regional uniqueness" through serving "a generalized Indian food from no area whatsoever," she faulted the cooks as ill equipped to do justice to the foods they prepared because of their lack of skills. "Often former seamen or untrained villagers who have come to England in the hopes of making a living, somehow or other," upon opening restaurants they simply copied their competitors' menus. In consequence, sauces "inevitably have the same colour, taste, and consistency; the dishes generally come 'mild, medium or hot'" (1978: 11–12).

As will be explored further below, Jaffrey's critique of "second-class" restaurants and her promotion of regional cuisines share much in common with later assessments by other middle- and upper-class Indians opening restaurants in late-twentieth-century Britain. She had never been the sole detractor, however; accusations of inauthenticity by other self-styled connoisseurs already abounded at the very moment when these restaurants' popularity rose most sharply. Critics in the early 1980s disparaged restaurant fare as a "terrible parody of Indian food" in which "a common sauce is slopped on" and "everything tastes the same" (N. Khan 1982: 10–11; Chapman 1983: 12).

The timing of these attacks was by no means accidental. Arjun Appadurai has argued that authenticity, which "measures the degree to which something is more or less what it *ought* to be," is a criterion apt to "emerge just after its subject matter has been significantly transformed" (Appadurai 1986a: 25). The changes made to South Asian food by members of a diaspora settled in Britain with an eye towards generating and retaining new business marks just such a historical shift, one which worried and offended individuals within and outside the diverse community of South Asian origin. Claiming superior knowledge became a marker of distinction at a time when ever greater numbers of Britons became familiar with, and appreciative of, the versions of Asian food made available to them—what Appadurai termed a "political economy of taste" or a "politics of connoisseurship" revolving around commodities that had travelled far from their place of origin (Appadurai 1986b: 44). Brian Spooner's work similarly asserts that authenticity is never simply an objective measurement but rather is determined by the choices and desires of persons seeking to establish, or strengthen, an elevated social position. When possessing a type of object in and of itself ceased to qualify as a sign of status thanks to its general proliferation and adaptation, the processes of knowing, searching for, and even (arguably) finding authenticity differentiates those with privileged access from those willing to accept generic varieties available to the supposedly undiscerning and ignorant majority (Spooner 1986). The act of consuming South Asian restaurant food in Britain involved precisely such forms of separation and association.

Stock accusations of poor, nongenuine offerings were part of the curry house's generally downmarket image that encompassed restaurant staff, diners, and their spaces of interaction.[8] Critics complained that most owners and chefs had arrived in Britain as workers and lacked formal catering qualifications, hence proving unable or unwilling to provide "the real thing"—which, in any case, few of their ignorant customers appeared to want. Waiters, meanwhile, bore little resemblance to the "servile" staff Jim Taylor remembered at 1960s Birmingham establishments, and instead were commonly accused of being "surly" and providing "service with a leer" (Restaurant Roundup 1982a). Mutual contempt characterized relations between curry's producers and consumers at many restaurants. Public understandings of mainstay curry house diners focused on the white male clientele who took advantage of late-night hours of operation to arrive drunk after pubs or clubs closed, behave disrespectfully, if not violently (most characteristically by racially abusing the staff), and possibly try to leave without paying (Monroe 2005; Alibhai-Brown 1998; Midnight Cowboys 1996).

Many customers found curry houses attractive because they were cheap, filling, informal, and open late—circumstances in which food quality often proved secondary (Shah Knows What's What 1985). As several Bradford restaurant reviews summarized when praising particular establishments, they offered "good value for a fiver" despite dishes having proved a "let down . . . no real sauce [and] too much oil"; "good grub in copious quantities"; a chance to "fill your boots for under £2"; or qualified as a reliable "soak-up curry after the pub" (Good Value for a Fiver 1989; Man! What a Great Nan 1988; Cheap without Frills and Thrills 1989; Rajshahi 2003). Epitomizing how an establishment could be damned and praised simultaneously, one 1988 review read: "Steve couldn't remember whether he'd ordered a murgh massala or the murgh korma—and was left none the wiser when his dish arrived. . . . Either way it went down well," given the price (Striking a Balance 1988). "Value for money" proved a continual source of attraction, regardless of whether the food, service, or atmosphere was assessed as good or indifferent. Curry's supposed drawbacks and risks never faded fully into the background, and anxieties about restaurants' standards of hygiene and their dishes' effects on digestion resiliently remained part of public discourse. Newspapers periodically reported establishments which violated health and environmental codes and alluded to the Asian staff's ignorance of sanitation requirements, while diners' comments about digestive "suffering the next day" featured regularly in reviews (Restaurant Food Cooked in Garage 1983; Dirty, Filthy and Disgusting 1988; Restaurant Roundup 1982b).

However much curry houses were habitually lampooned and critiqued, by the 1980s they nonetheless had acquired a loyal mass following that had diversified to include families and a cross-class clientele. Some diners may have poked fun at their kitsch décor and staff demeanor, yet most would not have patronized these establishments had they not enjoyed the cuisine on offer—regardless of its oft-proclaimed inauthenticity. British South Asian food aficionados included both those who condemned restaurant versions as nongenuine and those who actively sought out "the restaurant curry" and valued it highly in its own right. Indeed, a writer in the Curry Club's magazine commented how difficult it was to satisfy those members who sought to "recreate the flavours they have become used to in restaurants and at the same time supply authenticity" (Aziz 1982: 8). The magazine thus featured articles on "genuine" regional specialties alongside restaurant reviews and recipes instructing readers how to prepare the "definitive Indian restaurant-curry" at home (Ivan Watson Defines the Indian-Restaurant Curry 1983). Polarized attitudes remained common during the 1990s. As a reader of *Tandoori Magazine* protested in 1998, "Indian restaurants have swept to the No. 1 position in dining out choice because customers like it as it is" (Fairall 1998: 11).

Although their image was resolutely downmarket in some eyes, Asian restaurants thus acquired a range of positive associations as well. As a result, between the 1980s and the present Britain's curry tradition was reconfigured in two ways. On the one hand, standard offerings became elevated to a new pride of place by those who considered them a valued part of national or local multicultural life, while on the other, an emerging and distinct group of entrepreneurs opened new restaurants explicitly intended to challenge stereotyped, "inauthentic," and routinely disparaged establishments.

CURRY CAPITALS AND CONDITIONAL MULTICULTURALISM

In stark contrast to the hesitancy and indeed the hostility with which many white Britons greeted the smell of curry—let alone its taste—several decades ago, South Asian food is no longer widely viewed as a social problem or an indicator of immigrants' repugnant cultural traits and unwillingness to integrate. Its mass popularity enabled fans to draw positive conclusions from the way Asian restaurateurs altered their cuisine to accommodate British tastes and, to reiterate Robin Cook's claims, made chicken tikka masala into a distinctly "British national dish."[9] What is more, selected cities and neighborhoods with sizeable Asian populations came to view their numerous restaurants as an opportunity to tell an affirmative story about local ethnic diversity. Indeed, they did so precisely in areas plagued with social and economic problems and where "race relations" proved persistently precarious. Styling themselves as Britain's "Curry Capitals" became a central plank in a succession of local regeneration efforts.

In Bradford and Birmingham, the Asian restaurant sector's expansion tellingly occurred in the same years as Bradford's textile mills and Birmingham's motor, metal, and engineering industries went into steady and irreversible decline. In the 1970s and 1980s, many immigrants and their children who initially had worked in booming traditional industries turned to catering and other forms of self-employment and service-sector jobs after being made redundant with deindustrialization (Kalra 2000; Metcalf, Modood, & Virdee 1996; Srinivasan 1995; Ram & Jones 1998). In an economically depressed city like Bradford, curry became drawn into an attempt to redefine the area in more positive ways. Starting in the mid- to late 1980s, local newspapers and the city's tourist office began promoting curry houses and producing "Flavours of Asia" brochures meant to attract visitors to Bradford on account of its restaurants, as well as other "colourful" offerings including Asian fabric, clothing, and grocery shops. Embarking on the "curry trail" offered residents and prospective visitors alike "a feast that only Bradford can offer" at one of its scores of Asian restaurants (which numbered over fifty in the late 1980s and over two hundred today).[10] Optimists described curry as enabling a "trade renaissance for Bradford" (Curry: A Trade Renaissance for Bradford 1997). Asian families running flourishing chains like Aagrah and Mumtaz became fêted as success stories in their own right—Aagrah's owners, for example, had arrived in Britain from Kashmir in the early 1960s and started out as bus drivers and mill workers—as well as commended for bringing hundreds of new jobs to a city in dire need of employment opportunities (Aagrah 2004; A. Khan 1997a, 1997b).

Enthusiasts celebrated curry as having become central to Bradford's economic and cultural traditions. After the virtual disappearance of textiles, South Asian restaurants came to count as one of the city's "traditional industries," while the Aagrah restaurant chain earned praise as "a Yorkshire institution" (Giving a Trendy Edge to Tradition 2001; Aagrah 2004). Curry was added to the moors, the dales, and the Brontë sisters' home in the nearby town of Haworth as West Yorkshire highlights. Fresh from their visit to the Brontë Parsonage Museum, tourists could eat a meal at the Raj Mahal and enjoy "traditional Indian cuisine in the heart of Brontë country" (Raj Mahal 1998; Restaurant of the Month 2004). What was named as "Indian" became partly stripped of its foreign aspects to become appropriated within newly reconfigured constructions of Bradford's and Yorkshire's heritage. Thus familiarized and localized, curry's popularity and growing economic presence in and around Bradford made it "the positive side of the city's multiculturalism" (Cope 2002).

Bradford was not alone in actively promoting curry as part of its newly reinvented local tradition. Other cities like Manchester and Leicester followed suit, the former advertising the more than fifty restaurants serving 65,000 diners a week on a street known as the "Curry Mile" and the latter offering "Taste of Asia" weekend package tours.[11] Similarly, since the late 1990s local authorities in east London's Tower Hamlets borough have embarked on a concerted campaign to promote the Brick Lane area as "Banglatown"—on account of having the largest Bangladeshi population in Britain—or "London's Curry Capital." Efforts to publicize the scores of Bangladeshi-run restaurants and cafés alongside other Asian shops and cultural offerings in the East End aimed at de-emphasizing poverty and ethnic conflict in favor of stressing vibrant cultural diversity (Carey 2004; Tower Hamlets Council 2005; Sahid 1988; Banglatown Plan Comes Under Fire 1997; Dench, Gavron & Young 2006).

Birmingham's incorporation of South Asian food as part of its identity is arguably the most distinct example of an ethnically diverse city deploying minority cultural products for self-promotion (Ram, Jones, Abbas, & Sanghera 2002). Home to one of the nation's most populous Asian communities, Birmingham's restaurant sector developed its own distinctly local form of curry known as *balti*. *Balti*—which translates as "bucket"—refers to the wok-like dish in which food is prepared and served in a manner that differed from other styles of South Asian restaurant fare. Developed in the 1970s and 1980s by the city's restaurateurs from northern Pakistan, it spread throughout Britain in the 1990s but remained seen and celebrated as something that emerged in Birmingham—"a Brummie thing."

Just as Asian restaurants in and around Bradford became subsumed within local and regional culture, so too did Birmingham's, with the *balti* designator foregrounding their development within a local British context as much as, and usually more, than their specifically Pakistani roots. The account provided by Jim Taylor, the early curry convert introduced above, who subsequently became one of balti's foremost champions and unofficial publicists, typifies the tendency to highlight local English particularities. While many Asian restaurants throughout Britain added balti dishes to their menus during the height of the "balti craze" in the mid- to late 1990s, Taylor noted, few offered balti cooked in "the correct way" as done by Birmingham's first- and second-generation Pakistani community. Bangladeshis who dominated the Asian restaurant sector on the national level and introduced balti dishes failed, in the eyes of Birmingham balti enthusiasts, to serve "the real thing." As he and others like him put it, restaurants outside Birmingham were "trading in on Birmingham's heritage" (Taylor interview with author; Tredre 1995).

Starting in the mid-1990s, Birmingham's local authorities began to consider how the "run-down Sparkbrook area" with its many Asian residents and restaurants might be transformed from an urban blight into a selling point (Percival 1995; Hussain 1997a; Rex & Moore 1967; Rex 1987). The Asian Balti Restaurant Association worked together with the organization Marketing Birmingham to generate promotional materials drawing attention to the Asian shops and the more than fifty eateries located within what became restyled as the "Balti Quarter," or "Balti Triangle." As the 2004–2005 guide asserted, "no longer perceived as a grey, industrial city, Birmingham has emerged as an exciting and vibrant city. . . . Canals, Cadbury's, cars and jewelry have long been synonymous with Birmingham, but undoubtedly Balti is now equally part of Birmingham's tradition" (Marketing Birmingham 2004–2005). In a city suffering from persistent and deep-seated economic problems, the Balti Triangle's annual £8.5 million restaurant turnover made it a valued player in a local economy where regeneration has been an urgent albeit often elusive goal (Ram et al. 2002: 26).

Celebratory narratives of these restaurants' spread and popularity enlist them as illustrations of Asian entrepreneurial achievement and economic success, not to mention as evidence of a thriving multicultural outlook and improving race relations. Yet such evaluations have proven overly optimistic. In economic terms, while many Asian families have built modestly successful businesses and a small proportion have become prosperous, many restaurateurs lead a precarious existence, earning low profits in a saturated catering market and struggling to stay afloat (Ram et al. 2002; Rafiq 1988). Notorious for long, antisocial hours and low pay for kitchen staff and waiters, the drawbacks of restaurant work have caused many owners' children to contemplate taking over the family business with reluctance (Hussain 1997a; Kalra 2000, 2004). A study of Bangladeshi-run Brick Lane establishments in east London revealed that those working in catering found themselves ridiculed back home as "OCs (onion cutters) and DCs (dish cleaners)"—the former an ironic allusion to "the big district police head" and the latter to the administrative district commissioner (Dench, Gavron, & Young 2006: 130). Many Bangladeshi men who start out working in restaurants upon arrival—often through kinship ties with the owners—correspondingly seek other work when, and if, more promising opportunities arise.

Furthermore, however affectionately the white British public has come to view its curry experiences, racism has never fully receded from the restaurant encounter. Rudeness and racial verbal abuse to the staff continue, although this now occurs less frequently; less common but far more serious are the ongoing incidents of racially motivated assault, arson, and other forms of violence that occur at some restaurants (Assault Fears at Balti Houses 1997; Chalmers 2000). Additionally, as most curry or balti houses are run and staffed by Muslims of Bangladeshi or Pakistani origin, they are prime targets for Islamophobia. As two second-generation restaurateurs in Birmingham's Balti Triangle reported, although most of their customers are friendly, they still periodically hear comments such as "go back to Pakistan," or get called "Paki" or "Osama bin Laden" by aggressive passers-by.[12] This has increased since September 11, 2001, the wars in Afghanistan and Iraq, and the July 2005 suicide bombings by British Muslims on the London transport network. Anti-Muslim sentiments had been apparent since at least the late 1980s, however, with the Rushdie Affair (in which protests in Bradford attracted international attention) and the Gulf War serving as critical turning points (Asad 1990; Back et al. 2002; Modood 1992a, 2005; Abbas 2005; Amin 2002).

Such episodes count among the few direct references to the fact that nearly all of Britain's South Asian restaurants are owned and operated by Muslims. With the sharpest surge in their popularity taking place during the same years as anxieties about Muslim extremism in religious, political, and cultural terms became a recurring feature of British life, commentators worrying about British Muslims' loyalty to the nation and capacity for integration failed to give them credit for shaping Britain's now highly valued curry culture. Muslims in the restaurant sector had indeed assimilated South Asian cuisine into the British mainstream by catering to white British tastes, yet public attention remained focused on cultural practices that were seen to demonstrate that Muslims isolated themselves and lacked appropriate political and religious moderation (A. Basu 2002). South Asian food may have become seen as integrated into the nation and its localities, but not its purveyors, who still stand accused of self-segregation (Abbas 2005; Amin 2002). Multiculturalism as developed by a largely Muslim group of South Asian restaurateurs thus could be construed as reflecting a tolerant British society's success in "absorbing and adapting external influences" rather than as an indicator of producers' own agency and flexibility. Popular understandings of the curry house as "Indian," "British," or culturally hybrid equally serve to obscure Muslims' leading role within a celebrated aspect of a national culture that has grown accustomed to viewing Muslims—most of whom originated in Pakistan or Bangladesh—as marginal, intolerant, regressive, and dangerous.

Multiculturalism emerges as highly qualified, partial, and conditional in its application, both discursively and in the realm of everyday life, even in Britain's proud "Curry Capitals." Bradford's incidences of racialized civil strife in July 2001 provide further evidence of its selective nature. Riots occurring there followed other episodes in Oldham and Burnley, two other northern English former textile centers with large Asian populations. These outbreaks of civil unrest in economically depressed, ethnically diverse, and deeply divided communities attracted national attention and condemnation, resulting in a protracted struggle to assess their causes and implications. As analyses by Arun Kundnani and Ash Amin cogently stress, the roots lay in deprivation, high unemployment, and the competition for scarce jobs and social assistance. Discriminatory policies meant that social housing had largely been allocated to whites, who thus lived in separate areas from Asians.

"It was 'white flight' backed by the local state," Kundnani summarizes (2001: 107). But rather than attribute divisions and unrest to socioeconomic problems, institutional racism, and "the cultural exclusions associated with White Englishness," as Amin phrases it, many commentators placed the blame on Muslims, who were accused of self-segregation and stubbornly refusing to integrate (Amin 2002: 963).

As a sign that Bradford's longstanding ethnic divisions were not reducible to the violence of July 2001 but had already attracted considerable scrutiny, the Ouseley Report following an intensive official review appeared that same month. White Bradfordians, the report noted, often felt that Asians received disproportionate public assistance "at their expense," while Asians believed widespread Islamophobia and racism combined to create an atmosphere of "harassment, discrimination and exclusion" that resulted in unequal treatment and public marginalization. The social consequences were summarized thus: "Different ethnic groups are increasingly segregating themselves from each other and retreating into 'comfort zones' made up of people like themselves. *They only connect with each other on those occasions when they cannot avoid each other, such as in shops, on the streets, at work, when travelling and, perversely, in Asian-owned restaurants by choice*" (Community Pride not Prejudice 2001: 16, emphasis added).

While the Ouseley Report deemed the contacts with other ethnic groups occurring at Asian restaurants "perverse," they come as no surprise in light of the history of white patronage of curry houses outlined above. By 2001, voluntarily eating out at Asian-run restaurants had long been the exception that proved the rule, and was subsequently to remain so. On the first anniversary of the unrest, one Bradford Asian restaurant owner offered free food to members of different ethnic communities—"provided they spoke to each other over lunch." "Restaurants are often the only place where white people mix with Asians so it is important we present a positive image," he continued (I Provide the Food 2002; Cope 2002). Albeit intended optimistically, his point underscored the limited degree of meaningful interaction between most Asians and whites as well as the curry interface's inability to signal, or to effect, substantive positive change. As an Asian waiter interviewed several years earlier reflected, "mainly I have good contact with the white people who are customers at the restaurant. But sometimes when I meet them in the market place or in a shop, I feel like they don't want to know me" (Whitehorn 1997). Far more cynically, an Asian complained in a letter to the editor of one newspaper that "it embarrasses me greatly to hear about the 'enrichment' of multi-culturalism in Bradford. I think the sum total of enrichment for the average indigenous person is a 'drunken curry'" (Stop Pretending 2002).

South Asian food's white British following counts as a key example of how, as Paul Gilroy suggests, "exciting, unfamiliar cultures can be consumed in the absence of any face-to-face recognition or real-time negotiation with their actual creators. The intensified desire for what was formerly stigmatized and forbidden can also be interpreted as a part of the collapse of English cultural confidence that has fed the development of anxious and insecure local and national identities" (Gilroy 2004: 137; Hooks 1992). While the profusion of self-proclaimed "Curry Capitals" within postindustrial Britain was undertaken with the aim of reinvigorating beleaguered local identities in ways that draw upon Asians' presence and contributions, the extent to which these efforts can be considered successful or merely superficial remains highly debatable.

Indeed, in the wake of the watershed events of 2001 (and again following the London bombings of 2005), multiculturalism suffered severe setbacks at the level of national government rhetoric. In moments of crisis, New Labour retreated from earlier proclamations valuing cultural and ethnic diversity, veering instead towards what Tahir Abbas, Les Back, and other scholars have likened to 1960s-style assimilationism (Abbas 2005; Back et al. 2002; Great Britain Home Office 2001). Yet in this atmosphere ridden with mistrust, food survived as a source of enjoyment and celebration when so much else that was culturally associated with Britain's South Asian community attracted increased suspicion. In part, it did so via attempts to further marginalize and discredit the contributions made by British Muslims of Bangladeshi and Pakistani origin.

FRACTURES, DIVERSIFICATION, AND AUTHENTICITY

Despite curry houses having achieved local and national prominence, their image remains predominantly a downmarket one. As such, it has come under attack from a new front opened up from within a socially and nationally divided Asian business community (Brown 2006: 111). Beginning gradually in the 1980s in London's West End, new restaurants opened for wealthier customers, joining the long-established Veeraswamy's in catering to affluent Londoners. Discerning "experts" who claimed to know how South Asian cuisine *should* be greeted the opening of the Bombay Brasserie in 1982 as an oasis in a culinary desert. Prominent restaurant critic Fay Maschler responded ecstatically: "the grip of the conventional menu was shattered and instead of the predictable list of mainly Northern Indian dishes there were dishes from Goa and the Punjab, traditional Parsi food and Bombay street snacks. . . . It will give you some idea of the incredible variety to Indian cuisine, a fact that has tended to be swamped by the popular notion of a curry." The Bombay Brasserie, moreover, moved away from the ridiculed flock wallpaper décor, opting instead for a Raj "colonial style" ambiance. "Wicker chairs, revolving ceiling fans, brass-bound chests, potted banana palms, sepia-tinted photographs," Maschler continued, "[come] off convincingly and romantically" (Maschler 1986: 30–31; Chapman 1983: 9).

The Bombay Brasserie marked the beginnings of the gradual bifurcation of the South Asian restaurant scene, in which new entrepreneurs dissociated themselves from the curry house norm on every level. Allusions to French restaurants—traditionally associated with wealth and gastronomic sophistication—through recourse to the "brasserie" appellation connoted prestige, as did invoking British colonial lifestyles of previous generations. In the 1980s and early 1990s, the image of choice was often Raj-style décor, reflecting the current of colonial nostalgia apparent elsewhere in British culture (Dyer 1997; Burton 2001; Buettner 2004, 2006). Opened in 1990, Chutney Mary similarly opted for a Raj look, "Anglo-Indian cuisine," and a "Verandah bar" to suggest affluence to its well-off clientele (Chapman 1991: 8; Hashmi 1998).[13]

Owners of such new, largely London-based establishments and their chefs seldom resembled the Bangladeshis, Pakistanis, and their British-born children running most curry and balti houses; rather, most had come from India as middle- or upper-class professionals who had begun their careers working at five-star hotels and restaurants in Bombay and New Delhi (Taj Restaurant 1999: 5; Monroe 2005). One of the most explicit statements meant to elevate newer arrivals above the "curry house formula" appeared in 2004 on the website for Masala World, a company whose portfolio includes London's revamped Veeraswamy, Chutney Mary, and the more modestly priced Masala Zone. "Owned by Namita Panjabi and her investment-banker husband Ranjit Mathrani," the site insisted on the genuine Indianness, regional specificity, and high-status origins of the cuisine served. Dishes from "regional gourmet families [and] Maharajas' palaces" made by directly recruited "Indian regional specialist chefs" were "prepared authentically, as in Indian homes, and no short cuts are taken." The result, in sum, was "very different from the inexpensive neighbourhood curry restaurants started in Britain by enterprising non-Indian entrepreneurs who developed their own brand of curry totally different from the tastes of real Indian food."[14]

Authentic and regional Indian cuisine, elite professional Indian purveyors, and establishments serving discerning, better-off connoisseurs thus characterized one type of establishment, while fabrications made by Bangladeshis and Pakistanis of working-class origin who provided cheap food to unsophisticated customers constituted their disreputable "other." Affluent and sophisticated owners and customers alike engaged in acts of distinction vis-à-vis their curry house counterparts as a means of proclaiming social and cultural superiority (Spooner 1986: 223–26). Interviewing another British Asian culinary "moderniser"—"dressed in Paul Smith" designer clothing—in 2001, Yasmin Alibhai-Brown quoted him as wanting "to take this business away from Pakis and Banglis who are just junglee peasants with rough habits. We want to appeal to the people who spend money going to the palaces of Rajasthan, bon vivant people. This is about rebranding the food, making it 21st century" (Alibhai-Brown 2001a).

Exclusive new restaurants thus asserted their distinction in social and national terms that were often implicitly religious as well. The desire for social differentiation plays a central role in shaping this attitude, reflecting the fact that the main South Asian Muslim communities in Britain from Pakistan and Bangladesh lag far behind Hindus and Sikhs from India or East Africa in terms of upward social mobility. The association of Britain's Muslims with economic disadvantage—by whites and other Asians alike—is strong (Modood 1992, Ballard 2003, Alexander 1998). Anti-Muslim attitudes in Britain described above also arguably influence decisions by some upmarket restaurant owners and managers of Hindu, Parsi, or Sikh Indian origin to distance both their establishments and their cuisine from the mainstream eateries run by Pakistani and Bangladeshi Muslims. India's own recent troubled history of sectarianism exhibited through Hindu communalist politics—which shape politics and culture among Hindus in the diaspora as much as they do at home—as well as diplomatic tensions between India and Pakistan also stoke such outlooks (van der Veer 1994, 2000).

Insistence that they serve "real Indian" food that curry houses do not provide also stems from the perception that the "discerning" customers in Britain they hope to attract are likely to be more familiar with Indian than with Pakistani or Bangladeshi culture, often through travel. Invoking

Maharajahs' palaces in Rajasthan or focusing on southern Indian regional dishes from Goa or Kerala mirrors these regions' importance as likely tourist destinations for the growing numbers of Britons visiting the subcontinent in recent years (Ramusack 1995; Tharav Roast 1999). Moreover, neither Goa nor Kerala sent many immigrants to Britain, thereby facilitating the act of dissociating such establishments from Britain's largest South Asian communities.[15] Emphasizing the Sylhetti or Kashmiri regional origins of the vast majority of Bangladeshi and Pakistani restaurant owners, by contrast, was deemed unlikely to appeal to an upmarket clientele. Not only had these establishments become firmly associated with a standardized and Anglicized cuisine, but neither Sylhet nor Kashmir rank high on tourists' itineraries. The former remains largely unheard-of by non-Asians in Britain, while the latter is predominantly associated with chronic violence resulting from its status as a disputed territory between India and Pakistan.

Owners of newer, purportedly authentic restaurants repeatedly stake claim to their modernity by reference to their "traditional" dishes, and assiduously avoid aesthetic associations with the curry house stereotype that go beyond the menu. In naming their restaurants they steer clear of ubiquitous monikers such as Taj Mahal or Koh-i-Noor, as well as names reminiscent of the Raj, like Passage to India, as these too became clichéd choices. Instead, Indian-language words with culinary associations or English-language spice names have become popular options for higher-status restaurants, as they connote a more cultivated cultural awareness of the subcontinent and knowledge of sophisticated gastronomy—hence the arrival of restaurants called Cumin, Lasan (meaning "garlic"), Tamarind, the Cinnamon Club, and Rasa (meaning "taste" or "essence") (Wahhab 1997; Hussain 1998). Nor is interior decoration that became mocked as part of the curry house tradition anywhere to be seen. Instead, the preferred style combines a backdrop of modernist minimalism interspersed with selected Indian—largely Hindu—artistic signifiers, ideally antiques (Interior Motives 1998; Vegetarian Wonders 1998; Zaika 1999).

Lastly, in defining their restaurants in opposition to the ridiculed curry house image, such newcomers universally omit dishes labeled "curry" or "balti" from their list of options. Chicken tikka masala is decidedly absent from their menus, which instead might inform diners that dishes are prepared according to Ayurvedic principles (Good for What Ails You, 1999). Ironically yet tellingly, hybrid offerings acclaimed for exemplifying multicultural Britishness, associated with working-class immigrants, and eagerly consumed by countless "balti addicts" and "curryholics," were precisely those to which high-status Asian restaurateurs and their clientele took exception (Stein 2003). Unworthy of celebration, they were dismissed as authenticity's poor relation.

CONCLUSION

A variety of actors thus assert the value of Britain's curry tradition at the same time as others vigorously contest it, condemning its failure to be "genuine." A popular activity among much of white British society that once found the smell of curry repellent, "Going for an Indian" is now a multi-billion-pound service industry whose significance is economic and cultural alike. Yet interactions between Asians employed in the restaurant sector and white customers remain largely skin deep, with multiculturalism having become acceptable as consumer practice, yet remaining seen as disconnected from its producers. As playwright and director Jatinder Verma reflected, "I do not think that imaginatively we have become multicultural. I think that in diet we have, absolutely, but I don't think that has translated from our stomachs to our brains yet" (Alibhai-Brown, 2001b: 110).

While the profile of South Asians in certain cities and neighborhoods with large minority communities has become more prominent through the branding of these areas as "Curry Capitals," this has come at the price of incorporating and largely submerging their restaurants within local British contexts. Thus, diners in and around Bradford can enjoy "traditional Indian cuisine in the heart of Brontë country" or visit a restaurant chain promoted as "a Yorkshire institution," while balti qualifies as part of Birmingham's heritage. Within these geographical framings, a generic, homogenized "Indianness" is deployed to attract white customers and the specifically British terrain in which they are situated is foregrounded. Despite widespread liking for their cuisine, many white diners remain ignorant about, and intolerant of, Britain's diverse South Asian population, having gained little in terms of enhanced awareness or meaningful social interaction from their dining experiences. Like the multicultural policies that emerged after the 1960s, consumer multiculturalism has proven inadequate to the task of combating racism and inequality, further vindicating the doubts voiced by antiracists in the 1980s. South Asians are still commonly perceived as an undifferentiated group separate from mainstream British society that remains imaginatively white, even now that their restaurateurs are routinely commended for reconfiguring national culinary preferences.

Indicatively, when the central role played by restaurateurs of Bangladeshi or Pakistani origin in developing Britain's curry culture has been noted, it has often been by elite Indians and affluent white "connoisseurs" engaged in the act of disparaging familiar offerings as downmarket and inauthentic. Mainstream curry and balti restaurants simultaneously became condemned for being too Bangladeshi, too Pakistani, and too British to properly qualify as "Indian." Indeed, from the 1980s on, the contest within Britain over what should properly count as "Indian" food became increasingly pronounced in tandem with the proliferation, rising popularity, and eventually the diversification of restaurants categorized as such. With many South Asians eagerly asserting their distinction not only from white Britons but also from each other in terms of their national, social, and religious origins, restaurant and gastronomic trends reveal multiple ethnic absolutisms at work within a purported multiculture that severely circumscribe what convergences and transformations have occurred.

Nonetheless, multiculturalism continues to serve as a powerful myth in contemporary Britain—despite, and largely because of, its limited impact on everyday social realities. Projecting a national self-image in which tolerance of ethnic diversity and cultural changes predominates remains as appealing today as it was for Robin Cook in early 2001 immediately prior to the challenges posed by the riots in northern England and September 11. Reminders of this purported acceptance and openness have acquired greater urgency at precisely the time when suspicion of ethnic differences has mounted, with the war in Iraq and the London bombings of July 2005 having made Muslim extremism both within and outside Britain an increasingly prominent political and social concern.

Ongoing instances of racism and social fears revolving around ethnicity necessitate repeated recourse to myths that emphasize the opposite. This became visible in 2007 when *Celebrity Big Brother,* a popular British "reality television" program, became mired in controversy surrounding racist insults directed at one of the contestants, the Indian Bollywood star Shilpa Shetty. Following a dispute about supposedly undercooked chicken, several British contestants, including Jade Goody, targeted Shetty for a protracted wave of abuse in which many of the slurs directed against her revolved around food. Refusing even to learn Shetty's surname let alone try to pronounce it, Goody angrily referred to her as "Shilpa Fuckawallah" and "Shilpa

Poppadom"—poppadom being a typical curry house appetizer. Other comments about Shetty included that she should "go home" and that she "wanted to be white"; another contestant warned against eating the dinner she had prepared, saying "you don't know where her hands have been" (Gibson 2007; Jacques 2007).

The British public responded vigorously, with tens of thousands complaining to the channel broadcasting the program about its airing of racial bigotry. For days, the story dominated the British media as well as Chancellor of the Exchequer Gordon Brown's official visit to India, which coincidentally overlapped with the *Celebrity Big Brother* incidents. When questioned there about the shabby treatment of one of India's film stars, Brown underscored that countless Britons, "like me, are determined to send a message worldwide that we want nothing to interfere with Britain's reputation as a country of fairness and tolerance. We are against any forms of racism and intolerance" (Nathan & Robertson 2007). In the end, eighty-two per cent of viewers phoning in succeeded in voting Goody off the show, and Shetty emerged the winner. Many commentators condemned such views, effectively using Goody's behavior as a platform to demonstrate their own multicultural credentials and argue that her attitudes were those of a disreputable minority (Vasagar 2007).

Later asked why she called her "Shilpa Poppadum," Goody explained that "she wanted to use an Indian name and the only word she could think of was an Indian food" (Kirby 2007). When interviewed following her departure from the show, Goody unsurprisingly denied that her comments were racist, immediately adding, "I love chicken curry" (J. [Jade] Goody 2007). Within a Britain sharply divided about the extent of racism and its forms of expression, South Asian cuisine's familiarity and popularity continues to generate narratives proclaiming tolerance at the same time that it inflects and structures racist outbursts. Once marginalized within British culture, curry became a primary vehicle for denying, masking, and articulating racism, demonstrating the mutually constitutive nature of intolerance and multicultural celebration.

NOTES

1. The spread of "ethnic" restaurants does not invariably correspond with the presence of a substantial immigrant population of the same origins within a national

or local context. As Turgeon and Pastinelli (2002: 255) argue, in Quebec "the demand for ethnic restaurants appears highest where immigrants are few and far between. When foreign people are absent, they are represented, even given material form, by way of the restaurant."

2. Between 1810 and 1812, Dean Mahomed ran the "Hindostanee Coffee House" in London, which offered Indian cuisine, décor, and hookahs to customers, many of whom were men who had once served in India.

3. Other edible colonial products first found their foothold in Europe through tastes cultivated among returned colonizers. On the introduction of chocolate into Spain see Norton 2006.

4. That many of Britain's Asian eateries opening in the 1950s and 1960s owed their origins to the needs of itinerant men who moved far from their families to find work bears resemblance to the spread of what Frank Conlon calls "utilitarian public dining" within India (Conlon 1995: 98–99).

5. Portrayals of the entry of foreign food as akin to assault have recurred in other national contexts (Ferguson 2005).

6. *British Eating Out* (1966) found that 8 percent of Britons had visited an Indian restaurant at some point, with regional variations reflecting immigrants' geographical concentration. In London and Birmingham 11 and 9 percent, respectively, had done so.

7. Gender issues within the curry house culture merit far more attention than they can receive here. While the "boys' night out" clientele has been joined by more women diners, couples, and families in recent decades, what has changed little is the rarity of Asian women seen working at such establishments. Visible owners, managers, and waiters are almost exclusively male. The fact that "Indian" restaurants are largely run by Muslim families of Bangladeshi and Pakistani origin is clearly relevant in determining the inputs of family labor at these businesses—not only by restricting the visible roles of women, but also by relying upon an extended kinship network more generally (U. Narayan 1997; Srinivasan 1995; Brah & Shaw 1992; Ram, Abbas, Sanghera, Barlow, & Jones 2001; A. Basu 2002; Basu & Altinay 2003).

8. Scholars differ markedly in their assessments of the status implications of patronizing "ethnic" restaurants (contrast Warde, Martens, & Olsen 1999; Warde & Martens 2000; with Finkelstein 1989). Although many Britons opting for Asian restaurants in the 1980s appear to have been middle class, many seemingly ranked such visits as an everyday, and rather lowly, dining event as opposed to a "fancy" meal eaten on a special night out. The social position of the ethnic groups both producing and consuming the food in question, as well as the occasions when diners patronize particular establishments, clearly play a role in shaping how these dining experiences are evaluated both by the individuals involved and a wider public.

9. The emphasis placed upon Asian restaurateurs having adapted their cuisine to suit Britons is revealing. As Will Kymlicka has argued, the British government's "idea of respecting diversity is not defended as something whose benefits outweigh its costs, but rather as something that costs nothing to native-born citizens, and asks or expects nothing from them in terms of adaptation" (2003: 205).

10. For tourism information, see www.visitbradford.com.

11. See "Rusholmecurry.co.uk: An Online Service for Manchester's Curry Mile," http://www.rusholmecurry.co.uk, accessed on June 8, 2005; "Taste of Asia Weekend Restaurant Offers," http://www.visitleicestershire.com/shortbreaks/asia restaurants.htm, accessed on June 6, 2005.

12. Yunus Khalil and Omar Shakur, interviews with the author, Birmingham, England, May 26 and June 14, 2005.

13. Many "high street" curry houses also adopted colonial-inspired names as well, with establishments called Passage to India, Last Days of the Raj, Memsahib, et cetera opening throughout the 1980s.

14. http://www.realindianfood.com, accessed on June 22, 2004.

15. Foreign cuisines not associated with large immigrant groups whose members commonly arrived to work in factories may well stand better chances of gaining a reputation as cosmopolitan and upscale. Sushi's sophisticated connotations in North America and Western Europe can be linked to cultural imagery surrounding Japan (as a wealthy, high-tech nation visited by Western business travelers) without contending with the burden of a contentious history of immigration (see Bestor 2000).

NINE

Global Flows, Local Bodies

DREAMS OF PAKISTANI GRILL IN MANHATTAN

Krishnendu Ray

A DEFINITIVE STUDY of immigration proposed by the Committee on International Migration of the Social Science Research Council of the United States, titled *Immigration Research for a New Century* (Foner, Rumbaut, & Gold 2000), underlines the saliency of race, language, and gender, yet it lists neither the body nor embodiment in its index and section bibliographies.[1] Such an omission has greater significance when it persists in the new edition of a self-consciously interdisciplinary and theoretically attuned volume such as *Migration Theory* (Brettell & Hollifield 2008), where the migrant's body is once again only indirectly visible and never an object of theoretical attention. Another current instance invokes the missing immigrant body. The September 2009 issue of the *Asian Studies Review* highlights "Globalization and Body Politics," drawing attention to "how global processes play out in specific sites" especially at the level of the body (Mackie & Stevens 2009: 257). A final instigation for underscoring the need for theoretical attention to immigrant bodies is the 2011–2012 call for dissertation proposals by the Social Science Research Council of the United States, which contends that "Research on migration and gender has changed considerably since the 1980s," and yet, it goes on to argue, few scholars of migration have drawn on sophisticated theories of embodiment to investigate processes of movement.[2]

It is now almost three decades since Bryan S. Turner published *The Body and Society* (1984), which was one among a number of early sociological texts to pay sustained theoretical attention to the body.[3] Turner's synthesis sought to account for the path-breaking theorizations of Michel Foucault and practices of the social movements of feminism and civil rights that centered on this tactile, tangible thing, the color, texture and gender of the body. Now the field is crowded theoretically,[4] yet it is apparent that the sociology of immigration on the one hand, and theories of taste, embodiment, and practice on the other hand, are developing in separate realms. Much of the sociology of the body continues to be devoted to broad theoretical speculation focused on gender, sexuality, and disease, belying the sense that all social action, including immigration, is always embodied.[5] I think studies of immigration demand a dose of corporeality, and that theories of embodiment could benefit from a diverse body of empirical research, and that is what I will do in this chapter.[6]

Immigrant foodways should provide a naturally fecund site to interrogate such an intersection, yet, in the sociology of food we have learned a lot about what customers seek and get in eating ethnic food (typically assumed to be the food of recent and diacritically marked immigrants), which nevertheless summarily dismisses any volition or aspiration on the part of the immigrant producer of food, outside of economic necessity (Johnston & Baumann 2007; Warde & Martens 2000; Warde, Martens, & Olsen 1999). Even when born of economic necessity, there is more to the story of immigrant restaurants than distinction, domination, and deployment of cultural capital. By inserting the habits, memories, work, and dreams of immigrant entrepreneurs into the discussion of taste, this study contributes to a fuller understanding of global flows and modes of localization—bodies are always somewhere, and, as we shall see, they are often trying to make room for themselves in that place.

My work focuses on the "ethnic" restaurateur because he or she is the hinge between taste and toil, globalization and localization, two streams of theoretical accounts that could be put in productive conversation with each other. I am interested in the process of designing a restaurant by an immigrant entrepreneur. By design I mean not only the physical infrastructure, but the concept, the menu, and the ways of reproducing it through investment, recruitment of labor, recipes, and cooking. I use the word *design* because it relates the body to space, economics to aesthetics, habits to consciousness, inhabitance in a locale to global gastronomic discourse.

The immigrant body is imprinted with the history of its unconscious habits, made visible and audible by its displacement. An immigrant is an inverted anthropologist, flowing in the wrong direction in the incline of global hierarchies, but with the same advantages of awareness of the tacit dimensions of a practiced body and everyday experience because of the very act of displacement. An accent is nothing but the memory of an old language; posture and gesture a dated hexis; tastes, those of a misplaced locale. Yet, those very tastes, now demanded by a roving cosmopolitan appetite, must be fed in a furious gesture of appeasement. Immigrant hands and imaginations must be put to work. We have heard a lot about the body and food from anthropologists, it is time to hear from immigrants precisely about that experience of displacement and the kinds of knowledge that might produce, with or without disciplinary consecration. That is where Muhammad Rasool enters the picture.

. . .

Muhammad Rasool, the owner of Bread & Butter, came to New York City from Lahore, Pakistan, in the summer of 1988.[7] "Never, ever, get into the restaurant business" he insists, laughing out loud. Nevertheless, when asked, "So, how did you get into the restaurant business?" he launches into a tale of some depth and density:

MUHAMMAD RASOOL (MR): You see I did odd jobs. Worked in a gas station for a couple of months. I had been driving a Yellow Cab for six to seven months. That is when I ate at a restaurant on Forty-second Street. It was very crowded and the people were rude. That is where I got the idea that I should have a restaurant. I drove taxi for nine more months, saved some money. I didn't know anything about restaurants. I had never cooked. I drove taxi at night to pay my workers.

INTERVIEWER (I):[8] *How would you characterize your restaurant?*

MR: Fast food restaurant. Indian, Pakistani spicy food. I also carry less spicy Spanish American food.

I: *Spanish American?*

MR: Yes, because you see we have rice and we have beans and chicken, of course, everyone eats. It is the same food without spices. Spanish food.

I: *How did you come to name your restaurant Bread & Butter?*

MR: You see, I used to call it Taj Mahal, but my business was not working and I was unhappy. Day after day I dragged my tired body home on that [commuter] train. One day I fell asleep. The train jolted to a halt. I woke up and looked around . . . which is when it came to me. No one, not one person in this compartment knows what Taj Mahal is, but each one of them knows about bread and butter, so to make my business run I had to change the name to Bread & Butter!

Bread & Butter sits at a dense intersection of a cross-street and an avenue in Lower Manhattan. It is barely visible from across the wide street, caught in a whirl of honking cars, buses spewing fumes, and illegally parked trucks on hurried delivery runs. A crush of pedestrians weave their way to and fro from the subway station, stepping among untreated epileptics dozing off mid-pavement, and mistreated schizophrenics reduced to panhandling. Among them Nigerian, Bangladeshi, and Chinese vendors peddle fruits and veg-etables, knock-off handbags, pirated DVDs, cheap jewelry, and knick-knacks. The physical pressure of the packed sidewalk brings the customers stumbling across the threshold of Bread & Butter. The storefront restaurant never takes the customer very far from the dust and noise of the pavement.

As I enter the long narrow store, the steam table is on my left behind a glass counter and a sneeze-guard, with its row of twenty cooked items ready to be ladled onto styrofoam plates. The whole length of the wall on the right is covered with mirrors. Squeezed between the mirrored wall and the steam table are eight two-tops (small tables) with sixteen chairs, and a narrow path leading to the kitchen. When asked about the particulars of the venture he responds:

MR: I need a place until my children finish school. I have to make it work. This place was being run by a friend of mine who was taking in $500 a day. He wanted to get out. I sold some family property in Pakistan to pay down the $20,000. I put in $10,000, maybe $15,000, to renovate the place. My rent is $8,000 a month. I sell on average $6.00 per customer. I have about one hundred customers a day. Twenty for breakfast, sixty for lunch, twenty for dinner.

I: *Do you cook at home?*

MR: No.

I: *Where did you learn how to cook?*

MR: It is easy. I know it.

I: *Did you train for it?*

MR: No.

I: *You just know it?*

MR: Yes. . . . It does not take a genius.

I: *Who cooks at home?*

MR: My wife.

I: *Did your wife give you the recipes?*

MR: No.

I: *Do you consult cookbooks?*

MR: No.

I: *Did you watch your wife cook?*

MR: No, but she gave me confidence. She didn't tell me how to cook, but she gave me confidence. If you don't know how to cook then your partners take advantage of you. Once I called my wife on the phone and asked her how to make *aloo-gobi* and she told me how to do it. Then I did it. I ask her, how do I cook this, how do I cook that? She tells me. I do it. It does not take a genius you know. . . . You see this Mexican guy who works for me? He learned just by watching me. Now he is my best cook. It is business. It is only business. It is not real. People come in, they take a look at it and think it must take all these people to make complicated things. But it is simple. It is business. It is just business.

There are a number of things to note here. First, the failure of the interview as a tool to elicit tacit knowledge about cooking, which forced me to redesign the study to deploy more ethnographic techniques to get at doing. Second, there is something more going on here; something about language (that I cannot press on without Punjabi—the interviews were conducted in Hindi and English), something about doing, about the social embarrassment of cooking and middle-class Lahorean masculinity that I cannot put my finger on. Rasool does not embody the skills of cooking that his wife can lay claims to, what he does incorporate is the taste of the real thing and he tries to mobilize that memory to feed his imagined cabbie customer. Furthermore, Rasool's insistence that what we have here is mere commerce and not culture is echoed in diasporic Indian newspapers' sparse coverage of commercial cookery. For instance, two major expatriate Indian weekly newspapers—*India Abroad* and *India Tribune*—have carried about two dozen stories on the culture of cooking per year from 2000 to 2010. Yet every issue has numerous advertisements from people hoping to buy or sell restaurants, and many classifieds looking for tandoor and curry cooks.

Based on a systematic analysis of the coverage of food articles in *India Abroad* over the last decade I can say that there are at least three kinds of food-related copy. The most common are advertisements for sweetshops such as Rajbhog Sweets, and restaurants such as Hot Wok Village, which serves "authentic Bombay style Chinese cuisine." All of this talk about food is situated in the realm of commerce, not culture, in Rasool's words. Then there are occasional interviews with food writers with excerpts from their cookbooks (Pais 2003: M14). Most of those write-ups conclude with a page of recipes written by women for women (if one follows the pictures). In a typical year there are also a handful of articles about the virtues of Ayurveda, such as "Food that Heals" (Krishnan 2003). Finally, there are rare features on restaurants such as Café Spice, written by Arthur Pais (2003), and Café Goa, by Jeet Thayil, (both men), or "A Bite of Tamarind" by Pais (2010) and "The Magic of Tabla" by Aseem Chhabra (2010).

The primary focus of the food articles in these newspapers is to collate a pan-Indian cuisine in the diaspora, introducing the readers to dishes from "elsewhere" in India, such as Goan fish curries, Bengali sweets, Andhraite pickles, and so on—a theme Arjun Appadurai noted in his seminal article on cookbooks in the Indian national space in 1988, which appears to have been extended to the diaspora today. The addressee is the female domestic cook who wishes to introduce some regional variation into her cooking for her family or for a party. The assumption is that the audience of her food will be mostly her children and expatriate Indians from her own linguistic state or elsewhere in India.

Unlike what has happened in major American newspapers (see K. Ray 2008), aesthetic and gastronomic discussions centered on restaurants are relatively rare in *India Abroad* and *India Tribune*. Both these expatriate newspapers have a cautious, middle-brow approach to food, contained mostly within discourses of domesticity, and reflect the tastes of Anglophone, achieving, middle-class Indian men in the United States. That approach sits quite well with Rasool's valorization of his wife's cooking, the presumed realm of culture in his understanding, which he will not put up for sale.

FOOD MATTERS

No one orders the vindaloo at Bread & Butter. It is too expensive at $7.95. It may also be a bit too much for the crowd it caters to, but it is right there in smudged ink at number twenty-three on the menu: "A piquant Chicken/Lamb/Goat curry from the famed Beach City of Goa, meat marinated in a unique spicy 'masala' w/Cumin seeds & Potatoes." The language is formulaic, magical, ritual-like in its ubiquity here and in all low-cost Indian restaurants, and points to something sad and touching, obvious and insistent, revealed by the momentary confusion of a young man. Sebastian D'Souza is an American-born Bangladeshi, who manages Sonar Bangla, one of the downtown Indian restaurants along with a group of six intricately linked brothers and uncles. When asked whether some of the food in the restaurant is similar to the food served at home, he surprisingly picks the vindaloo. He says, "Yes, of course, we have it often at home. . . . My mother cooks it. Like most Bengalis we love our vindaloo." His father hastens to explain, "We are Catholic Bangladeshis, and vindaloo is Portuguese. So we have it often." The vindaloo partly refers to an imagined geography of South Asia for people who have never crossed national borders (because we reserve special suspicions for each other).

Then there are problems of translation. On studying the menus of 188 Indian restaurants in Manhattan, I was intrigued to find that kachori was listed on the menu in the following way:[9] "too different to put into words, but recommended" at Amin; "too difficult to put into words, but recommended" at Bombay Grill, Baluchi's, India Place, Indigo, Indian Bistro, Sitar; Kachori Chaat "ask an Indian friend" at Chennai; "deep fried lentil pastry w/mash potatoes, chic peas, & 3 sauces" at Kinara's. It is interesting how kachori got on the menu and came to be named through a series of borrowings; and why is it so susceptible to plagiarism? What are the specific problems of translation that motivates the restaurateur to give up (and then try to seduce us with his cheekiness)? Analogously, I was drawn to how the vindaloo got on the menu; what the recipe for it is; how it is made at Bread & Butter and at Sonar Bangla; how that vindaloo relates to Sebastian's mom's cooking in Queens; how Floyd Cardoz's "South Indian Mushroom Soup" with tamarind at the high-status and high-priced Tabla may or may not be a riff on it, while simultaneously fleeing from it; why Madhur Jaffrey's menu at Dawat (an association she now disavows) puts its duck "vindaloo" within quotation marks? I pursue these questions elsewhere. But for now I can see that such issues point to a ratio of configuration between immigrant bodies, urban demand, and cosmopolitan gastronomic discourse through which the menu is constructed. The story of the kachori and the vindaloo connects the problem of transplanting durable dispositions, failure of language, to inhabitance in a new place, and the social work of the imagination of migrants. But dreams are not only made of the quest for a better analogue for the kachori. They are more substantial.

DREAMS OF PAKISTANI GRILL: "BEAUTIFUL LIKE AN AMERICAN PLACE"

I: *If you could change this place . . . to make it your dream place, what would you do?*

MR: I will take this mirror out and put the picture there such as the scenery of Mohenjodaro that hangs in the Pakistan Consulate.

I will put a small stand there with three containers of soup. I will sell cheap soup, self-service soup, pita bread and put a grill there: serve shawarma, chicken shawarma, lamb shawarma. I will put the clay oven, the tandoor, there. I will get a young guy with a cap [toque] on his head. We will just have meats in the tandoor and salads. I will call it Pakistani Grill!

I would open a big restaurant . . . still an Indian Pakistani place but beautiful like an American place. I might even be able to name it Pakistani Grill, now I cannot call this place Pakistani. I write that in my language [Urdu], but if I write it in any other language it will drive some of my customers away. I can't afford that.

The sociological discussion of taste after Pierre Bourdieu (1984) has developed as a retort to philosophical concerns. In philosophy, there is a long discussion on the distinctions between sensory taste and aesthetic taste, as recuperated by a number of recent theorists such as Carolyn Korsmeyer (1999) and Allen Weiss (2002). In *Distinction,* Bourdieu critiques aesthetic taste as nothing more transcendental than durable class dispositions, which he polarizes between the tastes of necessity—heavy, sweet, rich, unselfconscious comestibles—and tastes of luxury, which is the realm of choice and restraint that involves the preference for smaller, bitter, lighter, subtler flavors and portions. Parts of Bourdieu's theory of distinction could be criticized for tying class too closely to certain foods eternally, when things, such as polenta, could begin as the heavy food of the poor, but over time climb up the class hierarchy, and whole cuisines could fall down the ladder, such as Continental, say, among American gastronomes. But Bourdieu's more powerful argument is one about relative position-taking in the field of gastronomy. Tastes can change, some things find greater favor among gastronomes and some things fall in estimation, but a hierarchy remains in place in spite of the changes. Bourdieu's field theory can account for such changes as polenta climbing up and iceberg lettuce falling in estimation.

Yet the status hierarchy as such does not interest me, partly because it has been overworked in the sociological literature. What does intrigue me is the toil—practice, repetitions, rehearsals, imaginative leaps (Calhoun & Sennett 2007)—that goes into the entrepreneurial deployment of immigrant understandings of metropolitan tastes. There is a substantial sociological discussion of entrepreneurial toil, especially of immigrants. There are a number of parts to the theory of ethnic entrepreneurship. The commonalities persist despite the nuanced distinctions between, say, Ivan Light's ethnic entrepreneur model, Alejandro Portes' ethnic enclave frame, and Roger Waldinger's ethnic niche theory (Heisler 2008; Zhou 2004; Granovetter 1995; Portes 1995; Sassen 1995; Light and Bonacich 1988; Waldinger 1986; Landa 1981; Light 1972). For the purposes of this chapter those distinctions do not matter. For the level of analysis that is productive to my purpose here, a number of things must be noted. First, low capital cost makes it relatively easier for ethnic entrepreneurs to enter into the business of feeding others. Cultural capital—knowledge about unfamiliar foods—gives them a competitive edge over better-capitalized mainstream entrepreneurs in the niche market. Social capital—kin or fictive kin (unrelated members of village, town, neighborhood or caste who are treated as if they are family members) networks of loyalty that allows the lending of money on a rotating basis without collateral—enables ethnic entrepreneurs to raise the necessary cash for a small eatery without the required assets. Self-exploitation—long hours of work and unpaid labor of kin and fictive kin—permits these enterprises to compete with better-capitalized businesses, and turns sweat and loyalty into capital. Finally, and most importantly for our purposes, both migration and entrepreneurship exhibit serial patterns. That is, people who know each other and come from the same regions work in and own similar enterprises, built with money and expertise borrowed from co-ethnics. They effectively develop an informal, intra-ethnic consulting and banking system. Paucity of assets to collateralize loans and unfamiliarity with language and norms of a consumer society deepens the dependence on co-ethnic money, information, and cultural expertise.[10] This, of course, is a broad prototype of an explanation, and a structural one, that needs to be fleshed out with the real activity of real agents. The structural model cannot explain, for instance, why and how the first Bangladeshi or Pakistani entered into the Indian restaurant business in New York City. That demands biographies and interpretive inquiries, which brings us back to Rasool.

Rasool came to the United States with the burdens of feeding his body and using it to feed his customers and his household. He came with his morals, motivations, and aesthetic standards, all practically developed in the preceding social context. His tongue, taste, and hands were tied to the Lahorian lower-middle-class milieu when he immigrated at the age of thirty-seven. He learned to deploy his body, especially his hands and his tongue (both for talk and taste) in the midst of a dispositional crisis under the scrutiny of others. He brought memories of things he had eaten, but never cooked, morals entwined with a division of labor at home and at work, and an insistent distinction between commerce and culture. He has crafted his place in this world that is not of his own making, and in the process has supplied what was demanded of his labors, turning his culture into commerce, which he resists and profits from. Rasool had to develop a sense of his city, and yoke his senses to the making of a living in that city.

The ongoing sociological discussion—of taste, ethnic entrepreneurship, changing gastronomic categories, field theory, shared meaning in restaurant work, and professional identity—can only partially account for Rasool.[11] Not in the sense that no sociology can ever fully explain an individual and his trajectory, but in the sense that sociologists have failed to stop by his eatery, look at his menu, ask for his recipes, or even ask him to explain transformations of taste in the city.[12] Let me illustrate the problem of the current discussion on "ethnic food" as developed without asking immigrants like Rasool, who design the entrepreneurial venture to supply that ethnic food (which is different still from those who work the grills and tandoors, but I do not have the space to develop those differences here).

. . .

Rasool and many like him have peopled American cities for centuries. They have cooked, developed recipes in an implicit dialogue between their bodies and others, crystallized that dialogue in thousands and thousands of menus strewn in archives, on the web, and many more erased without a trace, thrown away as ephemera. Rarely have we ever taken the practical knowledge of a person like Rasool as a point of departure for social scientific analysis.[13] That may be a product of the tendency to see discussions of taste as marginal to the real lives of marginal peoples. In this habit of mind, taste is a matter of elites and emulation—a continuing shadow of the notion of Culture with a capital C, which is precisely the target of Bourdieu's *Distinction*. Sociologists have been so busy proving over and over again that taste is still hierarchical, in spite of apparent omnivorousness, that they have not bothered to listen to people trapped at the receiving end of the sociological hierarchy. In this conception, poor people can only teach us about poverty and suffering, hierarchy and symbolic violence, maybe even racism, but never about taste. That blindness is a function of the exclusive focus on consumption, rather than the production of possible options. It is a problem that is prefigured in Bryan Turner's contention that the recent eruption of the body in academic studies is related to the transition whence the "laboring body has become a desiring body" in advanced, Western, postindustrial, consumer societies (1984: 2). Yet, there is work to be done, and if we forget the conditions of production of possibilities of leisure and pleasure we are liable to be blind to the transactions in taste between producers, consumers, and numerous consecrated and consecrating intermediaries.[14] As a consequence, taste loses its contested, dynamic, and, I would argue, even fundamentally sociological nature and become a mere means in the metaphysics of endless oppression or varieties of virtuous consumption.[15]

Taste is transactional and people who deploy taste, literal taste, as cultural capital, do not do so under conditions of their choosing. Even when we are acquiring cultural capital through our talk of taste, the choices of what cuisine we use to make such an argument are neither infinite nor randomly open to us. They are framed within the historical structure of immigration, conquest, tourism, and trade. What does the entrepreneurial immigrant body and memory bring to the metropolitan transaction in taste? That is the central question that needs to be addressed.

VADA PAO: MUMBAI STREET FOOD IN NEW YORK CITY

When Rasool was asked, "Do you look at online reviews of your restaurant?" he provided a desultory response. It was clear that the social location of Rasool, who was unable or unwilling to play in the gastronomic discourse of Manhattan and Brooklyn, is very different from the position of another entrepreneur I want to bring into the picture now. She also conveys a very different approach to the embodied materiality of cooking and entrepreneurship. She carries much of the palatal sense of her preimmigration being and is also successful in translating her practices to perform in the gastronomic field of Manhattan. And she has the advantages of a little more money than Rasool, and a lot more cultural capital. Her location is also quite distinct from Rasool's.

Vada Pao is indistinguishable from any small West Village eatery. It is narrower than Bread & Butter, sitting more tightly between a number of restaurants—some Indian, others not. The sidewalk is slender but less crowded, with hardly a delinquent in sight. The foot traffic is younger, calmer, and whiter, wandering rather than headed anywhere with grim purpose and raw ambition. When we entered Vada Pao in the early afternoon, the sidewalk was devoid of traffic and the place appeared to be slowly stirring from a tropical siesta. The only things missing were a slowly whirring ceiling fan muddling the heat amongst the creeping bougainvillea.

Chitrita Mukherjee (CM) is the entrepreneur behind Vada Pao.[16] She is thirty-four years old, a comfortably anglophone Indian immigrant, born in Calcutta (now Kolkata), but dreaming up a place like Mumbai (Bombay) in New York City. When we asked her, "What would be your ethnic self-identification?" she seamlessly suggested the more transnational and cosmopolitan phrase "South Asian," rather than the narrower "Indian." Rasool's imaginary was tied to the nation and the taxi-driver's occupation in the big city. Mukherjee's connection was to the world and her professional training as a designer. Her culinary handiwork has garnered substantial critical attention in the world of gastronomic discourse as "a sleek sandwich shop that specializes in upmarket spins on Bombay-style street food, with a focus on pao—meat and vegetable sammies served like sliders on ghee-griddled buns."

A Portion of Vada Pao's Menu

Pao Sliders or Kathi Roll: Choose any filling below:

Vada

Potato, chickpea flour, coconut garlic chutney

Bhaji

Mix vegetables, kutchumber salad, lemon juice

Chappli Kebab

Ginger, chilli garlic ketchup, tomatoes, lettuce

Shami Kebab

Minced lamb, lentil, kutchumber salad, mint yogurt

Tandoori Pulled Goat Leg

Kutchumber salad, cilantro, lemon juice, Mexican sour cream

Parsi Beef Keema
Mince beef, coriander cumin masala, tomato

I: *What is the concept here?*

CM: Vada pao has a very strong, authentic, regional identity as Mumbai street food. Plus we wanted to streamline our operations. We went with our interpretation of the pao as a slider.

I: *What brought you to this?*

CM: I came to the United States to do my master's in architecture and urban design at Columbia University. I was attracted by the Parson School's program in lighting. I got my master's in lighting design.

I: *How did you get to food?*

CM: I was fascinated by the food scene here [in the United States]. We loved all the choices available to us. We thought Indian food had this market gap where you could find very expensive, good Indian food, or two-day-old curries. We wanted fresh Indian food, which would be portable, sold at a value price, to students and young professionals. To people like us.

I: *How did you get the original idea of Naanini [her concept prior to Vada Pao]?*

CM: Once I was sitting around with my friend. We were trying to brainstorm. There happened to be a naan at home. We had some curries too, so we wrapped it in a naan and grilled it on a tawa—which is essentially an Indian griddle. We thought "Okay, this would make a good sandwich." This is where the whole idea of the naanini came about. We called up our girlfriends and offered it to them. They liked it. We developed the concept further.

I: *So that is not something you would get in India?*

CM: No, that is not something that you would get in India.

I: *Were you thinking about doing traditional Indian food at all?*

CM: No, we were thinking of basically using our experiences and our backgrounds. The kind of foods we would like to eat—the global Indian with a background in India coming here, exposed to different food and different cultures, and therefore more willing to try out different foods.

I: *You are Bengali, why not a Kolkata (Calcutta) concept?*

CM: I don't think the repertoire of Kolkata street food is large enough to provide us with a range. You have kathi roll (which we have), jhaal muri, puchka. The Bombay repertoire both works better and is underserved. For instance, a Delhi concept would also work with parathas and kebabs. But no one does vada pao—only two or three places do it in Queens, but they don't do it right. Plus a slider works as a good translation of pao.

I: *Is the Delhi concept crowded?*

CM: Yes. . . . In a sense that is generic Indian restaurant food now.

I: *I was surprised by the name Vada Pao, because it is so local and specific. Weren't you afraid that it might not make any sense to your audience?*

CM: Yes, I worry about it. My fallback position [laughs] is that I can always go back to lighting design if the concept fails.

I: *How many customers do you have on a typical weekday and on the weekend? If you were to guess their demographics, what would it be? What is your check average?*

CM: We have about 100 customers on a typical weekday. And about 150 customers on an average weekend day. My weekday and late night customers are about 30% visibly Indian and 70% non-Indian, probably young professionals and students. On weekends I have more Indian families coming from New Jersey and Philadelphia for the stuffed parathas and now vada pao. My check average is between $8–$9.

I: *What were your thoughts in designing this place?*

CM: Lower-end version of high-end cuisine. A lot of our design was influenced by trying to do it in the cheap and yet make a statement. Since the concept is Mumbai street food, we wanted to put up a large image of the VT train station [in Mumbai]. Earlier, this wall had a plain finish, now it is a textured finish, a slightly unfinished look, a little like a *dhaba*. For the tables I wanted to get a distressed look as in a *dhaba*—Indian street food eatery—where tables have a lot of graffiti. But instead of graffiti we wanted iconic Mumbaiker imageries, such as of the cricketer Sachin Tendulkar.

I: *Are the cooks Indian?*

CM: I have two Indians (one Gujarati, one Mumbaiker), one Mexican, and one Nepali in the kitchen. The cook is Indian, Goanese, who has cooked at the Taj in Bombay, then he worked on a ship (that is how he came here), and he has worked in a couple of restaurants here in the United States.

I: *Did the cook bring his recipes or did you teach him all the recipes?*

CM: Well, a little of both. He knew how to make chicken tikka, achari chicken, and bhaji. We asked him to follow our recipes, and the spice mix is our own.

I: *Did you consider hiring a chef who was not of Indian origin?*

CM: We didn't know where to source the chef. We were asking our friends in the Indian restaurant business and putting ads in Indian newspapers. That is where we were getting our chefs. That is how we got Mohan.

I: *You said you cook at home. How did you learn to cook?*

CM: I come from a joint family with 13–14 people. Sunday would be a day when everyone cooked something. It was very competitive. I had an uncle who had studied for a hotel management degree, but did not pursue a career in it. Yet, every time we would make a dish he would ask us to break it down, analyze it. That is something I took for granted. I thought if this is going to be my vision, then I should put together the menu and the recipes.

I: *How would you characterize your relationship to the media?*

CM: For the first time we have a PR rep. We were covered very early on by *New York Magazine*. It seems Florence Fabricant came and ate here and wrote about us. I did not even know that she had eaten here until I saw the write up.

I: *Do you read online reviews?*

CM: Yes, all the time. We have a Google alert; every time someone posts something on Yelp or Menupages we get a notification. I read it.

I: *Has customer feedback influenced your concept?*

CM: No, I wouldn't say that it has. But it has influenced our service. Most of the feedback is that the food is good, but the wait is too long or the service is bad. I make use of customer feedback to inform the cooks and servers.

TRANSACTIONS IN TASTE

Rasool and Mukherjee have designed their restaurants in Manhattan within the constraints of their material, symbolic, and bodily resources (of skill and imagination). One started with a $35,000 investment, a bachelor's degree (from Pakistan), and the limits of his Punjabi-Pakistani masculine habitus. He didn't know how to cook and he still doesn't. He doesn't want to cook. That is women's work, maybe even servant's labor (perhaps commerce, but differently configured). His food, his location in the city, his labor force, the limits of his skills and imagination has set his restaurant adrift from even any generic notion of Indian food. I walk past his restaurant almost every day, morning and evening. He is there outside on the phone, never cooking or serving. I have rarely seen a visibly South Asian customer in there. Rasool characterizes his customer base as "5% Indian and 95% local." What he is selling more than anything else is gyros, french fries, and chicken curry and rice for lunch and dinner; eggs, toast, and coffee for breakfast. Less than six months after the interview, the Urdu sign was gone, replaced by two large signs announcing "$5.00 lunch or dinner." Since he does not cook, his menu and recipes are drifting more and more towards the habitus of his "Mexican" cooks and their joint understanding of American tastes. With less capital and less embodied skill, Rasool's transaction with his customer has to concede a lot more ground than Mukherjee's. She, on the other hand, responds to her customers' demands for better service, but not for different food. She is more successful at translating the pao as a slider, which is a product of her greater familiarity with Anglophone American popular culture than Rasool's.

Rasool does not want his three grown children or his wife to work in his restaurant. He has enough resources to be able to keep them away, unlike, for instance, the twelve Latino vendors of tacos, tamales, and pupusas in Red Hook, Brooklyn, studied by Sharon Zukin (2010). What those vendors paid to regularize their carts wasn't much different from what Muhammad Rasool paid up front (about $35,000).[17] The financial difference is Rasool's rent of $8,000 per month. And Rasool's bachelor's degree, which gave him his competency in spoken English (although his first language is Punjabi), and his legal status made some difference in terms of applying for various permits and paperwork. Yet Zukin (2010) shows that the materially impoverished Red Hook vendors were quite successful in latching on to the gastronomic discourse of the city.[18] They effectively used numerous intermediaries, such as immigrant advocates and foodie bloggers, to successfully legitimize their vending and accumulate substantial cultural capital as an authentic urban space. In contrast, Rasool fails to draw himself into that discourse. Yet, he does have some degree of cultural capital, some of it embodied in his tongue as language and as taste, which he can remember but which his hands cannot replicate. Furthermore, he is forced to fit his somatic experience of Pakistani food into the category of Indian food, which for reasons either of translation or global hierarchical valuation appears to work better in Manhattan. Given the relative paucity of national cultural capital as a Pakistani, his origin is something else he has to concede to the demands of his audience. He resents that, given the work of imagining contested national communities in South Asia.

Rasool's cultural advantages are less than Mukherjee's, who came with almost $100,000, a master's degree from a premier American university, and the vocabulary of design that allowed her to connect the rough newness of the vernacular to the smooth texture of the cosmopolitan omnivore. Hence she can imagine that the common street foods of India can become containers of capital. For Rasool, they are a source of personal relish and social embarrassment. Approached through a designer's eyes, Mukherjee grasps their pop-cosmopolitan possibilities. But those are not her only advantages. She can cook, partly because as a South Asian woman of a particular cohort, she must. She could explain to us the art of making good stuffed parathas and the analogic taste of a kathi roll. Yet she also claims more than she can legitimately command when she erases her cook's somatic memory of making "chicken tikka, achari chicken, and bhaji" by suggesting that it is adequate to remember the process: "We asked him to follow our recipes, and the spice mix is our own."

But that is not the whole story either—of gender, generation, and class. In her words, her "hotel management uncle" in a large, middle-class Bengali family delivered an unusual familiarity with cooking, which is an extraordinary accomplishment against the grain of *bhadrolok* (proper, middle-class) masculinity. This is partly where biography exceeds sociology. Cooking skills and the ability to access what she calls a "global Indian" imaginary, accentuated by an accidental catering gig for the New York premier of *Slumdog Millionaire* (after which the call of the vada pao was more insistent), connects her to networks that are crucial to her self-conception as a successful entrepreneur and designer. As a designer, she has coped very well with fitting her bodily habits into a new, albeit tight, space in this large city, hinging her economics to aesthetics, habits to consciousness, and inhabitance in a locale to global gastronomic discourse.

Yet as a particular economic enterprise, Vada Pao failed to meet Mukherjee's income expectations and she had to close down her business. Rasool's restaurant survives today, two years after our interview, while Vada Pao was sold, replaced by another Bollywood concept. Rasool is more successful in his practice on that street corner between Papaya Dog and CVS, perhaps because he was never attuned to the global gastronomic "discourse" on Indian food. What I initially presumed to be Mukherjee's advantage—attention to the global hierarchy of taste—turned out to be her precise disadvantage, making her unfit to occupy the street corner she had landed on.

CODA

This chapter presses the argument beyond Bourdieu towards Loïc Wacquant's terminus at the black boxer's body in *Body & Soul,* where in an attempt to understand his milieu of young black men on the South Side of Chicago he had to take up boxing and build a reputation as Brother Louis (2004). Inversely, I have sought to understand what was obscure and confusing to me—my bodily practices as an immigrant. I have learned much about my body's place in a new world by following the bodies of other immigrants, which has driven me "to thematize the necessity of a sociology not only *of* the body, in the sense of object, but also *from* the body, that is, deploying the body as tool of inquiry and vector of knowledge" (Wacquant 2004: viii).

Furthermore, written words so define what we do in the university that there is a temptation to turn every aspect of the world into a text, and write the body out of it. Hence it is not at all a surprise that a cultural frame such as anthropology, in which tacit everyday knowledge is more important has most fully engaged with the body compared to almost any other discipline (see Connerton 1989; Lock 1993; Lock & Farquhar 2007; Seremetakis 1994; Counihan 1999; Sutton 2001; Herzfeld 2004). I show how recent sociological work on taste has gone about its task as if the corporeality of the body and the materiality of food didn't matter. I argue that the sociology of immigrant entrepreneurship must be stitched to theories of embodiment, and we must relearn to weave the sensual materiality of food into the analysis. The flaky puff of the kachori, laced with the brittle heat of dried red chilies, can be one tool in the transaction in taste between native and immigrant, even when the translation fails. Rasool and Mukherjee show us ways they use their bodies as tools and carry its burdens, animating their desires with the hunger of others, so that they can seed the new world with old habits and new aspirations. Globalization has spiked their dreams of elsewhere with new sensory demands on their bodies. Finally, in spite of all the global flows, locality still matters and it is constructed by cross-stitching the body to place over time.

A different version of this chapter was published in the journal *Food, Culture & Society* June 2011.

1. At the time of its publication (2000), Hancock et al. were already writing about how the somatic turn had compelled sociologists "to interrogate the place of embodiment in social life" (Hancock, Hughes, Jagger, Paterson, Russell, Tulle-Winton, & Tyler 2000: 10–11).

2. http://www.ssrc.org/fellowships/subcompetitions/dpdf-fellowship/4C9 C26B8-59F2-DF11-9D08-001CC477EC84/6CFB1EF9-5EF2-DF11-9D08 -001CC477EC84/

3. Norbert Elias's work, leading to (the late translation of) *The Civilizing Process* (1982) prefigured much of the sociological interest on the body, but was mostly ignored by anglophone sociologists. Although first published in 1939, it was not fully engaged with until the publication of Stephen Mennell's *All Manners of Food* (1985).

4. Within a decade there was an outpouring, such as Jaggar and Bordo (1989); Featherstone, Hepworth, & Turner (1991); Giddens (1991); Haraway (1991); Crownfield (1992); Butler (1993); Shilling (1993); Synnott (1993); Falk (1994); Grosz (1994); Winkler & Cole (1994). This outpouring was preceded by Foucault's writings (1967, 1980a, 1980b, etc.).

5. See critiques in B. S. Turner (1996); and Wacquant (1995 and 2004).

6. For a recent attempt in that direction, see Mackie and Steven (2009). See Mauss (1935/2007); Connerton (1989); Lock (1993); Seremetakis (1994); Sutton (2001); Herzfeld (2004); and Lock & Farquhar (2007).

7. Both the names of the owner and the restaurant have been changed.

8. All interviews were conducted by me and/or my research assistants, Sierra Burnett and Jaclyn Rohel.

9. Figuring out the answer to the simple question, how many Indian restaurants are there in New York City, turned out to be quite complex. Lists of Indian restaurants in Manhattan and Brooklyn, such as on MenuPages.com, were mostly accurate and updated. In November 2009 there were 202 such restaurants. The number of Indian restaurants in Queens was the most difficult to ascertain. First, there are no comprehensive lists. Combing through YellowPages, Yelp, and City Search we could identify 139 self-described Indian restaurants in Queens. But we soon realized that many of these Indian restaurants identified to be in Queens were often in New Jersey and other surrounding areas. So we had to match addresses with zip code and census tract data to impose county and city boundaries on the data. Furthermore, we realized that the YellowPages list was seriously outdated. We would often call the establishments listed as an Indian restaurant to find out that an Italian restaurant had replaced an Indian restaurant at that address over a decade ago. It appears then that YellowPages has no system of excising outdated information from its pages. A round of telephone calls reduced that list of 139 to 85 Indian restaurants in Queens—23 of these clustered in Jackson Heights, with

smaller clusters of about a dozen each in Richmond Hill, Flushing, and neighborhoods such as Long Island City. Adding all the numbers for all the counties that constitute New York City our best estimate is that there were 290 Indian restaurants in New York City in November 2009.

10. There is also some work on why and how some groups are better at converting cultural and social capital into financial capital, while others cannot do the same (Small 2009); and on conflicts between groups with differential entrepreneurial outcomes, such as African-Americans and Koreans (Light 1972; Park 1997).

11. Johnston & Baumann 2007; Rao, Monin, & Durand 2003, 2005; Warde & Martens 2000; Warde, Martens, & Olsen 1999; Ferguson 1998, 2004; Ferguson & Zukin 1995; Fine 1996; Waldinger 1986, 2001; Aldrich & Waldinger 1990; Bailey 1987; Berger & Piore 1980.

12. Gary Alan Fine (1995, 1996), Priscilla Parkhurst Ferguson (2004), and Rao et al. (2005) do pay attention to the details of menus, media, and recipes. But their concerns do not include immigrants and the processes of transplanting bodies. Sharon Zukin (2010), on the other hand, does consider immigrants, but not the processes of cooking, skill, and embodiment.

13. Since occupations and birthplace have been identified, beginning with the 1850 Census, the data shows a strong correlation between food service occupations and new immigrant groups. The foreign-born numerically dominate certain occupations, such as domestic servants, hotel and restaurant employees, hotelkeepers, saloon keepers and bartenders, traders and dealers in groceries, and bakers. In contrast, members of the so-called white-collar occupations, such as the clergy, lawyers, school teachers, government officials, and physicians, have mostly been native born. For example, in New York City in 1850, 70 percent of hotel and restaurant employees, and 80 percent of hotelkeepers were foreign born, mostly of Irish and German heritage. (This is in a context where the foreign born constituted about a third of the labor force.) Fifty years later, according to the 1900 Census, 63 percent of Hotel and Restaurant employees were foreign-born (Irish and German) and 65 percent of hotelkeepers were foreign-born (mostly German). Restaurant-keepers, a newly significant occupation by 1900, were 67 percent foreign-born at a time when foreign-born were about 50 percent of the population. Even by the 1950 Census, when the immigration wave had subsided, 64 percent of cooks in restaurants were foreign-born (Italians now at the top, followed by Greeks, Chinese, and Germans). The trend continues: according to the 2000 Census, 75 percent of cooks in New York City are foreign-born, but the dominant countries and regions of origin are now Mexico, Central America, the Caribbean Basin, South America, China, and the countries of the former USSR (Ruggles, Alexander, Genadek, Goeken, Schroeder, & Sobek 2010).

14. I have borrowed the very productive phrase "transactions in taste" from the title of Manpreet Janeja's book, *Transactions in Taste* (2009).

15. I recognize that my contention makes it necessary to listen to consumers in this transaction, and I will do so as I develop my project further, but for now, for

reasons of space and time, and given the underappreciation of the entrepreneurial immigrant project, I will concentrate on that interlocutor, to the exclusion of the customer and the cook.

16. Once again, the names and identities have been changed.

17. According to Sean Basinski of the Street Vendor Project, there are about 12,000 vendors in NYC (in 2009) out of which, in all probability, about 5,000 are food vendors (no one knows exactly, because more than one-half are illegal due to license caps). Major vendor languages of Lower Manhattan in 2009 were Bengali (21%), English (20%), Mandarin or Cantonese (15%), Farsi (10%), Fulani (8%), Arabic (7%), Spanish (6%), French (2%), Tibetan (2%), Urdu (2%), Wolof (2%) and other (5%). All data from Center for Urban Pedagogy and the Street Vendor Project (Center for Urban Pedagogy 2009).

18. The Red Hook vendors also don't seem to create a dichotomy between culture and commerce, and in fact frame their commercial venture as a cultural one, and I think that is one of the reasons they are more successful in playing to the gastronomic audience.

TEN

From Curry Mahals to Chaat Cafés

SPATIALITIES OF THE SOUTH ASIAN
CULINARY LANDSCAPE

Arijit Sen

ETHNIC RESTAURANTS and grocery stores play an important role in the creation of contemporary American urban culture. Difference, both symbolic and real, is expressed through cuisine and culinary practices in these sites. Increasingly such spaces are emerging in neighborhoods impacted by demographic, economic, and political restructuring and urban revitalization in American cities. Hole-in-the-wall eating spots, gourmet ghettos, and foodie places have become part of our urban experience. Various social stakeholders—what Nancy Fraser would call multiple publics (Fraser 1992)—interact and meet in these places making these locations part of a larger public realm where ethnic worlds intersect mainstream landscapes, and global culture is articulated in local forms. Sharon Zukin argues that such spaces serving global cuisine are sites where power, politics, and social and cultural hierarchies are made physical through architecture (Zukin 1995). Valle and Torres (describing Mexican restaurants in Los Angeles) argue that ethnic restaurants provide a critical infrastructure of conspicuous consumption and manufacture "the edible multicultural texts and symbols upon which a global city's pluralistic self image is constructed" (2000: 69). In these discussions one finds a common refrain that ethnic culinary spaces in urban America cannot be read as part of a landscape that is segregated, circumscribed, and distinct from mainstream. Rather these are sites of hybridity and cultural contact where multiple worlds, networks, processes, and agents interact with each other. These spaces, indeed, are contemporary multicultural public spaces.

In this chapter I will examine a South Asian Indian ethnic grocery store and fast-food restaurant called Vik's Distributors (henceforth Vik's) in the city of Berkeley. The following discussion will argue for a method of analysis that puts the material and symbolic processes of producing place as the primary analytic focus. Ethnicity is creatively reproduced during everyday life and social interactions between various individuals and groups (Barth 1969; Conzen, Gerber, Morawska, Pozzetta, & Vecoli 1992; Gans 1996; Sollors 1989; Stern & Cicala 1991; Waters 1990). The production of ethnic places involves an interactive and performative process during which various individuals and groups actively negotiate social boundaries (C. T. Sen 2009; Goffman 1959; Brubaker, Feischmidt, Fox, & Grancea 2006). A large part of my argument comes out of the theoretical position of scholars of interactionalism (Goffman 1973; Brubaker et al. 2006). Rogers Brubaker explains the performative production of culture and identity among ethnic groups can "best be understood if studied from below as well as from above, in microanalytic as well as macroanalytic perspective" (2006: xiv). He argues that if we only examine rhetorical production of ethnicity and culture at a macro level we encounter an illusion that erases beliefs, desires, hopes, and interests of ordinary people on the ground. Erving Goffman, in his work on behavior in social institutions, demonstrated how sociospatial boundaries sustain human interactions during everyday life. Front and back territories help maintain boundaries between multiple domains such as inside/outside, private/public, informal/formal, and community/civic. Places are like stages, encouraging interactive performances from users.

In addition, this chapter argues that in order to understand contemporary public places we need to understand the multiple forms of spatial behaviors that frame the experience of these sites (Bhabha 1994; Clifford 1997; Gupta & Ferguson 1992). In geographical literature one hears the term "spatialities" to explain the myriad perceptions, character, and lived experiences of the world around us (Bhaba 1994; Clifford 1997; Gupta & Ferguson 1992). This chapter ends with a discussion on the need to study multiple spatialities in order to understand contemporary ethnic food landscapes.

Dolores Hayden's and Setha Low's analyses of how identity is produced during concrete everyday activities and human interaction in specific places documents methods of analyzing spatiality (Hayden 1995; Low 2000). During such practices, architectural locations are imbued with meanings and memories, a process Hayden calls the production of place. Many such "places"—like the one described in this chapter—are not built by immigrants. Rather, place making refers to a process by which meaning, identity, and memories are attached to a place, even if these places were originally built by others.

Places can be read as evidence of human culture. Material culture scholars such as Bernard Herman have shown that buildings, objects, and landscapes can serve as valuable evidence to read culture practices and cultural encounters (Herman 1984). Others have analyzed taste (Ames 1992) and symbolic content of interior objects and furnishing (Grier 2010), buildings (Bishir, Brown, Lounsbury, & Wood 1990; Glassie 1975) layout (plan and juxtaposition of interior spaces) (Hubka and Kenny 2000; Groth 1994) and landscapes (Upton 1994) as material registers of cultural contact. In her description of Mississippi blues joints, Jennifer Nardone examines human experiences of material landscapes (Nardone 2003). According to her, the location, interior layout, signage, and lights on the building facade and the experience of walking through a juke joint reproduce familiar and recognizable spaces for members of the in-group. However, outsiders are oblivious of these places, or they feel unwelcome because of their unfamiliarity with the ambiance of these spaces. Jessica Sewell shows us how at the turn of the twentieth century, department stores staged a highly visible storefront along main streets in order to encourage women customers to come in (Sewell 2011). These storefronts were filled with "objects of desire" meant to incite potential consumers. But the storefronts also became a political space where posters and information about suffrage was prominently displayed.

The importance of food in immigrant culture makes restaurants, grocery stores, and kitchens important sites where ethnicity is practiced and reproduced on a daily basis (Gabaccia 1998; Bonus 2000). Immigrant stores, described in ethnic enterprise literature, serve as sites of social, political, and economic transactions. These places promote in-group solidarity and sustain a robust ethnic economy (Bonacich & Modell 1980; Light 1972; Aldrich & Waldinger 1990). The above works just cited are concerned with social and economic processes and do not consider the role of architectural and material environment in the production of ethnic spaces. More recently works on immigrant stores and markets have shown how the visual staging of signage, exotic goods, and merchandise on storefronts are important strategies used to solicit potential customers (C. T. Sen 2009; Mankekar 2002). Purnima Mankekar argues that Indian grocery stores in the Bay Area "enable the production and consumption of a range of texts, images, and commodities that participate in this ongoing construction of India and Indian culture." (Mankekar 2002: 76) Mankekar demonstrates that these stores are important nodes within a global network of circulating images, objects, and texts. She also claims that the objects sold and exchanged in these stores produce *"regimes of value"* even as they travel and circulate. As loci where circulating people and goods converge, they are spaces where gender, class, and race are reconfigured. Although Mankekar doesn't discuss the spatial and architectural qualities of these spaces, she carefully examines the experience of shopping. "India Shopping," as she calls it, involves a complex consumption and reproduction of home, homeland, memory, and identity.

Agius and Lee (2006), describing the behavior of cashiers in Latino-owned ethnic markets, demonstrate that in addition to being in-group spaces, ethnic stores are contact zones where multiple social groups interact. The authors demonstrate how cultural roles and norms of behavior and interaction, inflected by class, race, and gender identities, are reinforced and reproduced during interactions in ethnic grocery stores. Turgeon and Pastinelli's work on Quebec City's ethnic restaurants (Turgeon & Pastinelli 2002) and Sharon Zukin's work (Zukin 1995) on similar spaces in New York show that these spaces act as sites where global culture is consumed, commodified, and produced, and are arenas where changes due to globalization and the new economy are made manifest. Turgeon and Pastinelli's work shows that the layout of the restaurant interior is often implicated in the race and class differences underpinning ethnic enterprise: the interior ambiance and material culture of front spaces in the restaurants cater to a non-ethnic (and white) clientele. The back spaces are occupied by ethnic workers (often people of color). The layout of restaurant controls the nature of contact between various social groups.

NEW CUISINE, OLD PLACES, AND THE NEW ECONOMY

Every weekend afternoon, an odd but now-familiar sight awaits residents of Berkeley's west side. Single individuals and families of different racial, ethnic, religious, and national backgrounds line up patiently in front of Vik's. Some engage in conversation, a babel of languages animating a slowly moving line. The line is made of smaller groups. Families, groups of friends, acquaintances, and regulars gather in sociopetal clusters. Occasionally, agile individuals leap out of the line to grab an emptying table for their group while others stand dumbfounded at the confusion and chaos produced by many pulsating worlds—a winding queue, waiting customers on the side, jostling children, and cross traffic—coinciding simultaneously on a narrow crosswalk.

The crowd in front of 724–726 Allston Way is, however, very different from the one we see in the neighboring Fourth Street retail shops, zoned by the city of Berkeley as a region-serving commercial zone. Compared to the more homogenous clients on Fourth Street (mostly young urban professionals, white, and upper- and middle-income couples), the crowd on Allston Way is younger, multicultural, and clustered in groups. Some seem to be part of large Indian families in festive gear. Women in saris and *salwar* suits and a rather large contingent of loud children sit around tables. Americans of non–South Asian backgrounds, sometimes led by their South Asian friend, try out this new multicultural experience. After they order food, customers hover around unable to find a place to sit in the crowded interior. A few appear to be regulars. They walk straight in and cleverly maneuver themselves in order to reserve open tables before others can get to them. Locating, reserving, and occupying seats is a big part of the experience of this space and one can identify various groups by the ease with which they work their way through this consumer ballet.

The majority of the customers frequenting this business on weekdays work in nearby media, advertising, legal, consultancy practices, real-estate industries, and banking and economic services. They are young, well traveled, and mixed in their racial, ethnic, and national origins. They experience and sustain a new economy that is variously referred to as the post-Fordist, flexible, the informational, or the global economy. The cooks and preparation staff in the kitchen area of Vik's are mixed—most from India and a few of Mexican and Central American origin.

The citizens of Berkeley are no strangers to South Asian culture. During the first two decades of the twentieth century, Berkeley was the intellectual center of Indian immigration. Students enrolled in the University of California made Berkeley the center of their cultural and political world as they staged nationalist activities against British Colonial rule in India from this city. The counterculture movement in the city during the 1960s popularized Indian culture, religion, music, dress, and food to local residents. N is an old resident of Berkeley who is Jewish-American. She moved from Los Angeles to Berkeley as a student at the University of California during the sixties. She remembers a South Asian store from the sixties, a store that (she thinks) was located on the 2400 block of Telegraph Avenue. She believes that this store disappeared sometime in the seventies: "Going back to the 1960s there was a place called India Imports on Telegraph that was frequented by all the hip people. And I was laughing because it just occurred to me that

India Imports and India did not have anything to do with each other [in my mind at that time]. It was just that everyone had to wear those shirts, and everyone had to buy sandalwood incense. Some place around the 2400 block. It was the biggest store in terms of volume and in terms of trade."

Between 1946 (with the Luce-Celler Act) and 1965 (with the Immigration and Nationality Act) major changes in immigration laws permitted skilled Indian immigrants to enter the United States. Berkeley became one of the major urban destinations for students and new immigrants, and between 1975 and 1980, pioneering Indian grocery stores opened along University Avenue (Bazaar of India, 1801 University Avenue, started in 1975; Milan, 990 University Avenue, started in 1975; Ajanta Enterprise, 1624 University Avenue, started in 1970; and Shrimati's Sari Store, 2011 University Avenue, started in 1977).

In 1987, when Vinod and Indira Chopra rented the warehouse on Allston Way, south of University Avenue, for their wholesale distributorship, there already existed a thriving concentration of ethnic stores along nearby University Avenue. These years were important for the South Asian community in the Bay Area. The family reunion clause in the immigration act was bringing many South Asians into the Bay Area. Political unrest in Fiji and parts of Africa was pushing out South Asians from these areas. New refugees and immigrants settled in the region. Consequently, during the late eighties and early nineties, the population of South Asians in East Bay and South Bay cities grew at a rapid pace. Residential enclaves developed in cities such as Fremont, Richmond, and El Cerrito along U.S. Interstate 80. Vinod Chopra's plan was to cater to the wholesale needs of the newly emerging restaurants located in the extended region and suburbs of Northern California where the new population lived.

Just north of Allston Way, University Avenue of Berkeley continued to grow as a regional ethnic retail strip. New South Asian stores emerged on the western end of the street (nearer to the freeway exit) and clustered around rented storefronts below the U.A. Homes building owned by a South Asian. The older stores produced a perfect anchor for the new generation of Indian stores to develop along this busy corridor. Being next to the interstate exit ramp and located in a city already known for its ethnic South Asian stores, University Avenue quickly developed as an attractive venue for Indian stores selling clothes, food, music, baggage, jewelry, and other cultural artifacts (A. Sen 1998). The customers included South Asian immigrants living in the extended hinterland, Middle Eastern and African immigrants from neighboring cities, and local Indophile Anglo residents of Berkeley and Oakland.

Yet Vik's, compared to the stores along University Avenue, had a different trajectory and reason to be there. The lack of signage on its façade visually distinguished this store from those located along the University Avenue corridor. The reason for this visual austerity was not incidental. As a wholesale distributor for spices and beer, storeowner Vinod Chopra had intended to supply local and regional restaurants and Indian grocery stores. In contrast to most ethnic stores along University Avenue that catered to a growing clientele of South Asian families who drove down to Berkeley on weekends, Chopra's business did not target individuals and families as primary customers. The stores along University Avenue would clamor for attention, trying to attract these potential clients in their cars via large signage. Vik's constituency of restaurateurs and storeowners already knew where the store was located. They were not impulse buyers. In fact, the mere location of Vik's gives us an idea of the nature of its initial clients. In those days before GPS, one needed prior knowledge in order to navigate the complex set of one-way streets in order to get to Vik's. The geographical location of Vik's and the visual character of the storefront distinguished it from other ethnic retail stores in the vicinity.

The west side of Berkeley, where Vik's is located, used to be an abandoned gritty industrial neighborhood until the late twentieth century. We still see corpses of the industrial past in the form of large empty warehouses, unused factory buildings, boarded up worker cottages and empty lots. Things have changed in the last thirty years. Today, the residents of this area are a mixed lot: many older residents remain, but since the late nineties new young, professional, middle-class residents have occupied newly redesigned and renovated warehouses, lofts and live-work units. West Berkeley is like a palimpsest where past and present coexists. One such renovated warehouse on Allston Way houses Vik's South Asian Indian ethnic grocery store (left) and a fast-food restaurant called Vik's café (right).

The South Asian cultural landscape in the Bay Area exemplifies a geographical settlement pattern that Melville Webber calls "a community without propinquity" (Webber 1963). In a more recent work on "heterolocalism," Wilbur Zelinsky (2001) identifies contemporary immigrant landscapes as networked and argues that the experience of such a landscape is very different from that of territorially bounded ethnic enclaves. Today's ethnic residential settlements are dispersed in suburbs (Wei Li calls them ethnoburbs) while cultural, business, and work spaces are spread across the region (Li 1998;

Fong 1994; Dunn 1998; Anderson & Gale 1992; Poulsen & Johnston 2000; Newbold & Spindler 2001). Nodes within this network are accessed via the automobile. As a result of this dispersed nodal geography, the spatial experience of traversing this landscape is considerably different from the way, say, Boston's West Enders experienced the cultural geography of Italian immigrants (Gans 1962). This novel geography also impacts the way we read, study, and talk about ethnic landscapes of immigrants in contemporary cities. For instance, it is impossible to talk about Vik's in geographical isolation from its many constituent networks. This store sells merchandise from across the world and is thus tied into transnational networks of goods, capital, culture, images, and people. But, being located in Berkeley, Vik's is influenced by local laws, economics, and politics. Being attached to a regional ethnic political geography ties Vik's to the culture and politics of the region. Ethnic groups that patronize this space come from a vast hinterland and their lifestyles influence how the store is inhabited at different times. Since the store is accessed by out-of-town customers traveling in their automobiles, customer experience is related to the way they emerge from their automobiles, cross the street, and enter the store through a series of sequential, transitional, and experiential boundaries. Each of these frameworks provides us with a different sense of location, geography, and spatial experience. I argue that production, reproduction, and consumption of "cultural difference" in ethnic restaurants should be confused neither with cultural and ethnic authenticity nor with a singular causal reference (ethnicity). Rather as Arjun Appadurai shows in his discussion of scapes and flows, chaat restaurants like Vik's are local sites where global flows of images, cultural forms, culinary practices, and taste meet crisscrossing flows of capital, resources, and labor. The following discussion therefore suggests a method to read ethnic sites as a product of simultaneous macro- and microcontexts/processes.

CHAAT CAFÉ, A CONSTANTLY TRANSFORMING PLACE

The side-by-side juxtaposition of the restaurant and the ethnic grocery store in Vik's is important because it brings together two very important spatial types within the South Asian immigrant foodscape. On the one hand, the Indian grocery store has a long history and is one of the most distinct place-types within South Asian cultural landscapes across the world. These stores

FIGURE 1. Grocery store entrance on the left and café entrance on the right, 2004. Photo by Arijit Sen.

sell groceries, beverages, spices, grains, toiletries (often made in the subcontinent), and seasonal fruits and vegetables used in South Asian cuisine. Generally, merchandise sold in these stores is not available in mainstream American stores. Elsewhere I have shown how the unique sensorial qualities of the Indian grocery store give meaning, sense of place, and value to these locations among immigrant customers (A. Sen 2006, 2009). Indian grocery stores appear regularly in literature, popular culture, and media as symbols of the exotic ethnic landscapes of expatriate Indians.

On the other hand, the chaat café is a new type of place to appear in the United States. Until recently most Indian restaurants in the United States were famous for their curries that required skilled kitchen staff. For example, between 1980 and 2002 there were eight to ten Indian restaurants in the city of Berkeley serving the traditional fare of North or South Indian curries. By 2003 a fast-food restaurant type called *chaat* cafés overtook them and a total of eleven such cafés appeared in the city, some of them often only a counter inside a preexisting restaurant or grocery store.

Made of a crunchy mix of stuffed fillings and topped with a tangy sauce, *chaat* is a kind of food that is preprepared and mixed fresh on the spot. A *New York Times* article mentions that "Chaat is made of fried bits of chickpeas, puffed rice, browned mashed-potato patties, fresh ginger, mung bean sprouts, spice-dusted toasted lentils and topped with a tangy powder made from green mangoes, mint, cumin, pomegranate, black salt, cilantro, tamarind sauce, and yogurt." Chaat is part of an emerging menu of global cuisine that has appeared in American cities. It belongs to a growing list of popular food—wraps, organic snacks, fusion food, finger-food, and small plates that attract cosmopolitan urban professionals. Most chaat cafés are places that accommodate everyday practices of immigrants while also catering to the needs and activities of nonimmigrant customers and other stakeholders in a multicultural city. Increasingly, in cities across the world we encounter chaat cafés sporting similar décor, store names, and menus.

Chaat originated as a roadside snack food in North India. *Chaat* means to "lick" or "taste" in Hindi. The word *chatpata*—from where the term originates—refers to tingling hot and sour flavors. In India most chaat restaurants were roadside vendors. They were not sit-in, formal places. Going for a chaat "is a social act with the same casual sociability as going for a beer. (Most Indians are Hindus and Muslims and drink little or no alcohol.) After work a group of men will buy each other rounds of chaat on the way to the train and sometimes even have competitions over who can eat more. Piyush Sukhadia, an owner of chaat-and-sweet stores, said 'In India a guy might have a Mercedes and live in a house on a hill, but he still puts on his slippers and goes to eat chaat'" (quoted in Moskin 2005).

As a circulating cultural phenomenon, the chaat café has returned to India as a fashionable gourmet restaurant type. Unlike traditional Indian "curry-restaurants," new *chaat* cafés sport self-serve delis and informal decor. The small serving portions, distinct recipes, absence of specialized culinary skills, location, and interior space requirements differentiate the latter from former (Moskin 2005; Holbrook 2007; Mochon 2007). Upscale restaurants in five-star hotels in Indian cities now sport chaat counters and chaat cafés. However, in the unstable economy of ethnic restaurant businesses of Berkeley, changing clientele and fluctuating urban rent create constant renewal and change in the *chaat* café business. *Chaat* cafés appear and disappear with alacrity.

After a few years of its inauguration the news of Vik's spread within the community. Initially, on weekends few Indian families driving down to Berkeley from the surrounding cities began to include Vik's in their itinerary. Although intended only as a wholesale business, Chopra's retail business had taken off and by 1992 Chopra added a small weekend fast-food counter near the entrance in order to serve a quick lunch to the growing clientele.

Chopra reasoned that if he could serve a quick snack for the immigrant families who drove down on Sundays to shop, he could produce loyal and

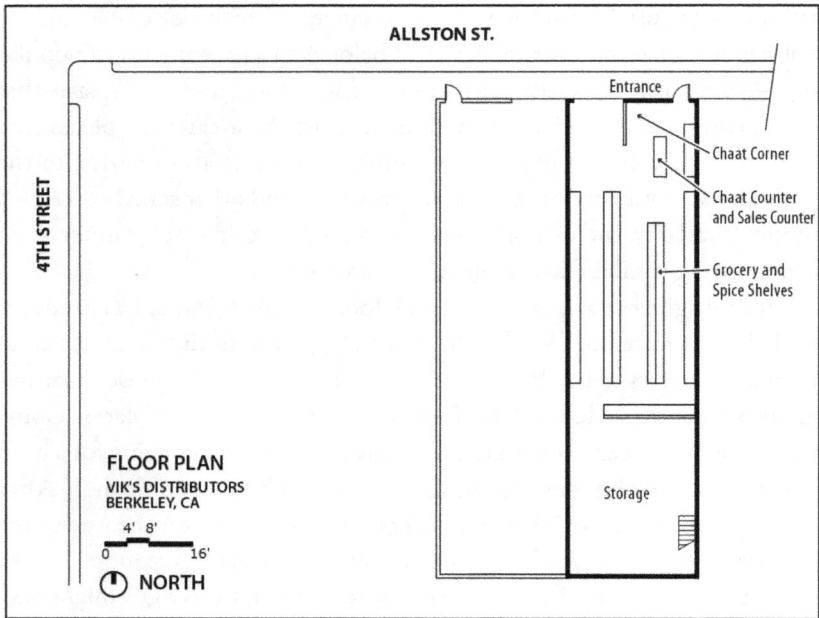

FIGURE 2. Vik's interior layout, 1992. Drawing by Andy Blaser.

returning customers. What started as a trickle grew and the popularity of Vik's transformed it into a well-known retail grocery store. Vinod Chopra's initial decision to start a small food counter came out of his prior experience of a kind of fast food that was popular in North India, where he grew up. The chaat counter in Vik's recreated the informal layout of North Indian chaat stores with the food being prepared, sold, and consumed in the same front part of the store. Relatively simple to make, Chopra's wife, Indira could supervise the service from the front counter. Chaat was a novelty in America during the eighties. It was not something one got in local Indian restaurants.

Soon, the front counter could no longer accommodate the increasing number of customers. By the late 1990s redevelopment and gentrification efforts by the city of Berkeley started to transform West Berkeley. The West Berkeley Plan, a long-term development plan for the area between San Pablo Avenue and the Eastshore Freeway, was a policy document drawn up by the city in 1997 in response to the economic boom in Silicon Valley. This boom had resulted in high property rents in the South Bay. Easy access to San Francisco and South Bay made the West Berkeley neighborhood very desirable for information technology (IT) businesses, advertisement agencies, graphic design offices, architectural and landscape architectural firms, artist units, and professional services. The West Berkeley Plan encouraged in-fill developments with light industrial, small-scale office, and live-work uses. In 2001 the Berkeley city manager reported to the city council that in 2000 there was "a greater level of construction of new offices and conversion of warehouse and light industrial space to office uses in the MU/LI [Mixed-Use, Light Industrial Zoning Code] district as well as in other West Berkeley manufacturing districts than in the previous three years" (Rucker 2001). The plan also specified that new retail establishments should not spread south of University Avenue. Therefore while restaurants developed north of University Avenue—along Fourth Street earmarked for such growth—no new restaurants appeared in the vicinity of the office developments.

Because of its location, by 1999 Vik's was one of the few lunch destinations for the local professional customers. Realizing the potential of serving lunch to the burgeoning customers, the Chopras decided to keep the food counter open during lunch on weekdays as well as weekends. The interior layout of Vik's changed to cater to this new lunch crowd. By 1999, the weekday lunch crowd consisted of mainly non–South Asian customers. The owners decided to move the chaat counter to the back of the store in order to avoid the crowding and confusion in the front that resulted out of the Indian grocery store customers jostling with the café customers. By 2000, Vik's owners separated the restaurant section from the grocery store and moved the former to the adjacent warehouse space.

Vik's popularity led to many copycat chaat cafés in Berkeley in special locations such as near downtown—to cater to lunch crowds. Chaat was fast gaining acceptance among non–South Asians and chaat cafés were making their appearance across the country in cities such as Phoenix, Los Angeles, Houston, Chicago, and New York. By 2008 franchise opportunities for chaat cafés appeared in the United States as well as in India under Chaat Café Inc.

A common back space was shared by the café and the grocery store. This space was closed to the public and was generally used for storage and food preparation. These changes transformed the nature of the chaat café while keeping the grocery store the same.

By 2003 the *New York Times* reported with wonderment that this Indian café has become a popular local hangout even for the staff of Alice Water's upscale French restaurant Chez Panisse (Apple 2003). Vik's had entered the urban gourmet world—it was now ready to be explored and discovered by young urban Bay Areas foodies. In 2004, the continuing popularity of Vik's

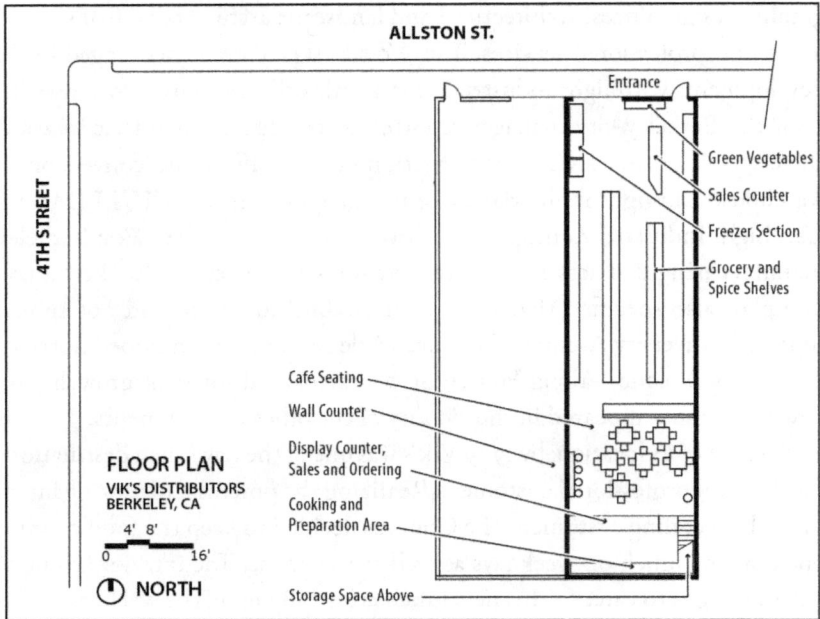

FIGURE 3. Vik's interior layout, 1999. Drawing by Andy Blaser.

made further demands on its interior space. By 2005, Sam Whiting wrote in the *San Francisco Chronicle*, "On weekends, it is mobbed. . . . You can stand in line for half an hour, [and] you'll see everybody in the neighborhood" (Whiting 2005).

Soon Vik's expanded again. The 2006 layout of the café no longer resembled a chaat house in India or the original chaat counter of 1992. Rather it reflected the changing business, clientele, and neighborhood economy. While the grocery and spice store interiors remained exactly as it was ten years ago, the café saw renovations. A blogger described in 2008, "Now, *Vik's is an institution*. Despite several expansions into the warehouses next door, there are still impossibly long lines on the weekends. On Sundays, it feels as if the entire South Asian community and all the hippie wannabes of Telegraph Avenue have descended upon the place" (Emerson 2005).

The entrance to the grocery store used to be a large warehouse door with overhead rolling shutters. That entrance was redesigned in 2006 and the overhead shutter in front of the café was substituted with a door and an entry vestibule. The community bulletin board added to this vestibule made this an extended transitional space between the café and the street and allowed

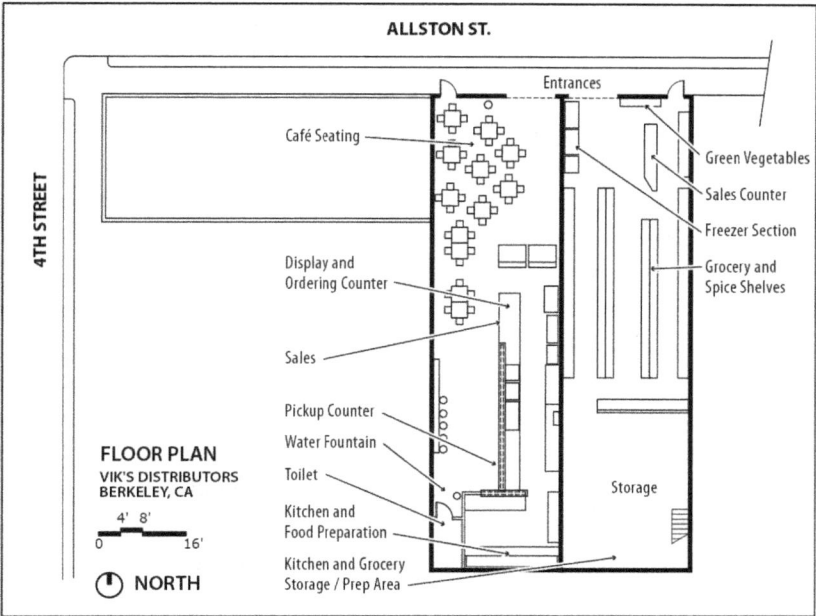

FIGURE 4. Vik's interior layout, 2000. Drawing by Andy Blaser.

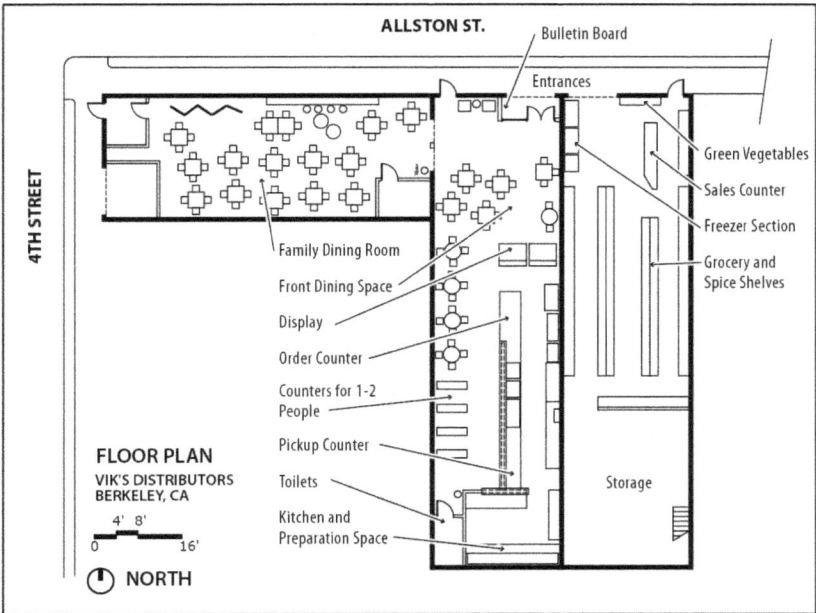

FIGURE 5. Vik's interior layout, 2004–2006. Drawing by Andy Blaser.

the interior of the café to be air-conditioned and meet code requirements for a restaurant. The entry to the grocery store remained as it was.

By 2008 two separate and distinct kinds of spaces existed side by side. The grocery store interiors resembled the quintessential niche market ethnic grocery store. It was part of an immigrant community domain. An elderly lady at the counter spoke to customers in her native tongue (Gujarati). On weekend and evenings Indira, Vinod Chopra's wife, would manage the counter. She engaged customers in friendly banter, asking them personal questions about their family and trips to India. She would remind some women customers when herbs like *methi* and curry leaves would come in fresh and chide others for buying the wrong brand of spices. She whispered in a conspiratorial tone advising regular clients to choose alternate brands of oil (even though she carried the brand she was advising against). An Indian helper, who did not speak fluent English, clearly knew the names of the goods held at the back and scurried back and forth to retrieve these items for customers. The grocery store employees spoke a language of the insider and employed a tone that gave an impression of familiarity.

In contrast, the material culture of the café was cosmopolitan. The café customers displayed racial, occupational, ethnic, and age diversity. Festive wall colors, posters of exotic locales in India, and the Air India Maharaja doll sustained a symbolic economy of cultural difference oriented towards westerners—similar to what Kay Anderson terms "a Western construction" in her work on Vancouver's Chinatown (K. J. Anderson 1987: 591). The bulletin board space near the entrance to the café was very different from the similar space near the entrance to the grocery store. In the former there were displays and announcements of neighborhood new age yoga and meditation classes, self-realization workshops, local meetings, and organic food. In the latter one found untidy piles of ethnic newspapers printed in Northern California, the regional Indian American Business directories, old newspapers, advertisements for Bollywood movies, advertisements for South Asian cultural events in the Northern California Bay Area region.

The café sales counter was neatly separated from the preparation area and seating space producing order in this chaotic environment. A self-serve silverware and plate counter ran against the back wall. At the café counter the server spoke fluent English and took orders with speed not matched by their counterparts in the grocery store. Ready orders were announced by the loudspeaker system and customers lined up along the east wall to collect

FIGURES 6A AND 6B. Grocery store interiors. Photos by Arijit Sen and Chris Pelli.

FIGURE 7. Café interior before remodeling. Photo by Arijit Sen.

the goods with the efficiency of a production line. View lines and surveillance was carefully manipulated via the layout. Customers got a controlled glimpse of the back kitchen where Mexican and Central American immigrants worked alongside the elderly Indian Amma Chennale. Mixing chaat required fewer skills than preparing food in traditional restaurants and hence non-Indian workers did just fine. There was no communication between the customers and the back kitchen workers. No one knew what went on in the storage and food preparation back zone (the space at the back of the grocery store adjoining the café).

Yet the café was no more local than the grocery store and the experience in the two spaces were not segregated. People in the café mistakenly slipped into the grocery store (the common refrain being that the two adjacent entrances, lacking signage, was very confusing). For many non–South Asians this unintentional entry into this new world became an instructive experience. As they threaded their way past Indian groceries and peered through the exotic merchandise, they experienced the Indian grocery store for the first time. Repeated over time, the once newcomers became familiar with the musty world of spices and over the years the number of non–South Asian customers in the grocery store increased.

FIGURE 8. Café interior after remodeling. Photo by Chris Pelli.

Amanda Berne of the *San Francisco Chronicle* describes the atmosphere in the café/grocery store on a weekend:

> The Viks' dining room, if you can call it that, is filled with a mix of students, couples and Bay Area natives either from the area or making the trek for chaat. It's a weekend morning ritual, so the tables fill up quickly and spill out on sunny days to the parking lot.... The kitchen has more energy than an airport during the holidays, and as soon as the doors open, the automated machines go into action, flashing orders on flat-screen panels. Staff members man various stations, while a few work in the back on preparing for the next day. Amod [Chopra's son] expedites, calling out names on a microphone for people to come back to the counter to pick up orders. Vinod and Indira arrive on the weekends around 11 a.m., and Vinod immediately starts greeting the customers. He's all over the place, tasting sauces, sitting in the sun chatting with groups of men, while Indira sneaks off to help work the store, her own meeting point to catch up. When he's not at the counter, Amod dips into every curry pot, sambar or biriyani pan in the kitchen, tasting for balance of flavors, spice and salt. Pakoras fry in the giant karahi, a cast-iron wok used in Indian cooking, and as they turn gold, the vegetable dumplings come out. Amod barely waits for them to cool before cracking one open. He adds more

salt and celery seed to the rest, then repeats the process, until they are perfect. (Berne 2006)

Clearly Berne read the café as the public dining room and the grocery as Indira's place. This apparent front and back experience was reiterated in the layout of the two spaces.

During weekdays, out-of-town visitors parking their cars in the adjacent private parking lot created some conflict among neighbors by inconveniencing people working in nearby offices on a daily basis. Local residents often had to call the police and tow unauthorized vehicles away. As a result Chopra erected signs warning potential customers that if they parked in nonspecified locations their cars could be towed. On weekends the lot was free, and Vik's customers drove into the lot through the lot's exit (nearer to store entrance). In doing so the visiting cars moved in the opposite direction than the normal weekday traffic flow. The drivers ended up parking at an angle that was different from the direction indicated by the lot signs. There was a different spatial order to this occupation, a temporary spatial change that marked the parking lot during the weekends as part of this ethnic landscape. By 2006 Vik's had rented out a large section of the parking lot to avoid this continuous bother. Yet conflict over parking continued to fester. In 2008, the owners of Vik's (now Vinod, Indira, and their son Amod) wrested the chaat restaurant premises from the grocery store. Now located a few blocks south of the original location, with its own parking lot, Vik's chaat house is a separate entity no longer attached to the ethnic grocery store.

MULTIPLE SPATIALITIES AND MULTICULTURAL CONTACT ZONES

An emphasis on "place-making" is a good point of entry into the analysis of immigrant landscapes, as well as of the urban culture of contemporary American cities. The editors of this volume posit that due to globalization, neat separations between the global and local are complicated, the "categories of the local and the global, which previously appeared to be distinct, now become increasingly interwoven and reproduce each other" (see chapter 1). The preceding discussion partially unravels this interwoven nature of urban ethnic landscapes by tracking and correlating the physical transformation of the built environment within larger political-economic processes. Place and place-making allows us to examine how global practices are being rearticulated at a local setting. The interior environment of Vik's is akin to an ever-changing stage that accommodates everyday events, shifting practices, and changing identities and political negotiations between various social constituencies. Vik's is a node where multiple worlds overlap and the public realm of the immigrant community confronts the urban public domain. Ethnic networks of friends and family intersect with networks based on nonethnic relationships and professional liaisons. Understanding place-making allows us to see how culture and ethnicity are negotiated and learned. Changes instituted in the store (interior layout, merchandise, and business practices) were more than an attempt to solve a crowding or a space problem. By constantly redefining the boundaries between the grocery store and the café, between the street (outside) and store (inside), between front and back, the ethnic entrepreneurs mediated the many conflicting domains within which their business operated. The reconfiguration of the interior space became a way by which the Chopras and their cosmopolitan clientele negotiated contingencies of daily life, needs of the market, and policies of the state and urban governance. Ethnicity and indeed the immigrant cultural landscape became a site of capitalism's creative destruction where the market incessantly redefined itself (Schumpeter 1942).

In addition to the expansion and locational displacement of the café, the edges between the grocery store and the café underwent repeated mutations. The transitional space between the street and the café became what Borden calls *thick edges* (Borden 2000). In the first instance, when the café was a weekend snack counter, the edge served as the transition between the store and the street, a point where customers paused before leaving (or after entering). The move to the back during its initial transformation as a lunch counter was an attempt to wrest the interconnectedness between the store and the café. By placing the café in the "back-zone," this functional space was separated from the social space of the store. Yet, since the credit card machine was located in the front store counter, cross-traffic between café customers and store customers became intertwined. At this point the café had the quality of a private back room, from which one could hear sounds and laughter, but which was disconnected from the street by the intervening interior space of the grocery store. The imagery of the private back room gives us a glimpse of how the owners thought of the café at a time when it was becoming popular among Anglo and non–South Asian clients. They saw it as a *bracketed space* ensconced at the back within the larger ethnic retail and wholesale context. Access to it was controlled and under surveillance. Later the move to the neighboring premises coincided with an acknowledgement of the unique interdependent yet independent nature of the chaat café. The shared back space, storage, and food preparation area provided an umbilical cord between the store and the café—the position of the café counter along the back wall was a result of the existence of a common back zone.

The many interior rearrangements of Vik's also produced changing temporal experiences in the store and the café. In Vik's, the weekday rhythms of customers created crowded hours during lunchtime at the chaat counter. That crowd dwindled down by the afternoon and spiked again in the evening with customers coming in for groceries on their way back from work. In each instant different parts of the store become operational and people performed and consumed ethnicity in different ways. With the shifting of the chaat counter (relative to the store counter) the locus of activities shifted too. Groceries produced a "seasonal" cycle that impacted the experience of space—mangos in summer took over the front of the grocery counter while seasonal vegetables were spread out next to the entrance. Frequent customers knew when a certain green leafy vegetable called *methi* became available and when curry leaves came in fresh. What looked to outsiders as clutter as they negotiated the strewn merchandise was a heartwarming reminder of home to others.

The acts of the government imposed a different, albeit longer beat to the system. For instance, the urban development schemes and plans of the city influenced the popularity of Vik's as a lunchtime destination. Yet the impact of these factors operating within long-term planning cycles, determined at the urban government level, also coincided with an even larger international migration pattern. The immigration patterns of Indians in the Bay Area, national economic cycles, the digital revolution, and the real estate boom in the region were intertwined factors.

Like the forums and plazas of yesteryear and the privatized public spaces, malls, and amusement parks of a consumer society, Vik's café is indeed the new public space of a global city. Unlike the adjoining grocery store that (despite many non–South Asian customers) caters mainly to a more-focused community of clients (mostly immigrants from out of town), the café is a meeting point for immigrants, natives, men, women, bureaucrats, entrepreneurs, the powerful, and the powerless. Communities without propinquity negotiate territorial control with neighborhood groups and urban publics. The sequential entry and the watchful surveillance of the grocery store clerk discipline the customers and educate the uninitiated about a highly constructed world of Indianness. The bustling market place with an ambiguously transforming edge between the grocery store and café simultaneously sustains the divided worlds of the cab driver, the computer scientist, and the Anglo neophyte.

Vik's displays what Lefebvre calls polyrhythmia, an overlay of multiple rhythms producing a complex spatial and temporal rhythmic field (Lefebvre 2004: 16–17). Understanding Vik's therefore requires us to examine the conditions of polyrhythmia. The experience of spatial change and temporalities inside Vik's are embodied in diverse ways as people move through the store, experience the changing smells, sounds, and ambient qualities of the interior, and approach different destinations. As users use these spaces they internalize the rhythms and orders within them. Experiencing these rhythms also creates a certain kind of memory. A memory of time and place that repeated, adapted, or transformed in cycles, produce a log of what has occurred before, different experiences of social circles and networks within the store. Paul Connerton shows how persistent bodily enactments—incorporating and inscribing practices—produce and sustain memories (Connerton 1989: 72–73). Such memories sustain imagined communities and shared and collective knowledge. These memories and embodied forms of knowing are not produced in conscious and predetermined ways. Rather, they are haptic.

It is here that the concept of multiple spatialities becomes relevant to our discussion. The internalization and experience of these rhythms and temporalities as embodied spatial knowledge is not fixed. Many customers come from suburban and urban areas across the Bay Area. They visit Vik's primarily on weekends. They come in automobiles, often in groups, and use the chaat café as a place to meet friends. They drive down from distant locations to stock up on groceries and goods on weekends. To these customers Vik's is a node within a regionally reticulated landscape of ethnic spaces. The network includes places of worship, work places, residential spaces, retail and business sites, and cultural institutions. The experience of Vik's as part of a network is not the same as the experience of being a part of a neighborhood fabric. Such a spatiality contrasts with that generated by territorially bounded experiences of place that one finds in an ethnic enclave or a neighborhood café. Local residents' experience of Vik's as part of an everyday neighborhood fabric falls under the latter.

By simultaneously mapping Vik's at multiple scales—within a global public culture, an automobile-based networked geography of Indian immigrants in the Bay Area, a local pedestrian-based area from which majority non-ethnic customers come, and the personal scale of the store interiors where Anglo, Indian, and Mexican individuals consume and reproduce immigrant culture in different ways, we generate systemic cartographies that challenge the way we understand the relationship between place and culture, between ethnic and mainstream domains, between locality and globality (Rapoport 1993; Lynch 1960). Such mappings also bring forth complex local factors that ground global processes. The spatial development of a chaat café can then be read as the document of an unfolding history in which business needs, local government requirements, and cultural identities are all in a state of flux and dynamically related to each other. The clientele and the business incessantly redefine themselves, architectural and ethnic identities are constantly reinvented. What on first glance seems like bland global simulacra turns out to be a protean and creative rearticulation of place.

ELEVEN

Masala Matters

GLOBALIZATION, FEMALE FOOD ENTREPRENEURS, AND THE CHANGING POLITICS OF PROVISIONING

Tulasi Srinivas

THE CONTEXT FOR THIS exploration is the specific question of local and global articulation (Miller 2005: 55) of prepackaged Indian food and its shifting meanings as it travels across the globe. Sidney Mintz noted in his pathbreaking study of the ethnohistory of sugar that studying the consumption of food constitutes the "inside meaning of food," but the socioeconomic contexts of the larger "institutional changes" of the production of food—the "outside meaning" of food—(1996: 10) are equally important, as they are in fact structures of power (1996: 22 quoting Eric Wolf 1990: 586–587) and shape "the field of action so as to render some kinds of behavior possible, while making others less possible or impossible" (Wolf 1990: 586–587). It is the untold connections between the inside and outside meanings of food and the power relations embedded in globalization that this chapter explores, using the lens of prepackaged Indian food.

Globalization has been seen by theorists as the dominance of the culture of Euro-America (Appadurai 1996; Barber 1996; Berger 1997; Friedman 2000), that is, the center dominating the periphery. This chapter seeks to expand on an understanding of a network form of cultural globalization—where goods and ideologies move through the network in many directions, leading perforce to plural forms of cultural globalization—that I have argued elsewhere (T. Srinivas 2001), which stands in opposition to this cultural homogeneity model. In a previous article on packaged food consumption among diasporic Indians, I argued that such consumption was fuelled by a "meta-narrative of loss" engaging several narratives within it (T. Srinivas 2006). I suggested that the movement of Indian packaged foods across international borders allows for a "utopic consumption" by cosmopolitan Indian families, where local food is culturally inserted into the global space (Appadurai 1996;

Hannerz 1992). This insertion enables South Asian families to conceptually sidestep the confrontation between the local and the global, and engage what Lakshmi Srinivas calls the "translocal" (L. Srinivas 2005: 319–321). Agreeing with Appadurai that cultural mediation lies at the center of the problem of transnationalism (1996), I suggested that the packaged food became—in its familiarity and its distance—a mediating model for these cosmopolitan families and is simultaneously seen as of a place and placeless (Giddens 1991: 26), leading one not only to question the empirical value of these categories, but also to question the nature of embeddedness and authenticity. But at the most immediate level the changes of eating prepared packaged food implicate a new model of factory production for packaging and preparing the foods, and at the more distant level the development of an agro-industrial complex.

And so this chapter is drawn from a larger project that examines ethnic food consumption, gendered labor of food production, and the evolving status of South Asian women from domestic provisioners to food entrepreneurs. A twinned examination of food in the cities of Bangalore and Boston, a microethnography of the lives and emotions of women as they provision, and a multi-sited transnational study of the flows of capital and labor in the mass production of food, this study considers the development of women's work in a global economy. This chapter explores a few of these changes in the production of the foodscape of urban India and their implications for middle-classness, particularly as it deals with the production of Indian food. The study critiques contemporary theory on Indian food that focuses on nation-building (Bubinas 2005; Mankekar 2002) by drawing on the work of feminist scholars. It examines the production of Indian food as constituted by the social, political, and economic transformations of postmodern India and argues that the food creates alternate "regimes of value" (Paxson 2006, 2008) located in regional and caste discourses. It parses the process by which provisioners turn into producers, identifying attitudes toward tradition and modernity, negotiations between Indian and Western values, all of which condense as discourses about and around gender. Beyond the obvious fact that women are still the provisioners in most families, neoliberal conceptions of internationality seem to offer a disciplinary regime for women that reveal how gendered spaces are reflected, constructed, and transformed, or transgressed. Counterintuitively, the study shows that Indian food discourse is influenced by a multivalent and conflicting definitions of modernity and identity, with locus points both in indigenous practices (of caste and regionality) and Western influences, leading to a fluid understanding of womanhood, domesticity and gastronomic knowledge.

I argue that women translate their embedded traditional knowledge (recipes and methods) of caste based food into a postmodern capitalist product; engage traditional female homosocial spaces (food preparation spaces) as spaces of gendered politics; and use Western populist feminist rhetoric to negotiate a powerful status for themselves as keepers of ancient tradition. So while domesticity has been viewed as oppressive from the perspective of feminist thought, the study shows that women are able to subvert the power dynamics and mobilize the opportunities produced as sources of personal empowerment. Feminist scholarship has shown that globalization is not a gender-neutral phenomenon (Butler 2004 and Benhabib 1995), but in the food arena it appears that the role of women as agents of change, cultural ambassadors who subtly create new definitions of desired food and methods of food presentation and preparation to present to the world, is acceptable.

FROM RATION CARDS TO CREDIT CARDS: THE CHANGING NATURE OF PROVISIONING

To set the stage for the more detailed discussion to follow I will here paint the picture of urban middle-class provisioning in very broad strokes. Beginning with the early 1950s, when India emerged as free country from its colonial past (India achieved its freedom in 1947), the goal of Indian leaders like Jawaharlal Nehru (a freedom fighter and later first prime minister of independent India) was to ensure national food security. At that time India was an agrarian society with over seventy-two percent of the population living in villages, and the "father of the nation" Mahatma Gandhi believed that India would be truly free when each one of its villages was economically independent and self-sufficient. It was a torturous path from the dream of autarkic villages to a planned economy, but following the Soviet model the dominant segment of the leadership of free India felt that a centralized Indian food and agricultural sector would make them independent of foreign food subsidies. So in the decades following Independence, segments of the Indian provisioning system was highly centralized following the Soviet model, with farmers paid fixed state prices for their crops, which were then distributed throughout India through largely inefficient state-run channels modeled on the British war system of rationing. Surpluses and shortages were often not managed effectively, and a corrupt parallel black market industry in food distribution emerged, run by the state distributors themselves.

In the 1980s a familiar sight for me as a child as I played with friends in the Jayamahal park neighborhood in Bangalore, South India, was a middle-class family's servant maid or errand boy waiting in an interminable line outside the government-run "ration shop" to collect the family's monthly allowance of provisions. They often waited for several hours for the shop to open and the goods to be weighed out and measured by the government clerk who operated the shop. The government-issued cards—ration cards—that gave one access to the "fair price" goods were closely guarded. I remember housewives shouting at family retainers to be careful with the ration card in case it was lost or stolen, as it listed family members and their food allowances. The family's diet depended on the ghee, sugar, pulses, rice, and other grains that were bought at the local ration shop. Families often retained members on the card who had left or were long deceased, to allow for larger allowances, and this often created confusion at election time, since the ration card rolls were often bought by parties as election master lists. The rations themselves were often not enough and would be supplemented with purchases from the black market at exorbitant prices. Gossip raged that the black market vendors were supplied by the government ration shop clerks, who siphoned off the supplies from the shop and sold them at a gargantuan profit on the "free" black market. Families would then in turn hoard the precious commodities of ghee and sugar from the ration shop to be used on certain festival occasions. The overwhelming emotions that I remember accompanying these transactions was anxiety and secrecy.

In the decades after Independence the agricultural sector in India underwent enormous structural change shaped in part by the state policy on farming combined with the efforts of nongovernmental organizations. The Green Revolution in India, though often thought of as one continuous revitalization of the agricultural sector, appears to have three distinct waves: the staples wave, the produce wave, and the fruit wave. The first wave, between 1965 and 1970, yielded a spurt of growth in staple crops such as wheat and rice needed to feed India's millions. The second wave (still being developed) was an increase in vegetable and produce yields by using high-yield varieties and more fertilizers. The final wave, which is still being developed, seems to address the fruit and floriculture market. The evidence of this fruit revolution can be seen in any metropolitan city in India, where carts piled high with fruit, both cut and whole, stand all day. Such an abundance of indigenous fruits and vegetables has occurred over the past two decades. While the green revolution has yielded food for India and for export, environmentalist and other scholars of food sufficiency worry that the kind of intensive farming that the Green Revolution encouraged is unsustainable and externalizes costs.

Added to the Green Revolution was a white revolution in dairy farming. Initiated by the Indian government in 1950, "Operation Flood" as it came to be known, was the brainchild of one Dr. Kurien, who began to revamp the Indian national dairy development board located in Anand, Gujarat (later known as Amul, an acronym for Anand Milk Union Limited). Operation Flood was also a three-part venture between 1970 and 1996 where the premier "milkshed" of India was linked to large metropolitan outlets through a network of cooling plants and delivery systems. In the space of just twenty-five years India became the largest producer of milk in the world, overtaking the United States. In the metropolitan marketplaces, milk went from being a shortage commodity bought in buckets and pails in the mid-1970s to easily accessible and affordable sachet bought at local booths. These milk booths are seen in every metropolitan city and each state has their own state run dairy: Karnataka (my home state) has Nandini milk and Tamil Nadu (the neighboring state) has its AAVIN. The booths that dot every city sell butter, cream, flavored milks, milk-based sweets, ghee, and plain milk. Every year new products are introduced.

Allied with these changes in the agricultural industry, a whole range of social, economic, and cultural changes have taken place in India over the past fifty years, culminating in the economic boom of the past two decades. In 1989 the Indian economy was "liberalized" after nearly fifty years of Soviet style protectionism. Since then the Indian economy has seen significant growth, rising from 2% in 1990 to 8.5% in 2009–10.[1] While India is one of the world's leading food producers, it accounts for less than 1.5% of the US$500 billion trade in world food, since most of its products are consumed internally (Indianfoodindustry.net). Emergent during Liberalization was a new packaged food industry, which has grown rapidly in the past decade and a half. Independent research by the RNCOS group has projected that the Indian food, beverages, and tobacco market will grow at around 7.5% during 2009–2013 to around US$330 billion by 2013. However, the prepared food market in India is still in its nascent stage, with only 2.2% of fruits and vegetables being processed into prepared foods and about 35% of dairy products being packaged and branded (New Zealand Trade & Enterprise, 2009).

Much of the material for this chapter is based on ethnographic work in Boston and in Bangalore, both in observation of families and what they eat, as well as in informal and formal interviews of women as they shopped, cooked, and fed their families. I began the study of Indian packaged food in 1998 as part of a ten-nation study on globalization, but it is only in the past three years that I have actively thought about the world of packaged food in India, primarily because of the growing number of packaged products both in Bangalore, where I am from, and in Boston, where I now live.[2] Secondly, my Indian friends and colleagues are at an age when they all have young children, and I find that Indian mothers both in urban India and in America struggle to find foods that their children will eat and that have what they consider to be both nutritive and cultural content.

The comparison between the urban Indian and diasporic Indian communities is useful since both the Bangalore community and the Boston community are dealing with similar problems of cosmopolitanism arising from being an integral part of a transnational world. From an outsiders perspective one may say that these two communities are roughly similar. Both these cities are central to the global economy through their dynamic participation in knowledge capital industries: software and information technology services and biotech advancements. But the similarity between the two communities holds up only in a first approximation. The local patterning of the diasporic community has a complex relationship to the dominant Western Judeo-Christian culture of the United States. As a group one could argue that Indians in America are marginalized, both politically and socially, by the dominant culture, even though they, according to sociologist Nazli Kibria, suffer from the label of a "model minority," derived from their "cultural programming for economic success"(2003: 11).[3]

The middle-class professionals in Bangalore lead a similar cosmopolitan life in which they too are an essential part of transnational culture. In the late 1980s Bangalore became one of the hot zones (Friedman 2000; Heitzman & Schenkluhn 2004) of technology, and then in the 1990s attracted new software companies and their employees.[4] Today Bangalore is a center for all those interested in engineering, software technology, chip building, information technology, and related fields (S. Srinivas 2001; Heitzman 2004). Engineers and other professionals have poured into the city, and the population of Bangalore has grown from 3.4 million in 1985 to 5.5 million in 2000,[5] and is projected to reach 7 million in 2011 (Heitzman 2004, quoting Bangalore Development Authority 2000 statistics). There are believed to be more information technology engineers in Bangalore (150,000) than in Silicon Valley in the United States (120,000) (See Kripalani & Engardio 2003: 69–70). As a result of this economic spurt and increased monetization, a significant and growing Indian middle class[6] has been created with the power and cultural capital for global consumption. It is important to note that this middle class is a minority, as over one third of the Indian population is illiterate and the country's per capita income is $460 per annum (Kripalani & Engardio 2003).

In May 2009 I went back to Jayamahal, now an upper-middle-class neighborhood in Bangalore. I went shopping for food and groceries to the local Naamdari's supermarket, an organic grocery store that sells provisions, fruit, vegetables (neatly washed, sorted and packed in small plastic tubs and bags) and other packaged food items such as biscuits, bottled drinks, prepared and packaged Indian and Western chips and snacks. In order to pay, my friend (who lives in Bangalore and overruled everyone else in her desire to pay) whipped out her Citibank Visa card and swiped it in a practiced motion to pay for the two large cartfuls of food we had accumulated surprisingly quickly. The store clerk pushed over the electronic signature keypad in a bored fashion as the supermarket bagger filled giant plastic bags for us and helpfully pushed the overladen carts to our car. We could have been shopping in any part of the urban, affluent, world—the rituals of provisioning seemed to be global and homogenous across the urban middle-class world. What did the rapid shift over thirty some years in rituals of provisioning— from ration cards to credit cards—tell us about the provisioning experience in urban India? What did this provisioning anecdote reveal about the backstory of Indian agriculture and prepared foods that allowed for such a Naamdari shopping experience? This is an exploration of some of the ideas about the getting of food, its making, gender performance, and the making of a middle-class identity in post-Liberalization India. The middle class is a self-defined class and many people of different socioeconomic backgrounds define themselves as such.

The middle class has significant social and economic clout as they loom large in the public imagination of urban India. For decades now journalists have extolled this new consumer revolution in India. *The Wall Street Journal* wrote at the beginning of this trajectory that "a thriving middle class is changing the face of India in land of poverty; its buying spree promises economic growth" (19 May 1988). Popular news magazines since the late 1980s have focused several stories on the consumption mores of the new India, such as, "The New Middle Class" (*Hindustan Times,* 7 June 1987), "The New Millionaires and How They Made It" (*India Today,* 31 October 1987), and "The New Gold Rush" (*Sunday,* 13 December 1987). The popularity of new Italian restaurants, Thai restaurants, and the ubiquitous bars, discotheques, coffee shops and pubs, created the early image of Bangalore as a cosmopolitan location within India. The Bangalore cosmopolitans are often single people or young couples who often find themselves far from their home and larger family (T. Srinivas 2006). This "spatially mobile class of professionals" creates a small (by Indian standards) but culturally important consumer-base known for its knowledgeable, often westernized, taste, and is characterized by its "multi ethnic, multi caste, polyglot" taste (Appadurai 1988: 6).

THE MULTICUISINE WORLD OF INDIAN PACKAGED FOOD

On March 12, 2005, the Indian Union Minister for Commerce and Industry, Kamal Nath addressed a conference on processed food products in the South Indian city of Bangalore. Newspaper reports of his address state "Mr. Kamal Nath emphasized India's potential to create 'brands' for a variety of food categories. . . . Brands could be developed for other select products where the potential to create global differentiation is possible like Alphonso Mango and Shimla Golden Apple and Malabar Pepper, he pointed out" (*Deccan Herald* March 12, 2005). Packaged food sales in India are forecast to soar, according to research from industry analysts BMI (Business Monitor International). The analysts forecast that by 2012 packaged food sales will climb over 67% to US$21.7 billion (Just-Food.com 2008). India will thus be a key emerging market for multinational food manufacturers. With India's economy forecast to grow at 7.9% a year between now and 2012, multinational interest in the market is "massive," BMI said. However, local conglomerates are investing more in the country's food sector, the analysts added. Well-established Indian corporate houses Reliance Industries and RPG have broken into India's burgeoning organized retail sector, while the likes of cigarette giants ITC (originally Indian Tobacco Company) and Godfrey have made moves into packaged foods (Just-Food.com 2008).

The Indian Tobacco Industry, a recent entrant into the world of packaged foods, announced that they see a huge growing market potential for these "agri-exports" among the middle classes of urban India and among NRIs (nonresident Indians, the local term for the diaspora), and they anticipate their company share, which is already at 60% of the total market (valued then at US$3.2 billion for the decade), growing still further (Chairman Speaks 2008). The indigenous packaged food industry takes Indian recipes, simplifies them for fast production, and decreases the preparation time and cost for the consumer. The industry includes food products for immediate consumption, as well as prepared foods such as snacks, spice powders, lentil wafers, pickles, and chutneys. A brief survey of goods on the shelf in any urban supermarket suggests that the Indian prepared food industry is divided along caste, ethnic and microregional lines of affiliations (Srinivas 2006).

Preparation of these indigenous foods has become a local cottage industry for cooperatives of women (many of them homemakers or widows), who are subcontracted to work for larger local food preparation companies (Srinivas 2001). In making a particular ethnic or caste specialty, local entrepreneurs, many of them women, often employ poor women from the targeted caste or ethnic group to prepare the product so it has an authentic taste, it is argued. Today in local markets in urban India over three hundred companies do business, and middle- and lower-middle-class housewives rely on these mixes and snacks to provide food for the family.

The prepared food industry has a large and eager clientele in urban America in the South Asian diaspora. According to Neil Soni, vice president of House of Spices, for "wholesalers . . . it's possibly a $15 million market, while for the retailers it could be a $25 million market. It's a good component with lots of growth opportunities" (Melwani 2004). The February 2006 issue of *Little India,* which proclaims itself the "largest circulated Indian publication in the USA" aimed at the South Asian diasporic readership, ran a feature article titled "The Immigrant Thali" by Lavinia Melwani. In the article Melwani quotes Madhu Gadia, the health editor of "Diabetes Living," which states that Indians have started eating far more prepared foods than ever before. Gadia states that Indian food is catching on even in the heartland of America. In her hometown of Ames, Iowa, "many of the supermarkets and coops carry frozen and canned Indian foods." Gadia states that "these are becoming part of the everyday home food of busy Indian families." She says that she knows of many friends who "carry the shelf stabilized ready Indian meals to work often." In the same article, Julie Sahni, chef, author, food historian, and culinary celebrity, states, "I think what has happened is that they [Indians] are buying a tremendous amount of ready-made foods because people with busy schedules still need to have something nice to put on the dinner table. . . . These are family people buying ready-made food. So there is a need and it is being fulfilled. There are some very good products out there, very tasty and authentic tasting in both shelf stabilized and frozen." Food manufacturers in India and in the United States scour the Indian food market for prepared foods that can be marketed to the growing Indian diaspora. Shwetal Patel of Raja Foods says, "Our best bread is going to be something we discovered in Delhi, called the Papad Paratha, a paratha with papad inside it. Trust me, it's unbelievable! We're also coming out with paneer and potato wraps. These will be great for people on the go, like college students and the taste is really good. It's solid Indian paneer which tastes delicious" (Melwani 2004).

To understand the globalization of this "front end of production" a shift to biography may be helpful. Gujerati Dhokla mixes, handwa mixes, and pickles, made with the correct ingredients, are made by Swad, a Gujarati-owned food preparation company. On the other hand, South Indian Brahmin prepared food is dominated by the Bangalore-based MTR,[7] owned and operated by the Maiya family, an Udupi Brahmin family from coastal western Karnataka (see chapter 5 in this volume). The MTR plant is staffed by Brahmin product tasters, and equipped with modern and sophisticated technology, inclusive of a state-of-the-art plant for producing pasta/vermicelli based on a plant in northern Italy. With their wide range of product categories and with a consistent track record of good-quality products, the brands of MTR have made substantial inroads into markets overseas, such as the United States, United Kingdom, the Persian Gulf region, the Far East (such as Singapore and Malaysia), and Australia, for consumption by the Indian diaspora. Their packets are also visible on supermarket shelves in urban India. MTR was begun by Parampalli Yajnanarayana Maiya and his brothers in 1924. The prepared food business that MTR dominates (known as MTR Foods) was started by accident. In the mid-1970s, when India was under an emergency act sponsored by then Prime Minister Indira Gandhi, a food control act was introduced that mandated that food was to be sold at very low prices. This move made it difficult for MTR to maintain its high standards in its restaurant business and forced it to diversify into the instant food business, selling chutneys and spice powders. In 1999, when I began this study, it was owned and operated by Sadananda Maiya and Harishchandra Maiya, sons of Yajnanarayana Maiya. By then the MTR foods division was producing packaged foods in different ranges—spices, instant mixes, ready-to-eat foods, vermicelli, ready-to-cook gravies, a range of frozen products, papads, pickles, chips, snacks, and ice creams.

In 1999 Hema Nalini Maiya, the daughter of Harischandra Maiya, who had been schooled in engineering, was forced to step in to head the company when her father suddenly died. When interviewed she indicated that the male employees tried to bully her, initially often overruling her orders. She stated that she was forced to show her control of the business by banning some of the older male employees from entering the restaurant kitchen and from issuing counter orders. She added happily, "ten years later I'm still here." In 2007 Ms. Maiya sold MTR Foods to the global food giant Orkla of Norway for approximately US$100 million, as reported in Finance Asia (Sahad 2007). According to global business rumors the MTR brand was so strong and unique that the American spice giant McCormick Foods was also in the bidding, but lost to Orkla (Sahad 2007).

The rise of MTR to the level of a global player, while an iconic story, was echoed by the rise of relatively small women-led cooperatives that specialized in making prepared foods for the Indian marketplace. Between the late 1980s and the turn of the century preparation of these indigenous prepared foods became a local cottage industry for cooperatives of Bangalorean women. The women often form local neighborhood- or Taluk- (regional) based cooperatives and sell the handmade products to larger companies, where they are then packaged and shipped. The local boom in food products has led to older women finding secure jobs in these cooperatives, and also to the rise of the housewife entrepreneur. These women entrepreneurs often have small production facilities either in home kitchens or in small "factories" in the center of the city.

I met Shantamma, one of these women, in her home in the neighborhood of Malleswaram in north Bangalore in July 1999 as she was stirring rice *ganji* (a rice stew used to make dried snacks called *vadam,* which are later fried) in a pot and flavored it with salt, crushed green chilies, and other spices. While we spoke she patted out small flat discs onto thin clean white cloth sheets and took them up to her rooftop terrace to dry in the sun. When I met her later that week she had tins of these ready-to-fry vadam snacks, which she was weighing and packing (with a printed label of her production facility), and a young man on a cycle transported the bags for her to the local collection point. She led me to some four other such operations on her narrow street in Malleswaram. She told me it was good way for her to earn money ever since her husband had died. She also said in an informal interview that as a woman she felt it was something she could do easily from her home when her children were growing up.

There are many women like Shantamma in Bangalore. In the south of Bangalore in a locality called Gandhi bazaar is another globally known woman pioneer food entrepreneur. She is known for a fried savory peanut snack popularly called "congress kadlekai." She employs three men and two women who fry the peanuts and spice them in a small factory off the main street. Her peanuts make their way through unofficial channels to many Brahmin homes in the Boston area and in San Francisco. She double packs them in plastic bags for overseas customers so that they retain their freshness. Other women run food catering services and food production facilities that serve both local communities and the global marketplace.

So the production of these global packaged foods usually have two stages of production. In the first stage technology and efficiency may be low. I have seen women steaming rice on an ancient kerosene stove, grinding chilies in an ancient pestle and mortar, and drying *vadams* (rice-based fritters) on house rooftops in the sun as they have done for several generations. The second stage involves high-technology quality control, including taste tests and chemical testing of the product, followed by industrial packaging with vacuum-sealing plants. Thus for the Indian consumer the authenticity of production is maintained within the hygienic modern packaging.

When I surveyed the food "factories" in 2000 it seemed that most of the labor was performed by women, however, by late 2009 some of these factories were run by women but the food was made by men, often under the women's tutelage. Many of these smaller cooperatives have become global producers. One of the earliest—a small cooperative of women food producers who make *papads* (thin lentil and rice fritters)— Shri Mahila Griha Udyog Lijjat was begun in 1959 with a starting capital of Rupees 80 (then roughly US$3 then) and was the brainchild of seven semiliterate Gujarati housewives in Mumbai. It now has a turnover of Rupees 5 billion (approximately US$100 million). Half of its products are exported. It employs over forty-seven thousand women and is run by Jyothi Naik, a woman from Mumbai, though it still retains it cooperative flavor with all the women who work there being referred to as *Behen* (sister) and all accounts being transparent to all the member sisters. Scholarships are given to children of member sisters and women's empowerment schemes are regularly funded by the women of Lijjat. The women of Lijjat suggest in their marketing materials that as women "feeding people is what we do best."

When we look at Indian food produced outside India, for example, in the United States, the industry is still in its initial stages where it is managed by women. Deep Foods is an international family-owned packaged food company started by an Indian immigrant to New York, which sells packaged Indian food to other American cities and to other cities all over the world. It is probably the biggest manufacturer of Indian food in the United States. It has a one-hundred-thousand-square-foot facility in Union, New Jersey, where it produces several lines—Mirch Masala, Deep and Curry Classics, as well as the Green Guru International Cuisine line, other frozen food lines such as Maharani and Kawon Malaysian parathas and a popular ice cream line called Reenas. According to the narrative on the Deep Foods website, the company was begun by Bhagawati Amin, a worker in a clothing mill, in the 1970s as she "had a passion for sharing the cuisine and culture from her homeland" and in 1977 the company was incorporated. In the 1980s her son Deepak (after whom the company was named) joined them with a degree in food science from Cornell University.

So whether we discuss the small factories of Shantamma or the large-scale production of Deep Foods, we find that women food entrepreneurs shape a new understanding of food consumption through radically altered ways of understanding food production that conceptually delink it from the nation, linking it effectively to larger processes and politics of global neoliberalism. In actuality it appears that a complex maneuver is undertaken by these women that lets them convert the domestic power of traditional knowledge of food and cooking processes into public power of global food entrepreneurship. They are able to accomplish this without feeling any societal constraints or consequences to their nonconformist behavior because the narrative of this power shift is cloaked in the recognizable and seemingly traditional rhetoric of being a good wife and mother as it relates to cooking and provisioning, overlaid upon the global virtue of being able to become an innovative entrepreneur, which has taken hold of the Indian imagination. As such, women food entrepreneurs enable an idealized straddling of the categories of the traditional, equated with caste and region, and the modern, usually equated with the West. They convert domestic knowledge into portable public goods.

As the biographies of these women demonstrate, the domestic virtues of having the knowledge and skill to process foods into wholesome meals—an essential part of being a good wife and mother—has hitherto operated within domestic realms, but two decades into globalization women are using this inherited knowledge, (a) to harness a unique agency located in this knowledge of food processing to insinuate themselves in the global capital neoliberal marketplace and (b) to use these strategic maneuvers to shift women's power from a domestic realm into an emergent public realm, thereby forcing male chefs and producers either to compete, or to create alternate venues of food production. This process also appears to be unleashing an emergent neoliberal version of feminism by allowing other women to buy their products, thus releasing them from the drudgery of cooking and cleaning. Beyond the obvious fact that women are still the provisioners in most families, despite joining the workforce (see T. Srinivas 2006), neoliberal conceptions of internationality seem to offer a disciplinary regime for women that reveal how gendered spaces are reflected, constructed, and transformed or transgressed.

Counterintuitively, the study shows that Indian food discourse is influenced by a multivalent and conflicting definitions of modernity and identity, with locus points both in indigenous practices (of caste and regionality) and Western influences, leading to a fluid understanding of womanhood, domesticity, and gastronomic knowledge. So while domesticity has been viewed as oppressive from the perspective of standard feminist thought, this study shows that women are able to subvert the power dynamics and mobilize the opportunities produced as sources of personal empowerment.

INDIA'S EMERGENT AGRO-INDUSTRIAL COMPLEX

The reach of companies such as Deep Foods and MTR depends not only on their proximity to the consumer but also upon the strength of the India's agricultural sector. But due to arcane inheritance laws and the legal protection of land that tie land to the cultivator, land is often spilt into minute holdings rendering only small-scale agriculture possible. Thus nascent agro-industrial entrepreneurs feel limited by owner-cultivator land laws prompting them to acquire land in other countries. As the *Economic Times* reports, this global "land grab" is a recent phenomenon and many Indian companies are entering the food production and retailing market in a big way through the consolidation of land holdings and buying of cheap agricultural land in Africa and other developing nations (Ramsurya 2010). Reliance India, a telecommunications company, now owns or leases several thousand acres in the breadbasket of India—the state of Punjab—and has several hundred retail outlets for produce all over the country, called Reliance Fresh. The Reliance group of industries is believed to have invested over Rupees 2,500 crores (approximately US$250 million) in agribusiness, with special focus on Reliance Fresh. Bharti enterprises, in cooperation with Walmart, has invested over US$2.5 billion in a chain of small supermarkets through India, and has leased vast tracts of land from small farmers to grow vegetables and produce. The discussion in the newspapers has been about the small land holdings of Indian farmers and what the state will do to protect the Indian farmer from such predatory practices. No clear legislation has been announced.

An example of the globalizing impetus of India's agriculture can be seen in Karuturi Global limited, which has food-processing facilities in Tumkur (close to Bangalore) and Bangalore itself. Karuturi began as an India-based company that dealt primarily in floriculture: cut roses for the European marketplace. However, over the past five years they have expanded into the food-processing business, growing and exporting pickled vegetables, including, beets, radishes, and (most importantly) gherkins. Karuturi Global grows no food for the Indian marketplace, but is purely an export company. In September of 2009, they received a certification of HAACP clearance by the U.S. Department of Agriculture and also have Kosher clearances to export to western Europe and the United States. Ramakrishna Karuturi, the owner of the company, owns land eight times the size of the metropolis of Mumbai (Karuturi, undated).

A report on Indian companies by the India Infoline Group says that Karuturi owns one of the world's largest landbanks—over 3,000 square kilometers in 2009 and growing (Kohli 2009). His company, Karuturi Global, figures among the top twenty-five transnational agriculture corporations. He owns land in Kenya, Ethiopia, and is now in talks to lease land in Uganda. Karuturi is the tip of a significant phenomenon: a breathtakingly ambitious bid to enter the global food market by a number of players. As a World Policy Institute report states, "groups of Punjabi farmers are currently negotiating a deal with the Ethiopian government to lease 250,000 acres at astonishingly low rates—$3.60 per acre per year, for 25 to 40 years, with the first five years rent-free" (Parulkar 2011). Particularly those farmers who are cash-rich but land-poor (due to controlling legislation in their home countries) are buying up enormous swathes of farmland in the poorer nations. According to activists who worry about indigenous African farmers and their right to food, "in the last one-and-a-half years alone, over 33 million hectares of prime agricultural land in dozens of developing countries have been snapped up—roughly the size of Germany" (Goodspeed 2009).

Mindful of India's long struggle to free itself from British bondage, the Indian Government has carefully avoided any overt role in this rising wave of seeming neocolonization. "We are now in talks with Namibia, after their President's visit, to use land for our purposes," minister Shashi Tharoor said when the *Times of India* asked him for the External Affairs Ministry's view on the subject. The globalizing impetus of Indian agribusiness is clear. Where it lands up is yet to be seen.

CONCLUSION

The Indian kitchen and food processing is significant to a broader understanding of social history as it complicates the narrative of the cross-cultural encounter between India and global neoliberalism. An examination of the ways in which women and men manage production and provisioning illuminate some important themes—the radical transformation in the manner of food production; the emotions that women invest in the provisioning, preparing and eating of food; and the significance and symbolism of food for differing communities. I have tried in this chapter to tie together the threads of gendered work, global consumption and production, and ethnic identity of and in South Asia. I have attempted to close a gap in our knowledge about the contemporary world and the cultural environment we face in the future.

While domesticity has been viewed as oppressive, women sometimes use domesticated skills to subvert established power dynamics and mobilize the opportunities produced as sources of personal empowerment. Women translate their embedded traditional knowledge (recipes and methods) of caste-based food into a postmodern capitalist product, engage traditional female homosocial spaces (food preparation spaces) as spaces of gendered politics, and use Western populist feminist rhetoric to negotiate a powerful status for themselves as keepers of ancient tradition.

NOTES

1. The economic benchmark paper, Bloomburg, reports that India may exceed the government expected target growth of 8.5 % for the fiscal year 2010 (Goyal & Krishnan 2010).

2. This research was supported in part by the Pew Charitable Trust and the Smith Richardson Foundation. I thank Peter Berger of the Center for the Study of Religion and World Affairs of Boston University for his support of my interest in food in Bangalore and his encouragement when I decided to study the gastro-scapes of Bangalore as part of a ten-nation comparative study of cultural globalization that he directed in 1998 and 1999. Subsequent data collection has been funded in part by Wheaton College. I thank my colleagues at Boston University, Merry White and Charles Lindholm, for supporting me in writing this paper and for reading its many incarnations. I have benefited enormously from discussions with Lakshmi Srinivas, and many of these discussions were the fuel for this paper. I also would like to thank Professor Gopal Karanth of the Institute of Social and Economic Change, Bangalore, for his unstinting help in understanding the Bangalore food industry. Dhanvanti Nayak did the initial research on food in Bangalore that led me to look at packaged food. Jyothi Kadambi and Aruna and Krishna Chidambi brought some of these packaged foods to my attention. Kala Sunder helped me enormously by pointing out interesting articles on food in the Bangalore newspapers and sending me newspaper clippings.

3. Zolli (2006) states:

"Even as America goes gray (and promptly dyes its hair), its skin will become more polychrome. Buoyed by higher birth rates among minorities and increasing immigration from Latin America and Asia, parts of the United States will become as diverse as a New York subway car. Minorities will make up one-third of the U.S. population in 2016.... High schools will soon routinely offer Hindi and Mandarin as Asians become a still more influential slice of the populace. MTV is already launching new channels, MTV Desi, MTV Chi, and MTV K aimed at South Asian, Chinese, and Korean immigrant teens. We can expect a proliferation of culture not only pitched to Asians, but by them. The rise of these new blocs will change American diets, tastes, and cultural references—but it will also redefine the notion of race itself, perhaps permanently. The distinction between black and white will become an anachronism: Get ready for the politics of brown."

4. It was estimated in the 1990s that there were about between 150 and 300 software firms in Bangalore, the majority of which were medium-sized, i.e., had between 100 and 150 employees, and only about ten percent of these firms had over 500 employees (personal interviews). More than two-thirds of the companies in Bangalore are Indian. The foreign component of total investment in the software industry, however, is about seventy percent (*Economist,* March 23rd, 1996, p. 67).

5. Population statistics derived from Megacities Taskforce of the International Geographical Union. http://www.megacities.uni-koeln.de/internet/

6. Scholars put the number of the Indian middle class anywhere between 100 to 250 million, a significant number by any standards.

7. "Mavalli Tiffin Rooms," as it was known, was famous all over South India for cooking their food in clarified butter and serving their customers with silver utensils, practices associated with "good" and "pure" upper-caste Brahmin food ways. Rumors swirled that the Maiya's recipes came from the kitchens of the famous

Krishna temple at Udupi where over five thousand pilgrims are fed every day with fifty different kinds of rice, salads, vegetarian curries, fruit chutneys, and accompaniments. MTR's cuisine was and is very micro-region specific and is located in what is called Dakshina Kannada on the western coast of Karnataka. This region is famous in South India both for their innovative mixing of sweet, hot, and sour ingredients and the business acumen of their chefs. The popular joke in Karnataka acknowledging their ability is that if one climbed to the top of Mt. Everest one would find an Udupi hotelier there ready with a cup of steaming coffee to greet you in a spotless cotton dhoti. Cleanliness, commitment to quality, and business acumen characterize the Udupi Brahmin food enterprise (see chapter 5 in this volume).

Globalizing South Asian Food Cultures

EARLIER STOPS TO NEW HORIZONS

R. S. Khare

The anthropological study of human food systems, although carried out since the beginning of the field, is becoming an important subfield and is proving "valuable for debating and advancing anthropological theory and research methods" (Mintz & Du Bois 2002: 99; also Messer 1984: 205–249). This postscript cannot be comprehensive, so it will focus on a few trajectories in anthropological food studies that will help us connect a much longer tradition to the current iteration of South Asian "curried cultures," as currently imagined by the urban, middle-class Indians at home and in the diaspora. In such a pursuit, the anthropological approach is helpful, although in it the food has been often considered only as "an instrument for the study of other things. . . . It was not the food or its preparation that was of interest, so much as what, socially speaking, the food and eating could be used for" (Mintz 1996: 3–4; J. [Jack] Goody 1982; also see below).

However, for about thirty years, anthropology has comprehensively studied food, underscoring its ecological variability and material/caloric function as much as its highly valued religious-cultural-symbolic variability and significance (see Harris 1985; Douglas 1984a; Mintz 1996: 1–32). By the seventies, in the United States, the anthropology of food and nutrition was recognized as a disciplinary subfield by the American Anthropological Association (see Mead 1943; on nutritional anthropology, see Fitzgerald 1977; and Jerome, Kandel & Pelto 1980). Lately, as this volume illustrates, distinct new transnational food marketing and consumption models and their related global cultural and communicational structures have appeared. To view foods and foodways in these ways is also to avoid, both in theory and practice, treating segments of the subject for the whole. If this means including hunger or, in Mintz's terms, "our 'animal' need to eat" (1996: 6), then it also now means tracking the development of new mass-produced food markets alongside related industrial production and consumption of "fast" and other kinds of foods (e.g., Wilk 2006a). So pursued, we also avoid the theoretical "escapes too fully and easily executed" for Indian foods (see chapter 1 this volume).

Food- and nutrition-focused studies on India began to appear by the 1970s (e.g., see Khare 1976a, 1976b; Gopaldas & Seshadri 1987; Appadurai 1988; Achaya 1998a, 1998b; Khare 2004: 407–428; see below). The Indic world-views were found to give food and eating a central and abiding attention on the close spiritual-religious, regional ecological and caste-kinship, and the health care grounds. The texts provided overarching knowledge and thought-systems and highly diverse food distribution and sharing patterns (for food in the classical Indian texts, see Prakash 1961; food systems in Hinduism and Buddhism, Khare 1992; and food-handling issues in South Asian society and culture, Khare & Rao 1986). Aesthetically, culinary distinctions and excellence are long held interrelated to, and are treated on par with, other major Indian fine arts (e.g., music, dance, drama, and literature). Hindu devotionalism, over the centuries, has perhaps best elaborated and popularized this interdependence, linking "food taste" to the classical *rasa* schemes. Major Hindu religious sects and temples continue to observe a comprehensive sensorial aesthetics where the daily devotional prayers draw on sight, touch, food taste, and music to worship the regnant deity (for a recent account and analysis, see Prasad 2007).

During the last fifty years, modern urban India's food adaptations very often constituted interesting culinary-cultural additions and reconfigurations rather than radical breaks and departures. In food production, India also went through the Green Revolution and a government-controlled food distribution system. By the 1980s, multinational agribusiness and food processing companies began to penetrate a much wider India, pulling in village economies and challenging villagers to adapt to global pressures (A. Gupta 1998). With Liberalization in the 1990s, however, the expanding Indian urban middle classes embarked on the trans-regional Indian as well as transnational foods and food tastes. The metropolitan India's major newspapers and magazines also began to take note of the foreign food tastes impacting the local-regional Indian palates.

Sociologically, as "eating out" became first a middle-class "fashion" and then created room for "fast foods," those numerous restaurants, coffee houses and tea stalls, and the roadside *dhabas,* or eateries, mushroomed. These food outlets not only led to a relaxation of the local caste and other customary barriers to eating out, but they also prepared the ground necessary for a wider public appetite for, say, the Chinese, American, Italian, Thai, and many other foreign cuisines. However, such new entrants hardly if ever upset the much deeper culinary specialties associated with almost all major places and traditions of religious worship, sacrifice, and the cities of pilgrimage (e.g., Amritsar, Ajmer, Ayodhya, Mathura, Varanasi, and Jagannath Puri), and even the erstwhile regional ruling capitals and major market towns.

ANTHROPOLOGICAL INITIATIVES: CLAUDE LÉVI-STRAUSS WITH CURRY

In the mid-twentieth century, anthropologists were often focused on the intriguing Indian caste system, the most pervasive social, religious and political identifier of Indian-ness in the eyes of many. In the traditional perspective, family- and caste-regulated Indian foods and foodways appeared closely related to those about marriage. As I summarize the stance of three well-known anthropologists on approaching Indian foodways, I shall comment on some related informal and personal situations in food-sharing and eating, highlighting the eternal problem of maintaining formal systems in everyday practice.

In post–World War II anthropology, Claude Lévi-Strauss gave a distinct conceptual boost to the study of food and culture structurally, that is, as "raw vs. cooked," "women vs. men," or "nature vs. culture." A favorite shorthand formulation was: "raw is to cooked as nature is to culture" (for a distinct point of conceptual departure, see Lévi-Strauss 1965; for an early explication of this structural method, Yalman 1967: 71–89). Lévi-Strauss's own travel accounts, *Tristes Tropiques,* on South America and South Asia were no less distinct for grappling with the core disciplinary conundrum: an anthropologist accounts for his cultural other only by accounting for his self. Such concerns converged in the curry-eating Lévi-Strauss among the Indians of South Asia in the 1940s.

In a Dhaka flat Lévi-Strauss ate a meal offered by an unnamed "young teacher" host, living with his wife and several other relatives. The description is worth quoting: "Squatting on the concrete floor, in the dim light of a single bulb hanging by its flex from the ceiling, I once—oh, Arabian Nights!—ate a dinner full of succulent ancestral savors, picking up the food with my fingers: first, the *Khichuri* rice and small lintels. . . . Then *nimkorma,* broiled chicken;

then *chingri kari,* an oily fruity stew of giant shrimps, and another stew with hard-boiled eggs called *dimer tak,* accompanied by cucumber sauce, *shosha;* finally, the dessert, *firni,* made of rice and milk." The host's young wife, "a silent, frightened doe" for Lévi-Strauss, was made to show her latest personal underwear from a chest-drawer to the visiting anthropologist "to prove [the host's] esteem for Western ways, *of which he knew nothing*" (Lévi-Strauss 1974 [1955]: 129; added italics).

Here, a traveling wartime French anthropologist, yet to be famous, was quick and candid about how he had found and characterized his Indian host's food and social ways. The vital question has always centered on how an anthropologist processes cultural otherness. It prefigures in his subsequent explication that the ethnographic project is a delicate balancing act between exoticism and the self-reflection that comes with doing it, a form of knowledge that only anthropology willingly embraced, where other disciplines sought expertise beyond the everyday. "When you study different societies," he urged, "it may be necessary to change your reference, and that involves somewhat painful mental gymnastics which furthermore can be learned from experience in the field." However, "we cannot, at one and the same time, bring our minds to bear both on very different societies and on the one in which we live" (see Charbonnier 1961: 18).[1] Can such a segregation of the theoretical object hold, or do we live in a world and practice now in a field of knowledge that has been totally transformed by the jostling of nations, peoples, and ways of knowing the world? What have we gained in the process and what might we have lost?

CASTE-FOCUSED APPROACHES:
MCKIM MARRIOTT AND LOUIS DUMONT

I will discuss Marriott first as much because of his early detailed analysis of caste-ranked food exchanges as for writing about his personal experience in the field centered on sharing an intoxicating celebratory drink (see Marriott 1968: 133–171, 1966: 200–221).[2] If Dumont's work on India also approached foodways in the caste systemic context, it was not without some wider relevant cultural notes and comments.

Marriott's 1966 writing on India was innovative at the time for being both autobiographical and insistently anthropological (1966: 200–212). While doing his anthropological field work in a North Indian village, Kishan Garhi (near Mathura, Uttar Pradesh), Marriott experienced the annual Hindu Holi festival twice in the village, and it centered on sharing an intoxicating celebratory drink and coping with its aftereffects. To the villagers, let us not forget, he was a foreigner, a "sahib" (especially in 1951–52, so soon after Indian Independence), attracting special attention. After the drink, Marriott, in his own words, "floated that afternoon [in the four villages], towed by my careening hosts.... My many photographs corroborate the visual impressions that I had of this journey: the world was a brilliant smear.... My face in the morning was still a brilliant vermillion, and my hair was orange from repeated embraces and scourings with colored powders...." Marriott, the anthropologist, coped with the experience anthropologically: though he was "unable at once to stretch my mind so far as to include both 'love' and these performances in one conception, I returned to the methodological maxim of Radcliffe-Brown [of learning about 'all the contexts' of a ritual's occurrence]" (Marriott 1966: 204–205; my interpolation).

A year later, at the next Holi, he recorded: "Who was it who was made to dance in the streets, fluting like Lord Krishna, with a garland of old shoes around his neck? It was I, the visiting anthropologist, who had asked far too many questions, and had always to receive respectful answers." Still, as an anthropologist in the field learns to take the strange and the unwelcome in stride, Marriott remarked: "The observing anthropologist, inquiring and reflecting on the forces that move men in their orbits, finds himself pressed to act as a witless bumpkin" (Marriott 1966: 212).

Unfortunate for food anthropology, however, Marriott did not write about his other Indian experiences of food sharing and feasting. Unlike Lévi-Strauss, Marriott thus skipped writing about himself as an eater, a guest, or a food giver/receiver during his Indian fieldwork, or any other visit to India. Nor was there ever any published evidence that the Indian food and foodways elicited distinct cultural-aesthetic responses from him (compare Dumont below).

His next publication (Marriott 1968: 133–171), a formal study and analysis of inter-caste ranking, started by noting that he was a visiting "sahib" in the village, and the villagers eventually accorded him a caste rank: "As soon as I began residing in the village called 'Kishan Garhi,' I found that the persons of different castes were struggling to assert and establish a caste-ranked order of social relationship around me, governing the activities of my employees, and affecting my personal uses of food and water, house, furniture, automobile, household rubbish...." To fit into the village's caste world, he was "given" a caste rank—"next the Jat cultivators" (Marriott 1968: 134, 135).

Widely cited for years, this study carved out a distinct approach, a method, and an explanation of village inter-caste ranking, centered on studying the actual transactions of the caste-ranking "food types." In evidence, he produced a whole array of transactional "matrices" of the numerous local inter-caste food exchanges to highlight a procedure, a social logic and an explanation of how a multi-caste village in North India ranked its caste members, highlighting both the village caste structure and instances of limited mobility within it. He tracked how the highest, the middling, and the lowest caste villagers gave and/or received, in different social and ritual contexts, the ritually crucial five *food types*—the "raw," "water boiled" (*kaccā*) or "ghee fried" (*pakkā*) foods, alongside the "food remnants" (particularly the eaten "leftovers" or *juthā*), garbage (*kuda*), and feces (*gū*). Since the village studied had thirty-six different caste groups, Marriott had multiple, multi-transactional ranking matrices, rather than the usual binary food exchange scorings (see Marriott 1968: 142–146, 156–158).

Generalizing, as Marriott had pursued the caste rank–dependent logic for both the giving/receiving of foods and for other social services in the village, he noticed that the food exchange social logic was converse of the service-rendering one. Thus, in a caste society if high rank derived from "the giving, [and] low rank from receiving the foods," then, under a complementary logic, "givers of services are [found] lower than receivers, whatever the nature of the service" (Marriott 1968: 170). His method, he ambitiously argued in conclusion, should encourage the reader to study similarly the "systems of tribute, hypergamy, games, and competitive behavior generally" (Marriott 1968: 170).

In fact, such ever wider generalizations became a signature of Marriott's anthropological research. His later studies embarked on careful sociological explanations of selected crucial Indian cultural constructions and their transactional relationships, with "evidence" coming from the selected clusters of relevant published ethnographic accounts and anthropological studies. Marriott thus verified and argued for his ever-wider comparative Indian analytical formulations, stipulations, and explanatory transactional schemes, climaxing into what he called "an ethnosociology of India" (see Marriott 1989: 1–39; Marriott & Inden 1977: 227–238). Here, as Marriott deciphered "the Hindu world," he also, at a grander epistemic level, claimed that some "deep comparisons" were possible between "Western and Indian sciences." For, after all, some of the Hindu/Indian "presuppositions" were, for instance, found "compatible with the findings of current linguistics, of molecular biology and atomic physics, of ecological biology, and of social systems theory. . . ." (Marriott 1989: 2, 33).

For the present writing, the relevance of such transactional analysis and reasoning is more when those comprehensive conceptual, cosmologic schemes located at the core of the conception of Indian food systems and cultures are under emphasis. The major Indian cosmological, philosophical, and religious thoughts identifying Hindu food circulations and foodways are thus verified, one could argue, in another way (cf. Khare 1992: 201–220). Indian thought locates food within life's full range, whether these are struggles of all god's creatures or of the local-regional human caste-kinship-ritual ways, or of the social ordinary *(sadharana)* dharma under normalcy or under major natural vagaries and calamities.

Compared to Marriott, Dumont's magnum opus, *Homo Hierarchicus* (first English edition 1970), distinctly tackled the topic in its own way. While establishing his theory of hierarchical opposition in the Indian caste system, Dumont accorded a distinct structural-cultural placement to Indian foods and food-sharing rules for explicating the Indian caste system (e.g., see Dumont 1980: 130–151, including the related substantial endnotes).[3] Focusing on the intercaste rules for food sharing or its avoidance, Dumont accorded Hindu food rules a dependent (or an encompassed) structural position within the hierarchal caste order. Put another way, the enormous actual diversity of Indian foods, foodways, and the related value anomalies had also to uphold, ultimately, the primacy of caste hierarchical ideology.

However, if the range and depth of Indian historical, technological, and socioeconomic changes have substantially qualified Dumont's stand, we must suitably reevaluate —and, when necessary, step out of—Dumont's caste-bound assumptions, formulations, and explanations. We start in this direction once we let the Indian foods and foodways become a primary, comprehensive subject of study, and, accordingly, we carefully "reread" Dumont's treatment of Hindu and Indian foods and foodways for their wider content and conception. His text on the topic needs to be read in full (i.e., including his substantial endnotes; see Dumont 1980: 91–93, 137–151; also 382–388). By doing so, and also by learning from other writings on or about him, we get better glimpses not only of Dumont's scholarship on caste-bound Indian foods, but also about some of his wider food-related Indian cultural-culinary-aesthetic sensibilities.

Overall, we know that Dumont's ritual purity- and impurity-based approach to caste-bound Hindu foods in *Homo Hierarchicus* served best in establishing his caste theory. At the core, this meant Dumont should (a) explicate the crucial rules and practices of "Hindu commensalism"; (b) review the changing values shaping Hindu "vegetarian vs. nonvegetarian" foodways; and (c) limit and downgrade the intrinsic significance of any intruding modernity in Indian foods and foodways. Thus, for Dumont, Marriott's (1968) inter-caste ranking study was little more than a "factual" illustration of a northern regional-local version of Hindu commensalism (Dumont 1980: 141–146, including the relevant endnotes). And, finally, foods and food exchanges were found to be a weaker sociological predictor of the caste order than marriage. Hence, food rules might be "closer, rather to marriage rules, but here again one must be careful not to push the similarity too far" (Dumont 1980: 131).

Still, *Homo Hierarchicus,* on a closer reading, gives us some more on the topic of Indian food and foodways. After remarking on the foodways of some other distant peoples and cultures, Dumont's writing incorporates some closely observed ethnographic examples and anecdotes in the main text, and a few related Sanskrit textual references and popular cultural examples in his endnotes (1980: 131–146). He thus carefully remarks, for example, on the complex value trade-offs Indian foodways make around the ideologically vexing issue of vegetarianism among the Hindu, Buddhist, and Jain cultures. Similarly, as he comments purposefully on the meat, meat-eating, the Hindu sacrificial system, and the sacred cow, he also alludes to M. K. Gandhi's nonviolence and vegetarianism (for the relevant references, see Dumont 1980: 139–141, including the notes 63c, 63g, 63i on page 383–384; for all the relevant endnotes on foods and foodways, see pp. 382–388).

Since the informal, experiential side of Louis Dumont's approach to Indian foods is little known (in print so far), I refer here to one known to me. One evening in November 1972 in Paris, when he and Jenny (his first wife) had invited me (with my family) to their flat for dinner, they had not only prepared a vegetarian meal but also recalled how they had cooked, once in a while, Indian basmati rice and spicy *daal* in their flat. For Dumont, to do so was to celebrate the memories of his North Indian fieldwork. Throughout that evening, an aesthetic and thought-provoking ethnographer and a gracious, talkative host overtook that well-known erudite, reserved scholar. His conversations that evening centered on the northern Hindu culinary subtleties, *sans* complicated ritual purity-impurity issues.[4] As for Dumont's work and its influence on mine on Indian food systems, it is best summarized by referring to the three distinct kinds of points of departure. First, foods in India, once pursued beyond daily practices, is found intimately and pervasively related to the people's caste-kin-family and personal lives on the one hand, and to certain crucial cosmological and collective social-ceremonial value structures on the other (see Khare 1976b). Second, the actual cultural-ritual classifications of Hindu foods, foodways, and the related material culture are far more differentiated, by regions, values, and practices, than Marriott's and Dumont's studies indicate, hence requiring closer-fitting descriptive, conceptual, and analytical markers. And once done so, Indic foods and foodways reveal distinct—and indispensable—cultural, linguistic, moral, and material grammars of action patterns, purposes, and meanings (see Khare 1976b: 1–27, 47–80; Khare 1992).

Third, food and food availability issues in India constantly draw attention to the historically changing social life, and to related regional, economic, political, and natural vagaries (e.g., of rains and drought). Thus, however sliced, the Indian moral, mythical, social, and material economies reconfigured virtually every year, challenging Indian villagers to make sense while facing food abundance or scarcity (see Khare 1976b: 142–173). For instance, is there a suitably differentiated frame of moral compass available to the Hindu that is wider and more flexible than that of inter-caste morality? There is, some scholars have argued, once the far wider daily "ordinary" *(sahaj)* dharma is *not* aborted or neglected in favor of the "specialized," better emphasized *(varna-jati)* orders in routine eating, food sharing, and feeding spheres (see Khare 1998b: 253–278).

The preceding points of departure also underscored how my phenomenological approach to food in the Indian family-kin-community helped expose the hidden or neglected classificatory material, social, religious-ritual-philosophical, and linguistic orders that held keys to much more than just the caste order, whether it were the aphoristic Upanishads on the Indic conceptions of food, or the prevalent ways of Indian hospitality, the "Indian meal," and the abstemious Hindu saints (see Khare & Rao 1986; 1992: 27–52; 201–220). Indian food and food-sharing issues were about much more than the materialist vs. the moralist theoretical dichotomy. They rather irresistibly pulsated in ever-wider meaning-making waves, as under A. K. Ramanujan's creative collocated cultural approach, conjugating whole arrays of Indian religious-ritual-philosophical, literary-poetic, and oral cultures (see Ramanujan 1992: 221–250).

By 1977, not only a focus on "anthropology of food" in India and on South Asia had appeared, there also emerged an international and interregional focus on studying foodways and systems. This was started by the International Commission on Anthropology of Food (ICAF) at the behest of the International Union of Anthropological and Ethnological Sciences (IUAES).[5] The commission, with its several "regional working groups" (e.g., the North American, European, South Asian, and Southeast Asian) had started to encourage collaborative anthropological research on the regional foods, foodways, and food problems by pooling the new and the already available resources in research, teaching, and policy related work. Thus, for instance, the South Asian regional food commission had produced an edited volume, highlighting a comprehensive approach to study South Asian food systems, including the value of centuries-old historical records of "food offerings" in a major South Indian temple; operating strikingly elaborate foodways to identify distinct religious sects; interdependence between "the diet-health contingencies"; and the cultural-economic factors in the Indian government's food distribution issues to the poor (see Khare & Rao 1986).

Among a host of research conferences, collaborative projects, research reports, and publications, we also held, in January 1985, a Smithsonian Institution–sponsored "Conference on Food Systems and Communication Structures" in Mysore, India.[6] Concerned with the sociocultural, regional semiotic, and political communicational structures in Indian/South Asian food systems, the meeting resulted in a publication assembling together the studies of conspicuous "divine feasts"; foods with Hindu saints and the cosmic models of Hindu foods; anomalous food eating and status in Hindu mythology; the "essence and experience" food in Buddhism; and an insightful collage of "food images" in India (see Khare 1992: 1–25).

FOOD PROBLEMS IN SOCIAL AND MORAL ORDERS: MARY DOUGLAS

However, the preceding wider anthropological studies of foodways in India/South Asia were mostly rooted in the well-known anthropological studies of the Indian caste, kinship, and religious orders (e.g., M.N. Srinivas, 1965, along with the studies of Marriott and Dumont already discussed). Mary Douglas (1984b), with her fieldwork experience in Africa, was another anthropologist who, interested in comparing and generalizing from different socioreligious orders, gave attention to food as an integral part of the social-ritual-moral human order (see Douglas 1972). Her work on social order thus had a strong affinity to those on caste and food orders in India (in evidence: Dumont asked her to write a foreword to a printing of *Homo Hierarchicus*). Building on this convergence, I invited Mary Douglas to join the commission in 1978 as cochair. At the time, she had begun to explore "food in the social order" in a comprehensive way, including attention to issues of food availability.[7]

Her introduction to the resulting volume set forth in detail her interpretive approach and concerns (Douglas 1984a: 1–39), explicating "some elementary relations between food sharing and social integration. . . . It starts from the assumption that unlike livestock, humans make some choices that are not governed by physiological processes. They choose what to eat, when and how often, in what order, and with whom" (Douglas 1984: 2–3). Thus, whether it was a regular meal or a food availability problem, a crucial point was "to rectify thinking about food is to recognize how food enters the moral and social intentions of individuals" (Douglas 1984: 8, 9). This intention, she argued, also played a crucial role in food problems. For it could cause social and moral acceptance of food under one circumstance, or it could also mean rejection under another. Since the problems are further complicated when major gaps exist between "our" (i.e., the modern generalizing Western type) vs. "their" (i.e., from small-scale studies of remote, exotic places) views of the food problem, she concluded that we still lacked that "fine tuned relevance to the way that the great food problems are posed" (cf. A. K. Sen 1988).

Complementarily, Mary Douglas tended to express her personal reactions and opinions to different foods and culinary cultural and aesthetic preferences rather spontaneously. She did so informally, whether she was a guest, a host, or just a casual observer.[8] She was keenly observant and persistently curious whether she was eating informally at someone's home or was in a famous restaurant in New York. For instance, in a major New Delhi hotel (in December 1978), during an international conference, a hotel waiter's persistence in getting a hefty *bakhshish* (tip) from her, a foreign visitor, elicited her comment on the Indian food-serving aesthetics and its hierarchical expectations.[9] And, not unlike Lévi-Strauss decades ago, she also commented on how some Indians freely ate with their fingers in a major Indian hotel while the others strictly went with forks and knives.[10]

Since Mary Douglas's cultural-religious-symbolic approach to food studies stressed the roles moral attitudes and values played in major foodways and food availability issues, it had a broad affinity with the anthropological approach developed by M. N. Srinivas, Dumont, and Marriott to study caste systems in India. My approach had also started from the same quarter.[11] Still, Douglas and I independently arrived at and stressed in our own way the crucial place of moral values and attitudes in devising practical ways to resolving food problems (compare Khare 2004: 426–427; Douglas 1984a: 8–9). By the nineties, my interest in food studies had changed once again.[12]

CURRY AS CULTURAL TASTE, GLOBALIZING MARKETS, AND NEW TRENDS

The term "curry," noted in use since the late seventeenth century, refers to "a food, dish or sauce in Indian cuisine seasoned with a mixture of pungent spices" (Webster International Dictionary 1993: 285).[13] In sensorial, biochemical, physiological, bio-psychological, and cultural-aesthetic terms, a "curry culture" is firmly rooted not only regionally and geographically in South Asia, but it is also embedded in the corresponding food habit forming *patterns of taste.* The distinct combinations of pungent spices, flavors, and aromas, often associated with distinct food dishes, tend to engrain distinct food habits among the eaters (potentially from anywhere in the world). Attracting synecdochical webs of South Asian culinary ways, tastes, and meanings during the last century, "curry" began to represent—and expand on—a regionally distinct culinary culture into a pan-Indian one. With recent cultural globalization, an expanding South Asian diaspora, and the internationally mobile westernized youth, "curry" has become culinary-cultural shorthand for the entire *desi* (native home recalling) foods and foodways. Put another way, such formations are ever-farther from any colonial era constructions.

Curry, as a noun or a verb, represents a distinctly civilizational (and pan-Indian) cooking and eating construction of history, culture, and food politics. The expanding and rising South Asian middle classes have pushed these distinct food tastes and food habits into ever-wider overseas food markets, creating correspondingly a demand for such cuisines in more restaurants, including that curry-eating habit (e.g., Conlon 1995). In India, if this has meant loosening of caste-kinship rules in eating and food sharing, it has also created room for that ever more regionally diverse national culinary smorgasbord. The urban middle-class South Asian, living at home, traveling, or settled abroad, now increasingly traverses such local-to-global-to-local food-sharing cycles. But these also show when and how globalization may fire, misfire, or fail. Thus, if globalizing modernity has, by expanding food business, brought ashore "fast foods," "organic foods," and "genetically modified foods," then it has also raised new concerns about healthy food, health, and the quality of life. The globalizing foods have deepened a counter-thirst for those "authentic grandmother- or mother-cooked meals."

As this volume demonstrates, "curried cultures," products increasingly of globalizing South Asian foodways, have already acquired, by their changing history, social, and market values, a distinct transnational culinary and cultural signature. They are quickly climbing over any remaining stereotypical colonial or even narrow postcolonial culinary-cultural politics. The new aesthetics derives from that distinct South Asian sensibility that places "food taste" amid inter-nestling touch, sight, smell, and hearing. Traditionally, in all major religious places and political ceremonies, for instance, food is offered accompanied by conspicuous ritually tactile, visual, and musical displays. This is unlike the Western counterpart that, as Korsmeyer (2005: 2) has noted, tends "to downgrade taste (along with touch and smell) as merely 'bodily' senses, in contrast to the more intellectually coordinate senses of sight and hearing."

Simultaneously, curried cultures are reaching the cosmopolitan, transnational elites and tourists at one end, and are multiplying amid the Indian diaspora as the competing roadside tea stalls and eateries *(dhabas)* at the other. Here, Sidney Mintz's studies of historically select, prized foods (e.g., sugar) and their widening socioeconomic production, values, and availability are useful to compare (see Mintz 1985, 2006: 3–11). More useful in studying Indian curry cultures might be Mintz's writings on the changing eating patterns amid different cuisine constructions (Mintz 1996).

Thus, some interesting globalized meaning-making frames are being attempted in India today. For instance, with Kraft Foods (India) recently buying the British Cadbury Chocolates, new Indian television advertisements are trying to culturally reframe chocolate. Though an increasingly "in" middle-class treat, it is still a culturally foreign sweet for most Indians. To widen its market, the company advertisements are now labeling chocolate "a celebratory Indian sweet" (personal observation in India, summer 2010). However, chocolate's desired entry might be still some time away, since no major traditional family and religious ceremonies let chocolate confections enter, much replace, the customary Indian sweets, the symbols of coveted auspicious celebratory values. In India, such ongoing "insider-outsider" culinary-cultural battles are frequent, even long term. For instance, M. K. Gandhi's "vegetarianism" (and all that it epitomizes to promote, for instance, cardiovascular health in urban middle-class India and to Indian morality on nonviolence), the creeping-up genetically modified foods, and the multiple fast food "food courts" in the Indian shopping malls are all jostling to keep their foothold.[14]

Outside India and the subcontinent, the multiplying South Asian food markets and their ready-to-heat-and-eat food-vending sections are among the major creative force multipliers for the curry culture. Supporting these is now an expanding international (and not only a South Asian) entrepreneurial class in mass South Asian food production, processing, and marketing. The South Asian and foreign entrepreneurs are found collaborating in ever-newer ways. For instance, "Darjeeling Tea," now often blended in and marketed from London today ends up serving pervasively not only the European and American food markets but also both the Indian and the British economies. The "authentic Patak's Indian Spices and curry powders" firm was honored (in 2002) with the OBE by the British queen. Such sustained successful efforts have opened up new consumers of "the authentic South Asian curries" in major retail American food stores and grocery chains.[15]

FROM THE AUTHENTIC TO THE "FAST" AND OTHER NOVEL FOODWAYS

Another related new development in South Asian cuisines juxtaposes the indigenous and the authentic to whatever is "fast food." However, as a business reality, *both* sides must find their customer niches at one level, and, at another, learn to live together, especially in large towns. The resulting Indian urban food fare is far more than just a clumsy traditional-modern "hybrid." By context and circumstance, it is, instead, often a consciously planned *gastronomic orchestration,* where from a chic elite restaurant to a McDonald's, to a casual vegetarian eatery, a road corner *dhaba,* an ordinary sweetshop, a *chaat* and *kulfi* stall, and a cluster of roadside sweet and savory snack sellers— all pitch their best today to retain as well as expand their customer base. Similarly, the bulk ready-to-eat food serving urban outlets also strategize on the authenticity and fast food–like convenience of their products, whether it is now New Delhi, London, Paris, New York, or Tokyo.

There is a whole "grammar of quality product, authentic taste, and inviting packaging management" in all such businesses today. If authenticity also sometimes requires "reproductions," "emulations," and "improvisations," then these must be handled by the outstanding cooks or chefs. Once the name recognition is firmly established in a major Indian city or a region for certain kinds of foods, curry sauces, pickles, or snacks, the transnational business footholds follow next (e.g., "Haldiram's Indian Snacks and Sweets" now have a sizeable presence in the Indian American food markets).

The Indian local-regional convenience foods and the international fast foods now openly compete in India. Though McDonald's, Dominos, Pizza Hut, and Ben and Jerry's ice cream shops, among others, are still a social, food, and culinary novelty for the middle class, they have not been able to replace the local-regional food companies selling customary convenience sweets, snacks, and ready-to-eat foods. The novelty of foreign fast food shops is most often found as much in their setup and selling-serving getup (for the urban youth and the middle class) as in the surrounding new social activities and meanings they generate. Still, these are hardly the places for routine everyday eating. They are for looking "cool" to the youth. Then there is also a wider critical social, health-nutrition, and moral commentary in India on the fast foods.

Still, metropolitan middle-class India is already under a sort of "McDonald's effect." All kinds of "fast foods" are now sought as much for novel taste and novel social ambience as convenience. However, India is very far from becoming a "fast food nation" (see Schlosser 2001), assuming that it ever would want to be one. Though foreign fast food companies have already quickly adapted to the Indian social, religious, and food-taste ways, the convergence is likely to have long-term limits. As the companies salivate at the new huge untapped Indian market, the Indian culinary cultures and the related substantial business interests reassert to control their markets. On the other side, with time, even the westernized young Indian families might also uncover the unhealthy food habits and associated rising risks in personal health. Though the Indian incarnation of Eric Schlosser has still to appear, it might be only a matter of time, underscoring how globalizing waves are seldom without some severe undertows. Over time, the major interests in both the Indian and foreign fast foods would have to seek a health-promoting and culturally and aesthetically convergent balance.

Whether India or the United States, fast foods thus can seldom qualify for a "regular," healthy, or "quality" meal. In fact, the more health-conscious upper-middle class American is found turning towards "natural and organic foods." Those ecologically conscious promote more local farm markets and some would even grow vegetables in their backyard. For instance, with the national media in attendance, and with school children's active involvement, Michelle Obama, the first lady of the United States, has planted a vegetable garden at the White House. With fast, fatty, and unhealthy food habits lurking, this is also for a fight against the increasing obesity among the nation's children. Sidney Mintz echoes a similar message from anthropology apropos of the American birth of fast foods: "Perhaps we need to know more than we do about the history and sociology of our own food practices. In our daily life we meet the enemy all the time, and indeed he probably is us" (Mintz 2006: 3). Hence, as a remedy, Mintz (2006: 3, 10–11) argues for "food at moderate speeds." To do so is to intensify the search for "that good and healthy food for more and more people . . . and that such foods can be made available fast enough—and more important, prepared at slow enough speeds—for all of us."

NOTES

1. In a personal meeting austere in speech and interaction, Lévi-Strauss recalled to me his visit to the Indian subcontinent one day in Paris in the autumn of 1972. As author of the "culinary triangle," he commented some on the distinct food culture of the subcontinent. But those of us working on India at the time endeavored to show why—and how—India's food categories did *not* neatly fit Lévi-Strauss's binary structural formulations (see Marriott 1968; Khare 1976b).

2. Broadly, if Dumont's emphasis on caste system prompted me in 1959 to study the Kanya-Kubja Brahman's intracaste social organization, with ritual food exchanges at its core, then the Marriott's anthology, *Village India* (1955), along with M. N. Srinivas (1955) and Majumdar (1958), encouraged me to study a village (nearby Lucknow) for its ritual purity and pollution issues in relation to the village's personal and public health problems. At the time, Marriott (1968) gave me the needed impetus to turn intensively to study the Indian food system.

3. For my approach to Dumont's works on both India and Europe, and on my contacts with him, see Khare 2006: 1–35. Briefly, Louis Dumont influenced my interests in the Hindu castes and Indian food systems most during the 1957–1966 decade. He was known in India at the time for the debates and discussions in his journal (initially coedited with David Pocock), *Contributions to Indian Sociology.* Some of these writings influenced my decision in 1959 to study the Kanya-Kubja Brahmans' caste organization in Lucknow. Though Dumont's influence on my trajectory of food studies, during the seventies, was less direct and sustained than

Marriott's, I was drawn to Dumont's studies of modern Western individualism and economy for related reasons (Dumont 1977).

4. Though Dumont, like Marriott, allowed little room in his published "scientific writings" for any field-related personal or informal social experiences, Dumont nevertheless gave occasional glimpses of how culturally and aesthetically finely attuned he was to Indian food culture. After studying both South and North India, he had a softer corner, we learn, for southern Indians and their cultural aesthetics (see Madan 1999: 473–501).

5. As chair of the Commission, I invited Mary Douglas (then at the Russell Sage Foundation, New York) to join the Commission in 1978, as cochair. We collaborated to further international research cooperation among anthropologists (and with other specialists) working on food and food problems (for initial details on the Commission, see Douglas and Khare 1979: 903–913; Khare 2008: 360–361).

6. The commission's early files, newsletters, and publications, including some of Mary Douglas's commission papers, are a part of the records my office has at the University of Virginia.

7. Her research project out of the Russell Sage Foundation in New York was concerned with three distinct American ethnic foodways (i.e., the Oglala Sioux of South Dakota, African Americans, and Italian Americans), deciphering their distinct consumption patterns. After summarizing the findings of her research team, and remarking on the related "culinary complexity" (a topic on which a professor of computer science had helped her), Douglas underscored the importance of the "lines of [social] solidarity and competition" in both food habits and food distribution (1984a: 35).

8. As collaborators, she and I had numerous occasions to share a meal and to be also a host or a guest to each other (or be cohosts to others), whether it was for a "quick working meal," a meal in an upper-crust New York restaurant, or in a New Delhi, Rome, Vienna, Paris, or London hotel. Wherever it was, Mary Douglas was quick to remark as often about the display and handling of foods as on the ambience of the place.

9. And the waiter, in turn, reproached me in Hindi for denying him his tip. He retorted, "Why are you spoiling my day? I did not ask anything of you."

10. Observing such differences was, of course, closely related to Mary Douglas's distinct interest in anthropology of everyday life, whether it related to pollution, dirt, body, food, social boundaries, fences, or the environmental risks. She often reflected on both the mundane and the profound in each other's terms.

11. Unlike Dumont and Marriott, Mary Douglas did influence my studies early on. I was in touch with her, for the first time, only in late 1977. Fortuitously, however, our approach to food had converging interests, allowing for the collaboration described here.

12. I repeatedly taught "dietary health and culture" courses at my university, with a focus on the construction/deconstruction of one's self-image around food, especially among the upper-middle-class American and Indian-American university students. With suitable interdisciplinary collaboration, the eating disorders were

pursued, arising out of trauma (e.g., the Cambodian refugees in the United States), and under anorexia nervosa and bulimia.

13. An "authentic curry" demands knowledgeable, measured use of the "curry powder" (i.e., a dry mixture of such spices as turmeric, cayenne pepper, fenugreek, and curry [in Tamil, *kari*] leaves from Indian tree *Murraya koenijii*). This spice use becomes a far subtler and much more adept art at the hands of Indian chefs-de-cuisine as much as at the hands of adept Indian grandmothers, mothers, and aunts.

14. However, neither side is still an easy pushover in the culturally and politically diverse India. For instance, Gandhi's vegetarianism and nonviolence may still link up with the cow protection politics of the Hindu right, showing limits to the Indian metropolitan culinary modernity and its unbounded liberalism (see Khare 2004: 424–427).

15. For instance, such major American bulk food retailers as the Sam's Club and Costco have begun selling certain Indian spices, heat-and-eat curry preparations, and the basmati rice. Such items are also becoming an "in-thing to have" in international food aisles of such grocery chain stores as Safeway.

REFERENCES

Aagrah. (2004, December 21). *Yorkshire Post.*

Abbas, T. (2005). Recent Developments to British Multicultural Theory, Policy and Practice: The Case of British Muslims. *Citizenship Studies, 9,* 154–159.

Abu al-Fazl ibn Mubarak. (1873). *The Ain i Akbari, by Abul Fazl translated from the original Persian by H. Blochmann (and Colonel H. S. Jarrett).* Calcutta: Baptist Mission Press.

Abu-Lughod, J. L. (1989). *Before European Hegemony: The World System A.D. 1250–1350.* New York: Oxford University Press.

Achaya, K. (1998a). *A Historical Dictionary of Indian Food.* New Delhi: Oxford University Press.

———. (1998b). *Indian Food: A Historical Companion.* New Delhi: Oxford University Press.

ACSA Annual Meeting, Froehlich, D., & Pride, M. (2008). Seeking the City: Visionaries on the Margins. 96th ACSA Annual Meeting. *Global Cultures in Local Economies: Case Study of Ethnic Fast Food Restaurants* (pp. 401–13). Ann Arbor, MI: College of Architecture and Urban Planning, University of Michigan.

Adams, C. (Ed.). (1987). *Across Seven Seas and Thirteen Rivers: Life Stories of Pioneer Sylhetti Settlers in Britain.* London: Eastside.

Agius, A. & Lee, J. (2006). Raising the Status of the Cashier: Latina-White Interactions in an Ethnic Market. *Sociological Forum, 21*(2), 197–218.

Aldrich, H. E., & Waldinger, R. (1990). Ethnicity and Entrepreneurship. *Annual Review of Sociology, 16,* 111–135.

Alexander, C. (1998). Re-imaging the Muslim. *European Journal of Social Sciences, 11,* 439–450.

Alibhai-Brown, Y. (1998, August 25). Whose Food Is It Anyway? *Guardian* (London), p. 2.

———. (2001a, July 13). Britain's Beloved Chicken Tikka Masala Is under Threat from a New Wave of Upmarket Curry Houses. *Annex Guardian.*

———. (2001b). *Imagining the New Britain.* New York: Routledge.

Allen, C., & Dwivedi, S. (1984). *Lives of the Indian Princes.* New York: Crown, in association with the Taj Hotel Group.

Allen, S. (1971). *New Minorities, Old Conflicts: Asian and West Indian Migrants in Britain.* New York: Random House.

Ames, K. (1992). *Death in the Dining Room and Other Tales of Victorian Culture.* Philadelphia: Temple University Press.

Amin, A. (2002). Ethnicity and the Multicultural City: Living With Diversity. *Environment and Planning, 34,* 959–980.

Amin, A., & Parkinson, M. (2002). *Ethnicity and the Multicultural City: Living with Diversity.* Swindon, UK: Economic and Research Council.

Anderson, B. (2006). *Imagined Communities: Reflections on the Origin and Spread of Nationalism.* London: Verso.

Anderson, E. N. (2005). *Everyone Eats: Understanding Food and Culture.* New York: New York University Press.

Anderson, K. J. (1987). The Idea of Chinatown: The Power of Place and Institutional Practice in the Making of a Racial Category. *Annals of the Association of American Geographers, 77*(4), 580–598.

Anderson, K., & Gale, F. (1992). *Inventing Places: Studies in Cultural Geography.* Melbourne, Australia: Longman Cheshire.

Anglo-Indian, An. (1882). *Indian Outfits and Establishments: A Practical Guide for Persons about To Reside in India; Detailing the Articles Which Should Be Taken Out, and the Requirements of Home Life and Management There.* London: L. Upcott Gill.

Anthias, F., Yuval-Davis, N., & Cain, H. (1992). *Racialized Boundaries: Race, Nation, Gender, Colour, and Class and the Anti-racist Struggle.* London; New York: Routledge.

Appadurai, A. (1981). Gastro-Politics in Hindu South Asia. *American Ethnologist, 8*(3), 494–511.

———. (1986a). On Culinary Authenticity. *Anthropology Today, 2,* 4.

———. (Ed). (1986b). *The Social Life of Things: Commodities in Cultural Perspective.* Cambridge: Cambridge University Press.

———. (1988). How to Make a National Cuisine: Cookbooks in Contemporary India. *Comparative Studies in Society and History, 30*(1), 3–24.

———. (1990). Disjuncture and Difference in the Global Cultural Economy. In M. Featherstone (Ed.), *Global Culture: Nationalism, Globalization and Modernity* (pp. 295–310). Newbury Park, CA: Sage.

———. (1995). Playing with Modernity. The Decolonization of Indian Cricket. In C. Breckenridge (Ed.), *Consuming Modernity* (pp. 23–48). Minneapolis: University of Minnesota Press.

———. (1996). *Modernity at Large: Cultural Dimensions of Globalization.* Minneapolis: University of Minnesota Press.

———. (2000). Spectral Housing and Urban Cleansing: Notes on Millennial Mumbai. *Public Culture, 12*(3), 627–651.

———. (2001). *Globalization.* Durham, NC: Duke University Press.

———. (2006). *Fear of Small Numbers: An Essay on the Geography of Anger.* Durham, NC: Duke University Press.

Appadurai, A. & Breckenridge, C. (1995). Public Modernity in India. In C. Breckenridge. (Ed.). *Consuming Modernity. Public Culture in a South Asian World* (pp. 1–22). Minneapolis: University of Minnesota Press.

Appiah, A. (2006). *Cosmopolitanism: Ethics in a World of Strangers.* New York: W.W. Norton.

Apple, R. W., Jr. (2003, January 17). Journeys: In Berkeley, Strollers Find Art with Curb Appeal. *New York Times,* Travel Section.

Armstead, H. C. H. (1987). *Princely Pageant.* London: T. Harmsworth.

Arnold, D. (Ed.). (1988). *Imperial Medicine and Indigenous Societies.* Manchester: Manchester University Press.

———. (1993). *Colonizing the Body: State Medicine and Epidemic Disease in Nineteenth-century India.* Berkeley: University of California Press.

———. (1994). The "Discovery" of Malnutrition and Diet in Colonial India. *Indian Economic & Social History Review, 31*(1), 1–26.

Arunachalam, M. (1980). *Festivals of Tamil Nadu.* Tiruchitrambalam, Tanjavur District: Gandhi Vidyalayam.

Asad, T. (1990). Multiculturalism and British Identity in the Wake of the Rushdie Affair. *Politics & Society, 18*(4), 455–480.

Ashcroft, B., Griffiths, G., & Tiffin, H. (1995). *The Post-Colonial Studies Reader.* London; New York: Routledge.

Ashton, S. R. (1982). *British Policy towards the Indian States, 1905–1939.* London: Curzon.

Asians Have Made This Place Thrive. (1976, July 13). *Birmingham Evening Mail.*

Assadi, M. (1999). Communal Violence in Coastal Belt. *Economic and Political Weekly, 34*(8), 446–448.

Assault Fears at Balti Houses. (1997, September 23). *Birmingham Evening Mail.*

Aurora, G. S. (1967). *The New Frontiersmen: A Sociological Study of Indian Immigrants in the United Kingdom.* New York: Humanities.

Axtmann, R., & Houbert, J. (1998). *Globalization and Europe: Theoretical and Empirical Investigations.* London; Washington, DC: Pinter.

Aziz, K. (1982). Indian Restaurants in the West. *Curry Magazine, Spring* (8), 130.

Back, L., Keith, M., Khan, A., Shukra, K., & Solomos, J. (2002). New Labour's White Heart: Politics, Multiculturalism, and the Return of Assimilation. *Political Quarterly, 73,* 445–454.

Bailey, T. R. (1987). *Immigrant and Native Workers: Contrasts and Competition.* Boulder, CO: Westview.

Bakhle, J. (2005). *Two Men and Music: Nationalism in the Making of an Indian Classical Tradition.* Oxford; New York: Oxford University Press.

Ballard, R. (Ed.). (1994). *Desh Pardesh: The South Asian Presence in Britain.* London: Hurst.

———. (2003). The South Asian Presence in Britain and Its Transnational Connections. In B.C. Parekh, G. Singh, & S. Vertovec (Eds.), *Culture and Economy in the Indian Diaspora* (pp. 197–222). London: Routledge.

Bandyopadhyay, B. (1872). *Swasthyakaumudi: Arthat Sarbasadharaner Abashya Gyatabya Bishayak Nutanbidha Grantha* [A Manual of Health: The New Essential Guide for the Common Man]. Dacca.

Banerjee, S.M. (2004). *Men, Women, and Domestics: Articulating Middle-Class Identity in Colonial Bengal.* New Delhi: Oxford University Press.

Banerji, C. (1997). *Bengali Cooking: Seasons and Festivals.* London: Serif.

———. (2006). *Feeding the Gods: Memories of Food and Culture in Bengal.* London; New York: Seagull.

———. (2007). *Land of Milk and Honey: Travels in the History of Indian Food.* Oxford; New York: Seagull Books.

———. (2008). *Eating India: Exploring the Food and Culture of the Land of Spices.* London: Bloomsbury.

Banglatown Plan Comes under Fire. (1997, January 16). *East London Advertiser.*

Barber, B.R. (1996). *Jihad vs. McWorld.* New York: Ballantine Books.

Barndt, D. (1999). *Women Working the NAFTA Food Chain: Women, Food & Globalization.* Toronto: Second Story.

Barnett, S.A. (1973). The Process of Withdrawal in a South Indian Caste. In M. Singer (Ed.), *Entrepreneurship and Modernization of Occupational Cultures in South Asia* (pp.179–204). Durham, NC: Duke University Press.

Barth, F. (1969). *Ethnic Groups and Boundaries: The Social Organisation of Culture Difference.* Boston: Little, Brown.

Basu, A. (2002). Immigrant Entrepreneurs in the Food Sector: Breaking the Mould. In A.J. Kershen, (Ed.), *Food in the Migrant Experience* (pp. 149–171). Aldershot, UK: Ashgate.

Basu, A., & Altinay, E. (2003). *Family and Work in Minority Ethnic Businesses.* Bristol, UK: Policy.

Basu, R. (1866). Prospectus of a Society for the Promotion of National Feeling among the Educated Natives of Bengal. *National Paper,* unpaginated.

———. (1873). *Se kal ar E kal.* Calcutta: Bangiya Sahitya Parishad.

Basu, S. (2003). *Curry: The Story of the Nation's Favourite Dish.* Stroud: Sutton.

Batmanglij, N. (1992). *The New Food of Life: A Book of Ancient Persian and Modern Iranian Cooking and Ceremonies.* Washington, DC: Mage.

Baudrillard, J. (1998). *The Consumer Society: Myths and Structures.* New Delhi: Sage.

Bayart, J. (2007). *Global Subjects: A Political Critique of Globalization.* Cambridge: Polity.

Bayly, C.A. (1986). The Origins of Swadeshi (Home Industry): Cloth and Indian Society, 1700–1930. In A. Appadurai (Ed), *The Social Life of Things. Commodities in Cultural Perspective* (pp. 285–321). Cambridge: Cambridge University Press.

———. (1988). *Indian Society and the Making of the British Empire.* Cambridge: Cambridge University Press.

————. (2004). *The Birth of the Modern World, 1780–1914: Global Connections and Comparisons*. Malden, MA: Blackwell.

Beames, J. (1961). *Memoirs of a Bengal Civilian: The Lively Narrative of a Victorian District Officer*. London: Beames.

Belasco, W. J., & Scranton, P. (2002). *Food Nations: Selling Taste in Consumer Societies*. London: Routledge.

Bell, D. (1986, September 13). Row over Curry on the Rates. *Birmingham Evening Mail*.

Bell, D., & Valentine, G. (1997). *Consuming Geographies: We Are Where We Eat*. London: Routledge.

Benhabib, S. (1995). Subjectivity, Historiography, and Politics. In S. Benhabib, J. Butler, D. Cornell, & N. Fraser (Eds.), *Feminist Contentions: A Philosophical Exchange* (pp. 107–126). London: Routledge.

Bennett, J. (2010). *Vibrant Matter. A Political Ecology of Things*. Durham, NC: Duke University Press.

Bennett, J. W., & Harris, M. (1967). On the Cultural Ecology of Indian Cattle. *Current Anthropology, 8*(3), 251–253.

Benyon, J., & Solomos, J., (Eds.). (1987). *The Roots of Urban Unrest*. Oxford: Pergamon

Berger, P. L. (1997). Four Faces of Global Culture. *The National Interest, 49*, 23–29.

Berger, P. L., & Huntington, S. P. (2002). *Many Globalizations: Cultural Diversity in the Contemporary World*. Oxford; New York: Oxford University Press.

Berger, S., & Piore, M. J. (1980). *Dualism and Discontinuity in Industrial Societies*. Cambridge: Cambridge University Press.

Berne, A. (2006, April 19). Master of Spices: How One Man's Vision Became the Most Celebrated Little Chaat House in the Bay Area. *The San Francisco Chronicle*, pp. F1.

Bestor, T. C. (2000). How Sushi Went Global. *Foreign Policy, 121*, 54–63.

————. (2001). Supply-side Sushi: Commodity, Market, and the Global City. *American Anthropologist, 103*(1), 76–95.

Between Two Cultures. (1968, November 27) *London Times*.

Beynon, J. & Dunkerley, D. (Eds.). (2000). *Globalization: The Reader*. New York: Routledge.

Bhabha, H. K. (1994). *The Location of Culture*. London: Routledge.

Bhatnagar, S., & Saxena, R. K. (1997). *Dastarkhwan-e-awadh*. New Delhi: HarperCollins.

Bhatt, C., & Mukta, P. (2000). Hindutva in the West: Mapping the Antinomies of Diaspora Nationalism. *Ethnic & Racial Studies, 23*(3), 407–441.

Bishir, C. W., Brow, C. V., Lounsbury, C. R., and Wood, E. H. III. (1990). *Architects and Builders in North Carolina: A History of the Practice of Building*. Chapel Hill: University of North Carolina Press.

Bonacich, E. & Modell, J. (1980). *The Economic Basis of Ethnic Solidarity. Small Business in the Japanese American Community*. Berkeley: University of California Press.

Bonanno, A., Busch, L., Friedland, W. H., Gouveia, L., & Mingione, E. (1994). *From Columbus to ConAgra: The Globalization of Agriculture and Food*. Lawrence: University Press of Kansas.

Bonus, R. (2000). *Locating Filipino Americans: Ethnicity and the Cultural Politics of Space*. Philadelphia: Temple University Press.

Bon Viveur. (1937). *Where to Dine in London*. London.

Borden, I. (2000). Thick Edge: Architectural Boundaries in the Postmodern Metropolis. In I. Borden & J. Rendell (Eds.). *InterSections: Architectural Histories and Critical Theories* (pp. 221–246). New York: Routledge.

Bordo, S. (1993). *Unbearable Weight: Feminism, Western Culture, and the Body*. Berkeley: University of California Press.

Borthwick, M. (1984). *The Changing Role of Women in Bengal, 1849–1905*. Princeton: Princeton University Press.

Bose, C. (1930). *Food*. Calcutta: University of Calcutta.

Bose, P. K. (Ed.). (2006). *Health and Society in Bengal: A Selection from Late 19th-century Bengali Periodicals*. New Delhi and Thousand Oaks, CA: Sage.

Bourdieu, P. (1984). *Distinction: A Social Critique of the Judgement of Taste*. Cambridge, MA: Harvard University Press.

Bowman, C. (1997, October 17). Whole Indian Access: Shiva Statues Join Saris and Spice on Berkeley's University Avenue. *The San Francisco Chronicle*, p. EB2.

Boxer, C. R. (1969). *The Portuguese Seaborne Empire, 1415–1825*. New York: A.A. Knopf.

Brah, A. (1996). *Cartographies of Diaspora: Contesting Identities*. London and New York: Routledge.

Brah, A., & Shaw, S. (1992). *Working Choices: South Asian Young Women and the Labor Market*. Sheffield: Employment Department.

Bray, F. (1997). *Technology and Gender*. Berkeley: University of California Press.

Breckenridge, C. A. (1986). Food, Politics and Pilgrimage in South India, 1350–1650 A.D. In R. S. Khare & M. S. A. Rao (Eds.), *Food, Society and Culture. Aspects of South Asian Food Systems* (pp. 21–53). Durham, NC: Carolina Academic Press.

———. (Ed.). (1995). *Consuming Modernity: Public Culture in a South Asian World*. Minneapolis: University of Minnesota Press.

Breckenridge, C. A., Pollock, S., Bhabha, H. K., & Chakrabarty, D. (Eds.). (2002). *Cosmopolitanism*. Durham, NC: Duke University Press.

Brettell, C., & Hollifield, J. F. (2008). *Migration Theory: Talking across Disciplines*. New York: Routledge.

British Eating Out: A Report from Britain's National Catering Inquiry. (1966). London: Smethursts Foods.

Brosius, C., & Butcher, M. (1999). *Image Journeys: Audio-visual Media and Cultural Change in India*. New Delhi: Sage.

Brown, J. M. (2006). *Global South Asians: Introducing the Modern Diaspora*. Cambridge: Cambridge University Press.

Brown, L. K., & Mussell, K. (Eds.). (1997). *Ethnic and Regional Foodways in the*

United States: The Performance of Group Identity. Knoxville: University of Tennessee Press.

Brubaker, R. Feischmidt, M., Fox, J., & Grancea, L. (2006). *Nationalist Politics and Everyday Ethnicity in a Transylvanian Town*. Princeton: Princeton University Press.

Bubinas, K. (2005). Gandhi Marg: The Social Construction and Production of an Ethnic Economy in Chicago. *City & Society, 17*, 161–179.

Buettner, E. (2004). *Empire Families: Britons and Late Imperial India*. Oxford: Oxford University Press.

———. (2006). Cemeteries, Public Memory and Raj Nostalgia in Postcolonial Britain and India. *History & Memory, 18*(1), 5–42.

———. (2008). "Going for an Indian": South Asian Restaurants and the Limits of Multiculturalism in Britain. *The Journal of Modern History, 80*(4), 865.

———. (2009). "Would You Let Your Daughter Marry a Negro?" Race and Sex in 1950s Britain. In P. Levine & S. Grayzel (Eds.), *Gender, Labour, War and Empire: Essays on Modern Britain* (pp. 219–237). New York: Palgrave Macmillan.

Burke, P. (1978). *Popular Culture in Early Modern Europe*. New York: Harper Torchbook.

Burnett, J. (2004). *England Eats Out: A Social History of Eating Out in England from 1830 to the Present*. New York: Pearson/Longman.

Burt, A. (1785). *A Tract on the Biliary Complaints of Europeans in Hot Climates Founded on Observations in Bengal, and Consequently Designed to Be Particularly Useful to Those in That Country*. Calcutta: John Hay.

Burte, H. (1996). Launching off from the Backyard: Towards a Theoretical Basis for the Design of Public Places in India. In R. Mehrotra & G. Nest (Eds.), *Public Places: Bombay* (pp. 45–49). Mumbai: Max Mueller Bhavan.

Burton, A. M. (1998). *At the Heart of the Empire: Indians and the Colonial Encounter in Late-Victorian Britain*. Berkeley: University of California Press.

———. (2001). India, Inc.? Nostalgia, Memory, and the Empire of Things. In S. Ward. (Ed.), *British Culture and the End of Empire* (pp. 217–232). Manchester: Manchester University Press.

Burton, D. (1993). *The Raj at Table: A Culinary History of the British in India*. London; Boston: Faber.

Butler, J. (1987). *Subjects of Desire*. New York: Columbia University Press.

———. (1993). *Bodies That Matter: On the Discursive Limits of "Sex."* New York: Routledge.

———. (2004). *Undoing Gender*. New York and London: Routledge.

Cağlar, A. (1995). McKebap: Döner Kebap and the Social Positioning of German Turks. In J. A. Costa & G. J. Bamossy. (Eds), *Marketing in a Multicultural World: Ethnicity, Nationalism, and Cultural Identity* (pp. 209–230). London: Sage.

Caldwell, M. L. (2000). The Anthropology of Food and Body: Gender, Meaning, and Power. *American Ethnologist, 27*, 990–991.

Calhoun, C. J. (Ed.). (1992). *Habermas and the Public Sphere*. Cambridge, MA: MIT Press.

———. (2007). *Nations Matter: Culture, History, and the Cosmopolitan Dream*. London: Routledge.

Calhoun, C., & Sennett, R. (Eds.). (2007). *Practicing Culture (Taking Culture Seriously)*. London: Routledge.

Cannadine, D. (1994). *Aspects of Aristocracy: Grandeur and Decline in Modern Britain*. New Haven, CT: Yale University Press.

———. (2001). *Ornamentalism: How the British Saw Their Empire*. Oxford: Oxford University Press.

Carey, S. (2004). *Curry Capital: The Restaurant Sector in London's Brick Lane*. ICS Working Paper 6 (April). London: Institute of Community Studies.

Carney, J. A. (2001). *Black Rice: The African Origins of Rice Cultivation in the Americas*. Cambridge, MA: Harvard University Press.

Caroline, A. (Ed.). (1987). *Across Seven Seas and Thirteen Rivers: Life Stories of Pioneer Sylhetti Settlers in Britain*. London: THAP.

Carrin, M., & Tambs-Lyche, H. (2003). "You Don't Joke with These Fellows": Power and Ritual in South Canara, India. *Social Anthropology, 11*(1), 23–42.

Castells, M. (1989). *The Informational City: Information Technology, Economic Restructuring, and the Urban-Regional Process*. Oxford: Blackwell.

Center for Urban Pedagogy. (2009). *Vendor Power! A Guide to Street Vending in New York City*. New York: The Center for Urban Pedagogy.

Cerny, S. D., & Berkeley Architectural Heritage Association. (1994). *Berkeley Landmarks: An Illustrated Guide to Berkeley, California's Architectural Heritage*. Berkeley: Berkeley Architectural Heritage Association.

Certeau, M. de., Giard, L., & Mayol, P. (1998). *The Practice of Everyday Life*. Volume 2. *Living and Cooking*. Minneapolis: University of Minnesota Press.

Chairman Speaks. (2008). http://www.itcportal.com/about-itc/chairman-speaks/ ChairmanSpeak.aspx?id=103&type=B&news=chairman-2008.

Chakrabarty, D. (1989). *Rethinking Working-Class History: Bengal, 1890–1940*. Princeton: Princeton University Press.

———. (1994). The Difference-Deferral of (A) Colonial Modernity: Public Debates on Domesticity in British Bengal. In D. Arnold & D. Hardiman (Eds.), *Subaltern Studies VIII: Writings on South Asian History and Society* (pp. 50–88). New Delhi: Oxford University Press.

———. (2007). *Provincializing Europe: Postcolonial Thought and Historical Difference*. Princeton, NJ: Princeton University Press.

Challapalli, S. (2004, 20 March). Tasty Bites and Titbits. *The Hindu*.

Chalmers, R. (2000, April 13). The Vindaloo Squad. *The Independent* (London), pp. 1, 7.

Chapman, P. (1983). Fay Maschler Looks for Clues in Search of Good Food. In *The Good Curry Guide 1984*. Haslemere, UK: Regional Foods.

———. (Ed). (1991). *The Cobra Indian Lager Good Curry Restaurant Guide*. London: Piatkus.

Charbonnier, G. (1961). *Conversations with Claude Lévi-Strauss*. London: Cape.

Chateau Indage. (2003). *Invitation to a Walk in the Clouds*. Mumbai: Chateau Indage.

Chatterjee, P. (1989). The Nationalist Resolution of the Women's Question. In K. Sangari & S. Vaid (Eds.), *Recasting Women: Essays in Colonial History* (pp. 233–253). New Delhi: Kali for Women.

———. (1993). *The Nation and Its Fragments: Colonial and Postcolonial Histories*. Princeton: Princeton University Press.

———. (1998). Our Modernity. In *The Present History of West Bengal. Essays in Political Criticism* (pp. 193–210). New Delhi: Oxford University Press.

Chaudhuri, K. N. (1985). *Trade and Civilisation in the Indian Ocean: An Economic History from the Rise of Islam to 1750*. Cambridge: Cambridge University Press.

Chaudhuri, N. (1992.) Shawls, Jewelry, Curry and Rice in Victorian Britain. In N. Chaudhuri & M. Strobel (Eds.), *Western Women and Imperialism: Complicity and Resistance* (pp. 231–246). Bloomington: Indiana University Press.

Chaudhuri, N., & Strobel, M. (Eds.). (1992). *Western Women and Imperialism: Complicity and Resistance*. Bloomington: Indiana University Press.

Cheah, P., & Robbins, B. (Ed.) (1998). *Cosmopolitics: Thinking and Feeling Beyond the Nation*. Minneapolis: University of Minnesota Press.

Cheap without Frills or Thrills. (1989, May 27). *Bradford Telegraph and Argus*.

Chelkowski, P. (2006). Monumental Grief: The Bara Imambara. In R. Llewellyn-Jones (Ed.), *Lucknow: City of Illusion* (pp. 101–133). Munich: Prestel.

Chhabra, A. (2010). The Magic of Tabla. *India Abroad, 41*(5), M11.

China Report, Special Issue on Kolkata-China Exchanges, December 2007.

Choudhury, Y. (2002). *The Roots of Indian Sub-Continental Catering in Britain*. North Kazitula, Bangladesh: City Offset.

Choudhury, Y., & Sylheti Social History Group. (1993). *The Roots and Tales of the Bangladeshi Settlers*. Birmingham: Sylheti Social History Group.

Chowdhury, I. (1998). *The Frail Hero and Virile History: Gender and the Politics of Culture in Colonial Bengal*. New Delhi: Oxford University Press.

City of Berkeley Planning Commission. (1996, June). *University Avenue Strategic Development Draft Plan*. Developed by Calthorpe Associates with Bay Area Economics.

Clayton, J. (1964, November 16). The Newcomers Keep to Their Old Food Habits. *Birmingham Post* (Birmingham, England).

Clifford, J. (1997). *Routes: Travel and Translation in the Late Twentieth Century*. Cambridge, MA: Harvard University Press.

Clothey, F. W. (2006). *Ritualizing on the Boundaries: Continuity and Innovation in the Tamil Diaspora*. Columbia: University of South Carolina Press.

Coe, S. D., & Coe, M. D. (1996). *The True History of Chocolate*. London: Thames & Hudson.

Cohen, A., (Ed.). (1974). *Urban Ethnicity*. London: Tavistock.

Cohen, B. (2006). *Kingship and Colonialism in India's Deccan: 1850–1948*. Gordonsville, VA: Palgrave Macmillan.

Cohn, B. S. (1987). *An Anthropologist among the Historians and Other Essays*. New York: Oxford University Press.

———. (1996). *Colonialism and Its Forms of Knowledge: The British in India*. Princeton: Princeton University Press.

Collingham, E. M. (2001). *Imperial Bodies: Physical Experience of the Raj, c. 1800–1947*. Cambridge: Polity.

Collingham, L. (2006). *Curry: A Tale of Cooks and Conquerors*. New York: Oxford University Press.

Colpi, T. (1991). *The Italian Factor: The Italian Community in Great Britain*. Edinburgh: Mainstream.

Community Pride Not Prejudice: Making Diversity Work in Bradford. (2001). Report Presented to Bradford Vision by Sir Herman Ouseley, July, accessible via *http://www.bradford2020.com/pride/report.pdf*

Conlon, F. (1977). *A Caste in a Changing World: The Chitrapur Saraswat Brahmans, 1700–1935*. Berkeley: University of California Press.

———. (1995). Dining Out in Bombay. In C. A. Breckenridge (Ed.), *Consuming Modernity: Public Culture in a South Asian World* (pp. 90–127). Minneapolis: University of Minnesota Press.

Connell, R. W. (1990). I am Man: The Body and Some Contradictions of Hegemonic Masculinity. In M. A. Messmer & D. F. Sabo (Eds.), *Sport, Men and the Gender Order*. Champaign: University of Illinois Press.

Connerton, P. (1989). *How Societies Remember*. Cambridge: Cambridge University Press.

Conzen, K. N., Gerber, D. A., Morawska, E., Pozzetta, G. E., & Vecoli, R. J. (1992). The Invention of Ethnicity: A Perspective from the U.S.A. *Journal of American Ethnic History, 12*(1), pp. 3–41.

Cook, I., Crang, P., & Thorpe, M. (1999). Eating into Britishness: Multicultural Imaginaries and the Identity Politics of Food. In S. Roseneil, & J. Seymour (Eds.), *Practising Identities: Power and Resistance* (pp. 223–248). Basingstoke: Macmillan.

Cook, I. & Harrison, M. (2003). Cross over Food: Re-materializing Postcolonial Geographies. *Transactions of the Institute of British Geographers, 28*(3), pp. 296–317.

Cooper, D. (1967). *The Bad Food Guide*. London: Routledge & Kegan Paul.

Cooper, F. (2001). What Is the Concept of Globalization Good For? An African Historian's Perspective. *African Affairs, 100*(399): 189–213.

Cope, S. (2002, July 8). Dozens "Eat for Peace" on City's Riot Anniversary. *Yorkshire Post,*

Copland, I. (1997). *The Princes of India in the Endgame of Empire, 1917–1947*. Cambridge: Cambridge University Press.

Corn, C. (1998). *The Scents of Eden: A History of the Spice Trade*. New York: Kodansha International.

Costa, J. A., & Bamossy, G. J. (1995). *Marketing in a Multicultural World: Ethnicity, Nationalism, and Cultural Identity*. Thousand Oaks, CA: Sage.

Counihan C. (Ed.). (2002). *Food in the USA: A Reader.* New York: Routledge.

———. (1999). *The Anthropology of Food and Body: Gender, Meaning and Power.* New York: Routledge.

Counihan, C., & Van Esterik, P. (Eds.). (1997). *Food and Culture: A Reader.* New York: Routledge.

Crackdown on Illicit Slaughter. (1984, November 30). *Birmingham Evening Mail.*

Crownfield, D. (Ed). (1992). *Body/Text in Julia Kristeva: Religion, Women and Psychoanalysis.* Albany, NY: SUNY Press.

Curry: A Trade Renaissance for Bradford. (1997, October 24). *Yorkshire Post.*

Curtis, C. (1807). *An Account of the Diseases in India, as They Appeared in the English Fleet, and in the Naval Hospital at Madras, in 1782 and 1783; with Observations on Ulcers, and the Hospital Sores of That Country.* Edinburgh: W. Laing, Longman, and J. Murray.

Cusack, I. (2000). African Cuisines: Recipes for Nation-Building? *Journal of African Cultural Studies, 13*(2), 207–225.

Cwiertka, K.J., with Walraven, B. (Eds.) (2001). *Asian Food: The Global and the Local.* Honolulu: University of Hawai'i Press.

Dahya, B. (1974). The Nature of Pakistani Ethnicity in Industrial Cities in Britain. In A. Cohen (Ed.), *Urban Ethnicity* (pp. 77–118). London: Tavistock.

Dalby, A. (2000). *Dangerous Tastes: The Story of Spices.* Berkeley: University of California Press.

Dalrymple, W. (2003). *White Mughals: Love and Betrayal in the Eighteenth-century India.* New York: Viking.

Danger of Too Much Chapatti, The. (1972, November 4). *Yorkshire Post.*

da Orta, G. (1996). Colloquies on the Simples and Drugs of India: Cinnamon, Cloves, Mace and Nutmeg, Pepper. In M. Pearson (Ed.), *Spices in the Indian Ocean World* (pp. 1–49). Brookfield, VT: Variorum.

Das, V. (Ed.). (2003). *The Oxford India Companion to Sociology and Social Anthropology.* New Delhi; Oxford: Oxford University Press.

David, K.A. (1977). *The New Wind: Changing Identities in South Asia.* Paris: Mouton.

Davis, M. (2001). *Late Victorian Holocausts: El Niño Famines and the Making of the Third World.* London: Verso.

Davis, R.H. (1997). *The Lives of Indian Images.* Princeton: Princeton University Press.

Davison, R.B. (1964). *Commonwealth Immigrants.* London: Oxford University Press.

Day, H. (With the collaboration of Sarojini Mudnani). (1955). *Curries of India: Book One.* Mumbai: Jaico.

———. (Assisted by May Ewing). (1964). *The Fourth Book of Curries.* London: Kaye.

Debi, P. (1900/1995). *Amish o Niramish Ahar* [Nonvegetarian and Vegetarian Cuisine]. Vol. 1. Calcutta: Ananda.

Delfendahl, B. (1981). On the Cow-Slaughter and Beef-Eating Interdiction. *Current Anthropology, 22* (3), 296–297.

Dench, G., Gavron, K., & Young, M. D. (2006). *The New East End: Kinship, Race and Conflict.* London: Profile.

Derné, S. (2008). *Globalization on the Ground. New Media and the Transformation of Culture, Class, and Gender in India.* New Delhi: Sage.

Derrett, J. D. M. (1968). *Religion, Law and the State in India.* London: Faber & Faber.

Derrida, J. (1980). The Law of Genre. *Critical Inquiry, 7*(1), 55–81.

———. (1991). Eating Well, or the Calculation of the Subject: An Interview with Jacques Derrida. In E. Cadava, J-L. Nancy, & P. Conner (Eds.), *Who Comes After the Subject?* (pp. 96–119). New York: Routledge.

Desai, G. (2004). Old World Orders: Amitav Ghosh and the Writing of Nostalgia. *Representations, 85*(1), 125–148.

Desai, R. C. (1963). *Indian Immigrants in Britain.* Oxford: Oxford University Press.

Deshpande, S. (2003). *Contemporary India: A Sociological View.* New Delhi: Viking.

Desmond, R. (1992). *The European Discovery of the Indian Flora.* Oxford: Clarendon Press.

Devi, G. (1969). *Gourmet's Gateway.* Jaipur: Virasat.

———. (1995). *A Princess Remembers.* Calcutta: Rupa.

Dewey, S. (2008). *Making Miss India Miss World: Constructing Gender, Power, and the Nation in Postliberalization India.* Syracuse, NY: Syracuse University Press.

Dhamija, J. (2007). *Kamaladevi chattopadhyay.* New Delhi: National Book Trust.

Dharker, A. (2005). *The Romance of Salt.* New Delhi: Roli Books.

Dharwadker, V. (2000). *Cosmopolitan Geographies: New Locations in Literature and Culture.* New York: Routledge.

Dickey, S. (2000). Permeable Homes: Domestic Service, Household Space, and the Vulnerability of Class Boundaries in Urban India. *American Ethnologist, 27*(2), 462–489.

———. (2007). *Cinema and the Urban Poor in South India.* Cambridge: Cambridge University Press.

———. (2011). The Pleasures and Anxieties of Being in the Middle: Emerging Middle-Class Identities in Urban South India. *Modern Asian Studies, 45*(6).

Dietler, M. (1996). Feasts and Commensal Politics in the Political Economy: Food, Power and Status in Prehistoric Europe. In P. Weissner & W. Schiefenhövel (Eds.), *Food and the Status Quest: An Interdisciplinary Perspective* (pp. 87–125). Providence, RI: Berghahn Books.

Digby, A., Ernst, W., & Muhkarji, P. (Eds.). (2010). *Crossing Colonial Historiographies: Histories of Colonial and Indigenous Medicines in Transnational Perspective.* Cambridge: Cambridge University Press.

Diner, H. R. (2001). *Hungering for America: Italian, Irish, and Jewish Foodways in the Age of Migration.* Cambridge, MA: Harvard University Press.

Dining Out at Veeraswamy's. (1982). *Curry Magazine,* Spring, 28–29.

Dirty, Filthy and Disgusting. (1988, February 12). *Bradford Telegraph and Argus,* 29.

Divakaruni, C. B. (1997). *The Mistress of Spices.* New York: Anchor Books.

Dixit, R. (2008). Give Us Our Daily Sushi! *The Weekend Report (ABC News Transcripts), 9*(11), 6.

D'Monte, D., & Kakodkar, P. (2002). Bye-bye Bombay? *Outlook, 42*(4), Feb. 4.

Donald, J., & Rattansi, A. (Eds.). (1992). *"Race", Culture, and Difference*. London; Newbury Park, CA: Sage Publications, in association with the Open University.

Donner, H. (2008). *Domestic Goddesses: Maternity, Globalization and Middle-class Identity in Contemporary India*. Burlington, VT: Ashgate.

Don't Turn Your Back on Us. (1980, March 11). *Birmingham Evening Mail*.

Döring, T., Heide, M., & Mühleisen, S. (Eds.). (2003). *Eating Culture: The Poetics and Politics of Food*. Heidelberg: Universitätsverlag.

Douglas, M. (1972). Deciphering a Meal. *Daedalus, 101*(1), 61–81.

———. (1975). *Implicit Meanings: Essays in Anthropology*. London: Routledge & Kegan Paul.

———. (Ed.). (1984a). *Food in the Social Order: Studies of Food and Festivities in Three American Communities*. New York: Russell Sage Foundation.

———. (1984b). *Purity and Danger: An Analysis of the Concepts of Pollution and Taboo*. London: Ark.

———. (1997). Deciphering a Meal. In C. Counihan and P. Van Esterik (Eds.), *Food and Culture: A Reader* (pp. 36–54). New York: Routledge.

Douglas, M., & Isherwood, B. C. (1996). *The World of Goods: Towards an Anthropology of Consumption*. New York: Routledge.

Douglas, M., & Khare, R. S. (1979). Commission on the Anthropology of Food: Statement on its History and Current Objectives. *Social Science Information, 18*(6), 903–913.

Drèze, J., Sen, A., & Hussain, A. (1995). *The Political Economy of Hunger: Selected Essays*. Oxford: Clarendon Press.

Dubois, A. J. A. (1906). *Hindu Manners, Customs and Ceremonies*. Oxford: Clarendon Press.

Dumont, L. (1970). *Homo Hierarchicus: An Essay on the Caste System*. Chicago: University of Chicago Press.

———. (1977). *From Mandeville to Marx: The Genesis and Triumph of Economic Ideology*. Chicago: University of Chicago Press.

———. (1980). *Homo Hierarchicus: The Caste System and Its Implications* (rev. ed.). Chicago: University of Chicago Press.

Dunn, K. M. (1998). Rethinking Ethnic Concentration: The Case of Cabramatta, Sydney. *Urban Studies, 35*(3), 503–527.

Dwivedi, S. (1999). *The Maharaja And the Princely States of India*. New Delhi: Lustre Press.

Dwyer, R. (2000). *All You Want is Money, All You Need is Love: Sex and Romance in Modern India*. London: Cassell.

Dwyer, R., & Pinney, C. (Eds.). (2001). *Pleasure and the Nation: The History, Politics and Consumption of Popular Culture in India*. New Delhi: Oxford University Press.

Dyer, R. (1997). *White*. London: Routledge.

Eade, J. (1989). *The Politics of Community: Bangladeshi Community in East London.* London: Gower.

Economist, The. (1996, 23 March), Software in India: Bangalore Bytes, p. 67.

Elias, N. (1982). *The Civilizing Process.* New York: Pantheon Books.

Emerson, B. (2005, September 13). *You and I Need to Sit Down and Have a Little Chaat.* Retrieved December 15, 2008, from *http://inpraiseofsardines.typepad.com/ blogs/destinations_san_francisco/index.html.*

Evans, P. (1973, March 26). A Kind of Café Conspiracy. *London Times.*

Fairall, C. (1998). Reader's Letters. *Tandoori Magazine, 5*(3), 11.

Falk, P. (1994). *The Consuming Body.* Thousand Oaks, CA: Sage.

Farquhar, J. (2002). *Appetites: Food and Sex in Postsocialist China.* Durham, NC: Duke University Press.

Farrer, J. (2010). Eating the West and Beating the Rest: Culinary Occidentalism and Urban Soft Power in Asia's Global Food Cities. In *Globalization, Food and Social Identities in the Asia Pacific Region* (pp. 1–21). Tokyo: Sophia University. Available at: http://icc.fla.sophia.ac.jp/global%20food%20papers/pdf/2_3_FARRER.pdf.

———. (Ed.). (2010). *Globalization, Food and Social Identities in the Asia Pacific Region.* Tokyo: Sophia University. Available at: http://icc.fla.sophia.ac.jp/global %20food%20papers/pdf/intro.pdf.

Favell, A. (1998). *Philosophies of Integration: Immigration and the Idea of Citizenship in France and Britain.* New York: St. Martin's Press, in association with Centre for Research in Ethnic Relations, University of Warwick.

Fay, E. (1908). *The Original Letters from India of Mrs. Eliza Fay.* Calcutta: Thacker, Spink.

Featherstone, M. (Ed.). (1990). *Global Culture: Nationalism, Globalization and Modernity.* Newbury Park, CA: Sage.

Featherstone, M., Hepworth, M., & Turner, B. S. (1991). *The Body: Social Process and Cultural Theory.* Newbury Park, CA: Sage.

Ferguson, P. P. (1998). A Cultural Field in the Making: Gastronomy in 19th-century France. *American Journal of Sociology, 104*(3), 597–641.

———. (2004). *Accounting for Taste: The Triumph of French Cuisine.* Chicago: University of Chicago Press.

———. (2005). Eating Orders: Markets, Menus, and Meals. *Journal of Modern History, 77*(3), 679–700.

Ferguson, P. P., & Zukin, S. (1995). What's Cooking? *Theory & Society, 24*(2), 193–199.

Fernandes, L. (2006). *India's New Middle Class: Democratic Politics in an Era of Economic Reform.* Minneapolis: University of Minnesota Press.

Fernandes, L., & Heller, P. (2006). Hegemonic Aspirations. *Critical Asian Studies, 38*(4), 495–522.

Ferrero, S. (2002). *Comida Sin Par:* Consumption of Mexican Food in Los Angeles: "Foodscapes" in a Transnational Consumer Society. In W. Belasco & P. Scranton (Eds), *Food Nations: Selling Taste in Consumer Societies* (pp. 194–219). New York: Routledge.

Ferro-Luzzi, G. E. (1977). Ritual as Language: The Case of South Indian Food Offerings. *Current Anthropology, 18*(3).

———. (1981). The Food of the Gods versus Human Foods in South India. *L'Uomo, 5*(2), 239–266.

Findley, C., & Rothney, J. (Eds.) (1998). *Twentieth-Century World*. Boston: Houghton Mifflin.

Fine, G. A. (1995). Wittgenstein's Kitchen: Sharing Meaning in Restaurant Work. *Theory and Society, 24*(2), 245–269.

———. (1996). *Kitchens: The Culture of Restaurant Work*. Berkeley: University of California Press.

Finkelstein, J. (1989). *Dining Out: A Sociology of Modern Manners*. New York: New York University Press.

Fischer, E. P & Benson, P. (2006). *Broccoli and Desire. Global Connections and Maya Struggles in Postwar Guatemala*. Stanford, CA: Stanford University Press.

Fischler, C. (1988). Food, Self and Identity. *Social Science Information, 27*(2), 275–292.

Fish, S. (1997). Boutique Multiculturalism, or Why Liberals are Incapable of Thinking about Hate Speech. *Critical Inquiry, 23*(2), 378–395.

Fisher, M. H. (1991). *Indirect Rule in India: Residents and the Residency System, 1764–1858*. New Delhi: Oxford University Press.

———. (1996). *The First Indian Author in English: Dean Mahomed (1759–1851) in India, Ireland, and England*. Oxford: Oxford University Press.

———. (2004). *Counterflows to Colonialism: Indian Travellers and Settlers in Britain, 1600–1857*. New Delhi: Permanent Black.

Fitzgerald, T. K. (1977). *Nutrition and Anthropology in Action*. Amsterdam: Van Gorcum.

Flandrin, J-L., & Montanari. M. (1999). *Food: A Culinary History from Antiquity to the Present*. New York: Columbia University Press.

Foner, N., Rumbaut, R. G., & Gold, S. J. (2000). *Immigration Research for a New Century. Multidisciplinary Perspectives*. New York: Russell Sage Foundation.

Fong, T. P. (1994). *The First Suburban Chinatown: The Remaking of Monterey Park, California*. Philadelphia: Temple University Press.

Food and Agriculture Organization (FAO), http://www.fao.org/docrep/011/i0291e/i0291e00.htm.

Forrest, D. M. (1973). *Tea for the British: The Social and Economic History of a Famous Trade*. London: Chatto and Windus.

Foucault, M. (1967). *Madness and Civilization: A History of Insanity in the Age of Reason*. London: Routledge.

———. (1980a). *The History of Sexuality*. Vol. I: *An Introduction*. New York: Vintage.

———. (1980b). *Power/Knowledge: Selected Interviews and Other Writings 1972–1977*, trans. Colin Gordon et al. New York: Pantheon.

Frank, A. G. (1998). *Re-Orient: The Global Economy in the Asian Age*. Berkeley: University of California Press.

Fraser, N. (1992). Rethinking the Public Sphere: A Contribution to the Critique of

Actually Existing Democracy. In C. J. Calhoun (Ed.), *Habermas and the Public Sphere* (pp. 109–142). Cambridge, MA: MIT Press.

Freed, S. A., & Freed, R. S. (1981). Sacred Cows and Water Buffalo in India: The Uses of Ethnography. *Current Anthropology, 22*(5), 483–502.

Freedman, P. H. (2008). *Out of the East: Spices and the Medieval Imagination.* New Haven, CT: Yale University Press.

Freidberg, S. (2004). *French Beans and Food Scares: Culture and Commerce in an Anxious Age.* New York: Oxford University Press.

Friedman, T. L. (2000). *The Lexus and the Olive Tree: Understanding Globalization.* New York: Anchor.

———. (2005). *The World Is Flat: A Brief History of the Twenty-First Century* (1st ed.). New York: Farrar, Straus and Giroux.

Fruzzetti, L., & Östör, Á. (1984). *Kinship and Ritual in Bengal: Anthropological Essays.* New Delhi: South Asian Publishers.Fryer, J. (1698). *A New Account of East-India and Persia, in 8 Letters. Being 9 years Travels, Begun 1672, and Finished 1681.* London: Chiswell.

Frykenberg, R. (1982). On Roads and Riots in Tinnevelly: Radical Change and Ideology in Madras Presidency during the 19th century. *Asia Monitor: South Asia Monitor, 4*(2), 34–52.

Fu, Z. (2009). *Ageing in East Asia: Challenges and Policies for the Twenty-first Century.* London: Routledge.

Fukuyama, F. (1992). *The End of History and the Last Man.* New York: Free Press.

Fuller, C. J., & Narasimhan, H. (2007). Information Technology Professionals and the New-Rich Middle Class in Chennai (Madras). *Modern Asian Studies, 41*(1), 121–150.

———. (2008). From Landlords to Software Engineers: Migration and Urbanization among Tamil Brahmins. *Comparative Studies in Society and History, 50*(1), 170–196.

Fussell, B. (2004). *The Story of Corn.* Albuquerque: University of New Mexico Press.

Gabaccia, D. R. (1998). *We Are What We Eat: Ethnic Food and the Making of Americans.* Cambridge, MA: Harvard University Press.

Gahlaut, K. (2002). *Among the Chatterati: The Diary of a Page Three Hack.* New Delhi: Penguin Books.

Galanter, M. (1972). The Abolition of Disabilities—Untouchability and the Law. In J. M. Mahar & S. Chandrasekhar (Eds.), *The Untouchables in Contemporary India* (pp. 227–313). Tucson: University of Arizona Press.

Ganguly, K. (2001). *States of Exception: Everyday Life and Postcolonial Identity.* Minneapolis: University of Minnesota Press.

Gans, B., Jokela, J., & Limnell, E. (Eds). (2009). *The Role of the European Union in Asia: China and India as Strategic Partners.* Surrrey: Ashgate.

Gans, H. J. (1962). *The Urban Villagers: Group and Class in the Life of Italian-Americans.* New York: Free Press of Glencoe.

———. (1996). Symbolic Ethnicity: The Future of Ethnic Groups and Cultures in

America. In W. Sollors (Ed.), *Theories of Ethnicity* (pp. 436–448). New York: New York University Press.

Gardner, K. & Shukur, A. (1994). "I'm Bengali, I'm Asian, and I'm Living Here": The Changing Identity of British Bengalis. In R. Ballard (Ed.), *Desh Pardesh: the South Asian Presence in Britain* (pp. 142–164). London: Hurst & Co.

Garhasthya Darpan [The Mirror of the Household], (1874, June). *Bmabodhini Patrika, 10,* 130.

Geertz, C. (1973). *The Interpretation of Cultures: Selected Essays.* New York: Basic Books.

Ghatak, K. K. (1991). *Hindu Revivalism in Bengal: Rammohun to Ramakrishna.* Calcutta: Minerva.

Ghose, G. C. (1972). Female Occupations. In B. D. Gupta (Ed.), *Sociology in India: An Enquiry into Sociological Thinking and Empirical Social Research in the Nineteenth Century, with Special Reference to Bengal* (pp. 58–59). Calcutta: Centre for Sociological Research.

Ghosh, A. (2006). *Power in Print: Popular Publishing and the Politics of Language and Culture in a Colonial Society, 1778–1905.* New Delhi: Oxford University Press.

Ghosh, D. (2006). *Sex and the Family in Colonial India: The Making of Empire.* Cambridge: Cambridge University Press.

Ghosh, L., & Chatterjee, R. (2004). *Indian Diaspora in Asian and Pacific Regions: Culture, People, Interactions.* Jaipur: Rawat Publications.

Gibson, O. (2007, January 20). So Was It a Tipping Point in Race Relations ... or Just Ratings Viagra? *Guardian.*

Giddens, A. (1991). *Modernity and Self-Identity: Self and Society in the Late Modern Age.* Stanford, CA: Stanford University Press.

Gilroy, P. (1987). *"There Ain't No Black in the Union Jack": The Cultural Politics of Race and Nation.* London: Hutchinson.

———. (2004). *Postcolonial Melancholia.* Abingdon: Routledge.

Giving a Trendy Edge to Tradition. (2001, January 15). *Telegraph and Argus.*

Glassie, H. H. (1975). *Folk Housing in Middle Virginia: A Structural Analysis of Historic Artifacts.* Knoxville: University of Tennessee Press.

Glazer, N., & Moynihan, D. P. (Eds.). (1975). *Ethnicity: Theory and Experience.* Cambridge, MA: Harvard University Press.

Gleason, P. (1980). Americans All: Ethnicity, Ideology, and American Identity in the Era of World War II. In R. Kroes (Ed.), *The American Identity: Fusion and Fragmentation* (pp. 235–264). European Contributions to American Studies 3. Amsterdam: Amerika-Instituut.

Goffman, E. (1959). *The Presentation of Self in Everyday Life.* Garden City, NY: Doubleday.

GOI (Government of India). Foreign Department. (1860). Despatch No. 43A to S/S, (30 April), PCI, 1792–1874, Vol. 85.

Goldberg, D. T. (Ed.). (2002). *A Companion to Racial and Ethnic Studies.* Malden, MA: Blackwell.

Good for What Ails You. (1999). *Tandoori Magazine*, 5(11), 7.

Good Value for a Fiver. (1989, April 29). *Bradford Telegraph and Argus*.

Goodspeed, P. (2009, October 21). South Africa's White Farmers Prepare to Trek to the Congo. *National Post* (Toronto). http://farmlandgrab.org/8443.

Goody, J. [Jack]. (1982). *Cooking, Cuisine, and Class: A Study in Comparative Sociology*. Cambridge: Cambridge University Press.

Goody, J. [Jade]. (2007, January 19). Interview with Davina McCall. *Celebrity Big Brother*. Channel Four (Great Britain).

Gopaldas, T. & Seshadri. S. (1987). *Nutrition: Monitoring and Assessment*. New Delhi: Oxford University Press.

Gowariker, A. (Director). (2008). *Jodhaa Akbar*. [Video/DVD] England: UTV Motion Pictures: Big Home Video [distributor].

Goyal, K. & Krishnan, U. (2010, December 1). Growth May Surpass Government Target for Year, Ushering Higher India Rates. *Bloomberg.com*, http://www.bloomberg.com/news/2010-11-30/india-economy-grows-faster-than-estimated-8-9-adding-inflation-pressure.html.

Grace, H., Hage, G., Johnson, L., Langsworth, J., & Symonds, M. (Eds.). (1997). *Home/World. Space, Community and Marginality in Sydney's West*. Annandale, NSW: Pluto.

Granovetter, M.S. (1995). The Economic Sociology of Firms and Entrepreneurs. In A. Portes (Ed.), *Economic Sociology of Immigration* (pp. 128–165). New York: Russell Sage Foundation.

Great Britain Home Office. (2001). *Community Cohesion: A Report of the Independent Review Team Chaired by Ted Cantle*. London: Home Office.

Great Divide, The (2002, February 15). *Bombay Times*, (Times of India), 2.

Grier, K.C. (2010). *Culture and Comfort: Parlor Making and Middle-Class Identity, 1850–1930*. Washington DC: Smithsonian Books.

Grihasthalir Katha [Tales of the Household]. (n.d.). *Antahpur, 5*, 5–6.

Grosz, E. (1994). *Volatile Bodies. Towards a Corporeal Feminism*. Bloomington: Indiana University Press.

Groth, P.E. (1994). *Living Downtown: The History of Residential Hotels in the United States*. Berkeley: University of California Press.

Grove, C. (1998, August 27). Letter: Spicy Food for Thought. *Guardian* (London), 17.

Grove, P., & Grove, C. (2005). *Curry Culture: A Very British Love Affair*. England: Surbiton.

Guha-Thakurta, T. (1992). *The Making of a New "Indian" Art: Artists, Aesthetics, and Nationalism in Bengal, c. 1850–1920*. Cambridge: Cambridge University Press.

Guibernau, M., & Rex, J. (Eds.). (1997). *The Ethnicity Reader: Nationalism, Multiculturalism, and Migration*. Cambridge: Blackwell Publishers.

Gupta, A. (1998). *Postcolonial Developments: Agriculture in the Making of Modern India*. Durham, NC: Duke University Press.

Gupta, A. & Ferguson, J. (1992). Beyond "Culture": Space, Identity, and the Politics of Difference. *Cultural Anthropology, 7*(1), 6–23.

————. (1997). *Culture, Power, Place: Explorations in Critical Anthropology.* Durham, NC: Duke University Press.

Gupta, B. D., & Ghose, G. C. (2007). *Sociology in India: An Enquiry into Sociological Thinking and Empirical Social Research in the 19th Century with Special Reference to Bengal.* Calcutta: Centre for Sociological Research.

Gupta, C. (2002). *Sexuality, Obscenity, Community: Women, Muslims, and the Hindu Public in Colonial India.* New York: Palgrave.

Habermas, J. (1991). *The Structural Transformation of the Public Sphere.* Cambridge, MA: MIT Press.

Hage, G. (1997). At Home in the Entrails of the West: Multiculturalism, "Ethnic Food" and Migrant Home-Building. In H. Grace, G. Hage, L. Johnson, J. Langsworth, & M. Symonds (Eds.), *Home/World. Space, Community and Marginality in Sydney's West.* (pp. 99–153). Annandale, NSW: Pluto.

————. (2000). *White Nation. Fantasies of White Supremacy in a Multicultural Society.* New York: Routledge.

Hall, S. (2000). Conclusion: the Multi-Cultural Question. In B. Hesse (Ed.), *Un/Settled Multiculturalisms: Diasporas, Entanglements, Transruptions* (pp. 209–241). London: Zed.

Hanák, P. (1982). The Relationship between Family Enterprise and Managerial Enterprise: Hungary in the Nineteenth and Early Twentieth Centuries. In L. Hannah (Ed.), *From Family Firm to Professional Management: Structure and Performance of Business Enterprise* (pp. 39–49). B9 papers organized by L. Hannah, Eighth International Economic History Congress, Akadémiai Kiadó, Budapest.

Hancock, M. E. (1999). *Womanhood in the Making: Domestic Ritual and Public Culture in Urban South India.* Boulder, CO: Westview.

————. (2001). Home Science and the Nationalization of Domesticity in Colonial India. *Modern Asian Studies, 35*(4), 871–903.

Hancock, P., Hughes, B., Jagger, E., Paterson, K., Russell, R., Tulle-Winton, E., & Tyler, M. (2000). *The Body, Culture and Society: An Introduction.* Buckingham: Open University Press.

Hannerz, U. (1992). *Cultural Complexity: Studies in the Social Organization of Meaning.* New York: Columbia University Press.

————. (1996). *Transnational Connections: Culture, People, Places.* New York: Routledge.

Hansard's. (1876). *Hansard's Parliamentary Debates,* 3rd ser., vol. 227, 409.

Haraway, D. J. (1991). *Simians, Cyborgs, and Women: The Reinvention of Nature.* New York: Routledge.

Hardyment, C. (1995). *Slice of Life: The British Way of Eating since 1945.* London: BBC Books.

Harlow, B., & Carter, M. (1987). Queen Victoria's Proclamation, 1 November 1858. In B. Harlow & M. Carter (Eds.), *Imperialism and Orientalism: A Documentary Source Book* (210). New York: Methuen.

———. (1999). *Imperialism and Orientalism: A Documentary Sourcebook.* Oxford: Blackwell.

Harris, H., & Lipman, A. (1984). Social Process, Space Usage: Reflections on Socialisation in Homes for Children. *British Journal of Social Work, 14,* 49–65.

Harris, M. (1985). *Good to Eat: Riddles of Food and Culture.* New York: Simon and Schuster.

———. (1992). The Cultural Ecology of India's Sacred Cattle. *Current Anthropology, 33*(1), 261–276.

Harrison, M. (1994). *Public Health in British India: Anglo-Indian Preventive Medicine, 1859–1914.* Cambridge: Cambridge University Press.

———. (1999). *Climates and Constitutions: Health, Race, Environment and British Imperialism in India, 1600–1850.* New Delhi: Oxford University Press.

Harriss, J. (2003). The Great Tradition Globalises: Reflections on Two Studies of "the Industrial Leaders" of Madras. *Modern Asian Studies, 37*(2), 327–362.

———. (2006). Middle-Class Activism and the Politics of the Informal Working Class: A Perspective on Class Relations and Civil Society in Indian Cities. *Critical Asian Studies, 38*(4), 445–465.

Harvey, D. (1992). *The Condition of Postmodernity.* Oxford: Blackwell.

———. (2001). *Spaces of Capital: Towards a Critical Geography.* New York: Routledge.

———. (2008). *The Condition of Postmodernity: An Enquiry into the Origins of Cultural Change.* Cambridge: Wiley-Blackwell.

Hashmi, A. (1998). A Tale of Two Cities. *Tandoori Magazine, 4*(1), 43.

Hattox, R. S. (1985). *Coffee and Coffeehouses: The Origins of a Social Beverage in the Medieval Near East.* Seattle: University of Washington Press.

Hayden, D. (1995). *The Power of Place: Urban Landscapes as Public History.* Cambridge, MA: MIT Press.

Heisler, B. S. (2008). The Sociology of Immigration. In C. B. Bretell and J. F. Hollifield (Eds.), *Migration Theory. Talking Across Disciplines* (pp. 83–111). New York: Routledge.

Heitzman, J. & Schenkluhn, S. (Eds.). (2004). *The World in the Year 1000.* Lanham, MD: University Press of America.

Held, D., McGew, A., Goldblatt, D., & Perraton, J. (1999). *Global Transformations: Politics, Economics and Culture.* Stanford, CA: Stanford University Press.

Heldke, L. M. (2003). *Exotic Appetites: Ruminations of a Food Adventurer.* New York: Routledge.

Henisch, B. A. (1976). *Fast and Feast: Food in Medieval Society.* University Park, PA: Pennsylvania State University.

Herman, B. (1984). Multiple Materials/Multiple Meanings: The Fortunes of Thomas Mendenhall. *Winterthur Portfolio, 19*(1), 67–86.

Herzfeld, M. (2004). *The Body Impolitic: Artisans and Artifice in the Global Hierarchy of Value.* Chicago: University of Chicago Press.

Hesse, B. (Ed.). (2000). *Un/settled Multiculturalisms: Diasporas, Entanglements, Transruptions* London: Zed Books.

Hill, C. S. (1965). *How Colour Prejudiced is Britain?* London: Gollancz.

Hiro, D. (1993). *Black British, White British.* New York: Monthly Review Press.

History and Origin of Dasaprakash. (2009). *http://www.dasaprakash.com/history/*

Hobsbawm, E. J., & Ranger, T. (1983). *The Invention of Tradition.* Cambridge: Cambridge University Press.

Holbrook, S. (2007, August 1–7). Fast Food Notion. *MetroActive.* Retrieved November 20, 2007, from *http://www.metroactive.com/metro/08.01.07/chaat-0731.html.*

Holkar, S. R., & Holkar, S. D. (1975). *Cooking of the Maharajas: The Royal Recipes of India.* New York: Viking Press.

Hooks, B. (1992). *Black Looks: Race and Representation.* Boston, MA: South End.

Hopkins, A. G. (Ed.) (2002). *Globalization in World History.* London: Pimlico.

Horn, B. M. (2000). Understanding Cultural Diversity: Culture, Curriculum, and Community in Nursing. *Journal of Transcultural Nursing: Official Journal of the Transcultural Nursing Society, 11,* 308–309.

Houbert, J. (1998). Decolonization in Globalization. In R. Axtmann (Ed.), *Globalization and Europe: Theoretical and Empirical Investigations* (pp. 43–58). Washington, DC: Pinter.

Housing Plight—All Combines to Create Ghettoes. (1965, 22 January). *Times.*

Howes, D. (1996). *Cross-Cultural Consumption: Global Markets, Local Realities.* New York: Routledge.

Hubka, T. C. & Kenny, J. T. (2000). The Transformation of the Workers' Cottage in Milwaukee's Polish Community. In S. McMurry & A. Adams. (Eds.), *People, Power, Places: Perspectives in Vernacular Architecture VIII* (pp. 33–52). Knoxville: University of Tennessee Press.

Humphrey, T. C., & Humphrey, L. T. (1988). *We Gather Together: Food and Festival in American Life.* Ann Arbor: UMI Research Press.

Huntington, S. (1993). The Clash of Civilizations? *Foreign Affairs, 72*(3) (Summer), 22–49.

———. (1996). *The Clash of Civilizations and the Remaking of the World Order.* New York: Touchstone.

Hussain, H. (1997a). Balti Cultural Birmingham. *Tandoori Magazine, 3*(5), 20–21.

———. (1997b). At Your Service. *Tandoori Magazine, 3*(3), 17.

———. (1998). Good Karma. *Tandoori Magazine, 4*(11), 23.

Imran, I., Smith, T., & Hyslop, D. (1994). *Here to Stay: Bradford's South Asian Communities.* Bradford, UK: City of Bradford.

Inda, J. X., & Rosaldo, R. (Eds.). (2002). *The Anthropology of Globalization: A Reader.* Malden, MA: Blackwell.

Inden, R. 1999. Transnational Class, Erotic Arcadia and Commercial Utopia in Hindi films. In C. Brosius & M. Butcher. (Eds.), *Image Journeys: Audio-visual and Cultural Change in India* (pp. 21–40). Delhi: Sage Publications.

Indianfoodindustry.net, http://www.indianfoodindustry.net/ Accessed September 11, 2011.

Indian Restaurant and Its Menu. (1983). *Curry Magazine, 4,* 12.

Inglis, D., & Gimlin, D. L. (Eds.). (2009). *The Globalization of Food.* Oxford: Berg.

Interior Motives. (1998). *Tandoori Magazine, 4*(2), 32.

International Food Policy Research Institute (IFPRI): http://www.ifpri.org/sites/default/files/publications/2020anhconfpaper01.pdf.

I Provide the Food, You Talk It Over. (2002, June 10). *Yorkshire Post.*

Irani, M. (1991, 21 April) Udupi Hotels in Bombay: Changing Styles and Tastes. *Udayavani.*

Irschick, E. F. (1986). *Tamil Revivalism in the 1930s.* Madras: Cre-A.

Islam, A., & Sarker, P. C. (2010). Linking Food Security and Nutrition: Conceptual Issues. *South Asian Anthropologist, 10*(2), 129–134.

Ivan Watson Defines the Indian-Restaurant Curry—How They Do It. (1983). *Curry Magazine, 5,* 9–10.

Iversen, V., & Ghorpade, Y. (2010). Misfortune, Misfits and What the City Gave and Took: The Stories of South-Indian Child Labour Migrants 1935–2005. *Modern Asian Studies, 45*(5), 1177–1226.

Iversen, V., & Raghavendra, P. S. (2006). What the Signboard Hides: Food, Caste and Employability in Small South Indian Eating Places. *Contributions to Indian Sociology, 40*(3), 311–342.

Jacques, M. (2007, January 20). British Society is Dripping with Racism, but No One is Prepared to Admit It. *Guardian.*

Jaffer, A. (2007). *Made for Maharajas: A Design Diary of a Princely India.* London: Lustre.

Jaffrey, M. (1978). *An Invitation to Indian Cooking.* New York: Knopf.

———. (1981). *Madhur Jaffrey's World-of-the-East Vegetarian Cooking.* New York: Knopf.

Jaggar, A. M., & Bordo, S. (1989). *Gender/Body/Knowledge: Feminist Reconstructions of Being and Knowing.* New Brunswick, NJ: Rutgers University Press.

Jain, R. K. (1970). *South Indians on the Plantation Frontier in Malaya.* New Haven, CT: Yale University Press.

Jamal, A. (1996). Acculturation: The Symbolism of Ethnic Eating among Contemporary British Consumers. *British Food Journal, 98*(10), 12.

James, A. (1996). Cooking the Books: Global or Local Identities in Contemporary British Food Cultures? In D. Howes (Ed.), *Cross-Cultural Consumption: Global Markets, Local Realities* (pp. 77–92). London: Routledge.

Jameson, F. (1986). Third-World Literature in the Era of Multinational Capitalism. *Social Text, 15,* 65–88.

———. (1998). Notes on Globalization as a Philosophical Issue. In J. Jameson & M. Miyoshi (Eds.), *The Cultures of Globalization* (pp. 54–77). Durham, NC: Duke University Press.

Jameson, F., & Miyoshi, M. (1998). *The Cultures of Globalization.* Durham, NC: Duke University Press.

Janeja, M. K. (2010). *Transactions in Taste: The Collaborative Lives of Everyday Bengali Food.* New York: Routledge.

Janer, Z. (Ed.). (2006). Culinary Crossings: A Symposium on the Globalization of Indian Cuisine. *Seminar, 566* http://www.india-seminar.com/2006/566.htm.

Jasanoff, M. (2005). *Edge of Empire: Lives, Culture, and Conquest in the East, 1750–1850*. New York: Knopf.

Jayasuriya, S. D. S., & Pankhurst, R. (2003). *The African Diaspora in the Indian Ocean*. Trenton, NJ: Africa World Press.

Jenkins, V. S. (2000). *Bananas: An American History*. Washington, DC: Smithsonian Books.

Jenks, C. (2004). *Urban Culture: Critical Concepts in Literary and Cultural Studies*. New York: Routledge.

Jerome, N., Kandel, R. F., & Pelto, G. H. (1980). *Nutritional Anthropology: Contemporary Approaches to Diet and Culture*. Pleasantville, NY: Redgrave.

Jhala, A. D. (2008). *Courtly Indian Women in Late Imperial India*. London: Pickering & Chatto.

Johnson, D. (1983). *Body*. Boston: Beacon Press.

Johnson, J. (1837). *The Economy of Health or the Stream of Human Life from the Cradle to the Grave with Reflections Moral, Physical and Philosophical on the Successive Phases of Human Existence, the Maladies to Which They Are Subjected, and the Dangers That May Be Averted* (2nd ed). London: Highley.

Johnston, J., & Baumann, S. (2007). Democracy versus Distinction: A Study of Omnivorousness in Gourmet Food Writing. *American Journal of Sociology, 113*(1), 165–204.

Johnston, J., Gismondi, M. A., & Goodman, J. (Eds.). (2006). *Nature's Revenge: Reclaiming Sustainability in an Age of Corporate Globalization*. Peterborough, ON: Broadview Press.

Jones, T. P., Abbas, T., Ram, M., & Sanghera, B. (2009). Ethnic Minority Enterprise in Its Urban Context: South Asian Restaurants in Birmingham. *International Journal of Urban and Regional Research, 26,* 24–40.

Joshi, S. (2005). *Fractured Modernity: Making of a Middle Class in Colonial North India*. New Delhi: Oxford University Press.

Just-Food.Com. (2008, July 25). India: Packaged Food Sales to Soar by Two-Thirds—Study. http://www.just-food.com/news/packaged-food-sales-to-soar-by-two-thirds-study_id103210.aspx.

Kahn, J. S., & Loh, F. K. (1992). *Fragmented Vision: Culture and Politics in Contemporary Malaysia*. Honolulu: University of Hawai'i Press.

Kalb, D. (Ed.). (2000). *The Ends of Globalization: Bringing Society Back In*. Lanham, MD: Rowman & Littlefield.

Kalra, J. I. S., & Das Gupta, P. (1999). *Prashad: Cooking with Indian Masters*. New Delhi: Allied Publishers Private.

Kalra, V. S. (2000). *From Textile Mills to Taxi Ranks*. Aldershot: Ashgate.

———. (2004). The Political Economy of the Samosa. *South Asia Research, 24*(1), 21–36.

Kanwar, D. (2006). *Palace on Wheels: A Royal Train Journey*. New Delhi: Prakash Books.

Kapurthala, B. (1954). *Maharani: The Story of an Indian Princess,* as told to Elaine Williams. New York: Henry Holt.

Karanth, S. (1975). *Yaksagana*. Mysore: Institute of Kannada Studies, University of Mysore.

Karuturi. Undated. http://www.karuturi.com/index.php.

Kent, S. (1990). *Domestic Architecture and the Use of Space: An Interdisciplinary Cross-Cultural Study*. Cambridge: Cambridge University Press.

Kershen, A. J. (Ed.). (2002). *Food in the Migrant Experience*. Aldershot, England: Ashgate.

Keshani, H. (2006). Architecture and the Twelver Shi'i Tradition: the Great Imambara Complex of Lucknow. *Muqarnas* 23: 219–250.

Khan, A. (1997a, May 15). £5M Curry House Plan. *Telegraph and Argus*.

———. (1997b, August 14). New Jobs Linked to Food Chain Deal. *Telegraph and Argus*.

Khan, M. (2006). *An Extraordinary Life: Princess Mehrunissa of Rampur*. Noida: Blue Leaf.

Khan, N. (1982). The Food of India: Punjab and the North. *Curry Magazine*, Spring: 10–11.

Khan, S. M. (2000). *The Begums of Bhopal: A Dynasty of Women Rulers in Raj India*. London: I.B. Tauris.

Khan, V. S. (1977). The Pakistanis: Mirpuri Villagers at Home and in Bradford. In J. L. Watson, (Ed.), *Between Two Cultures: Migrants and Minorities in Britain* (pp. 57–89). London: Basil Blackwell.

Khana Khazana. (2002, November 24). *Sunday Mid Day*.

Khare, R. S. (1966). A Case of Anomalous Values in Indian Civilization: Meat-eating among the Kanya-Kubja Brahmans of Katyayan Gotra. *The Journal of Asian Studies, 25*(2), pp. 229–240.

———. (1976a). *Culture and Reality: Essays on the Hindu System of Managing Foods*. Simla: Indian Institute of Advanced Study.

———. (1976b). *The Hindu Hearth and Home*. New Delhi: Vikas.

———. (1992). *The Eternal Food: Gastronomic Ideas and Experiences of Hindus and Buddhists*. Albany: State University of New York Press.

———. (1993). The Seen and the Unseen: Hindu Distinctions, Experiences, and Cultural Reasoning. *Contributions to Indian Sociology* 27 (2), 191–212;

———. (1994). *On and About Postmodernism: Writing/Rewriting*. Baltimore: University Press of America.

———. (1998a). *Cultural Diversity and Social Discontent: Anthropological Studies of Modern India*. New Delhi, London, and Thousand Oaks, CA: Sage.

———. (1998b). The Issue of "Right to Food" Among the Hindus: Notes and Comments. *Contributions to Indian Sociology, 32*(2), 253–278.

———. (2002). Two Disengaged Cultures, Two Distant Democracies. In A. Kapur, Y. K. Malik, H. A. Gould, & A. G. Rubinoff (Eds.), *India and the United States in a Changing World* (pp. 245–296). New Delhi and Thousand Oaks, CA: Sage.

———. (2004). Anna. In S. Mittal & G. Thursby (Eds.), *The Hindu World* (pp. 407–428). New York: Routledge.

———. (2006). *Caste, Hierarchy, and Individualism: Indian Critiques of Louis Dumont's Contributions*. Oxford: Oxford University Press.

———. (2008). Anthropology, India, and Academic Self: A Disciplinary Journey between Two Cultures over Four Decades. *India Review, 7*(4), 349–377.

Khare, R. S., & Rao, M. S. A. (Eds.). (1986). *Food, Society, and Culture: Aspects in South Asian Food Systems*. Durham, NC: Carolina Academic Press.

Kibria, N. (2003). *Becoming Asian American*. Baltimore, MD: Johns Hopkins University Press.

King, A. D. (1990). *Urbanism, Colonialism, and the World-Economy: Cultural and Spatial Foundations of the World Urban System*. New York: Routledge.

Kirby, T. (2007, January 19). Police Launch Investigation of Big Brother "Racism" as Sponsors Desert Contestants. *Independent*.

Kohli, J. (2009). Sri Ramakrishna Karuturi, Founder, Managing Director, Karuturi Global Ltd. http://www.indiainfoline.com/Research/LeaderSpeak/Sai-Ramakrishna-Karuturi-Founder-Managing-Director-Karuturi-Global-Ltd/6369363.

Korsmeyer, C. (1999). *Making Sense of Taste: Food & Philosophy*. Ithaca, NY: Cornell University Press.

———. (2005). *The Taste Culture Reader: Experiencing Food and Drink*. Oxford: Berg.

Kraidy, M. M., & Murphy, P. D. (2008). Shifting Geertz: Toward a Theory of Translocalism in Global Communication Studies. *Communication Theory, 18*(3), 335–355.

Kripalani, M. & Engardio, P. (2003). The Rise of India. *BusinessWeek,* December 8, 66–73.

Krishnan, S. (1983). *Host to the Millions. The Story of Krishna Rao of Woodlands, Madras: New Woodlands Hotel. http://www.newwoodlands.com/*

Krishnan, S [Sunil]. (2003, 4 April). Food that Heals. *India Abroad,* p. M2.

Kroes, R. (Ed.). (1980). *The American Identity: Fusion and Fragmentation*. European Contributions to American Studies 3. Amsterdam: Amerika-Instituut.

Kundnani, A. (2001). From Oldham to Bradford: The Violence of the Violated. *Race & Class, 43* (2): 105–131.

Kymlicka, W. (2003). Immigration, Citizenship, Multiculturalism: Exploring the Links. *The Political Quarterly, 74*(Supplement 1), 195–208.

Lakoff, G., & Johnson, M. (1999). *Philosophy in the Flesh: The Embodied Mind and Its Challenge to Western Thought*. New York: Basic Books.

Lal, R. (2005). *Domesticity and Power in the Early Mughal World*. Cambridge: Cambridge University Press.

Lamb, S. 2000. *White Saris and Sweet Mangoes: Aging, Gender and Body in North India*. Berkeley: University of California Press.

Landa, J. 1981. A Theory of the Ethnically Homogenous Middleman Group: An Institutional Alternative to Contract Law. *Journal of Legal Studies* 10, 349–62.

Landladies' Colour Bar on Students. (1966, March 5). *Times* (London), 6.

Latour, B. (1993). *We Have Never Been Modern*. Cambridge, MA: Harvard University Press.

Laudan R. (2000). Birth of the Modern Diet. *Scientific American, 283*(2), 76–81.

Laxman, R. K. (1988). *The Hotel Riviera*. New Delhi: Penguin Books.

Layton, R., Manley, G., Harris, O., Palmer, S., & Appadurai, A. (1986). Letters. *Anthropology Today, 2*(4), 24–25.

Layton-Henry, Z. (1992). *The Politics of Immigration*. Oxford: Blackwell.

Leach, E. R. (1967). *The Structural Study of Myth and Totemism*. London: Tavistock Publications.

Lee-Warner, W. (1899/1910). The Native States of India. *British Empire Series, Volume 1: India, Ceylon, Straits Settlements, British Northern Borneo, Hong-Kong*. London: Kegal Paul, Trench, Trubner.

Lefebvre, H. (2004). *Rhythmanalysis: Space, Time, and Everyday Life*. New York: Continuum.

Lerner R. M., Karabenick S. A., & Stuart J. L. (1973). Relations among Physical Attractiveness, Body Attitudes, and Self-Concept in Male and Female College Students. *The Journal of Psychology, 85*(1st Half), 119–129.

Levenstein, H. (1985). The American Response to Italian Food, 1880–1930. *Food & Foodways, 1*(1), 1–24.

Levine, P., & Grayzel, S. R. (Ed.). (2009). *Gender, Labour, War and Empire: Essays on Modern Britain*. New York: Palgrave Macmillan.

Lévi-Strauss, C. (1965). Le triangle culinaire. *L'Arc, 26*, 19–29.

———. (1974). *Tristes tropiques*. New York: Atheneum.

Lewis, J., & Moorman, G. B. (2007). *Adolescent Literacy Instruction: Policies and Promising Practices*. Newark, DE: International Reading Association.

Lewis, P. (2002). *Islamic Britain: Religion, Politics and Identity among British Muslims*. London: I.B. Tauris.

Li, W. (1998). Anatomy of a New Ethnic Settlement: The Chinese Ethnoburb in Los Angeles. *Urban Studies, 35*(3), 479–501.

Liang, J. (2007). Migration Patterns and Occupational Specialisations of Kolkata Chinese: An Insider's History. *China Report 43*(4), 397–410.

Liechty, M. (2003). *Suitably Modern: Making Middle Class Culture in a New Consumer Society*. Princeton: Princeton University Press.

Light, I. H. (1972). *Ethnic Enterprise in America: Business and Welfare among Chinese, Japanese, and Blacks*. Berkeley: University of California Press.

———. (1981). Ethnic Succession. In C. F. Keyes (Ed.), *Ethnic Change* (pp. 54–86). Seattle: University of Washington Press.

Light, I. H., & Bonacich, E. (1988). *Immigrant Entrepreneurs: Koreans in Los Angeles, 1965–1982*. Berkeley: University of California Press.

"Little Harlems" Must Go: Two Views on Birmingham's Colour Question. (1955, February 25). *Birmingham Evening Despatch* (Birmingham, England).

Llewellyn-Jones, R. (Ed.). (2006). *Lucknow: City of Illusion*. Munich: Prestel.

Lock, M. (1993). Cultivating the Body: Anthropology and Epistemologies of Bodily Practice and Knowledge. *Annual Review of Anthropology, 22*, 133–155.

Lock, M.M., & Farquhar, J. (Ed.). (2007). *Beyond the Body Proper: Reading the Anthropology of Material Life.* Durham, NC: Duke University Press.

London News: India Restaurant Opens. (1926, May 17). *Englishman* (Calcutta).

Long, L.M. (Ed.). (2004). *Culinary Tourism.* Lexington: University Press of Kentucky.

Lovely People but We Want to Get Away. (1976, July 13). *Birmingham Evening Mail,* 10–11.

Low, S.M. (2000). *On the Plaza: The Politics of Public Space and Culture.* Austin: University of Texas Press.

Lupton, D. (1996). *Food, the Body, and the Self.* London; Thousand Oaks, CA: Sage.

Lynch, K. (1960). *The Image of the City.* Cambridge, MA: MIT Press.

Lytton, Viceroy. (1876). To Queen Victoria, 21 April, I.O.L.R., E218/518/1.

Mackie, V., & Stevens, C. (2009). Globalisation and Body Politics. *Asian Studies Review, 33*(3), 257–273.

Madan, T.N. (1999). Louis Dumont 1911–1998: A Memoir. *Contributions to Indian Sociology, 33*(3), 473–501.

Madsen, S.T. (1992). Udupi Hotels: A Case of Ethnicity Based Non-Virulent Development. *Research Report from the Department of Sociology, Lund University,* SMS, Social Movements and Strategies in Third World Development, publication no. 25, 1–17.

———. (2005). Religion *is* Danger: The Brass-Robinson Debate in a Darwinian Perspective. Unpublished paper.

———. (2009). EU-India Relations: An Expanded Interpretive Framework. In B. Gans, J. Jokela, & E. Limnell (Eds.), *The Role of the European Union in Asia: China and India as Strategic Partners* (pp. 77–94). Surrey: Ashgate.

Mahal, R. (1963). *Keighley News.*

Mahar, J.M., & Chandrasekhar, S. (Eds.). (1972). *The Untouchables in Contemporary India.* Tucson: University of Arizona Press.

Majumdar, D.N. (1958). *Caste and Communication in an Indian Village.* Mumbai: Asia Publishing House.

Malamoud, C. (1996). *Cooking the World: Ritual and Thought in Ancient India.* New Delhi: Oxford University Press.

Man Swallows a Restaurant Fork. (1968, December 2). *Times* (London), 10–11.

Man! What a Great Nan! (1988). *Bradford Telegraph and Argus,* 10–11.

Mankekar, P. (2002). India Shopping: Indian Grocery Stores and Transnational Configurations of Belonging *Ethnos, 67*(1), 75–98.

Mannur, A. (2010). *Culinary Fictions. Food in South Asian Diasporic Culture.* Philadelphia: Temple University Press.

Marketing Birmingham. (2004–2005). *The Balti Triangle Birmingham: Essential Guide.* Birmingham: Marketing Birmingham.

Marriott, M. (1955). *Village India: Studies in the Little Community.* Chicago: University of Chicago Press.

———. (1966). The Feast of Love. In M. Singer (Ed.), *Krishna: Myths, Rites and Attitudes* (pp. 200–212). Honolulu: East-West Center Press.

————. (1968). Caste Ranking and Food Transactions: A Matrix Analysis. In M. Singer & B. Cohn (Eds.), *Structure and Change in Indian Society* (pp. 133–171). Chicago: Aldine.

————. (1989). Constructing an Indian Ethnosociology. *Contributions to Indian Sociology, 23*(1), 1–39.

————. (1990). *India through Hindu Categories*. New Delhi: Sage.

Marriott, M. & Inden, R. (1977). Toward an Ethnosociology of South Asian Caste Systems. In K. David (Ed.), *The New Wind: Changing Identities in South Asia* (pp. 227–238). The Hague: Mouton.

Martin, J. (2007, January 20). British Society is Dripping with Racism, But No One is Prepared to Admit It. *Guardian* (London).

Martin, J. R. (1837). *Notes on the Medical Topography of Calcutta*. Calcutta: G. H. Huttmann.

Marx, K. (1853, August 8). The Future Results of British Rule in India. *New York Daily Tribune*.

Maschler, F. (1986). *Fay Maschler's Guide to Eating Out in London*. London: Century.

Massey, D. B. (1994). *Space, Place, and Gender*. Minneapolis: University of Minnesota Press.

Mathur, L. P., & Sukhwal, L. (1991). British Interference in the Internal Sovereignty of Princely States (1858–1885). In R. P. Vyas (Ed.), *British Policy towards Princely States of India* (pp. 62–108). Jodhpur: Rajasthan-Vidya Prakashan.

Mauss, M. (1935/2007). Techniques of the Body. In M. Lock & J. Farquhar, J. (Eds.). *Beyond the Body Proper. Reading the Anthropology of Material Life* (pp. 50–68). Durham, NC: Duke University Press.

May, S. (2002). Multiculturalism. In D. T. Goldberg, (Ed.), *A Companion to Racial and Ethnic Studies* (pp. 124–144). Malden, MA, and Oxford: Blackwell.

Mazzarella, W. (2003). *Shoveling Smoke: Advertising and Globalization in Contemporary India*. Durham, NC: Duke University Press.

McMichael, P. (1994). *The Global Restucturing of Agro-Food Systems*. Ithaca, NY: Cornell University Press.

————. (2000). *Development and Social Change: A Global Perspective*. Thousand Oaks, CA: Pine Forge Press.

————. (2010). *Contesting Development: Critical Struggles for Social Change*. New York: Routledge.

Mead, M. (1943). The Anthropological Approach to Dietary Problems. *Transactions of the New York Academy of Sciences, II* (5), 177–182.

Mehrotra, R., & Nest, G. (Eds.). (1996). *Public Places-Bombay*. Mumbai: Max Mueller Bhavan, Urban Design Research Institute.

Melwani, L. (2004). Hot and Cold. The Hottest Thing on Indian Grocery Shelves is Frozen. October 5, http://www.biggerindia.com/arts-entertainment/1508-hot-and-cold.html.

Mennell, S. (1985). *All Manners of Food: Eating and Taste in England and France from the Middle Ages to the Present*. Oxford; New York: Blackwell.

Merleau-Ponty, M. (1996). *Phenomenology of Perception*. Delhi: Motilal Banarsidass.

Messer, E. (1984). Anthropological Perspectives on Diet. *Annual Review of Anthropology, 13*, 205–249.

Messner, M. A., & Sabo, D. F. (Eds.). (1990). *Sport, Men, and the Gender Order: Critical Feminist Perspectives*. Champaign, IL: Human Kinetics Books.

Metcalf, H., Modood, T., & Virdee, S. (1996). *Asian Self-Employment: The Interaction of Culture and Economics in England*. London: Policy Studies Institute.

Metcalf, T. R. (1994). *Ideologies of the Raj*. Cambridge: Cambridge University Press.

Midnight Cowboys. (1996, May). *Tandoori Magazine, 18*, 6.

Miles, R. (1980). Colonial Immigrants in a British City: A Class Analysis. *Urban Studies, 17*(2), 241–242.

Miller, D. (2005). Coca-Cola: A Black Sweet Drink from Trinidad. In J. L. Watson & M. L. Caldwell (Eds.), *The Cultural Politics of Food and Eating: A Reader* (pp. 54–69). Oxford: Blackwell.

Milton, G. (2000). *Nathaniel's Nutmeg*. New York: Penguin Books.

Mintz, S. (1985). *Sweetness and Power: The Place of Sugar in Modern History*. New York: Penguin Books.

———. (1996). *Tasting Food, Tasting Freedom: Excursions into Eating, Culture, and the Past*. Boston: Beacon Press.

———. (2002). Eating America. In C. Counihan (Ed.), *Food in the USA. A Reader* (pp. 23–34). New York: Routledge.

———. (2006). Food at Moderate Speed. In R. Wilk (Ed.). *Fast Food/Slow Food: The Cultural Economy of the Global Food System* (pp. 3–11). New York: Altamira Press.

Mintz, S. W., & Du Bois, C. M. (2002). The Anthropology of Food and Eating. *Annual Review of Anthropology, 31*, 99–119.

Mitchell, L. (2009). *Language, Emotion, and Politics in South India: The Making of a Mother Tongue*. Bloomington: Indiana University Press.

Mittal, S., & Thursby, G. R. (Eds.). (2004). *The Hindu World*. New York: Routledge.

Mochon, D. (2007, October 4). Samosa House Menu Covers Indian Regional Specialties. *The Poughkeepsie Journal*.

Modood, T. (1992a). *Not Easy Being British: Colour, Culture and Citizenship*. Stoke-on-Trent: Runnymede Trust and Trentham.

———. (1992b). British Asian Muslims and the Rushdie Affair. In J. Donald & A. Rattansi (Eds.), *Race, Culture and Difference* (pp. 260–277). London: Sage.

———. (2005). *Multicultural Politics: Racism, Ethnicity, and Muslims in Britain*. Minneapolis: University of Minnesota Press.

Möhring, M. (2008). Transnational Food Migration and the Internationalization of Food Consumption: Ethnic Cuisine in West Germany. In A. Nutzenadel & F. Trentmann (Eds.), *Food and Globalization: Consumption, Markets and Politics in the Modern World* (pp. 129–150). New York: Berg.

Mongia, R. (2007). Historicizing State Sovereignty: Inequality and the Form of Equivalence. *Comparative Studies in Society and History, 49*(2), 384–441.

Monroe, J. (2005). *Star of India: The Spicy Adventures of Curry*. Chichester, UK: Wiley.

Moore, L. (2005). *Maharanis: A Family Saga of Four Queens.* New York: Penguin.

Moore, R. (1984). *Anthropology and the Study of Religion.* Chicago: Center for the Scientific Study of Religion.

Moro, J. (2006). *Passion India: The Story of the Spanish Princess of Kapurthala.* New Delhi: Full Circle.

Moskin, J. (2005, March 9). Mumbai to Midtown, Chaat Hits the Spot. *The New York Times,* pp. 1.

Mu'in, M. (1963). *Farhang-i Farsi.* Tehran: Amir Kabir.

Mukhopadhyay, B. [Bhaskar]. (2004). Between Elite Hysteria and Subaltern Carnivalesque: The Politics of Street-Food in the City of Calcutta. *South Asia Research, 24*(1), 37–50.

Mukhopadhyay, B. [Bipradas]. (1987 [1885–1902]). *Pak-pranali* [Recipes]. Calcutta: Ananda.

Mukhopadhyay, J. (1868). *Sarir Palan* [The Care of Our Body]. Chinsurah.

Mukhopadhyay, R. P. (1868). *Swasthya Raksha* [Health Care]. Calcutta.

Mukhopadhyay, S. S. (1960). Hindu Melar Bibaran: 1789–1791 Sakya [Description of the Hindu Mela: 1868–1870]. *Sahitya Parishat Patrika, 69* (2–4).

Murphy, D. (1987). *Tales from Two Cities: Travel of Another Sort.* London: Murray.

Murthy, U. R. A. (1989). *Samskara: A Rite for a Dead Man.* New Delhi: Oxford University Press.

Muthiah, S. (1989). *Tales of Old and New Madras: The Dalliance of Miss Mansell and 34 Other Stories of 350 Years.* New Delhi: Affiliated East-West Press.

Mutt, S. K. (1989). *Udupi. An Introduction.* Udupi: Navayuga Press.

Naipaul, V. S. (1990). *India: A Million Mutinies Now.* New York: Viking.

Nair, J. (2005). *The Promise of the Metropolis: Bangalore's Twentieth Century.* New Delhi: Oxford University Press.

Nanda, M. (2009). *The God Market: How Globalization is Making India More Hindu.* Noida: Random House India.

Nandy, A. (2003a). *The Romance of the State and the Fate of Dissent in the Tropics.* New York: Oxford University Press.

———. (2003b). Ethnic Cuisine: The Significant Other. In G. Sen (Ed.), *India. A National Culture?* (pp. 246–251). New Delhi: Sage.

———. (2007). *An Ambiguous Journey to the City: The Village and Other Odd Ruins of the Self in the Indian Imagination.* Oxford: Oxford University Press.

Nandy, A., Trivedy, S., Mayaram, S., Yagnik, A. (1995). *Creating Nationality: The Ramjanmabhumi Movement and Fear of the Self.* New Delhi: Oxford University Press.

Naoroji, D. (1901). *Poverty and Un-British Rule in India.* London: S. Sonnenschein.

Narayan, K. (1994). *Love, Stars, and All That.* New York: Pocket Books.

Narayan, U. (1997). *Dislocating Cultures: Identities, Traditions, and Third-World Feminism.* New York: Routledge.

Nardone, J. (2003). Roomful of Blues: Jukejoints and the Cultural Landscape of the Mississippi Delta. In A. K. Hoagland and K. A. Breisch (Eds). *Perspectives in*

Vernacular Architecture, Constructing Image, Identity, and Place (pp. 166–175). Knoxville: University of Tennessee Press.

Naregal, V. (2001). *Language Politics, Elites, and the Public Sphere.* New Delhi: Permanent Black.

Nash, M. (1989). *The Cauldron of Ethnicity in the Modern World.* Chicago: University of Chicago Press.

Nath, A., Holmes, F. R., & Holmes, A. N. (2008). *Jodhpur's Umaid Bhawan : The Maharaja of Palaces.* India: India Book House.

Nathan, S. & Robertson, C. (2007, January 19). I Did Call Her Shilpa Poppadum but It Was Not Racial. *The Sun* (London).

Nederveen Pieterse, J. (2004). *Globalization and Culture: Global Mélange.* Lanham, MD: Rowman & Littlefield.Nestle, M. (2002). *Food Politics: How the Food Industry Influences Nutrition and Health.* Berkeley: University of California Press.

Newbold, K. B., & Spindler, J. (2001). Immigrant Settlement Patterns in Metropolitan Chicago. *Urban Studies, 38*(11), 1903–1919.

New Zealand Trade & Enterprise. (2009). *Market Profile for Food Processing in India.* Auckland: New Zealand Trade & Enterprise. http://www.nzte.govt.nz/explore-export-markets/market-research-by-industry/Food-and-beverage/Pages/Food-processing-market-in-India. Accessed September 11, 2011.

Nilesh, P. (2008). Food Culture and Creativity: Tiffin Box Courier Services in Mumbai. Paper Presented at a Conference on Asian Creativity in Culture and Technology, Trondheim. *http://www.asiancreativity.niasconferences.dk/papers.php.*

Norton, M. (2006). Tasting Empire: Chocolate and the European Internalization of Mesoamerican Aesthetics. *The American Historical Review, 111*(3), 660–691.

Nussbaum, M. C. (1996). *For Love of Country: Debating the Limits of Patriotism.* Boston: Beacon Press.

Nutzenadel, A., & Trentmann, F. (2010). *Food and Globalization: Consumption, Markets and Politics in the Modern World.* New York: Berg.

Obeyesekere, G. (1991). Review: Hindu Medicine and the Aroma of Structuralism. *Journal of Religion, 73*(1), (July): 419–425.

O'Connor, K. (2009). The King's Christmas Pudding: Globalization, Recipes, and the Commodities. *Journal of Global History, 4,* 127–155.

Ong, A. (1999). *Flexible Citizenship: The Cultural Logics of Transnationality.* Durham, NC: Duke University Press.

Orme, R. (1971). *Of the Government and People of Indostan.* Lucknow: Pustak Kendra.

Orsini, F. (2002). *The Hindi Public Sphere 1920–1940: Language and Literature in the Age of Nationalism.* New Delhi: Oxford University Press.

Osella, F., & Osella, C. (2000). *Social Mobility in Kerala: Modernity and Identity in Conflict.* London: Pluto Press.

Ovington, J., & Rawlinson, H. G. (1689/1929). *A Voyage to Surat in the Year 1689.* London: Oxford University Press.

Pais, A. J. (2003, April 18). Cooking with Love. *India Abroad,* m14.

———. (2010). A Bite of Tamarind. *India Abroad* (New York Edition), 41.

Parekh, B. C., and the Runnymede Trust Commission on the Future of Multi-Ethnic Britain (2000). *The Future of Multi-Ethnic Britain: Report of the Commission on the Future of Multi-Ethnic Britain.* London: Profile Books.

Parekh, B. C., Singh, G., & Vertovec, S. (Eds.). (2003). *Culture and Economy in the Indian Diaspora.* London: Routledge.

Park, K. (1997). *The Korean American Dream: Immigrants and Small Business in New York City.* Ithaca, NY: Cornell University Press.

Parker, D. (1995). The Chinese Takeaway and the Diasporic Habitus: Space, Time and Power Geometries. In B. Hesse (Ed.), *Un/Settled Multiculturalisms: Diasporas, Entanglements, Transruptions* (pp. 73–95). London: Zed.

Parulkar, A. (2011). African Lands, Up for Grabs. *World Policy Journal,* March 28, 103–110.

Pat's Postbag. (1996). *Tandoori Magazine, 18,* 31.

Paxson, H. (2006). Artisanal Cheese and Economies of Sentiment in New England. In R. Wilk (Ed.), *Fast Food/Slow Food: The Cultural Economy of the Global Food System* (pp. 201–217). Latham, MD: Altamira Press.

———. (2008). Post-Pasteurian Cultures: The Microbiopolitics of Raw Milk Cheese in the United States. *Cultural Anthropology, 23*(1), 15–47.

Pearson, M. N. (1987). *The Portuguese in India.* Cambridge: Cambridge University Press.

———. (1996a). Introduction. In M. N. Pearson, (Ed.), *Spices in the Indian Ocean World* (pp. xv–xxxvii). Brookfield, VT: Variorum.

———. (Ed.). (1996b). *Spices in the Indian Ocean World.* Brookfield, VT: Variorum.

People's Union for Civil Liberties. (2009). *Cultural Policing in Dakshina Kannada. Vigilante Attacks on Women and Minorities, 2008–09.* Bangalore, Karnataka: PUCL. http://youngfeminists.files.wordpress.com/2009/04/cultural-policing-in-dakshina-kannada-book.pdf.

Percival, J. (1995, June 21). Balti Classes Could Put Meals on the Map. *Birmingham Post.*

Pettigrew, J. (2001). *A Social History of Tea.* London: National Trust.

Pilcher, J. M. (1998). *Que vivan los tamales! Food and the Making of Mexican Identity.* Albuquerque: University of New Mexico Press.

Pinney, C. (2001). Introduction: Public, Popular, and Other Cultures. In R. Dwyer & C. Pinney (Eds.), *Pleasure and the Nation* (pp. 1–34). New Delhi: Oxford University Press.

Piore, M. J. (1979). *Birds of Passage: Migrant Labor and Industrial Societies.* Cambridge: Cambridge University Press.

Pires, T. (1944). *The Suma Oriental of Tomé Pires.* (A. Cortesao, Ed.) London: The Hakluyt Society.

Pollock, S. I. (2006). *The Language of the Gods in the World of Men: Sanskrit, Culture, and Power in Premodern India.* Berkeley: University of California Press.

Portes. A. (Ed.). (1995). *Economic Sociology of Immigration: Essays on Networks, Ethnicity, and Entrepreneurship.* New York: Russell Sage Foundation.

Postgate, R. (1954). *The Good Food Guide. 1954.* London: Cassell.

———. (1955). *The Good Food Guide. 1955.* London: Cassell.

Poulsen, M. F., & Johnston, R. J. (2000). The Ghetto Model and Ethnic Concentration in Australian Cities. *Urban Geography 21*(1), 26.

Prajñasundari, D. (1995). *Āmisha o Nirāmisha āhāra* [NonVegetarian and Vegetarian Cuisine]. Calcutta: Ananda.

Prakash. O. (1961). *Food and Drinks in Ancient India, from Earliest Times to c. 1200 A.D.* Delhi: Munshi Ram Manohar Lal.

Prasad, L. (2007). *Poetics of Conduct: Oral Narrative and Moral Being in a South Indian Town.* New York: Columbia University Press.

Prasad, S. (2005). Sanitising the Domestic: Gender, Hygiene and Health in Bengal/India, 1885–1935. *Wellcome History, 28,* 6–7.

———. (2006). *Social Production of Hygiene: Domesticity, Gender, and Nationalism in Late Colonial Bengal and India.* PhD dissertation, University of Illinois at Urbana-Champaign.

Prem, D. R. (1965). *The Parliamentary Leper: A History of Colour Prejudice in Britain.* Aligarh: Metric Publications.

Prewitt, M. (2008, January 21). Opportunities for Growth Heat up in India's Rapidly Rising Economy. *Nation's Restaurant (News Brands in Foodservice Supplement), 1,* 31–34.

Procida, M. A. (2003). Feeding the Imperial Appetite: Imperial Knowledge and Anglo-Indian Discourse. *Journal of Women's History, 15*(2), 123–149.

Quataert, D. (Ed.). (2000). *Consumption Studies and the History of the Ottoman Empire, 1550–1922.* Albany: State University of New York Press.

Radhan, K. 1996. Urban Green Spaces and Bombay. In R. Mehrotra & G. Nest (Eds.), *Public Places: Bombay* (pp. 55–57). Mumbai: Max Mueller Bhavan.

Rafiq, M. (1988). *Asian Business in Bradford, West Yorkshire: A Study of Ethnic Entrepreneurship in Retailing, Manufacturing and the Service Industries.* PhD thesis, University of Bradford.

Rai, M. (2004). *Hindu Rulers, Muslim Subjects: Islam, Rights, and the History of Kashmir.* Princeton: Princeton University Press.

Rajagopal, A. (2001). The Violence of Commodity Aesthetics: Hawkers, Demolition Raids, and a New Regime of Consumption. *Social Text, 68,* 91–113.

Raj Mahal. (1998, November 20). *Keighley News* (Keighley, England).

Rajshahi. (1930, June 21). *Telegraph & Argus.*

Ram, M. (2002). Ethnic Minority Enterprise in Its Urban Context: South Asian Restaurants in Birmingham. *International Journal of Urban and Regional Research, 26:* 24–40.

Ram, M., Abbas, T., Sanghera, B., Barlow, G., & Jones, T. (2001). Apprentice Entrepreneurs? Ethnic Minority Workers in the Independent Restaurant Sector. *Work, Employment and Society: Journal of the British Sociological Association, 15*(2), 353–371.

Ram, M., & Jones, T. (1998). *Ethnic Minorities in Business*. Milton Keynes: Small Business Research Trust, Open University Business School.

Ram, M., Jones, T., Abbas, T., & Sanghera, B. (2002). Ethnic Minority Enterprise in Its Urban Context: South Asian Restaurants in Birmingham. *International Journal of Urban and Regional Research, 26*, 24–40.

Ramadas. (1976). *Kartārana Kammaṭa. Kādambari*. Udipi: Jyotismati Prakasana.

Ramanujan, A. K. (1992). Food for Thought: Toward an Anthology of Hindu Food Images. In R. S. Khare (Ed.), *Eternal Food: Gastronomic Ideas and Experiences among Hindus and Buddhists* (pp. 221–250). Albany: State University of New York Press.

Ramsurya, M. V. (2010). Indian Companies Buy Land Abroad for Agricultural Products. *Economic Times* January 2, http://farmlandgrab.org/10070.

Ramusack, B. N. (1978). *The Princes of India in the Twilight of Empire: Dissolution of a Patron-Client System, 1914–1939*. Columbus: Ohio State University Press.

———. (1995). The Indian Princes as Fantasy: Palace Hotels, Palace Museums, and Palace on Wheels. In C. A. Breckenridge (Ed.), *Consuming Modernity: Public Culture in a South Asian World* (pp. 66–89). Minneapolis: University of Minnesota Press.

———. (2004). *The Indian Princes and Their States*. Cambridge: Cambridge University Press.

Rao, H., Monin, P., & Durand, R. (2003). Institutional Change in Toqueville: Nouvelle Cuisine as an Identity Movement in French Gastronomy. *The American Journal of Sociology, 108*(4), 795–843.

———. (2005). Border Crossing: Bricolage and the Erosion of Categorical Boundaries in French Gastronomy. *American Sociological Review, 70*(6), 968–991.

Rao, K. (2009, February 8). Street Food without the Street. *The New York Times*, Travel Section, 5.

Rapoport, A. (1993). Systems of Activities and Systems of Settings. In S. Kent (Ed.), *Domestic Architecture and the Use of Space: An Interdisciplinary Cross-Cultural Study* (pp. 9–20). New York: Cambridge University Press.

Ratnawali. (2010). Supplementary Nutrition to Women and Children. *Social Change, 40*(3), 319–343.

Ray, B. (Ed.). (2002). *Nari o Paribar: Bamabodhini Patrika (1270–1328 Bangabda)* [Women and the Family: Selections from *Bamabodhini Patrika*, 1863–1921]. Calcutta: Ananda.

Ray, K. (2004). *The Migrant's Table: Meals and Memories in Bengali-American Households*. Philadelphia: Temple University Press.

———. (2006). Ethnic Succession and the New American Restaurant Cuisine. Paper presented at the annual meeting of the American Sociological Association, August 11, 2006. www.allacademic.com/meta/p97132_index.html. Accessed May 8, 2009.

———. (2007). Ethnic Succession and the New American Restaurant Cuisine. In D. Beriss & D. Sutton (Eds.), *The Restaurants Book: Ethnographies of Where We Eat* (pp. 97–114). Oxford: Berg Publishers.

———. (2008). Nation and Cuisine. The Evidence from American Newspapers ca. 1830–2003. *Food and Foodways, 16*(4), 259–297.

———. (2009). Sabina Sehgal Saikia. *Gastronomica, 9*(2), 1–4.

Raychaudhuri, K. C. (1900/1995). Foreword. In P. Debi, *Amish o Niramish Ahar* [Nonegetarian and Vegetarian Cuisine] (unpaginated). Vol. 1. Calcutta: Ananda.

Redon, O., Sabban, F., & Serventi, S. (1998). *The Medieval Kitchen: Recipes from France and Italy.* Chicago: University of Chicago Press.

Restaurant Food Cooked in Garage. (1983, December 8). *Yorkshire Post.*

Restaurant of the Month. (2004, April 16). *Keighley News.*

Restaurant Opportunities Center of New York. (2005). *Behind the Kitchen Door.* *http://www.urbanjustice.org/pdf/publications/BKDFinalReport.pdf.*

Restaurant Roundup. (1982a). *Curry Magazine,* Fall, 33–34.

Restaurant Roundup. (1982b). *Curry Magazine,* Summer, 28.

Restaurant Trade. (1982). *Curry Magazine,* Fall, i.

Restaurants Serve Up Aid for the Homeless. (2004, December 20). *Yorkshire Evening Post.*

Rex, J. (1987). Life in the Ghetto. In J. Benyon & J. Solomos (Eds.), *The Roots of Urban Unrest* (pp. 103–10). Oxford: Pergamon.

———. (1996). *Ethnic Minorities in the Modern Nation State.* London: Macmillan.

Rex, J., & Moore, R. S. (1967). *Race, Community and Conflict: A Study of Sparkbrook.* Oxford: Oxford University Press.

Rex, J. & Tomlinson, S. (1979). *Colonial Immigrants in a British City: A Class Analysis.* London: Routledge and Kegan Paul.

Risley, S. H. (1908). *The People of India.* Calcutta: Thacker, Spink.

Ritzer, G. (2001). *Explorations in the Sociology of Consumption: Fast Food, Credit Cards and Casinos.* Thousand Oaks, CA: Sage.

Robbins, B. (1998). Introduction, Part I: Actually Existing Cosmopolitanism. In P. Cheah & B. Robbins (Eds.), *Cosmopolitics. Thinking and Feeling beyond the Nation* (pp. 1–19). Minneapolis: University of Minnesota Press.

Roberts, J. A. G. (2002). *China to Chinatown: Chinese Food in the West.* London: Reaktion.

Robertson, R. (1992). *Globalization: Social Theory and Global Culture.* London: Sage.

Robin Cook's Chicken Tikka Masala Speech. (2001, April 19). *Guardian Unlimited* (London), *http://www.guardian.co.uk/racism/Story/0,2763,477023,00.html.*

Rösel, J. (1983). Landed Endowment and Sacred Food: The Economy of an Indian Temple. *Archives Européennes de Sociologie, 24*(1), 44–59.

Roseneil, S., & Seymour, J. (Eds.). (1999). *Practising Identities: Power and Resistance.* Houndmills, UK: Palgrave, Macmillan.

Rosselli, J. (1980). The Self-image of Effeteness: Physical Education and Nationalism in Nineteenth-Century Bengal. *Past and Present 86* (February): 121–148.

Roy, N. S. (Ed.). (2004). *A Matter of Taste: The Penguin Book of Indian Writing on Food.* New Delhi: Penguin Books.

Roy, P. (2002). Reading Communities and Culinary Communities: The Gastropoetics of the South Asian Diaspora. *Positions, 10*(2), 471–502.

———. (2010). *Alimentary Tracts. Appetites, Aversions, and the Postcolonial.* Durham, NC: Duke University Press.

Roy, R. T. (2003). *The Departed Melody: Memoirs.* Islamabad: PPA Publications.

Rozin, E. (1992). *Blue Corn and Chocolate* (1st ed.). New York: Knopf.

Rubies, J. (2001). *Travel and Ethnology in the Renaissance: South India through European Eyes, 1250–1625.* Cambridge: Cambridge University Press.

Rucker, W. (2001). *Proposed Moratorium on Office Uses and Conversion of Space to Office Uses in the MU/LI district. http://www.ci.berkeley.ca.us/citycouncil/2001city council/pdf/041701a.pdf*

Rudolph, L. I., & Rudolph, S. H. (1967). *The Modernity of Tradition: Political Development in India.* Chicago: University of Chicago Press.

Rudolph, S. H., & Rudolph, L. I. (1984). *Essays on Rajputana: Reflections on History, Culture, and Administration.* New Delhi: Concept.

Ruggles, S., Alexander, J. T., Genadek, K., Goeken, R., Schroeder, M. B., & Sobek, M. (2010). *Integrated Public Use Microdata Series: Version 5.0* [Machine-readable database]. Minneapolis: University of Minnesota.

Rushdie, S. (1991). *Imaginary Homelands: Essays and Criticism, 1981–1991.* New York: Viking.

Sabrang Communications Private Limited, Mumbai, India and The South Asia Citizens Web, France. (2002). *The Foreign Exchange of Hate. IDRF and the American Funding of Hindutva,* November 20, 2002.

Sahad, P. V. (2007). MTR Foods Sold to Norway's Orkla for $100 Million. *VC Circle,* February 12, http://www.vccircle.com/500/content/mtr-foods-sold-to -norways -orkla-for-100-million.

Sahib in a Graceful Thicket of Words, The. (1964, July 11). *Times* (London).

Sahid, A. (1988). "Banglatown"—What the People Think. *Asian Herald* (London), (Nov. 23–30), 6.

Said, E. W. (2001). *Orientalism: Western Conceptions of the Orient.* London: Penguin Books.

Sangari, K., Vaid, S., & Chatterjee, P. (1990). *Recasting Women: Essays in Indian Colonial History.* New Brunswick, NJ: Rutgers University Press.

Sarkar, N. (2004a). *Mangala pandera bicara.* Calcutta: Punasca.

———. (2004b). *Parara baiyera baire para.* Calcutta: Ananda.

Sarkar, T. (2001). *Hindu Wife, Hindu Nation: Community, Religion, and Cultural Nationalism.* Bloomington: Indiana University Press.

Sassen, S. (1991). *The Global City: New York, London, Tokyo.* Princeton: Princeton University Press.

——— (1995). Immigration and Local Labor Markets. In A. Portes (Ed.), *Economic Sociology of Immigration* (pp. 87–127). New York: Russell Sage.

———. (1996). *Losing Control? Sovereignty in an Age of Globalization.* New York: Columbia University Press.

———. (2000). *Cities in a World Economy.* Thousand Oaks, CA: Pine Forge Press.

Schivelbusch, W. (1992). *Tastes of Paradise: A Social History of Spices, Stimulants, and Intoxicants.* New York: Pantheon Books.

Schlosser, E. (2001). *Fast Food Nation: The Dark Side of the All-American Meal.* Boston: Houghton Mifflin.

Schumpeter, J. A. (1942). *Capitalism, Socialism, and Democracy.* New York: Harper.

Scindia, V. R. (1987). *The Last Maharani of Gwalior: An Autobiography.* Albany: State University of New York Press.

Scott, J. M. (1964). *The Tea Story.* London: Heinemann.

Seal, A. (1968). *The Emergence of Indian Nationalism: Competition and Collaboration in the Later Nineteenth Century.* Cambridge: Cambridge University Press.

Sen, A. K. (1988). *Poverty and Famines: An Essay on Entitlement and Deprivation.* Oxford: Clarendon.

———. (2006). *Identity and Violence: The Illusion of Destiny.* New York: W.W. Norton.

Sen, A. (1998). Ethnicity in the City: Reading Representations of Cultural Difference in Indian Storefronts. In H. C. Dandekar (Ed.), *City, Space and Globalization: An International Perspective* (pp. 132–135). Proceedings of an International Symposium. Ann Arbor: College of Architecture and Urban Planning, University of Michigan.

———. (2006). Methods of Reading the Cultural Landscape of South Asian Immigrants: The Jackson Heights Tour, New York. Conference Tour and Presentation. Vernacular Architecture Forum Conference, New York City, June 2006.

———. (2008). Global Cultures in Local Economies: Case Study of Ethnic Fast Food Restaurants. In D. Froehlich & M. Pride (Eds.), *Seeing the City: Visionaries on the Margin* (pp. 401–13). Proceedings of the 96th ACSA Annual Conference, March 27–30, 2008, Houston, Texas. Washington DC: ACSA Press.

———. (2009). Everyday Production of Ethnicity in Immigrant Stores. *InTensions* 2 (Spring), http://www.yorku.ca/intent/pastissues.html (accessed August 22, 2010).

Sen, C. T. (2004). *Food Culture in India.* Westport, CT: Greenwood Press.

———. (2009). *Curry: A Global History.* London: Reaktion Books.

Sen, G. (Ed.). (2003). *India. A National Culture?* New Delhi: Sage.

Sengupta, J. (2010). Nation on a Platter: The Culture and Politics of Food and Cuisine in Colonial Bengal. *Modern Asian Studies, 44*(1), 81–98.

Seremetakis, C. N. (Ed.). (1994). *The Senses Still: Perception and Memory as Material Culture in Modernity.* Boulder, CO: Westview Press.

Sewell, J. (2011). *Women and the Everyday City: Public Space in San Francisco, 1890–1915.* Minneapolis: University of Minnesota Press.

Shaffer, H. (2007). Nawabs and Kebabs. *Seminar* (New Delhi) (575), 27–31.

Shah Knows What's What. (1985, November 2). *Telegraph and Argus.*

Shalot, O. T. (1906). *Things for the Cook: In English and Hindustani.* Calcutta: Thacker, Spink.

Sharar, A. H. (2005). *Lucknow: The Last Phase of an Oriental Culture.* Oxford: Oxford University Press.

Sheth, N. R. (1974). Industrial Sociology: A Trend Report. In *A Survey of Research in Sociology and Anthropology,* vol. 1, ICSSR, New Delhi.

———. (Ed.). (1983). *Industrial Sociology in India: A Book of Readings*. New Delhi: Allied Publishers.

Shetty, R. (1991, April 17 & 23). Mumbai Badhuku. Mumbai yalli Dakshina Kannadigagara Hotel Udyama. [Bombay Life: Hotel Industry of South Kanara People in Bombay], trans. Sujatha M. Murthy. *Mungaru* (Mangalore).

Shields, R. (1989). Social Spatialization and the Built Environment: The West Edmonton Mall. *Society and Space, 2,* 147–164.

Shilling, C. (1993). *The Body and Social Theory.* Newbury Park, CA: Sage.

Shipley, T. (2007). *Understanding Events.* Oxford: Oxford University Press.

Shiva, V. (1993). *Monocultures of the Mind: Perspectives on Biodiversity and Biotechnology.* London: Zed Books.

———. (2005). *Earth Democracy: Justice, Sustainability, and Peace.* Cambridge, MA: South End Press.

Simoons, F. J. (1979). Questions on the Sacred-Cow Controversy. *Current Anthropology, 20,* 467–493.

Singer, M. B. (1966). *Krishna: Myths, Rites, and Attitudes.* Honolulu: East-West Center Press.

———. (1972). *When a Great Tradition Modernizes: An Anthropological Approach to Indian Civilization.* New York: Praeger Publishers.

———. (Ed.). (1973). *Entrepreneurship and Modernization of Occupational Cultures in South Asia.* Durham, NC: Duke University Press.

Singer, M. B. & Cohn, B. (Eds.). (1970). *Structure and Change in Indian Society.* Chicago: Aldine.

Singh, M. S. (2002). *Royal Indian Cookery: A Taste of Palace Life.* Mumbai: Zaika.

Sinha, M. (1995). *Colonial Masculinity: The "Manly Englishman" and the "Effeminate Bengali" in the Late Nineteenth Century.* Manchester: Manchester University Press.

Slater, D. (1997). *Consumer Culture and Modernity.* Cambridge: Blackwell.

Small, M. L. (2009). *Unanticipated Gains: Origins of Network Inequality in Everyday Life.* Oxford: Oxford University Press.

Smith, E. H. (1928). *The Restaurants of London.* New York: Knopf.

Smith, F. M. & Wujastyk, D. (2008). *Modern and Global Ayurveda: Pluralism and Paradigms.* Albany: State University of New York Press.

Sollors, W. (1989). *The Invention of Ethnicity.* New York: Oxford University Press.

———. (Ed.). (1996). *Theories of Ethnicity: A Classical Reader.* New York: New York University Press.

Somprakash. (1887, July 25). In *Report on Native Newspapers in Bengal* (1887, July 30).

South Asia: Journal of South Asian Studies. Special Food Issue, April 2008

South Asia Research. Special Food Issue, May 2004.

Spivak, G. C. (1999). *A Critique of Postcolonial Reason: Towards a History of the Vanishing Present.* Cambridge, MA: Harvard University Press.

Spooner, B. (1986). Weavers and Dealers: The Authenticity of an Oriental Carpet. In A. Appadurai (Ed.), *Social Life of Things* (pp. 195–235). Cambridge: Cambridge University Press.

Sreenivas, M. (2008). *Wives, Widows, and Concubines: The Conjugal Family Ideal in Colonial India*. Bloomington: Indiana University Press.

Srinivas, L. (2005). Communicating Globalization in Bombay Cinema: Everyday Life, Imagination and the Persistence of the Local. *Comparative American Studies, 3*(3), 319–344.

Srinivas, M. N. (Ed.). (1955). *India's Villages*. Bombay: Asia Publishing House.

———. (1965). *Religion and Society among the Coorgs of South India*. New York: Asia Publishing House.

Srinivas, S. (2001). *Landscapes of Urban Memory: The Sacred and the Civic in India's High-Tech City*. Minneapolis: University of Minnesota Press.

Srinivas, T. (2001). "A Tryst with Destiny": The Indian Case of Cultural Globalization. In P. Berger & S. Huntington (Eds.), *Many Globalizations. Cultural Diversity in the Contemporary World* (pp. 89–115). Oxford: Oxford University Press.

———. (2006). "As Mother Made It": The Cosmopolitan Indian Family, "Authentic" Food and the Construction of Cultural Utopia. *International Journal of Sociology of the Family, 32*(2), 199–221.

———. (2007). Everyday Exotic: Transnational Spaces and Contemporary Foodways in Bangalore. *Food, Culture & Society, 10*(1) (Spring), 85–107.

Srinivasan, S. (1995). *The South Asian Petty Bourgeoisie in Britain: An Oxford Case Study*. Aldershot, England: Avebury.

Sripantha [pseudonym of Nikhil Sarkar]. (Ed.). (2004). *Bangla Bhashar Pratham Duti Rannar Boi: Pakrajeswar o Byanjan Ratnakar* [The First Two Cookbooks in the Bengali Language: *Pakrajeswar* and *Byanjan Ratnakar*]. Calcutta: Subarnarekha.

Steensgaard, N. (1996). The Return Cargoes of the Carreira in the 16th and early 17th century. In M. Pearson. (Ed.), *Spices in the Indian Ocean World* (pp. 121–139). Brookfield, VT: Variorum.

Stein, M. (2003). Curry at Work: Nibbling at the Jewel in the Crown. In T. Döring, M. Heide, & S. Mühleisen (Eds.), *Eating Culture: The Poetics and Politics of Food* (pp. 133–149). Heidelberg: Universitätsverlag.

Steingass, F. J. (1892). *A Comprehensive Persian-English Dictionary, Including the Arabic Words and Phrases to Be Met with in Persian Literature*. London: Routledge & Kegan Paul.

Stern, S., & Cicala, J. A. (1991). *Creative Ethnicity: Symbols and Strategies of Contemporary Ethnic Life*. Logan: Utah State University Press.

Stoller, P. A. (1990). *The Taste of Ethnographic Things: The Senses in Anthropology*. Philadelphia: University of Pennsylvania Press.

Stop Pretending. (2002, June 10). *Telegraph and Argus*.

Striking a Balance. (1988, November 18). *Telegraph and Argus*.

Subrahmanyam, S. (1993). *The Portuguese Empire in Asia, 1500–1700: A Political and Economic History*. New York: Longman.

Sultaan, A. (2004). *Memoirs of a Rebel Princess*. Karachi: Oxford University Press.

Sutton, D. E. (2001). *Remembrance of Repasts: An Anthropology of Food and Memory (Materializing Culture)*. London: Berg.

Swaminathan, M. S. (2006, September 8). An Evergreen Revolution. *Crop Science* 46(5), 2293–2303.

Synnott, A. (1993). *The Body Social: Symbolism, Self, and Society*. London: Routledge.

Taj Restaurant. (1999). *Tandoori Magazine*, 5(9), 5.

Tannahill, R. (1995). *Food in History*. New York: Broadway.

Taylor, C. (2004). *Modern Social Imaginaries*. Durham, NC: Duke University Press.

Tharav Roast: Masala Roast Duck—A Specialty of Cochi. (1999). *Tandoori Magazine*, 5(3), 17.

Their British Paradise Was Waiting—and the Racketeers. (1965, January 25). *Times* (London).

Theophano, J. (2002). *Eat My Words: Reading Women's Lives Through the Cookbooks They Wrote*. New York: Palgrave.

Thernstrom, S., Orlov, A., & Handlin, O. (Eds). 1980. *Harvard Encyclopedia of American Ethnic Groups*. Cambridge, MA: Harvard University Press.

Tilly, C. (1990). *Coercion, Capital, and European States AD 990–1990*. Cambridge, MA: Blackwell.

Times of India. (2002). The Great Divide. *Bombay Times* February 15: 2.

Times of India. (2007, February 14). Norway's Orkla Buys MTR Foods for $100 million. http://timesofindia.indiatimes.com/articleshow/1606558.cms.

Times of India. (2008, September 5). NRIs to Aid of Muzrai Temples.

Tomlinson, J. (1999). *Globalization and Culture*. Chicago: University of Chicago Press.

Toomey, P. M. (1986). Food from the Mouth of Krishna: Socio-Religious Aspects of Sacred Food in Two Krishnaite Sects. In R. S Khare & M. S. A. Rao, (Eds.), *Food, Society and Culture. Aspects of South Asian Food Systems* (pp. 55–83). Durham, NC: Carolina Academic Press.

———. (1994). *Food from the Mouth of Krishna. Feasts and Festivities in a North Indian Pilgrimage Center*. Delhi: Hindustan Publishing Corporation.

Toussaint-Samat, M. (1998). *A History of Food*. New York: Barnes and Noble.

Tower Hamlets Council. (2005). *Cultural Walk 3: Exploring Banglatown and the Bengali East End*. London, 2005. http://static.visitlondon.com/assets/maps/guides/bengali_history_walk.pdf

Tredre, R. (1995, May 7). Pukka Masters of Balti Cast Their Chilly Gaze South. *London Observer*.

Troyna, B. (1993). *Racism and Education: Research Perspectives*. Philadelphia: Open University Press.

Troyna, B., & Williams, J. (1986). *Racism, Education and the State: The Racialisation of Education Policy*. London: Croom Helm.

True, M. (2004). Fragrant Feasts of Lucknow. *Saveur, 78*.

Tsing, A. (2000). The Global Situation. *Cultural Anthropology: Journal of the Society for Cultural Anthropology, 15*(3), 327–360.

———. (2002). The Global Situation. In J. X. Inda & R. Rosaldo (Eds.), *The Anthropology of Globalization* (pp. 66–98). Oxford: Blackwell.

Turgeon, L., & Pastinelli, M. (2002). Eat the World: Postcolonial Encounters in Quebec City's Ethnic Restaurants. *Journal of American Folklore, 115*(456), 247–268.

Turner, B. S. (1984). *The Body and Society: Explorations in Social Theory.* Oxford: Blackwell.

———. (1996). *The Body and Society: Explorations in Social Theory* (2nd ed.). Thousand Oaks, CA: Sage Publications.

Turner, J. (2005). *Spice: The History of a Temptation.* New York: Vintage.

Tyndale, G. (1976, January 22). Urdu Brightens Up Yorkshire Streets. *Yorkshire Post* (Leeds, England).

Ukers, W. H. (1936). *The Romance of Tea: An Outline History of Tea and Tea-Drinking through Sixteen Hundred Years.* New York: A.A. Knopf.

Umar, M. (1998). *Muslim Society in Northern India in the 18th century.* Delhi: MRML.

United Nations. (2008). Distributive Trade Statistics in India. http://unstats.un .org/unsd/Distributive_trade/EGM-DTS-webpage/Country%20Notes%20 INDIA.PDF

United States Department of Commerce, Bureau of Census. (1995). *Census of Population and Housing, 1990.* Washington, DC: United States Department of Commerce.

Upadhyaya, U. P., & Upadhyaya, S. P. (1984). *Bhuta Worship. Aspects of Ritualistic Theatre,* Rangasthala Monograph Series 1, The Regional Resources Centre for Folk Performing Arts, Udupi.

Upton, D. (1994). Another City: The Urban Cultural Landscape in the Early Republic. In C. E. Hutchins (Ed.), *Everyday Life in the Early Republic* (p. 61–117). Winterthur: Henry Francis du Pont Winterthur Museum.

Valle, V. M., & Torres, R. D. (2000). *Latino Metropolis.* Minneapolis: University of Minnesota Press.

van der Veer, P. (1994). *Religious Nationalism: Hindus and Muslims in India.* Berkeley: University of California Press.

———. (2000). Hindutva Movement in the West: Resurgent Hinduism and the Politics of the Diaspora. Special Issue, *Ethnic and Racial Studies, 32*(3).

van Otterloo, A. H. (2002). Chinese and Indonesian Restaurants and the Taste for Exotic Food in the Netherlands. In K. Cwiertka, with B. Walraven (Eds.), *Asian Food: The Global and the Local* (pp. 153–66). Honolulu: University of Hawai'i Press.

van Wessel, M. (2004). Talking About Consumption: How an Indian Middle Class Dissociates from Middle-Class Life. *Cultural Dynamics, 16*(1), 93–116.

Varma, P. K. (1998). *The Great Indian Middle Class.* New York: Viking.

Vasagar, J. (2007, January 20). Jade Evicted as Poll Reveals Public Anger with Channel Four. *Guardian.*

Veeraswamy, E. P. (1953). *Indian Cookery for Use in All Countries.* London: Arco Publishers.

Vegetarian Wonders. (1998). *Tandoori, 4*(11), 33.

Verma, A. A., Kandpal, V., Murry, B., & Saraswathy, K. N. (2010). G6PD deficiency and Haptoglobin Polymorphism Among Gaddis of Palampur, Himachal Pradesh. *South Asian Anthropologist 10*(2), 109–110.

Visram, R. (2002). *Asians in Britain: 400 Years of History*. London: Pluto Press.

Vivekananda, S. (1897/1987). *Patrabali* [Letters] (5th ed). Calcutta: Udbodhan.

Vyas, R. P. (Ed.). (1991). *British Policy towards Princely States of India*. Jodhpur: Rajasthan-Vidya Prakashan.

Wacquant, L. J. D. (1995). Pugs at Work: Bodily Capital and Bodily Labour among Professional Boxers. *Body & Society, 1*(1), 65–93.

———. (2004). *Body and Soul: Notebooks of an Apprentice Boxer*. Oxford; New York: Oxford University Press.

Wadley, S. (1980). Sitala: The Cool One. *Asian Folkore Studies, 39*(1), 33–62.

Wahhab, I. (1997). The Future of Our Industry. *Tandoori, 3*(6), 41.

Wake, C. (1996). The Changing Pattern of Europe's Pepper and Spice Imports, ca. 1400–1700. In M. Pearson (Ed.), *Spices in the Indian Ocean World* (pp. 141–183). Brookfield, VT: Variorum.

Waldinger, R. D. (1986). *Through the Eye of the Needle: Immigrants and Enterprise in New York's Garment Trades*. New York: New York University Press.

———. (2001). *Strangers at the Gates: New Immigrants in Urban America*. Berkeley: University of California Press.

Walsh, J. E. (1997). What Women Learned When Men Gave Them Advice: Rewriting Patriarchy in Late-Nineteenth-century Bengal. *Journal of Asian Studies, 56*(3), 641–677.

———. (2004). *Domesticity in Colonial India: What Women Learned When Men Gave Them Advice*. Lanham, MD: Rowman & Littlefield Publishers.

Ward, S. (2001). *British Culture and the End of Empire*. Manchester: Manchester University Press.

Warde, A. (2000). Eating Globally: Cultural Flows and the Spread of Ethnic Restaurants. In D. Kalb, M. van der Land, R. Staring, B. van Steenbergen & N. Wilterdink (Eds.), *The Ends of Globalization: Bringing Society Back In* (pp. 299–316). Lanham, MD: Rowan & Littlefield.

Warde, A., & Martens, L. (2000). *Eating Out: Social Differentiation, Consumption, and Pleasure*. Cambridge: Cambridge University Press.

Warde, A., Martens, L., & Olsen, W. (1999). Consumption and the Problem of Variety: Cultural Omnivorousness, Social Distinction and Dining Out. *Sociology, 33*(1), 105–127.

Warren, A. (1999). Disraeli, the Conservatives and the Government of Ireland: Part 2, 1868–1881. *Parliamentary History, 18*(2), 145–167.

Waters, M. C. (1990). *Ethnic Options: Choosing Identities in America*. Berkeley: University of California Press.

Watson, J. L. (Ed.). (1977). *Between Two Cultures: Migrants and Minorities in Britain*. Oxford: Basil Blackwell.

———. (Ed.). (1997). *Golden Arches East: McDonald's in East Asia*. Stanford, CA: Stanford University Press.

Watson, J. L., & Caldwell, M. L. (Eds.). (2005). *The Cultural Politics of Food and Eating: A Reader.* Malden, MA: Blackwell.

Weaver, W. W. (2000). *100 Vegetables and Where They Came From.* Chapel Hill, NC: Algonquin Books.

Webber, M. (1963). Order in Diversity: Community without Propinquity. In L. Wingo (Ed), *Cities and Space: The Future Use of Urban Land* (pp. 23–54). Baltimore: Johns Hopkins University Press.

Weber, M. (1958). *The Religion of India.* New York: Free Press.

Webster International Dictionary. (1993). New York: Merriam-Webster.

Weiss, A. S. (2002). *Feast and Folly: Cuisine, Intoxication, and the Poetics of the Sublime.* Albany: State University of New York Press.

Where to Eat in London (1955). London: Publisher Unknown.

Where to Eat in London (1960). London: Publisher Unknown.

Whitehorn, K. (1997, March 9). Blaming the Asians: Whatever Happened to the Melting Pot? *London Observer.*

Whiting, S. (2005, January 23). The Full Berkeley: Preserving West Berkeley's Colorful Past. *The San Francisco Chronicle.*

Wickizer, V. D. (1951). *Coffee, Tea, and Cocoa: An Economic and Political Analysis.* Stanford: Stanford University Press.

Wiessner, P. W., & Schiefenhövel, W. (1996). *Food and the Status Quest: An Interdisciplinary Perspective.* Providence: Berghahn Books.

Wilk, R. R. (Ed.). (2006a). *Fast Food/Slow Food: The Cultural Economy of the Global Food System.* Lanham, MD: Altamira Press.

———. (2006b). *Home Cooking in the Global Village: Caribbean Food from Buccaneers to Ecotourists.* Oxford: Berg.

Willard, P. (2001). *Secrets of Saffron.* Boston: Beacon Press.

Winkler, M. G., & Cole, L. B. (Eds.). (1994). *The Good Body: Asceticism in Contemporary Culture.* New Haven, CT: Yale University Press.

Wolf, E. (1990). Distinguished Lecture: Facing Power—Old Insights, New Questions. *American Anthropologist, 92*(3), 586–596.

Wood, J. (1997). *Vietnamese American Place Making in Northern Virginia.* New York: American Geographical Society of New York.

Worboys, M. (1988). The Discovery of Colonial Malnutrition between the Wars. In D. Arnold (Ed.), *Imperial Medicine and Indigenous Societies* (pp. 208–225). Manchester: Manchester University Press.

Wu, D. Y. H., & Cheung, S. C. H. (Eds.). (2004). *The Globalization of Chinese Food.* Honolulu, University of Hawai'i Press.

Wu, F. H. (2002) The Best "Chink" Food: Dog-Eating and the Dilemma of Diversity. *Yellow: Race in America Beyond Black and White.* New York: Basic Books.

Wujastyk, D. (2003). *The Roots of Ayurveda: Selections from Sanskrit Medical Writings.* New York: Penguin Books.

Wujastyk, D., & Meulenbeld, G. J. (2001). *Indian Medical History.* Delhi: Motilal Banarsidass.

Wyvern. (Kenney-Herbert, A). (1885/2007). *Culinary Jottings: A Treatise in Thirty*

Chapters on Reformed Cookery for Anglo-Indian Exiles. Devon, UK: Prospect Books.

Yalman, N. (1967). The Raw: the Cooked: Nature: Culture—Observations on *Le Cru et le cuit.* In E. Leach (Ed.), *The Structural Study of Myth and Totemism.* ASA Monograph 5. London: Tavistock Publications.

Younger, C. (2003). *Wicked Women of the Raj: European Women Who Broke Society's Rules and Married Indian Princes.* New Delhi: HarperCollins.

Zaika. (1999). *Tandoori, 5*(6), 24.

Zardini, M. (Ed.). (2005). *Sense of the City: An Alternate Approach to Urbanism.* Montreal: Canadian Centre for Architecture.

Zelinsky, W. (2001). *The Enigma of Ethnicity: Another American Dilemma.* Iowa City: University of Iowa Press.

Zelinsky, W. & Lee, B.A. (1998). Heterolocalism: An Alternative Model of the Sociospatial Behaviour of Immigrant Ethnic Communities. *International Journal of Population Geography, 4*(4), 281–98.

Zhou, M. (2004). Revisiting Ethnic Entrepreneurship: Convergencies, Controversies, and Conceptual Advancements. *International Migration Review, 38*(3), 1040–1074.

Zimmermann, F. (1987). *The Jungle and the Aroma of Meats: An Ecological Theme in Hindu Medicine.* Berkeley: University of California Press.

Zlotnick, S. (1996). Domesticating Imperialism: Curry and Cookbooks in Victorian England. *Frontiers: A Journal of Women Studies, 16*(3), 51–68.

Zolli, A. (2006, March 16). *The US's Future is Older, Browner, and Feminine.* New York: Rediff.com . http://inhome.rediff.com/money/2006/mar/16spec.htm

Zuckerman, L. (1998). *The Potato: How the Humble Spud Rescued the Western World.* New York: Faber & Faber.

Zukin, S. (1991). *Landscapes of Power: From Detroit to Disney World.* Berkeley: University of California Press.

———. (1995). *The Cultures of Cities.* Cambridge, MA: Blackwell.

———. (2010). *Naked City: The Death and Life of Authentic Urban Places.* Oxford; New York: Oxford University Press.

CONTRIBUTORS

ELIZABETH BUETTNER is senior lecturer in history at the University of York (UK) and the author of *Empire Families: Britons and Late Imperial India* (Oxford University Press, 2004). She is currently completing a comparative study entitled *Europe after Empire: Decolonization, Society, and Culture* for Cambridge University Press.

Cultural anthropologist SUSAN DEWEY is an assistant professor in gender and women's studies at the University of Wyoming. She has published three single-authored books that address the complex intersections between feminized labor and the state: *Making Miss India Miss World: Constructing Gender, Power and the Nation in Postliberalization India* (2008), *Hollow Bodies: Institutional Responses to Sex Trafficking in Armenia, Bosnia and India* (2008), and *Neon Wasteland: On Love, Motherhood and Sex Work in a Rust Belt Town* (2011). She has coedited three volumes that address gender, nationalism, and violence, and her articles have appeared in *American Ethnologist, Journal of South Asian Popular Culture, Labor: Journal of Working Class History in the Americas,* and *Ethnography and Education.*

A devoted student of Indian cuisine, GEOFFREY GARDELLA holds a master's degree in Asian studies from Lund University. His thesis explored the eating habits of South Indians living in Delhi. Geoffrey is currently a computer engineer living in Colorado.

AKHIL GUPTA is professor of anthropology at the University of California, Los Angeles, and director of the Center for India and South Asia (CISA). He is the author of *Red Tape* (Duke University Press, forthcoming), and *The State in India after Liberalization* (edited with K. Sivaramakrishnan; Routledge, 2010). He teaches a course on the anthropology of food, and has written extensively about agriculture in India.

ANGMA D. JHALA is an assistant professor of South Asian history at Bentley University. She received her D.Phil. from Oxford (Christ Church) and an M.Div. and A.B. from Harvard University. She is the author of *Courtly Indian Women in Late Imperial India* (2008) and *Royal Patronage, Power and Aesthetics in Princely*

India (2011). Her work has been published or is forthcoming in *The Indian Economic and Social History Review, South Asian History and Culture, South Asian Popular Culture,* the *Encyclopedia of Women in Islamic Civilizations* and various edited volumes.

R. S. KHARE, professor of anthropology at University of Virginia, has longstanding interest in studying food and culture in India, now globalizing. His relevant publications include *The Hindu Hearth and Home* (1976) and "Anna" ["Food"] in *The Hindu World* (2004).

STIG TOFT MADSEN is a Danish South Asianist affiliated to the Nordic Institute of Asian Studies (NIAS). He is the coeditor of *Tryst with Democracy: Political Practice in South Asia* (Anthem, 2011), which features his study of Ajit Singh, a politician in possession of a "hereditary" constituency in India. In "Being on and Being in: Exposure and Influence of Academic Experts in Contemporary Denmark," published in Livia Holden's anthology *Cultural Expertise and Litigation* (Routledge, 2011), Madsen draws on his experience as media commentator to discuss the role of the academic expert.

KRISHNENDU RAY is currently an assistant professor of food studies in the Department of Nutrition, Food Studies, and Public Health at New York University. Prior to that, he taught for a decade at the Culinary Institute of America at Hyde Park, New York. He is the author of *The Migrant's Table: Meals and Memories in Bengali American Households* (2004) and he is finishing a manuscript titled *Taste, Toil and Ethnicity: Immigrant Restaurateurs and American Chefs.*

ARIJIT SEN teaches architectural design, urbanism, and cultural landscapes at the University of Wisconsin–Milwaukee. He cofounded Buildings-Landscapes-Cultures (www.blcprogram.org), an interdisciplinary doctoral research area shared by the University of Wisconsin–Madison and Milwaukee. His writings include articles and book chapters on South Asian immigrant cultural landscapes in Northern California, retail spaces of ethnic immigrants in New York and San Francisco, Muslim cultural landscapes in Chicago, and early twentieth-century South Asian religious spaces in the United States.

JAYANTA SENGUPTA is assistant professor of history in the University of Notre Dame. He is currently finishing his first book, on the discourses of development, democracy, and regionalism in twentieth-century Orissa, and working on another on U.S. perceptions of India from 1850 to 1950.

HOLLY SHAFFER is a doctoral student in the history of art at Yale University. The research for this article was prepared on a Fulbright Research Grant to India and a Dartmouth Reynolds Grant. She thanks those two organizations as well as R. K. Saxena and the Institute of Hotel Management (Mumbai), Vijay and Sulaiman Khan of Mahmudabad, Imtiaz and Ishtiyaque Qureshi, and the many others who supported her research.

TULASI SRINIVAS is an assistant professor of cultural anthropology at Emerson College in Boston, whose research centers around religious experience and subjectivity in a globalizing world with specific reference to Indian religious traditions. She is the author of *Winged Faith: Rethinking Globalization and Religious Pluralism Through the Sathya Sai Movement* (Columbia University Press, 2010), and is currently working on a second monograph tentatively titled *Thresholds of Faith: Innovative Ritual and Ambivalent Globalization in Hindu Temples in Bangalore.* She is equally interested in food and culinary process as a whole and Indian food in particular, and its complex links to globalization, gender, power, and the sacred, and has published several essays on these topics in leading journals such as *Food, Culture and Society, Education About Asia,* and *Food and Foodways.*

INDEX

Bangalore packaged foods (*continued*)
and, 229, 230; middle class and, 222;
MTR and, 104, 228–29, 232, 235n7;
provisioning and, 25, 222, 225, 229–30;
purity of, 25, 228, 235n7; secrecy among
women and, 25, 104; transnationalism
and, 224–25, 235n4; women as domestic
provisioners and, 25, 229–30; women as
entrepreneurs and, 229–32
Bangalore Udupi restaurants, 100, 109n7.
See also Bangalore packaged foods
Bangladeshi restaurateurs: in Britain,
146–47, 148, 161–64, 166, 167–69, 171,
173nn7; in New York City, 180–81, 183
Basu, R., 78, 85
Bengal in colonial period. *See* cuisine in
colonial Bengal
Berkeley, CA, 200–202, 206–7, 216. *See
also chaat café;* ethnic grocery store
Bhabha, H. K., 4, 9
bhadralok (gentleman) nationalism, 21,
78–82, 85–86, 86n5
Billavas (Poojarys), 102, 103
biriyani, 50, 113, 124n3, 125n12. *See also dum
pukht*
Birmingham, and British South Asian
restaurateurs, 147, 150, 152, 153, 158,
160–63, 170, 173n6
the body and bodies: containment of, 6–7;
embodiment of immigrant NYC restaurateurs and, 175–76, 192, 193n3; food
connection with, 3, 131, 134–35; gendered politics of, 12–13, 21, 74–80, 86n5,
87n6; global flows and, 3, 24; locality
connection with, 6–7, 24, 132–33,
132–34; scapes and, 16–17, 24, 131–32
Bombay Udupi restaurants, 18, 93, 100–101,
102–4, 109n10
Bose, C., 79
Boston, MA, and packaged foods, 25, 203,
220–21, 224, 230
Bourdieu, P., 7, 182, 184
Boxer, C. R., 39, 45n20, 46n21
Bradford, and British South Asian restaurateurs, 147, 150, 151, 158–59, 160–66
Brahmins: caste groups and, 96; cooking at
Krishna temple by, 97–98, 106, 235n7;
cuisine and food practices and, 14, 81,

95–97, 109n5; cultural capital and,
98–99; entrepreneurs and, 95–96,
98–101, 105, 108; identity and, 108;
religious revitalization and, 106; Udupi
restaurants and, 21–22, 91–92, 93–94,
99–103, 109n5. *See also* vegetarianism
Bray, F., 9
Breckenridge, C., 9, 18, 96
British colonial period: British East India
Company and, 12, 52, 56, 59–60, 77,
109n12; British South Asian restaurateurs and, 148–49, 173nn2–3; ceremonial and public functions during, 58–59,
67; cuisine and crop movement and,
42–43; *dum pukht* historical context in,
23, 113, 117–21; hereditary Mumbai elite
in, 136–37; ostentatious eating habits
during, 12–13, 21, 74–77; *zenana* cuisine
in, 51–52, 54, 55–62, 72n2, 72n3. *See also*
cuisine in colonial Bengal; Great
Britain
British East India Company, 12, 52, 56,
59–60, 77, 109n12
British South Asian restaurateurs: overview
of, 23–24, 147–48, 170–72; aesthetic
taste and, 169; anti-Muslim attitudes
and, 148, 163–65, 168; Asian clientele
and, 150–51, 154, 173n4; authentic
cuisine and, 148, 157–60, 166–70, 169,
174n13, 174n15; *balti* restaurants and,
162–63, 167, 169–70, 171; Bangladeshi
restaurateurs and, 146–47, 148, 161–64,
166, 167–69, 171, 173nn7; in Birmingham, 147, 150, 152, 153, 158, 160–63, 170,
173n6; in Bradford, 147, 150, 151, 158–59,
160–66; in colonial period, 148–49,
173nn2–3; cuisine and, 147, 150, 151–52,
157, 171; diaspora and, 148, 153–55, 157,
173nn6–7; economics versus authentic
cuisine, 158–59; ethnic identity and, 158,
173n8; gender of clientele and, 153–54,
173nn7; global flows and, 8; hierarchies
and, 158, 173n8; Indian food, 155, 157,
168, 171–72; locality and, 8, 140, 145–
46, 158, 168, 173n8; marginalization of
clientele and, 149–50; multiculturalism
and, 143–45, 148, 153–55, 160–66, 170–
72, 173n7, 173n9; Muslims and, 147, 153,

Harriss, J, 108
Hayden, D., 197
health and dietary practices in colonial
Bengal. *See* cuisine in colonial Bengal
health and modern hygiene, 25, 133, 224,
230
Held, D., 35
heritage tourism, 71–72. *See also zenana*
cuisine
heterogeneity of *zenana* cuisine, 49, 50,
54–56, 59, 63–65, 72n2
hierarchies: British South Asian restaurateurs and, 158, 173n8; cuisine and crop
movement and, 35, 45nn10; food and,
127, 128; middle class and, 4–6; neoliberalism and, 133, 142; Udupi restaurants and, 92–93, 102, 105. *See also* social
class(es)
Hinduism: aesthetic taste and, 238; food
orthodoxies and, 92, 95–99, 105–6,
109n2, 109n5, 128; gendered architectural space and, 49, 72n1; globalization
measurement and, 45n10; identity and,
108; religious identities and, 42; religious revivalism due to remittances and,
22, 106–8; Udupi restaurants and,
98–99, 105–6. *See also* caste groups
Hindustan spice-laden dishes *(pulao)*,
112–13, 118, 122–23, 124n3, 125n12,
125n14
Hopkins, 35, 43, 44n5, 46n29
hunger and famines, 11–12, 17n5, 18, 27n10
Huntington, S., 7
hygiene and modern health notions, 25, 133,
224, 230

ICAF (International Commission on
Anthropology of Food), 246
identity constructs, 4–7, 108, 137, 141–42.
See also ethnic identity(ies)
imaginary: overview of, 26; British
national identity and cuisine connection claims and, 146–47, 160, 161–62,
166, 173n9; *dum pukht* and, 23, 111–17,
124nn7–8; ethnic grocery store and,
199, 217; globalization and, 249; of
immigrant NYC restaurateurs, 177,

179, 181, 183, 186, 189, 191; Udupi restaurants and, 105
immigrant NYC restaurateurs: overview
of, 24, 176–77, 192; aesthetic taste and,
176, 180, 182–85, 189–92, 194n15; Asian
clientele and, 188, 190; Bangladeshi
restaurateurs and, 180–81, 183; cuisine
and, 177; cultural capital and, 176,
178–80, 183, 185–89, 190, 191, 194n10,
195n18; design and, 176, 177, 178, 182,
186–88; displacement and, 176–77;
economics versus cultural capital, 176,
178–80; embodiment of, 24, 175–76,
185–89, 192, 193n3; "fast food" and, 177;
food matters and, 180–81; global flows
and, 8, 14, 176; imaginary and, 177, 179,
181, 183, 186, 189, 191; locality and, 14,
24, 176, 194; media and client influences and, 189; men's role in economics
and, 178–79, 180; non-Asian clientele
and, 188, 190; preparation of food and,
177–78, 189, 191; scholarship on, 184,
194n12; social capital and, 183, 188–89,
194n10; sociology of food and, 176,
180–81, 184; statistics, 181, 193n9,
194n13; transnationalism and, 184,
189–92; women's role as cooks in Asian
culture and, 178–79, 180, 189, 191. *See
also* British South Asian restaurateurs
immigrant populations: overview of, 16–17,
18, 23, 28n11; in Berkeley, 200–202;
diaspora and, 148, 153–55, 157, 173nn6–7,
227–29, 248–49; displacement and, 43,
176–77; locality and, 202–3
India and Indians: agro-industrial complex
and, 220, 232–34, 238; as clientele in
Britain, 150–51, 154, 173n4; as clientele
in U.S., 188, 190, 202, 203–4, 205–6,
210, 215; cuisine and crop movement,
41; effeteness notions about, 77–80,
86n5, 87n6; Green Revolution and, 12,
222–23, 238; middle class and, 225–26,
235n6, 238; as "model minority" in U.S.,
224, 235n3; provisioning in, 11, 12, 25,
221–26, 229–30, 234n1, 238; transnationalism and, 232–34, 233–134;
white revolution and, 223; women as

United States (*continued*)
ethnic grocery store; immigrant NYC restaurateurs; New York City (NYC); Pakistani restaurateur
upper class: in colonial Bengal, 12–13, 21, 74–77, 83–85; ethnic succession to lower castes in Udupi restaurants and, 102–4; Mumbai, 126–27, 136–37, 142. *See also* British colonial period; caste groups; Mumbai post-Liberalization; social class(es)
urban development schemes, in Berkeley, CA, 206–7, 216

vegetarianism: Bombay Udupi restaurants and, 103–4; dietary practices and health and, 82–85, 250, 254n14; historical context and, 12, 244, 250, 254n14; nonvegetarianism versus, 83–85, 93, 104, 244; Udupi restaurants and, 103–4, 109n7. *See also* Brahmins
"veil" (*pardah;* "seclusion"), 49, 52, 63, 67
Venice, Italy, 38, 40, 42–43
viceregal visits (*durbars;* state marriages), 20, 57, 60, 62. *See also zenana* cuisine
Vivekananda, S., 84–85

Wacquant, L., 192
Wadley, S., 128
Weber, M., 92, 108
West Indians (Afro-Caribbeans), 144, 151
white revolution (dairy farming; "Operation Flood"), 223
wine industry, in Mumbai, 129, 136–37, 139–41
women: as clientele in Udupi restaurants, 103, 109n10; as domestic provisioners, 25, 178–79, 180, 189, 191, 220–21, 229–32; as entrepreneurs, 185–92, 220–21, 227, 229–32; Mumbai cuisine restaurateur and, 185–92; neoliberal feminism

and, 220–21, 231–32, 234; secrecy in packaged foods and, 25, 104; symbolic space of domesticity and, 21, 80–82, 87n11. *See also* gender issues; men; Mumbai cuisine restaurateur; *zenana* cuisine

youth as non-Asian clientele, 153–54, 173n7

zenana cuisine: overview of, 20–21, 49–55, 71–72, 72n1; aesthetic taste and, 59; Awadhi region cuisine and, 49; banquets and, 69–70; British colonial period context and, 51–52, 54, 55–62, 72n2, 72n3; ceremonial and public functions in public sphere during colonial period and, 58–59, 67; in Chakma Raj Buddhist kingdom, 52, 56, 64–65, 68; cookbooks and, 54, 55; cosmopolitan European cuisine and, 52, 66–71; description of, 49–50, 72n1; dining styles and, 65–66; *durbars* and, 20, 57, 60, 62; European influences on, 51–52, 54, 63–64; gourmands and, 65; heritage tourism and, 71–72; heterogeneity and, 49, 53–54, 55–56, 63, 64–65; heterogeneity of, 55, 59, 72n2; Indian food, 65, 67–68; local and global place as interwoven and, 49, 54, 59, 70; Mughal empire and, 50–51; Muslim states and, 51; nation-states during colonial period and, 55–62, 72n3; *pardah*'s effects on, 49, 52, 63, 67; political marriages and, 50–51, 52–53, 64; power and, 49, 54, 59, 70; railway cuisine and, 62–63, 72n4; vegetarianism and, 51. *See also* women
Zimmerman, F., 13–14
Zolli, A., 235n3
Zukin, S., 24, 190, 196, 199

TEXT
11/14 Garamond Premier Pro
DISPLAY
Garamond Premier Pro
COMPOSITION
BookComp, Inc.
INDEXING
J. Naomi Linzer Indexing Services
PRINTING AND BINDING
IBT Global

www.ingramcontent.com/pod-product-compliance
Lightning Source LLC
Chambersburg PA
CBHW020336270326
41926CB00007B/204